"In an age where the 'body of knowledge' on Reformation and Transformation is actually characterized by 'dis-embodiedness' Elisabeth Gerle provides us with this book about Transformative Passion. In a critical dialogue with Luther and contemporary theologians she expands our thinking on Love, Body, and Sensual Presence that challenges nostalgic theological trends dreaming of the past."

—SAROJINI NADAR, Desmond Tutu Research Chair,
University of the Western Cape

"With the instincts of a jazz singer, Gerle weaves feminist, Lutheran and *eros* theologies together with political theory and ethics. Intentionally breaking the rules of patriarchal texts, her non-linear writing is designed to entice and evoke. Gerle's deep, broad research propose fresh resources for understanding grace-filled, embodied desire at the heart of theology. Passion draws us to one another and to God, healing and calling us to live more deeply into the world."

—MARIT TRELSTAD, Professor of Constructive Theology,
Department of Religion, Pacific Lutheran University

Passionate Embrace

Passionate Embrace

Luther on Love, Body,
and Sensual Presence

Elisabeth Gerle

CASCADE *Books* • Eugene, Oregon

PASSIONATE EMBRACE
Luther on Love, Body, and Sensual Presence

Copyright © 2017 Elisabeth Gerle. All rights reserved. Except for brief quotations in critical publications or reviews, no part of this book may be reproduced in any manner without prior written permission from the publisher. Write: Permissions, Wipf and Stock Publishers, 199 W. 8th Ave., Suite 3, Eugene, OR 97401.

Cascade Books
An Imprint of Wipf and Stock Publishers
199 W. 8th Ave., Suite 3
Eugene, OR 97401

www.wipfandstock.com

PAPERBACK ISBN: 978-1-5326-1599-3
HARDCOVER ISBN: 978-1-5326-1601-3
EBOOK ISBN: 978-1-5326-1600-6

Cataloguing-in-Publication data:

Names: Gerle, Elisabeth, author.

Title: Passionate embrace : Luther on love, body, and sensual presence / Elisabeth Gerle.

Description: Eugene, OR : Cascade Books, 2017 | Includes bibliographical references.

Identifiers: ISBN 978-1-5326-1599-3 (paperback) | ISBN 978-1-5326-1601-3 (hardcover) | ISBN 978-1-5326-1600-6 (ebook)

Subjects: LCSH: Luther, Martin, 1483–1546. | Human body—Religious aspects—Christianity. | Sex—Religious aspects—Christianity—History of doctrines—16th century. | Christian ethics.

Classification: BR333.5.S49 G475 2017 (print) | BR333.5.S49 G475 (ebook)

Manufactured in the U.S.A.   MAY 3, 2017

Scripture quotations are from the New Revised Standard Version Bible, copyright © 1989, Division of Christian Education of the National Council of the Churches of Christ in the United States of America. Used by permission. All rights reserved.

Contents

Acknowledgments and Thanks ix

A Short Introduction xi

1. The Contemporary Landscape:
   Body Worship and Body Loathing 1

2. Luther: Heroic Liberator or Oppressor? 15

3. Human Bodies as a Phenomenon:
   Body Theology and Longing for the Past 34

4. A Woman Reads Origen, Augustine, Bernard, and Luther 50

5. The Movement of the Senses: Towards the Everyday 93

6. Commercial Transaction or Loving Embrace? 130

7. *Eros* as Poisoned Chalice, Medicine, or Everyday Body?
   Eros and *Agape* in a New Light 152

8. *Eros* Theology Challenges Traditional
   Lutheran Binary Opposites 182

9. Body, Sexuality, and Institutions:
   Roads to Salvation, Disciplining, or Presence and Gift? 213

10. Passion That Transforms:
    Patriarchy and Paradise, Personal and Private 247

11. Birth and Blossoming:
    Passionate Vision for the Future and Contrast to Greed 284

Bibliography 307

Acknowledgments and Thanks

FRIENDS, MENTORS, AND COLLEAGUES, who have inspired and helped this study to mature, are too numerous to mention. Naming also involves the risk of oversight, for which I apologize. There are, however, certain contexts that I want to mention. One is the Nordic Lutheran network of women theologians that widened to a global network, which also included men with a shared interest in writing back to Luther, searching a constant reformation and renewal. Without this network this book would not have found wings to fly beyond its Swedish, Scandinavian origin. From my American, Latin American, African, and Asian friends I became aware that there did not seem to be any study focusing on love, body, sensuality, and Luther. For this inspiration I am truly grateful.

An international, English version would, however, not have been possible without the generous support from the foundations of Thora Ohlsson and Bo Håkan Ohlsson in Lund and from the Research Department of Church of Sweden, who's Director Cecilia Nahnfeldt has been a constant support and inspiration during the whole process. The whole research group has been a loyal cheer group as well and Göran Gunner spent long hours helping out with formatting in desperate moments. Thank you for sharing your talent with great patience! The excellent British translator Stephen Donovan made miracles. Despite pressure from approaching deadlines he always took the time to discuss and try to find the exact nuances in collaboration with me.

Colleagues at Aarhus University in Denmark have generously shared their great knowledge in Luther studies, friends and colleagues at the Center of Theological and Religious Studies at Lund University have given support and encouragement during long hours in the library and in my office there. Tomas Appelqvist has with great patience given advice and made sure that my references to Luther in the Weimar Ausgabe were correct and in correspondence to Luther's Work. Some of my writing and editing was done during recurrent periods as Visiting Scholar at Stellenbosch Institute of Advanced Study (STIAS) Wallenberg Research Centre at Stellenbosch University, Stellenbosch 7600 South Africa.

Last but not least, my most immediate family, Anders and Kristofer, have always encouraged and made me feel that this work was worthwhile despite sometimes suffering from my stress and fatigue. For this I am deeply grateful!

Elisabeth Gerle
Lund
February 2017

A Short Introduction

Health, beauty, strength, and sexual desire are today highly valued. The mannequin or model in beautiful clothes is not merely a person showcasing haute couture but a paradigm to aim for, an ideal of beauty. As long as we can remain healthy and sexually active, we are considered valid human beings. Having a fit and healthy body thus becomes completely essential, a virtual path to salvation. We imagine ourselves as controlling our future through our body.

It is through the human body that we experience pleasure. Our eyes help us to absorb beautiful views, the beauty of flowers, architecture, and other people. Taste sensations are released by delicious food, and the sensitivity of our skin relays the caresses of another person or the warmth of a beloved pet. Our ears register tone of voice as well as music. But the body also registers pain and vulnerability. Harsh sounds grate on the ear.

The human body is currently attracting considerable interest. Health studies offer tips on how to stay in shape. But the body has always been central to people's hopes for the future. In the Middle Ages, female mystics regarded Jesus not merely as an object of love but as a lover. Catherine of Siena saw herself as married to Christ in a vision. The ring she wears is made of skin—Christ's foreskin. Physical foreskin. Physical proximity to Christ and his physical body implies a bodily union.

In the history of the Church, the human body has often been viewed as something that a human being ought to control by means of the intellect. Human sexuality came into competition with devotedness to God. For this reason, a woman's body was often seen as threatening, since it risked arousing a man's desire. This attitude can be glimpsed in Origen, Augustine, and Bernard of Clairvaux, and is a continual motif in the history of mysticism.

Martin Luther initiates something new. He sees a human being as a whole. Body and spirit do not stand in opposition to each other. Nonetheless, when he speaks of flesh it has a negative connotation. What he has in mind is a human being's general tendency to fixate—body, spirit, and soul—upon itself and to turn away from life, fellow human beings, and God. And yet sexuality, body, and sexual desire do not represent obstacles to the spiritual. Luther rejects any such opposition. On the contrary, God often shows his love for human beings precisely through the material and the physical. The care and love provided by other people thereby become signs of God's own love. A meal of good food, beer, and wine brings us together with other people and drives away mistrust and depression. It is about community and joy. In the home of Katharina von Bora and Luther, the meal—supper—is closely associated with the meal in the church that has long been known as the Lord's Supper. Like the evening meal, the Eucharist is a sign of care, love, joy, and community—a meal of thanksgiving. The sharp boundaries between spiritual and material are dissolved in Luther's writings because he sees God's care and love in the material, the everyday. The Word of God becomes a message of love that helps people to make sense of what they encounter.

When theologians talk about the body, they are often referring to the Church as body and community. In this study, I want to restrict myself primarily to the human body and its senses. In contrast to the ascetic traditions, sensual presence for Luther is neither a sin nor a threat to our closeness to God.

The body is a mystery that can never be fully encompassed or described. And yet we take it as fairly self-evident what a body is. We are all also aware that the body changes during its lifetime. Time, age, and health all play their part. Our vulnerability is especially visible at the beginning and the end of life.

This represents a challenge in a culture that values strength and health. How should we treat vulnerability, suffering, and death? Luther surrenders neither to body cult nor to body loathing. He is not primarily concerned with the body, though it is a gift and a means of support. Rather, his interest is in our relationship to God as well as to other people.

In this book, I choose to read Luther's own texts in dialogue with scholars from our era who are interested in the body's significance for theology. Luther's view of gender, sexuality, and sexual desire are summarized against a background of intellectual history. I go on to read Luther through contemporary wounds associated with gender, sexual orientation, and ethnic and religious affiliation.

Luther uses the erotic language of mysticism when referring to relationships with God as well as relationships between people. He thereby passes on several important aspects of the mystical tradition. These include queer elements. Christ is described as both bride and bridegroom. Although Luther holds a fairly traditional view of women, they never become a threat to how human beings relate to God and the spiritual, but are instead regarded as partners and equals. Man and woman are seen as God's co-creators. They pass on life by giving birth and taking care of new lives.

In our era, symbols and concepts are being reformulated. Theologians are referring to God as a relationship. People without children of their own are also involved in creating and caring for new life. Luther thought highly of the work of the body. He valued the lowliest of tasks, which were often performed by women, and claimed that these were more important than those of monks and nuns. This poses a significant challenge for the present: to make visible the bodies which serve and give life so that others can live in comfort.

Luther recovered the language of eroticism for shared physical intimacy as well as for politics. In actualizing this theology of love, I want to provide inspiration for an impassioned politics and an erotic physical spirituality that sees and cares about real, physical bodies in our world.

1

The Contemporary Landscape: Body Worship and Body Loathing

Our era takes a great interest in the human body. The young and beautiful body is an object of desire and attraction. Advertising implies that certain products can give you this body or help you to come closer to one like it. The present does not engage in body loathing—quite the opposite. The body is central to the health cult of our time and its focus on sexuality, life affirmation, and sensuality. The healthy, strong, and toned body occupies center stage. One might almost call it a body cult.

At the same time, human bodies are everywhere being exploited as sexual objects and by trafficking. Poor and vulnerable children, women, and young men are allowed or forced to satisfy the desires of those with the means to pay for sex or for cleaning work and other jobs that no-one wants to do. These bodies are ignored and viewed with disdain. They are nowhere visible in display advertisements. But they can be glimpsed behind the scenes, back in the cleaning areas and utility rooms of restaurants and hotels. The idea is that they should be invisible.

In gyms and health clubs, bodies are being exercised in order to become better and stronger. From a theological perspective, this flawless body can be seen as a secular path to salvation. Being slim is supposed to bring health, success, happiness, and long life. Many people long for and pursue an attractive body. An ugly or old body, by contrast, is an object of contempt. It is seen as an accident and *calamity*.

British theologian Sarah Coakley describes the body as "sexually affirmed but puritanically punished in matters of diet or exercise." It is "continuously stuffed with consumerist goods, but guiltily denied particular foods, in aid of the 'salvation' of a longer life; taught that there is nothing *but* it (the 'body') and yet asked to discipline itself from some other site of control."[1] Clubs for those who want to lose weight sometimes use words such as confession, remorse, and penance in order to create the necessary degree of self-control.[2]

It would seem that many people in the richer parts of the world are obsessed with the body, which they treat as a highly calibrated sensorium for the full gratification of their own desires. The symptoms range from the endless proliferation of health clubs to the popularity of chefs promoting exquisite cookery advice. Popular cultural notions about genetic mapping, for example, suggest that it is thought to lead to greater life expectancy. Thanks to advances in technology, movements such as post- and transhumanism are pursuing a radically extended life expectancy, which they view as attainable. Beneath all of this can be discerned a fear of losing the body, of its disappearance.[3] In hospitals, bodies are cared for in order to become healthy. Bodies considered hopeless—those of the old and the dying—are perhaps hidden away for that very reason. They, and often their caregivers, too, become invisible. We lose the body in death but the body's strength ebbs away long before then. It would seem, then, that there is a deep ambivalence—worship but also loathing—in how we view the body.

Paradoxically, the tremendous interest in the body in contemporary culture may have something to do with the fact that growing numbers of bodies are being made invisible. The working bodies in countries around the world do not appear on the map of global trade.[4] Time and money are being saved in one place by having the work carried out somewhere else, where labor costs and raw materials command lower prices.[5] For theologian Sigurd Bergmann, this forms a part of an asymmetrical system of global trade. Economic growth is founded on technological development but also on an iniquitous flow of resources and global power relations.[6]

1. Coakley, "Introduction," 7.
2. Bacon, "Expanding Bodies, Expanding God."
3. Cf. Ward, "On the Politics of Embodiment," 85.
4. Ibid. When dressmakers in Bangladesh, or some other poor Asian country, are burned to death, locked up in a dangerous factory, the incident receives intense media attention but is easily forgotten. If companies are forced to take greater security measures in one country, they often move somewhere else.
5. Hornborg, "Technology as Fetish."
6. Bergmann, "'Millions of Machines Are Already Roaring.'"

For many people in affluent societies, work has become ever less physical thanks to the Internet and mobile telecommunications.[7] At the same time, bodies carrying out hard labor exist everywhere. They sustain life, including in rich areas. Machines and technology can never replace what the body provides in terms of desire, caring, and survival. Yet the fact that we increasingly relate to other people via the Internet creates a screen upon which color, smell, and taste either disappear or are embellished. An embedded theology must therefore once again ask questions about the meaning of the body, about *eros* and desire, but also about the vulnerable, worn-out, and crippled body.

Today, the body and its senses thus seem to attract greater interest than any spiritual kind of search. Such, at least, is the impression given by TV listings, film releases, music, and magazines. Taste and sight are satiated by one food program after the other. But the dualism of spirit and body does not appear to be doing justice to either. Both sides are needed, but must they be treated as competitors?

Spirituality and Sensuality

To refer to spirituality and sensuality in the same breath can seem contradictory. But the question is whether there has always been a contradiction between body and spirit. Historically, eroticism and sexuality have been regarded both as a path to the spiritual or divine and as threats or competitors for one's love of God.

Throughout the entire history of the church, theologians have had reasons for emphasizing that God created the world. Their insistence upon the body and the material as part of God's creation was a response to claims made by movements within early Christianity that God had only created the spiritual. They contended that the earth and the material had been created by a demiurge. Early Church Fathers such as Irenaeus (c. 130–202) thus waged an intensive campaign against Marcion and these gnostic tendencies. In his tract *Ad haereses*, Irenaeus writes that it is impossible to live as a body without being in a relationship with God the Creator.[8] Several theologians within the so-called Luther Renaissance allied themselves to this cause. Gustaf Aulén (1879–1977) emphasized

---

7. Ward, "On the Politics of Embodiment," 85.

8. Irenaeus, *Against the Heresies*; cf. Wingren, *Creation and Law*, 18, quoting Irenaeus, *Ad haereses* IV:34, 6.

that Christ was the victor of the forces opposed to God—sin, death, and the devil. Following Irenaeus, he saw the God of salvation as identical with the God of creation.[9]

Gustaf Wingren (1910–2000), who was strongly influenced by Irenaeus early in his career, argued that theology becomes incomprehensible if it does not start with a belief in creation. He asks what it means "that the body 'lives.'" His answer was that all life is received life, that "to live means to receive life from outside oneself."[10] This applied to "resurrection life" as well as "bodily life here and now."[11] He claimed that this

> holds good even now of bodily life, and not just that of believers but of all bodily life. Breathing, searching for food, protection from danger, and warmth, all these are conditions of our human, created life, and are afforded by the contact which human life has with other created things. This contact keeps life in being and sustains human weakness against death.[12]

Irenaeus held that "the flesh can really partake of life." The sign of this is that it is alive.[13] Wingren also describes the Hebraic view of life as regarding the body, though admittedly "frail," as being "not . . . of less worth than the less visible and 'more refined' soul. When the body is alive, it is wholly permeated by the life which God has breathed into it."[14] In the Hebrew Scriptures and the Old Testament, body and soul, or spirit, are not counterposed to each other. When they are portrayed as opposites, it is the human being, "the creature that is being contrasted with God, who is the giver of life."[15]

This creation theology emphasizes, then, that life is a gift that includes a relationship to God. Human beings live in a relation to the Creator of life that is as immediate as breathing. Children who play, cry, and are hungry; the laborer in the field or on the factory floor; the mother and father who take care of their children: all are living in relationships. Both with God, as Creator, and with their fellow human beings and all living things. Hence "we cannot isolate a 'religious' part, our soul, from

---

9. Aulén, *Christus Victor*, 19, 25, 56f.
10. Wingren, *Creation and Law*, 18.
11. Ibid., 18–19.
12. Ibid., 19.
13. Ibid.
14. Ibid.
15. Ibid.

the rest of us, or separate body from the soul on the false assumption that only the soul can have any relationship to God."[16] Every part of professing one's faith involves saying yes to the body. Wingren goes on to explain that it is for this reason that the early church has a fondness for the word "flesh." In the first century, the message of resurrection was truly a gospel, the good news. When Danish theologian N. F. S. Grundtvig (1783–1872) translated Irenaeus's fifth book, which emphasizes the resurrection of the flesh, Wingren proclaimed it a "clarion call of freedom for the enslaved." He went on: "It means that the downtrodden, the oppressed, and the imprisoned could not be broken but have risen up, healed and whole, from their oppression and praised Christ the Victor. To allow the body in its wretchedness merely to disappear would not have been freedom."[17] For him, then, emphasis on the body becomes a sign of redemption and liberation.

For me personally, the Irenaeic tradition that N. F. S. Grundtvig and Gustaf Wingren actualized has left an enduring impression. This means that I am critical of oppositions between spiritual and sensual, of which there is a long tradition throughout the history of the West. I also regard belief in God as a continually active Creator as an important starting point for understanding life, the church, and the future. Inspired by this approach, I seek to maintain the connectedness of creation, rehabilitation, growth, and fulfilment.

This interpretation of life is not self-evident, however. Not everyone sees life as a gift or as created. But Christian faith proceeds from the fact that human beings have a relationship to God as Creator, as liberator, and as Holy Spirit.

Theologian Sigurd Bergmann argues that the point of this Christian doctrine is that

> God's Holy Spirit can work in, with and through all places, spaces and scales of creation. Humans cannot put limits on God's work. The opposite of inner and outer does not represent any border for the Creator. All natural and human borders are always open for the transcending Spirit. We can meet the Life-Giver in the most unexpected places.[18]

---

16. Ibid., 27.
17. Wingren, *Människa och kristen*, 21.
18. Bergmann, "Fetishism Revisited," 207.

This trinitarian perspective is important. Yet many theologians speak only rarely about the ongoing creation or about the life-giving Spirit. They take their point of departure directly in Jesus, as human being and God. If they then immediately proceed from talking about Jesus to talking about the church as Christ's body, there is a risk of the human, created body disappearing from view. At the same time, the Holy Spirit that creates anew, which cannot be directed or controlled, has often been "instrumentalised into structures of ecclesially controlled spirituality, where the Spirit per se was limited to the church and its internal practices."[19]

In the following section, I call this "churchification." It is something I wish to avoid. Human beings as living bodies are always involved in relationships in various settings. No man is an island. I am therefore also doubtful about a rampant individualism that risks placing a decontextualizing and atomizing emphasis upon the singular person.

What Is the Problem?

Our era exhibits an ambivalent attitude towards completely ordinary, physical, human bodies. This equivocation is even more apparent when it comes to animals, which are on the one hand fussed over and loved, and on the other subjected to extreme cruelty by the meat production industry. Bodies are not interchangeable, then. They form part of different contexts. They have different preconditions in life while also sharing something with each other and with all living things. For a theologian and ethicist, this raises questions about our views of the body, historically and in the present. Which philosophical and theological notions have affected or created different attitudes towards the human body and towards what we today call desire, *eros*, and sexuality? Perhaps these phenomena, which human beings share with non-human animals, have brought with them a hesitancy about precisely desire, *eros*, sensuality, and sexuality— the principal objects of my study.

In the history of the Christian West, society, economics, and technology have worked together with philosophical and theological conceptions. The history of theology shows a need to indicate the special status of human beings with respect to the rest of creation. Philosophically and theologically, human beings have also been primarily conceptualized as men. Abrupt shifts have sometimes occurred, materially as well

19. Ibid., 196.

as spiritually. Despite this, certain attitudes, including that of the precedence of human beings and men, seem to die hard.

The history of Christianity is a tapestry made up of incompatible threads. Some filaments in the fabric encourage a reverence for the body and the material, while others pull in an opposite direction, towards, if not a contempt for the body, then a view of the material as something to be transcended in pursuit of something superior and more heavenly. My question is how these notions have affected views of the body, desire, and sexuality, but also attitudes towards the working, ageing, and damaged body. Does it matter how one refers to love, or which concepts are used? Are different kinds of love in competition? Is the emphasis on the proximity or the distance between God and human beings? How is the relationship of human beings to their surroundings, to other people, and to other living creatures presented? Which hierarchies are most important?

One of my aims in getting to grips with Martin Luther and several of his texts is to show the way in which views of the body, sensuality, and sexuality change. Are there any egalitarian and reciprocal aspects that might provide inspiration today? A question that emerges is how spirituality changes when our view of *eros* is renegotiated. Another concerns the degree to which Luther's view differs from, or builds on, the ideas of the early church and late-medieval practices.

I will therefore turn to some key figures from church history such as Origen, Augustine, and Bernard of Clairvaux in order to consider how they viewed the body and sexuality. I will analyze the way in which Luther's writings depart from the ascetic tradition with regard to the perception of the body and its senses. My choice of Church Fathers in chapter 4 was determined by their frequent citation. They form a sounding board for several of our era's most influential theological trends, which claim to represent "classical Christianity" and "orthodox" attitudes. The current renewal of interest in asceticism and spiritual exclusivity, an exclusivity that not infrequently emphasizes the church as a culture that presents an alternative to the world, makes it essential that we read them again. The strong affirmation of the body and the material represented by the Church Father Irenaeus forms the starting point of my conversation. This conversation extends to Luther and other scholars who align themselves with or are critical of these trends. In my reading, I have been influenced by the critique made by feminist theologians of the opposition between spiritual and physical.

An additional goal is thus to engage the help of several contemporary *eros* theologians in order to illuminate and challenge traditional oppositions between different forms of love. Although I do not examine in detail the contemporary debates over desire, I am particularly interested in the consequences that these contrasting views of different kinds of love have entailed for women and for all those who do not fit into the heteropatriarchal norm. I argue here that Luther's use of the erotic language of the nuptial mystery can make a constructive contribution. This forms the background for an argument about the ethical and political consequences of the language of love in our time. In the final chapters I discuss contemporary views of the body and the possible meaning of an emphasis upon God's presence in creation and incarnation.

This study has been carried out within the framework of a project on Lutheran ethics and theology in a post-Christian society, for which I have chosen to study views of the body and sexuality.[20] My interest in Luther stems from the fact that he is an intriguing theologian. This book is thus not a confessional study. On the contrary, I have chosen to highlight what is contradictory and ambivalent. Many of Luther's ideas are based on an extraordinary desire for freedom. They are nonetheless closely bound up with the period in which he lived. Nothing can be done about this. But it is fascinating to look for things in his writing that might be liberating today.

The Reformation's and Luther's experiences of divine presence proved to be revolutionary. A movement emerges out of the search for the unattainable, bittersweet *eros*. This movement emphasizes the present moment and the experience of love as a gift, present in the here and now. Erotic imagery is used by Luther to emphasize union and embrace and leads to a sensual presence. This also entails an affirmation of the body and the material. But what happened to *eros*? Here, too, *eros* theology may be able to help resolve unnecessary oppositions.

Methodological Reflections and Perspectives

My perspective has been formed by the insights that earlier feminist theologians have provided into the importance of the body's and one's

---

20. In 2006, I initiated a new research project on Luther and Lutheran theology and ethics in collaboration with Professor Carl-Henric Grenholm. One of its first results was the anthology: Gerle, *Luther som utmaning*. The project was later led by Professor Grenholm, with financial support from the Swedish Research Council.

own experiences and of the importance of interpreting these experiences. In dialogue with new voices that are challenging the dominance of Eurocentric theology, I want to read Luther partly against himself and partly in conversation with contemporary scholars. Postcolonial theory emphasizes ambivalence and hybridity. Old and new voices mingle. Different linguistic fields cross like overlapping intersections, creating something new, not merely in the meeting, but in the spaces in between. This has also affected my reading.

One of my starting points has been that a theologian's personal identity and struggles are of great significance for theology. The body, eroticism, and sexuality can never be excluded. At the same time, theology affects discussion of God and human beings as well as our views of the body and sensuality, as becomes apparent from any overview of the history of ideas. Origen and especially Augustine have shaped the West's view of the body and sexuality. With the help of various scholars, I will retrace some of mysticism's several strands. Which bodies receive attention? What purpose or goal is ascribed to the body? What aspect becomes paramount and is regarded as natural or desirable? How are the other senses and sensuality viewed? What is obscured in the writings of these Church Fathers and Luther? A reading of selected texts by Luther will serve as the starting point for an intertextual conversation with contemporary scholars as well as for an argument about views of different notions of love and of contemporary ambivalence towards the body and sensuality.

My interlocutor in all this will thus be Martin Luther, the chief inspiration and namesake of the Lutheran tradition, but also contemporary scholars with whom I engage in an intertextual conversation about attitudes towards the body, sexuality, eroticism, and vulnerability. Luther's texts will be interrogated on the basis of current issues and of seemingly self-evident notions of eroticism, sexuality, sensuality, and the body. In a dialogue with scholars interested in the body's significance for theology, I develop an argument around points of intersection that reveal affinities, tensions, and outright conflicts. Rather than allowing Luther or the present moment to define a norm for right and wrong, I engage in a dialogue with other scholars in order to tease out new patterns and new intersections in the juncture between them. Luther thereby becomes an interlocutor who at times directs critical questions toward the present and at other times serves as the object of my own critical questions.[21]

21. Cf. Tracy, *The Analogical Imagination*.

I have chosen to position myself at a point of intersection in order to listen to different voices and develop arguments from different perspectives. Needless to say, this comes at the price of a linear, traditional, and systematic exposition. In a conversation, certain themes will reappear in different contexts. As a writer, I often find myself within the in-between space where these questions are posed. My sometimes associative style is connected to the fact that I am also a jazz singer and thus think that improvisations and digressions are occasionally valuable. I have perhaps also been influenced by Martin Luther himself, who always prioritized responding to current events and developments over a more systematic exposition. He dared to be an existential theologian even when it meant challenging traditional forms.

Martin Luther always wrote in full awareness of the larger context of an issue and did not shy away from the great challenges of his time. This is apparent from his unsystematic working methods and the way in which his writings frequently engage with a pressing issue of the moment. This means that he sometimes changes his opinion and contradicts himself. For this reason I have pursued an intertextual dialogue between different texts from his pen.

Culture involves a set of related symbolic systems that create value in the present and legitimate certain forms of activity, while disparaging and denigrating their opposing values and stigmatizing activities deemed incompatible with the lifestyle being advocated. Within this process, certain symbols are given priority over others. Certain symbols are crucial and come to the fore. They are used to interpret and rank in order of precedence those symbols that are seen as less valuable. These priorities and their hierarchies are internalized by every human being, often without reflection. The result is a normalizing of specific cultural ideologies that are then recreated and reproduced in everyday life. In discussions and debates as well as in research, these particular approaches and perspectives can to some extent be made visible. Yet no one can entirely step outside this process and claim to represent objectivity or universality. This must always be sought from the starting point of the particular. In theology, it is important to ask what is important. Should theology concern itself with the body or our views on it?

In the work of Graham Ward we encounter the view of culture that I have just described.[22] It can be read as a part of a tradition going back

---

22. Ward, "On the Politics of Embodiment."

to Durkheim. An alternative way of talking about culture would involve including different points of departure, attitudes towards power, and opportunities for effecting change. My purpose in basing my interpretation on perspectives influenced by feminist and liberation theologies is to avoid a classless and Eurocentric reading. New movements are identifying power structures, with the result that what constitutes progress for some parties can also be a defeat for others.

I have chosen to read Luther intertextually, then. This means that I sometimes allow certain texts by Luther to speak to another Luther. Through my case studies and close readings of early Church Fathers, I show how Luther partly belongs to his tradition and partly does something new. In this encounter something unique is created.

By studying how Luther uses the erotic language of the nuptial mystery, I investigate whether a number of binary opposites that have long defined the Lutheran tradition can be interpreted less dualistically. I argue that his concept of love is considerably more multifaceted than the traditional opposition between *eros* and *agape*. I additionally consider Luther's ethical and political applications of eroticism's figurative language. Here I assess whether this can contribute to contemporary ethical and political discussions of shared life in close relationships as well as to societal and cosmic relations.

Gustavo Gutiérrez, one of the giants of liberation theology, argued that liberation comprises three levels.[23] The first level relates to the socio-economic. The second emphasizes a process of humanization that runs throughout history. Finally, the third aims to realize a full community with God beyond time and space, and thus contains a transcendent dimension. It is possible to read Luther as having been interested only in the third of these three generally accepted definitions of liberation,[24] that which concerns a human being's communion with God. I contend, however, that his understanding of communion with God as a gift in the here and now resulted in changes to societies and structures and contributed to making human beings independent. It thereby involved all three levels.

In my view, every text encapsulates a perspective, consciously or otherwise. A text is always accompanied by a pre-understanding and a subtext. It is never a *tabula rasa*. My pre-understanding includes the notion that Luther did indeed facilitate the empowering and authorizing of

23. Gutiérrez, *Theology of Liberation*, 36–37, 176, 235.
24. See Westhelle, *Eschatology and Space*, 83.

human beings and thereby, in the long run, contributed to a democratization of societies and structures. My perspective is theological even when interpreting secular or general cultural conceptions in the present.

Material

While looking for material suited to a study of attitudes towards the body's senses, sexuality, and eroticism in Luther, I have found relatively little relevant secondary scholarship. A few of Luther's writings take up the subject quite openly. To a greater extent, however, it takes the form of passing references in letters and table talk. Often it is visible in the interim spaces between statements, as something unstated that is nonetheless taken for granted, or in some aspect of practical life, such as the many letters Luther wrote to his wife Katharina von Bora during his long absences from home. My aim here is to reconstruct at least a part of this jigsaw. Because many of its pieces are awkward and contradictory, the resulting image is sketchy. In his 2011 doctoral dissertation, Charles Lloyd Cortright made a detailed study of the human body in Martin Luther's theology.[25] However, I have otherwise been unable to find any sustained analysis of Luther and the body in relation to contemporary theological trends.

By contrast, marriage has been examined by many commentators, as has the importance of the family, or, rather, the large household, for Luther and Lutheran theology. Despite having considered sexuality in relation to approaches to marriage, Lutheran theologians, with a few exceptions, have been largely silent on the issues of body and sexuality. In Luther's writings, however, both the body and sensuality are highly present. This is apparent in various of his texts that treat human shared life, but also in those in-between spaces where it is possible to detect turning points and contradictions. His table talk contains scattered references to both food and bodily closeness. These intersections stage encounters between then and now. Also visible are some of the theological origins of the societal changes that the Reformation and Martin Luther effected with regard to views of the body, sensuality, and sexuality.

The texts by Luther that will here serve as the basis for a dialogue between Martin Luther and contemporary scholars are, above all, those that contribute to how we view the body, sexual desire, and sexuality. They

---

25. Cortright, "'Poor Maggot-Sack that I Am.'"

include Martin Luther's tracts *On the Freedom of a Christian* (1520), *A Letter to Several Nuns* (1522), *The Estate of Marriage* (1522), and *Sermon on a Marriage* (1531). I will also make reference to Luther's commentaries on Genesis, which were compiled by his students between 1535 and 1545. Other texts, such as sermons and letters, will underpin a discussion of the part played by theology, that is, our attitude towards a relationship with God, in intersocial relations. In one of his more central texts, *On the Freedom of a Christian* (1520), he uses the erotic language of the nuptial mystery and images from the Song of Solomon. This connects to a tradition that has long interpreted these images as metaphors of the love between God and the believer, or between Christ and the church. So, too, did Martin Luther. But he emphasizes presence in a way that disrupts traditional frameworks. His experience of Christ's love becomes something that he applies politically as well as to earthly love.

Organization

Following this introductory chapter, I discuss views of Luther and why it is important to question established images and patterns. Our current image of Luther is ambiguous. He is seen as a champion of liberty and, alternately, as an oppressor. In the subsequent chapter I argue for the importance of focusing upon the human body. I do so partly in agreement with and partly in opposition to powerful theological trends of the present moment, which treat the body primarily as a symbol of the church. In chapter 4, I sketch out a concise intellectual history of the mystical tradition, using the work of international scholars such as Grace M. Jantzen, Caroline Walker Bynum, Bernard McGinn, and Andrew Louth. In chapter 5, I develop these themes further and summarize Martin Luther's view of the body, sexual desire, sensuality, and sexuality. I point out that sensuality is directed towards the everyday.

Chapter 6 comprises a study of the nuptial mystery as a theme of Luther's writings. Else Marie Wiberg Pedersen and Kathryn Kleinhans show how Luther aligns himself with traditional interpretative models while also doing something new with them. These ideas form the background for some normative arguments that highlight their inspirational possibilities for contemporary relationships.

Chapter 7 takes Nietzsche's challenge as its starting point. He claims that Christianity gave *eros* a poisoned chalice, which meant that "he" degenerated into a burden.[26] This chapter outlines a number of contributions to Scandinavian creation theology that provide a contrast to contemporary theological trends. The focus of the former is the everyday body rather than desire. A critique of Nygren's classic opposition between *eros* and *agape* forms a bridge to chapter 8, in which I introduce several key concepts in the work of representatives of so-called *eros* theology. These are shown to offer a challenge to the rigid distinction between different forms of love that have sometimes defined Lutheran theology. I enter here into a dialogue with American theologian Catherine Keller.

In chapter 9, I discuss views of the body in relation to concepts such as representation and presence, both then and now. Whereas the body in the late medieval period was regarded as a means for attaining eternal life through ascetic transformation, the healthy and physically fit body has now come to seem like the ultimate object of a kind of secular salvation. Making a Lutheran interpretation here becomes a challenge to both perspectives. Moreover, a close reading of Luther's own texts shows that he reapplies the intimate and erotic relationship, which has traditionally represented the bond between God and the soul, to intimate human relationships while retaining subjectivity for both parties. In the final chapter, I discuss the potential political consequences of views of the vulnerable, erotic, and sexual body in relationships. The presence of sensuality is significant for both body and spirit. Luther's writings present the relationship between God and human beings as a sensual and loving embrace in the here and now. Sensuality moves from the unattainable and bittersweet to a presence in the present. In so doing, it affirms human, sensual love. In the process, new themes emerge—prosperity and life in abundance.

Each chapter is written in a manner that it can be read independently, which explains some intentional repetitions.

---

26. Eros was at this time seen as referring to the Greek god of love—while, of course, also being a designation for desire—and thus referred to as "he" by Nietzsche.

2

Luther: Heroic Liberator or Oppressor?

Reading the classics is coming back. It is important to position oneself in relation to tradition, not least in order to make conscious that which is unconscious. We can find both inspiration and resistance by allowing chords struck in the past to be heard again in relation to contemporary questions. My hope is that Luther's breakthrough on key theological issues will be given a hearing in contemporary debate, and that its occasionally discordant tones will serve as a reminder that all instruments need continual retuning. Some strings may need replacing.[1] What should be viewed as essential is largely determined by our present moment, given that we have limited access to Luther's era. Yet, no more than the self-evident truths of our own, the values of Luther's day should not be allowed to serve as criteria for what counts as good in the present moment. Greater awareness of what has been considered self-evident or "natural" can, however, lead to a critical conversation that asks questions of his historical context as well as ours. Cultural critique offers a way out of our present moment's self-absorption.

Mediating a tradition involves both relaying something and betraying it. Allowing Martin Luther's ideas to be heard in the background is—to adopt Michel Foucault's celebrated formulation—one way to change history in the present.[2] Anders Mogård uses the term "rework-

---

1. The term *theology* is here used in its literal sense as talk about God. But to talk about God is also to talk about humans and the world. It is related to experience and context. See Ruether, *Sexism and God-Talk*.

2. Poster, "Foucault, the Present and History," 105–21; Foucault, *The Order of Things*.

ing tradition" to denote an "active, critical, and constructive approach" to tradition.[3] Mogård shows how Nathan Söderblom (1866–1931)—Swedish Nobel Prize laureate, archbishop, and professor—reads Luther, putting the latter and his ideas into historical context as a way to address important questions. In this way, Söderblom does something new with Luther. My view is that to some extent everyone does this, more or less consciously, by positioning themselves in relation to a strong tradition and a highly charismatic innovator. In joining this long succession of interpreters, including some pioneers, I do so consciously, as a woman with the advantage of often living close to extra-European perspectives.

Who Was This Luther, Then?

There are many images and readings of Luther. Some basic facts may nonetheless be in order. Luther was born on November 10, 1483, in Eisleben in Saxony and died on February 18, 1546. His father, a leaseholder of mines, was ambitious and wanted his son to become a lawyer. In accordance with his father's wishes, he registered for a university law degree, only to abandon it for philosophy and theology. His decision to leave academia in order to become a monk is sometimes attributed to a thunderstorm on July 2, 1505. When a bolt of lightning struck nearby, he is supposed to have made a promise to take holy orders.

Whether a stormy night or an interest in theology led him to become an Augustinian monk need not detain us here. But he has gone down in history as the German priest, monk, and theologian who initiated the Protestant Reformation. In 1517, as professor of theology, he attacked the church in Rome in his famous Ninety-Five Theses. In them, he polemicized against the church's sale of indulgences, a kind of letter that enabled one to buy oneself free from God's punishment for sins committed. Luther's theses provoked violent reactions, but he refused to apologize for his writings. He was subsequently excommunicated by Pope Leo X. At the Diet of Worms in 1521 he was pronounced an outlaw. Luther claimed, at the risk of his own life, that no one is saved by good deeds but that salvation is a free gift of God, which can only be received by grace through faith in Jesus Christ. He additionally argued that the Bible was the only source of divinely revealed knowledge. He also opposed the authority of the pope and the view that priests were intermediaries between

---

3. Mogård, *Förtröstans hermeneutik*.

God and people. Until that point the Bible had been read in Latin. Luther now translated it from Hebrew and Greek into German. In the reformed territories, mass began to be celebrated in the vernacular instead of Latin. Luther himself composed many psalms and songs in German in order to make his teachings more accessible. So that everyone could read and understand, he introduced literacy teaching for everyone, regardless of gender or social status.

As a monk, Luther strove for righteousness. He mortified himself more severely than others, fasted, and prayed to meet a merciful God. After several years' struggle, he had a breakthrough that allowed him to believe himself forgiven. This was a powerful experience. It transformed his life. Rather than trying to reach the divine and to find forgiveness by means of the monastic life and asceticism, he began to see faith as a gift to be received freely, by grace.

He began to encourage monks and nuns to leave the cloister if they had not themselves chosen to enter. There are sensational accounts of him helping nuns to escape. While tales of using herring barrels to escape are probably apocryphal, an open cart was used on at least one occasion. Covered with a canvas, this cart was used for deliveries to the convent. The nuns were helped to escape from the convent in it.[4] One of those nuns on the run was Katharina von Bora. Her companions in the convent were married off, one after the other, until finally only she was left. She then proposed that, if she were to get married, it would have to be to Dr. Martin Luther himself. And so it turned out. Within three weeks they were married. This apparently pragmatic marriage seems to have been very happy. In the eyes of the law, however, marriage with a priest was considered concubinage. This meant that any offspring could not inherit. Despite this, Luther suggested that Katharina should be the trustee of their children after his death; his will was not followed. Only after Luther's death was the law revised in the duchy of Saxony so that marriage with a Protestant priest became legally valid.[5]

For Luther, marriage became the locus of sexuality, just as it had been for Augustine long ago. His rejection of monastic life's claim to be more spiritual led to him defending marriage and sexuality. Luther interpreted this as a "natural" life. This became a key battle-line against Rome. Marriage was no longer regarded as a sacrament but as a good regulation.

4. Stolt, *Luther själv*, 183.
5. Ibid., 185.

However, Luther viewed marriage and the family as far more important than monastic life. In it lay people's vocation towards their fellow human beings. As he did not accept monastic life as a higher spiritual calling, the everyday became a mode of divine service.

Large Households for Support, Procreation, and Intimacy

In Luther's time, the large household provided economic support while meeting its members' needs for not merely accommodation but warmth, care, and intimacy. *Oeconomia* thus denotes both economics and family. Kekke Stadin has shown that households are erotically affirmative as well as controlling. Nonetheless, she argues that the "new, affirmative attitude towards sexuality" was not always apparent to the great mass of the people.[6] She points out that theological debate and the unconditional channeling of sexuality into marriage, which was governed by several different interests, only partially affected the legal and moral norms of society. All the "measures which were taken against extramarital sexuality—within the fields of ecclesiastical and temporal law alike—tended to overshadow the positive view of sexuality within marriage," she argues.[7] We will come back to these interpretations of sexuality and their significance. Just like sexuality and the body, the different estates can be interpreted as liberating, dynamic, and inclusive or as hierarchical, patriarchal, and exclusive.

The large household in Luther's day was a reproductive sphere that was responsible for economic support, procreation, and many of its members' physical and emotional needs. Sensuality occupied a prominent place. Within this sphere (*oeconomia*), intimacy had its place, while the political sphere (*politia*) was meant to maintain justice, peace, and order, and the sphere of the church (*ecclesia*) was expected to sustain people with words of forgiveness. While many scholars have written about the differing goal and logic of each estate, I am more interested in what unites them, since I see each of them as a sphere of promise intended to help people.[8]

---

6. Stadin, *Stånd och genus*, 44.

7. Ibid.

8. I have used the notion "spheres of promise" in several articles. See Gerle, "From Homogeneous Nations to Pluralism"; Gerle, "Eros, Ethics, and Politics"; Gerle, "Var dags."

In the sixteenth century, the distinction between private and public was very different from today. Our conception of the private simply did not exist. Luther described a human being as both a person and an office, "Person und Amt." But even in this official capacity, Christ's love was expected to influence people's lives.[9] Even being a child or a parent was seen as an office, no less than being a teacher or a jurist. The lines of demarcation were completely different, in other words.

Katharina von Bora supported not just Martin Luther but also a growing family. This escaped nun, who had learned Latin in the monastery, seems to have been a talented businesswoman. Through her lodging house for students in Wittenberg and her brewing business, she made it possible for Dr. Martin to write Bible commentaries, pamphlets, and theological tracts. He was thus dependent on his wife, whom he loved and respected and did not wish to exchange for either France or Venice.[10] He affectionately called her his very own Letter to the Galatians.[11] This Pauline letter, which describes being redeemed by grace rather than deeds, was Luther's favorite text in the whole Bible. It may even imply that he saw Katharina as a grace, a gift he had received without effort on his part.

Luther had the means to marry, perhaps thanks to Katharina and her enterprise. However, many others had to wait for a long time before they could wed. Others could not or would not. What was it like for them when sexuality was so closely aligned with marriage and everyone was expected to live the everyday life of a good Christian? The transformation brought about by the Reformation was not for the good of everyone.

Tradition and Freedom: Three Reasons to Reread Luther

There are at least three reasons to reread Luther. The first is that it is important for a general public who is interested in culture. Since the sixteenth century the Lutheran legacy has been influenced by its surroundings. From the vantage point of the present, it includes both good and bad patterns.

---

9. Hägglund, *Arvet från reformationen*, 136–42, 146.

10. WA TR 1, 17, (no. 49) 1531, "[10] Jch wolt mein Ketha nit vmb Frankreich noch vmb [11] Venedig dazu geben, zum ersten darumb, das mir sie Gott geschenkt hatt vnd [12] mich yhr geben hatt."

11. Stolt, *Luther själv*, 185.

Some elements must be rejected, above all the anti-Semitism and xenophobia that became part of the unitary Lutheran societies in which state and religion were closely tied. Anti-Semitism goes back to medieval traditions that began in the twelfth century. However, Luther articulates this with great venom in his 1543 treatise *Von den Juden und ihren Lügen* (*On the Jews and Their Lies*). Luther's polemical and in places savage attack on the pope and, even more, on Jews and the invading "Turk" should be understood in its historical context and is something we must today distance ourselves from. Even in debates today, diatribes are routinely launched at Catholics, Jews, and Muslims, albeit from a secular perspective. There are, then, special reasons for Lutheran national churches to be aware of their history and to distance themselves from the tendency to categorically identify particular people as undemocratic and less reliable on the grounds of their religion or faith.[12]

However, other aspects of the Lutheran tradition are a source of pride. These include the fact that the reformed territories led the way in implementing mass literacy for people of all social backgrounds.[13] It was equally revolutionary in the sixteenth century that girls as well as boys were taught to read. Luther, of course, maintained that all were equal before God, regardless of birth or gender. Every human being also had direct access to God. Life, but also the Bible, were important guides. Everyone should therefore learn to read and write at least a little: learning one's catechism and being able to read the Bible oneself were emphasized. Why was this so important? In 1684, Sweden's ecclesiastical law stated that people should "see with their own eyes what God is offering and commanding in his holy word."[14] Laypeople, those not ordained, should be able to determine whether the priest is preaching true doctrine—namely, that human beings were redeemed by faith, not by deeds.

This did not mean, however, that people were seen as equal in society. Even so, equality before God gradually came to affect relationships between people, too. Literacy and a fundamental conviction of the equality of all before God became important steps towards democracy.

---

12. In the Nordic region, e.g., in Denmark and Sweden, the Reformation was part of nation building. One consequence was that only Lutherans were treated as reliable citizens. See Gerle, *Mångkulturalism*; Gerle, *Mänskliga rättigheter*; Gerle, "Nationalism, Reformation"; Gerle, *Farlig förenkling*.

13. See, e.g., Lindmark, *Alphabeta Varia*.

14. Tegborg, "Från kyrkolag," 42.

Contemporary values can thus in part be shown to have deep roots in the Lutheran intellectual tradition.

Another reason to read Luther is that it is vital to identify different possible readings of what Martin Luther represented, not least for those who regard themselves as participants in an evangelical Lutheran tradition. Today, it is neither possible nor desirable to use Luther as a norm for what is right and wrong. Reading him in relation to what we are talking about now can both call into question and affirm contemporary values and attitudes. If one accepts the fact that traditions change, the question arises as to which narrative we should choose to tell. Using history consciously means trying to identify and reveal which history, which narratives and themes, we choose to emphasize and connect to in our tradition.

The concept "uses of history" is used widely among historians, among others, who grapple with the Reformation.[15] It is one way to indicate an awareness that there is no simple way to bridge the temporal and historical gap separating our era from that in which Martin Luther's texts were written. Even so, it can be argued, as Johanna Gustafsson Lundberg does, that for people's ability to live a good life it matters greatly whether only certain forms of historical memory are permitted, one particular version of history has a monopoly, or several forms of historical narrative are given a voice."[16] She contends that several kinds of historical narrative make possible a widening of perspective that can prevent the enshrining of a single approach.[17] I would also say that it not only affirms a liberal, pluralist multiplicity but makes it possible, in the cacophony of competing voices, to argue that some interpretations are more reasonable than others—and, above all, better for people and the world.

Thirdly, it is important for Christians from other traditions—such as the family of Orthodox churches, the Roman Catholic church, and the Reformed churches and societies—to see what they share with the Lutherans as well as what divides them. Much of what Luther stood for is not unique, but is shared by Christians from different traditions. At the same time, there is in his experience and in the appeal it makes a freedom that has often been lost for long periods in Lutheran unitary societies.

---

15. See, e.g., Nordbäck, "Kyrkohistorisk historiebruksforskning."
16. Gustafsson Lundberg, *Medlem 2010*, 12.
17. Ibid.

Many emphases that we today associate with Luther derive from his time and context. Moreover, they have been defined by how his message has been interpreted and used in different contexts.[18] This can seem passé or something that is shared by many others.

For me personally, all three of these tasks are vital. The writings of Luther and other reformers contain ideas that remain important. These include ideas about everyone being "equal" before God, the universal priesthood, and the belief that it is our fellow human beings, not God, who need our good works.[19]

Seeking Answers from the Perspective of a Wound, a Dilemma

Luther's method of taking his own and his contemporaries' questions seriously, and of seeking answers from new vantage points, is a source of inspiration. He is sometimes described as a situational ethicist. A situation can be described as an occasion when different issues, forces, and events in one's milieu come together and trigger a response.[20] A response can have different consequences and is therefore not the same thing as a cause. Many before Martin Luther had reacted to the decline of the church and to both existential and bodily poverty. What prompted Luther to initiate a reformation derived from his reading of the situation and from the forces and events around him. Creative thinking not infrequently takes place in the proximity of a wound, argues Mary McClintock Fulkerson.[21] When one experiences or recognizes a dilemma, it forcibly generates new ideas in relation to tradition. In the process, new patterns of insight and reality arise. Various kinds of liberation theology have arisen in precisely this way. When I read Luther, I do so through spectacles that are tinted by complex, overlapping, intersectional "wounds" that female scholars and theologians outside Europe have helped identify. Proceeding from wounds that do great harm to human bodies no less than to social bodies, I therefore approach Luther anew. Since our era gives special treatment to successful people with attractive bodies, a yearning is created in us to belong to precisely this group. Yet many are ending up outside and

---

18. See Blåder, *Lutheran Tradition as Heritage and Tool*.
19. WA 7, 12–38; cf. LW 31 "Von der Freiheit" (1520).
20. Fulkerson, "Interpreting a Situation," 38.
21. Ibid.

becoming increasingly invisible. In tandem with this, there is a growing risk of being exploited. My point here is that Luther's conviction that our lives are given and not an achievement, or performance, represents a cultural critique. Perhaps it can help heal one of our era's wounds.

There is inspiration in Luther's existential attempt to relate to what Paul Tillich calls "the ultimate concern."[22] Even though his attitude endangered his position, his career, and even his life, he dared to stand up for what he thought was right. Nevertheless, daring to risk one's life is in itself not a criterion of good or evil. It is therefore important to ask: for what?

In Luther's Shadow, or Luther in the Shade

And so we return to the question of what to do with Luther. In his own writings a contradictory image appears. Not infrequently the Luther we meet there is sensual and physical, a million miles away from puritanism and prudishness. He has *joie de vivre* and appreciates the good things in life. Despite this, he seems not to have entirely shed his ambivalent feelings about sexual desire. He accepts sexuality and reproduction, but often associates powerful, almost uncontrollable sexual desire with the immense power of sin.[23] At the same time, in his letter *To Several Nuns* he describes sexual desire as something natural for both men and women.[24]

How he really views *eros* or eroticism is harder to pin down. By the time the Hebrew Bible was translated into Greek, around 300 BC, the word *eros* as a designation for love had come to be associated with the Greek god of love. This made it difficult to use within the context of a monotheistic worldview such as Judaism or Christianity.[25]

And yet there is more *eros* in Luther's texts and in his everyday life than we tend to imagine. Further investigation is needed here: we need to interpret not merely what remains unsaid but also what lies in the spaces between his words, sometimes in his praxis. I contend that the tension between *eros* and *agape* in Luther's writings is not as great or as cut-and-dried as Anders Nygren paints it.[26] When Luther takes human life as his

---

22. See Tillich, *Dynamics of Faith*, 5.
23. WA 42, 53–54, "Genesisvorlesung" (1535–38); cf. WA 24:90–91.
24. WA Br 3, 327–28, (no. 766) "Luther an drei Klosterjungfrauen" (1524).
25. Jeanrond, "Kärlekens praxis," 231; cf. Rubenson, "Himmelsk åtrå," 231.
26. This will be analyzed in chapter 7.

starting point for describing God, what recurs is the motif of a mother's love and of people's everyday care for each other. As Luther asks rhetorically, if people show this much love to one another, how great must God's love be?[27] Luther's Christ mystery contains powerful erotic elements. At the same time, there is more reciprocity in our relationship to God than has traditionally been argued.

Three issues are important for Lutheran theology, namely, the doctrine of justification, the universal priesthood, and the doctrine of vocation. Each is significant for the way Luther uses erotic imagery in order to foreground a paradoxical view of freedom and constraint in relationships. Just as he faced opposition on different fronts, the mediation of tradition today finds itself in a relationship with its surrounding society and differing views of life. In our time a respectful conversation that avoids alienating or distancing itself from its counterpart has much to gain from knowledge.

What inspires or attracts me in all this comes down to the way that Luther is paradoxical and contradictory while all the time struggling with existential questions. He finds himself in a period of transition and is sometimes regarded as one of the initiators of modernity by virtue of emphasizing the authoritative individual. It is also this that makes him so intriguing. "Luther wanted to speak directly to God as an individual and without awkwardness," argued Nietzsche, according to Erik Erikson.[28] Luther is sometimes seen as representing the struggle for a human being with her own religious authority. At the same time, he was, like many innovators, contradictory. Authority did not apply to all areas and could not be treated in any fashion. Luther's contradictory tendencies make him existentially interesting. This has an interest that extends far beyond the confessional groups who see themselves as part of an evangelical Lutheran tradition. Just as Luther chose to align himself with particular strands within his tradition, partly in order to reinterpret and break with that tradition, I contend that we are doing the same thing today. We take a stance on the tradition of which we are a part, consciously or otherwise. Those of us working within Lutheran theology and ethics today are saying both more and simultaneously less than Luther himself did.

---

27. Cf. WA TR 1, 189 (no. 437) "Tischreden" (1533).
28. Erikson, *Kulturkris och religion*, 137.

Luther and Contemporary Voices: A Crossroads on Several Levels

In this book I am therefore discussing sensuality in a dialogue with Luther and our contemporaries, even if the latter are not easily identified. Present-day questions force us to interrogate history, partly in order to make visible our hidden cultural legacy, partly in order to gain some perspective on ourselves. One obvious starting point is that this cultural legacy comprises both good and bad.

Equally obvious is the fact that the unitary subject from which Lutheran theology has often proceeded does not exist, either in Luther's day or in the present.[29] People are not just male or female but more plural, with several overlapping identities in which gender, sexuality, ethnicity, and skin color interact. Some aspects of identity can reinforce exclusion and oppression while others confer status and belonging. A black lesbian is thus not only a woman. Her skin color and sexual orientation play a part in determining how she is perceived. Her place in society, which not infrequently is a marginalized one, is reinforced by the fact that she is a woman, black, and homosexual.

In corresponding fashion, it is still often the case that being male, white, and heterosexual confers greater advantages and a higher status. In contemporary scholarship, this is a way of describing people intersectionally, as bearers of many overlapping identities. The concept of intersectionality gestures towards the impossibility of analytically differentiating between certain categories, which instead work together in complex ways. Behind it lies an ambition to make visible specific situations of oppression that are created by the intersection of power relations based on race, gender, and class.[30] This can also provide a methodological perspective. It involves, then, new threads of the fabric becoming visible by virtue of overlapping with each other, but also catching a glimpse of what lies in the interstices, the cracks, and in that which remains unstated.

Historical Images

The year 2017 marks the five hundredth anniversary of Luther's nailing his Ninety-Five Theses to the church door in Wittenberg. It may therefore

---

29. The destabilized subject is often connected with the work of Judith Butler.
30. Reyes and Mulinari, *Intersektionalitet*, 18; Svalfors, *Andlighetens*, 14, 38–40f.

be worth recalling how each era has chosen to see Luther as the solution to its greatest problems.

Various Reformation anniversaries have passed and each has been defined by its historical moment, writes Margot Käßman.[31] She cites historian Hartmut Lehmann, who showed how, in 1617, people celebrated Luther and confessional self-confidence. In 1717, the emphasis was on stylizing Luther as a pietistic and devout man, or as an early Enlightenment figure standing up to medieval superstition. In 1817, the anniversary was held as a national celebration for the memory of those slaughtered at the Battle of Leipzig four years earlier. Luther became a German national hero.

In 1883, the quartercentennial of Luther's birth, Luther was promoted to the founder of the German Empire, and in 1917, he finally became, together with Hindenburg, savior of the German identity in a time of dire adversity. In 1933, Luther was decked in the aura of the divinely sent Führer, or made the latter's harbinger. And in 1946, on the quartercentennial of Luther's death, he was cast as comforter of the German people at a time when comfort was desperately needed. In 1983, a dispute over the Lutheran legacy broke out between East and West Germany. In the German Democratic Republic, Luther was now no longer a servant of the sovereign but a representative of the proto-bourgeois revolution.

This simple history should serve as a humbling object lesson for any scholar who wants to interpret Luther. I therefore make limited claims for my own reading. By highlighting certain themes that have only rarely commanded attention, I wish to nuance our image of Luther, but also to offer a constructive re-examination and reinterpretation. When reading Luther, I want to exercise both empathy and critical distance.

The various images of Luther alternate with each other.[32] This is important to note for all those who in any way emphasize, or seek to dissociate themselves from, the Lutheran legacy as culture and theology. Discussing contemporary issues using the writings of a great reformer is not a way to trace the origin of those issues genetically, or to find the right answers. Rather, the questions being asked today determine which questions strike us as relevant. The recent renewal of interest in physicality and *ascesis*, in both its secular and religious forms, makes it relevant to discuss the body, sexuality, sensuality, and eroticism. I do so in a setting

---

31. Käßmann, *Schlag nach bei Luther*, preface.
32. Aurelius, *Luther i Sverige*.

that is shaped by a discourse of deliberate uses of history. By this, I mean that we always use history in relation to the present and the future. I also believe that the historical other can shed light upon what we take for granted in the present.

The Whole World

The Reformation insisted that the whole world belonged to God. All people, not merely Christians or a chosen few, were seen as collaborators in an ongoing creation. Both the church and the world were viewed as God's creation, but also as a battlefield between God and the devil. Continual new creation stands against destruction, life against death.

And yet theological claims to let theology govern all of society run directly counter to Martin Luther's critique of subordinating everything to theology or to the rule of the church.[33] For him, the idea that God is at work within every station of society[34] represented a way to challenge the supremacy of Rome, but also to affirm a view of creation in which God works in different ways in different areas. Limitations of space prevent me from considering in greater detail what is known as the two kingdoms doctrine,[35] but I do want to refer to what is usually called the estates doctrine. The two kingdoms doctrine in our era risks being interpreted on the basis of the modern oppositions between private and public or between religious or secular, divisions that did not exist in Luther's time.

Luther's ideas about the two kingdoms—one spiritual and one worldly, running through everything, not only people's hearts but all institutions, ecclesiastical and temporal—have often served as a pretext for the church to care only about the spiritual. The nation-state's influence over the church did not result in a clear demarcation between church and state. It was rather the case that "subjects" were expected to belong to the "right church."[36] In the early stages of the Reformation, the church was anything but unpolitical. The division between state and church, law and gospel, often led to a passivity towards political and economic power so long as the latter did not interfere in the church's affairs and permitted it

---

33. This discussion will re-emerge in relation to Radical Orthodoxy.
34. B. Brock, "Why the Estates?," 179.
35. I analyze the Two Kingdom theory in "Lutheran Theology," 210–28.
36. Sigurdson, *Det postsekulära*, 350; cf. Gerle, "Kristna fristående," 70.

to preach the gospel.³⁷ However, such an understanding of the two kingdoms doctrine misses Luther's dialectic, which is often a matter of simultaneity, not either/or. God acts in different ways in different spheres, simultaneously. Such binaries, which are at once separate and connected, are plentiful in Luther's writing, observes Margareta Brandby-Cöster.³⁸ Everyone is seen as requiring to give an account of themselves to God, regardless of whether they are active in the temporal or the ecclesiastical sphere. Despite having different tasks, they are all supposed to protect life and God's ongoing creation.

Luther did not only have ideas about different kingdoms, however. He drew on Aristotle's thinking about given social orders. From the reformist point of view, these so-called estates were supposed to protect life against evil. I would argue that they can therefore be regarded as realms of promises. The fact that Luther refers here to three estates—*politia*, *oeconomia*, and *ecclesia*—makes it easier to avoid a reading of the different kingdoms as a simple opposition between private and public or between church and state. However, the estates have often been defined by hierarchical concepts and theories of natural superiority and subordination, especially between man and woman.³⁹

Changing Structures and Orders

Reading Luther through the filter of contemporary culture, we find much that is offensive. His worldview was filled with hierarchical notions. People related to each other as superiors and subordinates, in households as

37. As we know, several important Lutheran theologians adopted a passive or positive stance towards the Nazi regime in Germany by referring to the Two Kingdoms theory, whereas I claim that it is important to focus on the equal value of all human beings as created by God. This means not choosing the particular perspective where you react first when your own organization is threatened. During the Third Reich, this meant distancing yourself from the politics of separation that led to persecution of Jews, Romani people, and homosexuals. Cf. Lind, "Kristen," 30–42.

38. Margareta Brandby-Cöster comments, "Luther's *simul* is not about first being sinner and then righteous, but being both-and. For example, he refers to human beings as both sinners and righteous—simultaneously (*simul*) sinners and righteous. It is thus not a question of *first-then* but of *both-and*. (As a sinner, a human being is righteous because God makes both the sinner and the godless righteous.) You also find law and gospel, hidden and revealed God, God and devil, faith and deeds, etc. These are all opposites, both separated and held together." See Brandby-Cöster, "Sökvägar och ledtrådar," 55. When I refer to the dialectic in Luther I refer to this both-and, *simul*.

39. See, e.g., Thielecke, *Theologische Ethik*, 335f.

well as in politics. This was something Martin Luther accepted and even emphasized. Since the breakthrough of democracy we imagine that our leaders and managers are responsible to their boards or to a political assembly. They can be removed if they are negligent. Being in charge, notes Brandby-Cöster, thus confers only a limited mandate in the present day.[40] Luther, by contrast, viewed authority as having been given its responsibility by God. This entailed being a model and setting a good example. For they were God's servants. On this view, the sovereign is not merely "someone with *the right to decide for others*" but "someone who has *a duty to serve others*." This also went for parents' relation to their children. It was about being responsible and showing concern, something that is bound up with our dependence upon each other. For Luther, this was tied to our double relationship—to God and to our fellow human beings. Today, argues Brandby-Cöster, we can still talk about our connection to each other as "employer-employee, care giver-care recipient, teacher-pupil."[41]

Nevertheless, it is clear that Luther's thinking bears the hallmarks of another time, one that was both patriarchal and hierarchical. Issues of gender equality, including the view of man and women as complementary, thus arise with full force. Scholarship in our own era speaks of several genders. The binary thinking found in Luther thus sits awkwardly with contemporary scholarship. But, as we will see, there are aspects of Luther's thinking that go beyond gender polarities.

In the case of sexuality, the question arises of its role in life. How do views of what belongs with reproduction, intimacy, community, and even reciprocity differ between the present and the past? Is sexuality between man and woman, or, more narrowly still, between husband and wife, the only kind that can be considered good? Our era exhibits a far greater variety of relationships. Perhaps contemporary scholarship on *eros* spirituality and homoeroticism can offer a healthy challenge to Lutheran theology. My view is that there are linguistic potentialities in Luther for different kinds of relationships, including gender-transgressing and queer, in which the genders are seen as less static. In several countries same-sex relationships have made their way into established forms, such as marriage, but the question of the forms of shared life needs continually to be kept alive. During their lifetime, modern people meet infinitely more people than was the case just a few generations ago. What is more,

---

40. Brandby-Cöster, "Sökvägar och ledtrådar," 70f.
41. Ibid., 71.

most people live far longer and remain vital long after their reproductive capacity has ceased or dwindled. For many reasons, sexuality is associated not merely with reproduction but with intimacy and tenderness.

While prominent Lutheran theologians, long into the twentieth century, continued to defend divinely ordained hierarchies of creation, above all in the relationship between man and woman,[42] Lutheran theology also includes a strong critique of static orders. On this view, the latter are considered part of a simplistic idea of creation.

Lundensian theologian Gustaf Wingren is one of the most prominent representatives of a theology that challenged the traditional theology of orders as developed by Paul Althaus, Helmut Thielicke, Emil Brunner, and others during the first half of the twentieth century. Within the Lutheran tradition, one finds two different ways of interpreting creation: one in which created orders have been seen as a way of protecting what is given, and thereby becoming a bulwark of the existing state of things; the other as emphasizing continual new creation.[43] Wingren emphasizes the renewal and invokes Luther's notions of an ongoing creation, *creatio continua*. He argues that our starting point is not a book that refers to the creation (namely, the Old Testament) "but is in fact creation itself, i.e., the fact that man lives."[44] Wingren claims, then, that God is given with life itself.[45] As with Luther's lectures on Genesis, the starting point is that God is creating right now. For this kind of approach to creation, orders are also something that change, precisely because they exist to protect life against death.

As theologian Carl-Reinhold Bråkenhielm observes, the first of these two theological interpretations—that there is a given order of creation that finds expression in hierarchical social structures—has nonetheless exerted a tight grip over the theological and religious imagination. It can be found in the New Testament and the writings of the Church Fathers, particularly Augustine; it is systematized by Thomas of Aquinas and modified by the sixteenth-century reformers; it inspires the legal theoreticians of the seventeenth and eighteenth centuries; and it reappears in theology in the nineteenth century. At that point, Bråkenhielm notes,

---

42. See, e.g., Thielicke, *Theologische Ethik*, vol. 2, for his view on marriage.

43. Bråkenhielm, "Ethics and Ecclesiology," 30, 86–88.

44. Wingren, *Creation and Law*, 27.

45. Ibid., 27, 31. Here Wingren connects to Irenaeus from the Old Church, to Luther, and to the Danish theologians Grundtvig and Løgstrup.

it takes the form of church opposition to new reproductive technologies and, above all, to homosexuality.[46]

Gustaf Wingren criticized the idea that moral orders were established by God in this way. He argued that one can discern God's will in creation, in both nature and society. But God's will is not expressed in particular, unchanging orders, common to all historical periods, cultures, and ages. God's law is moveable, not static.[47] Instead, God's laws reveal themselves as God's by virtue of their changeability.[48] According to Wingren, God is continually involved in new acts of creation precisely because destruction always arises in new forms.[49] Wingren thus emphasized creation as the continual re-creation of life, in a struggle against the new forms taken by destruction.[50] It was a matter of a battle between life and death.[51] For Wingren, Christianity was not about attaining a Christian *gnosis* but about life and death. Only God can create anew, he used to say, echoing Augustine. The devil can only demolish and destroy.

Luther's own interpretation of creation in his Small Catechism is entirely focused on the here and now, on God having "made me and all creatures; given me my body and soul, eyes, ears, and all my members, my reason and all my senses, and still takes care of them; also richly and daily provides me with clothing and food, house and home"[52] The emphasis is on the existential, what it means today, for me. The signs of God's care are sensual and physical, here and now.[53] In this Christian understanding of life, observes Henry Cöster, there is "a faith that the worth and meaning of life are something freely given by God." This redemption or gospel message is fundamental for both church and individual, he argues, a foundation on which the church stands or falls. Since this reality, which is the basis for our capacity to face life, is threatened by dejection, we need a "language for encouraging life."[54] This faith that "the ultimate meaning of life consists not of what we do but of what we undeservedly

---

46. Bråkenhielm, "Ethics and Ecclesiology," 86.
47. Ibid., 88f.
48. Wingren, *Öppenhet och egenart*, 112.
49. Bråkenhielm, "Ethics and Ecclesiology," 89.
50. Wingren, *Växling kontinuitet*.
51. Wingren, *Creation and Law*, 2.
52. WA 30 I, 239–425, *Der kleine Catechismus* (1529); cf. LW 51, Small Catechism.
53. It is, however, not related to earthly success but rather experienced in the midst of difficulties.
54. Cöster, *Livsmodets språk*, 1–2.

receive" means that life can be lived freely and frankly.⁵⁵ Naturally, this also has consequences for how we interpret external orders.

Beyond Unitary Lutheran Societies

Martin Luther represents a vanished epoch. His critique of Rome meant that other marginalized voices gained a hearing. His passionate involvement is said to derive in part from an anger at indulgences because they seemed to make it easier for the rich to be saved. When he was translating the Bible from Hebrew and Greek, he liked to listen to how women in the street spoke so as to be able to render the Bible's nuance and tone in a way that everyone could understand. His pedagogical fervor was tireless.

Luther and other reformers retained much of the tradition from which they came but they rejected some parts. This can be described as a hybrid between the language of tradition and Luther's personal experiences and historical moment. Moreover, Finnish-American theologian Kirsi Stjerna has shown that women were very active during the first phase of the Reformation.⁵⁶ In the Nordic Lutheran countries, however, the writings of Luther and his fellow reformers became a new canon that determined who belonged and who did not. What was liberatory and innovative ossified into an orthodoxy, once again administered by men.

In these unitary societies, Luther was invoked against Jews, Catholics, and "the Turk." Indeed, for centuries Lutheranism was used in the construction of the nation as a way of distancing oneself from others.⁵⁷ Conservative Lutheran theology has not only used Luther to legitimize inequality between "people" and "people" but also between men and women. However, such readings have detached Luther's writings from their historical context and ignored his theological emphasis upon the radical equality of all people. The early women's movement was thus able to use Luther in order to promote demands for participation and democracy.⁵⁸

In my reading of Luther's texts, I therefore naturally proceed from the insights provided by feminist theologians during the twentieth century. An emphasis upon experience, context, and body then became an

---

55. Ibid., 10.
56. See Stjerna, *Women and the Reformation*.
57. See Gerle, "Nationalism, Reformation and the Other," 140–78.
58. See Hammar, *Emancipation och religion*.

important resource with which to question patriarchal interpretations. One example of the importance of context is when women have analyzed how men with power have referred to pride and revolt as original sin, and instead emphasized humility. For women, it is more often a matter of daring to make one's voice heard, to become a moral subject possessed of responsibility.[59] Though nothing new, an awareness of different positions and starting points nonetheless forms part of my analysis. We have, perhaps, too quickly forgotten the importance of our own experiences, of context, and of the importance of interpreting experiences and calling into question self-explanatory discourses. Together with postcolonial theory, feminist theologians and historians provide a perspective that I draw on in a dialogue with Martin Luther. My hope is that it will convey something new.

In part, it involves listening to and learning from others; in part, speaking respectfully in a way that makes it possible to reply. Ethics then becomes, not a matter of knowledge, but a call to enter a relationship. To see ethics as an embrace, an act of love in which each party learns from the other, is not the same as choosing to speak for an oppressed group. It is an invitation to a relationship.[60]

Physicality and sensuality are the guiding lights of this book. Its object is the human body, a body not ecclesiastical or heavenly but earthly, one capable of marking itself off and living in a relationship, in the spaces between. A body that is both material and spiritual.

---

59. See Keller, *From a Broken Web*.
60. Landry and MacLean, *Spivak Reader*, 4–5.

3

Human Bodies as a Phenomenon: Body Theology and Longing for the Past

In the previous chapter, I addressed the question of what Luther means today. As important as not living in Luther's shadow is allowing Luther to emerge from the shadows, free from stereotyping. Only then can we discuss what is liberatory and what is oppressive. In this chapter, I therefore expand upon why I am concerned with the debate about the human body. This happens partly in agreement and partly in polemic with powerful theological trends in our time.

Body and Theology = Church?

Contemporary theology talks a lot about the body. Not infrequently this involves a critique of the modern project's focus on intellect. However, discussion of the body often becomes abstract and invalidates the material body. The body is sublimated. Metaphoric language of the church as Christ's body sometimes displaces the attention to earthly bodies. Body theology turns into an ecclesiology, which levels criticism at a church resembling a head without body in which physical, social expressions are not sufficiently visible. The body then becomes a matter of organization. It can also contribute to what I call churchification, that is, when the focus is directed towards church as such. Church may also be described as a positive contrast to the world. However, in a world where evangelical Christians in the United States seem to have voted for the reinstallment of white male supremacy, and the sexual exploitation of children and women still is rampant, it is, in my view, important to acknowledge that Christians and churches sometimes are more of a reflection of values of the world than a divine contrast. The pride of churches and Christians is rather connected to the fact that they nurture narratives of something else, such as caring for the poor and excluded and seeing all as created in the image of God, a God going deeper into the vulnerability of the body than anybody else. Grace, not moral superiority, is key in the Lutheran tradition, emphasizing that Christians are both sinners and saved, simultaneously—*simul iustice et peccator*.

What is more, when the church is described as body, it is also presented as a single body. The image of the body as an organ slides imperceptibly into talk of incarnation and Christ's body and into the image of an organism. There is something insidious about this, because even if the church is to some extent always a single body, it expresses itself in different ways. Likewise with incarnation as the embodied presence of God in the now. For Luther, the essential question was the *location* of the church. His answer pointed to those places where rehabilitation takes place. By contrast, he did not argue that the church as an institution always pointed clearly towards Christ. This is quite explicit in his polemic against the degeneracy of the Roman Catholic Church and in the severity of the tone he takes with the pope. Nor did he argue, with Gregory of Nyssa, that to behold the church is to behold Christ.[1] Luther emphasized the living Word that made Christ present in hearts and lives. The kerygma and the rehabilitation of human beings were central for him. Although this was the church's primary task, the restoration of love was not limited to the church's actions. The living Word could no more be confined than could God's dealings with human beings. Theologians today are increasingly talking about the healing of all creation, about "reconstructing earth's body, the human body, and our relation with all living bodies."[2]

However, the focus of this study is not different views of the church, but rather our approach to human bodies. When the body in theology increasingly tends to be sublimated to the church as body, there is reason to ask how Luther regarded the human body. Instead of reducing the body to an ecclesiological category, I therefore want to confine myself to our view of ordinary, physical bodies and what different understandings entail for theology and practice.

---

1. Gregory of Nyssa claims in his thirteenth sermon on the Song of Songs that whoever sees the church looks directly upon Christ. See Ward, "Displaced Body," 177.

2. Gebara, *Longing for Running Water*, 6.

Simply Human Bodies

Human bodies in the here and now have been attracting increasing attention. As a movement within twentieth-century philosophy, phenomenology has claimed that the human body is the organ through which we apprehend the world around us. But just as the body is open to the world and its surroundings, so, too, is it a creative force. The body can recognize and be recognized at the same time. The hand that strokes the cheek feels the cheek, and the cheek feels the hand. The body and its senses are thus reflexive.

My intention in this book has therefore been to sustain this interest in human bodies. How they are regarded and described is of importance for how humans share their lives with each other, for liberation and healing, and for a view of what theology and church mean. Calls for a more conspicuous church, one visibly more physical and organic, may be in order. But this can also be turned around. Many people would perhaps appreciate the church being a cephalopod that makes no claims to control human bodies, particularly in the context of a practice in which church and state have exerted a strong influence over human beings' bodies and sexuality. Others yearn for a church that takes seriously human bodies and their hunger for food, intimacy, and healing.

Luther's focus was not the church but on human beings' salvation. When he refers to the body, it is his own or possibly other bodies in his immediate circle. The body was not the problem. He longed for grace, reconciliation. When he dared to allow himself to be absorbed by a faith in grace, body and sexuality were also freed. The *eros* that lies in deferral and continual longing was called into question. Deferral is essential for eroticism's striving for intimacy as well as for the avoidance of closure. This is presumably why *le petit mort*, which has often been a metaphor for orgasm, both appeals and terrifies. It may be here that we find a clue as to why the *eros* spirituality that is nurtured in monastic life does not manifest itself in the same way in Lutheran territories. In the latter, the emphasis lies rather upon a bodily relation to both the divine and the human. The everyday body is taking over.

Having or Being a Body

Since I am interested in the body, sexuality, sensuality, and eroticism, I want to turn now to a body theology that focuses on the physical body.

British theologians Elizabeth Stuart and Adrian Thatcher argue that for centuries theologians have treated the body as an object. Instead of thinking "I am a body," we have conceived of human beings as "having a body." When the body is sick, it betrays the ego. Sex is described as actions.[3] This, they argue, has led to difficulties, particularly for men, in assuming responsibility for the sins of the body. Instead, the body has been accused of leading the real subject into sin. What is more, a dualistic mode of thinking that has placed body and soul in opposition has also associated women with the physical.[4] This dualism of body and soul was reinforced by the growing scientific understanding of material as compact, dead matter. As Stuart and Thatcher note, even when churches seek to move beyond this dualism in order to discuss body and soul as a unity, body and soul continue to be described as discrete entities that will be separated at death, to be reunited at the Resurrection. Perhaps this has something to do with a desire to avoid a materialistic monism in which the body becomes nothing more than bone and tissue. They argue, however, that the body cannot be reduced to biology alone. Instead, they emphasize an understanding of what a person is that involves seeing a human being as both material and spiritual.[5]

Body theology, argue Stuart and Thatcher, has emerged from the insight that a human being is a body and from the problems entailed by the dualism of body and soul. It has roots within the feminist movement, which sought to recover the body from an objectifying male gaze. Like medieval mystics, who see the body as a locus of divine revelation, they contend that incarnation is a signifier of how God is revealed, namely, in and through the body.[6] Latin American theologian Marcella Althaus-Reid claims that there is an immediate connection between sexuality and theology. One's own experiences affect not only how one interprets God and human beings but also how one does theology.[7]

Such an understanding lies close to my own. It colors the way that I, as an ethicist, interpret the present moment and Luther's texts. Throughout this book I ask questions about values and views on people, and discuss the possible ethical consequences of different approaches. The

---

3. Stuart and Thatcher, *People of Passion*, 89, 98.
4. Ibid., 89.
5. Ibid., 90.
6. Ibid., 98.
7. Althaus-Reid, "Queer I Stand."

issue of what is regarded as natural and what is considered deviant or something that does not belong, will recur continually.

The Body Again Actualized in Theology

Theology and philosophy are again showing a burgeoning interest in the body, as well as for Jesus's body and physicality. New understandings of incarnation have been advanced by critical theorists such as Luce Irigaray, Julia Kristeva, and Judith Butler. Queer theologians such as Marcella Althaus-Reid are proposing Christian models of incarnation and embodiment. She is not alone in seeking to find a language that is culturally more convincing. However, theologian Graham Ward wonders whether there is a risk that theologians are merely reproducing bodies that are in fashion in the culture. If so, then theology has lost its critical voice. He therefore argues that there are grounds for returning to Jesus's wounded and violated body.[8]

In recent years, Anglo-Saxon body and *eros* theology have had a quite substantial impact in the world. Several scholars are applying feminist insights into the importance of experience as a means of challenging church practices. I have already mentioned the critique of objectifying the body in church teachings, where women are often associated with the bodily within dualistic thought, which counterposes body and soul.[9] Other theologians have launched themselves as radically orthodox and are exerting themselves to reconnect with the early Church Fathers, whom they present in a less dualistic fashion. From a body-theological perspective, I have therefore chosen to engage in a conversation with, among others, British theologians Sarah Coakley and Graham Ward, both of whom evince a strong fascination with the early Greek Church Fathers and their views on church. The background in history of ideas set out in chapter 4 offers a critical background to several of the pre-Reformation theologians who most frequently engage in conversation with, and sometimes give answers to, contemporary issues within Radical Orthodoxy and neo-Augustinianism. These contemporary theological perspectives thus form a framework for my dialogue with Luther's texts. Other key voices among the sharpest critics of Radical Orthodoxy include Marcella Althaus-Reid, Virginia Burrus, and Rosemary Radford Ruether. One of

---

8. Ward, "On the Politics of Embodiment," 85.
9. Stuart and Thatcher, *People of Passion*, 89, 98.

my key starting points is taken from Althaus-Reid, who claims that there is an intimate connection between bodies, sexuality, and theology.

Embodiment can be conceptualized in new ways. Likewise, bodies need not be seen as *tabulae rasae* that merely receive cultural information.[10] Ward claims that our current notions about the body are no truer than those about, say, embodiment or about the facticity of the body that have been in circulation since the Renaissance. Contemporary assessments of what a body is come from scientific estimates that have been institutionalized by medicine and governments. We can therefore no more presume to know what a body is than we can be confident of understanding what physicality entails. Ward accordingly proposes a thoroughgoing agnosticism—in theological terms, an understanding of the body as a mystery.[11] Theology needs to understand how dependent it is upon time and language. These assumptions must therefore be continually scrutinized. History, argues Ward, shows us how the Middle Ages created the anorexic body and the twentieth century the homosexual body.[12]

Why, then, do bodies play so important a role today, asks Sarah Coakley. She observes that in our era the body seems to be as difficult to pin down as it is continually present.[13] The body appears to be all we have. And yet, she argues, we cannot define it or "control the political forces that seek to regiment it." She puts this in the context of the virtual disappearance of any expectations for a life after death:

> Devoid now of religious meaning or of the capacity for any fluidity into the divine, shorn of any expectation of new life beyond the grave, it has shrunk to the limits of individual fleshliness; hence our only hope seems to reside in keeping it alive, youthful, consuming, sexually active, and jogging on (literally), for as long as possible.[14]

Coakley here describes a frame of mind, found primarily in the West, that in many respects can be described as post-Christian. It is a situation

---

10. Ward claims that Merleau-Ponty, *Phenomenology*, is most influential on the question of the sexual body. Ward, "On the Politics of Embodiment," 74.

11. Ward, "On the Politics of Embodiment," 74f. This view was originally developed by Gabriel Marcel.

12. Ibid.

13. Coakley, "Introduction," 2.

14. Coakley, "Eschatological Body," 155.

in which those distancing themselves from their Christian heritage do so in terms of issues that the Christian heritage itself once passed on.

I cited above both Coakley and Ward, who, together with John Milbank, were among the first to call themselves "radically orthodox." The Radical Orthodoxy group, which includes other scholars, less frequently appears as a group, but it can be viewed as one of many contemporary tendencies that are looking back in time for ways to revitalize archaic modes of thought and practices. Although I align myself with aspects of their social critique, I am more doubtful about their strong focus on the church and their somewhat nostalgic idealizing of the past.[15] Moreover, Latin American theologians in particular have pointed out that Radical Orthodoxy also includes substantial elements of Eurocentrism, something I seek to avoid by including non-European voices in the conversation.

The Desire for "Origins" Meets Voices from the Margins

In this book I pursue an argument on two fronts: partly against the churchification of the body; partly against an atomism that fails to appreciate that human beings are always in relationship and that they are made up of body, soul, and spirit.

My first battle line is drawn up against the reduction of body theology to a discourse on the church. The latter frequently includes illuminating descriptions of the early Church Fathers. This has long been a unifying force in so-called Radical Orthodoxy. The impressive erudition of its exponents attracts many people who long to be able to return to their theological roots and to take pride in a single church. This trend of romanticizing and idealizing the early centuries of Christianity as well as the theologians and practitioners of the late Middle Ages can be seen as a desire for the archaizing, the premodern, and the unified. It exhibits an enthusiasm for ecclesiastical theology and praxis prior to the great schisms and, above all, for the Church Fathers. By the time of the Reformation, it is argued, the decline had already set in.

The early church was not united, however, but taken up with intense theological conflicts. Furthermore, in a critical response to Radical

---

15. As pointed out in chapter 2, Luther rejected all efforts to place the church above everything. He emphasized instead that God is active in different ways and spheres through all human beings. I think that this is reasonable and a shield against the church's abuse of power.

Orthodoxy, American theologian Rosemary Radford Ruether argues that it seems to consider human rights, democracy, and gender equality—benefits we associate with the modern—as relatively unimportant.[16]

Since the Reformation is typically seen as inaugurating the modern era, it is necessary to take a stance on these tendencies, which not infrequently claim to be representing the original and genuine, so-called classical Christianity. Critics point out that there is a risk of pilgrimages and Desert Fathers becoming an escape from our own era's focus on democracy and equality. Nonetheless, there are many who combine an engagement in contemporary crises with a desire for early Christian practices of prayer and *ascesis*. The question that insistently presents itself, however, is whether these often patriarchally inflected practices can easily be transferred to a contemporary setting without posing a threat to all the good that modernity, despite everything, has realized. This is a discussion to which we shall return in the final chapter.[17]

Despite the fact that the loosely affiliated group that makes up Radical Orthodoxy also describes itself as having taken on board postmodern philosophy's critique of Enlightenment reason as simplistic, they claim to be launching an orthodox Christian alternative. Theologians associated with Radical Orthodoxy, who largely come from the Anglo-Catholic wing of the Anglican Communion, can be compared with the radical theology whose thinking proceeds from the "God is dead" movement. While the latter embraces the secular and seeks to introduce a mode of theological thinking that moves beyond notions of a transcendent God and received truths, the proponents of Radical Orthodoxy, who share the same philosophical and theoretical starting point, are reinstating a Christian foundation and a transcendent God.[18] Perhaps this is why John Milbank lays such emphasis upon a strong church. When Graham Ward describes his own relation to Gregory of Nyssa, he claims that to behold the church is to behold Christ.[19] While Sarah Coakley seems to be developing a more reflexive position, she nonetheless lays claim to a "*théologie totale.*"[20]

---

16. Ruether, "Interpreting the Postmodern as Premodern," 79.
17. See, e.g., Pamela Sue Anderson's critique of Coakley, discussed in chapter 10.
18. Carlsson, *Theology beyond Representation*, 17–18.
19. Ward, "Displaced Body," 177n2.
20. Coakley, *God, Sexuality*, 37f.

Radical Orthodoxy can also be interpreted as a way of reinstating a European dominance of theology. Latin American theologian Marcella Althaus-Reid claims that while they may move easily in the landscapes of premodern European and North African roads, they fail to hear the cries coming from contemporary Greece or North Africa. The critique leveled by these long-marginalized voices is a trenchant one. Thus Althaus-Reid claims, "Radical orthodoxy is a deeply colonial theology. It aims to represent the voice of the master, restoring theology to its 'queenly' (monarchic) role of sacralizing medieval European perspectives on culture, politics, even biology."[21] She thus holds that those associated with Radical Orthodoxy base their arguments on a privileged subject unconstrained by class differences. Their theological subject is indifferent "not just to the world's excluded masses but to the British underclass."[22] She claims that they use the archive to confine God within dogmatic, pre-modern formulas that take no account of human beings' suffering. For her, it is there, among the most vulnerable, that God is to be found. She describes the liturgical beauty of demonstrating for human rights and in people's resistance to tanks and the overwhelming force of state violence. Her imagery is deliberately polemical towards what she describes as Radical Orthodoxy's aestheticizing, one that comes from a comfortable class position.[23] Althaus-Reid claims that doctrines must be thought through and reformulated from a position of hermeneutic, theological awareness. Every kind of theology, in other words, is a locus of identity struggle. Doctrines must therefore "be rethought from sensuality outside class, sex, and cultural patterns."[24]

Incarnation, Althaus-Reid continues, is a "first rebellion" since it "deprives theology of a sense of fixed identity in the past, as a contained divinity in Jesus." Instead of a legitimate God, Christ is "an unstable, overflowing God and, as such an outlawing of God occurs." "In this outlawing," she claims, "justice remains, but the law is deconstructed." "This restlessness in theology" is a "source of poiesis and subversion. There is something within theology that tends "to overthrow its own power settings." Every theology "must transgress its own boundaries and outlaw

---

21. Althaus-Reid, "'Saint and a Church,'" 112.
22. Ibid.
23. Ibid., 113.
24. Ibid.

itself. This is the messianic movement from law to justice, which does not allow theological identities to settle."[25]

This is an example of how Western theologians today are being challenged by the voices of "self-legitimating theological subjects." They are asking new questions of the theological "archive" on the basis of memories of a "silenced knowledge." Althaus-Reid is claiming, then, that Radical Orthodoxy is not even present on the fringes of poverty in Greece or among the excommunicated, itinerant medieval population that roused Martin Luther's compassion and indignation.[26]

Australian sociologist Melinda Cooper is also sharply critical of Radical Orthodoxy, in particular John Milbank and his approach. She analyses the consequences of religion's return in the field of social policy and their claims to be bridging the left-right divide. Their critique of neoliberalism is primarily a moral one, however. They contend that economic liberalism has shattered the ties of "custom, tradition, family," leading to a demoralization of working class life in particular. Cooper claims that Milbank and others in the Radical Orthodoxy movement exhibit a puritanical theology that lies close to that of former Pope Benedict XVI. Cooper offers the following summary of Milbank's construction:

> Harking back to the patristic roots of early modern theology, beyond what he perceives to be the rationalist compromises of late scholasticism, Milbank seeks to revive an Augustinian theology of participation that sees all "science" emanating from the truth of divine illumination. Milbank's vision of the proper sphere of the theological is nothing less than totalizing. Theology must be restored to its place as "queen of the social sciences." indeed as inner truth and foundation of the social itself, via the wholesale remoralization promised by faith-based welfare.[27]

Cooper points out that Milbank himself describes his own views as "extremely conservative," despite his critique of neoliberalism and support for Blue Labor. He is an opponent of abortion, embryonic stem cell research, and any suggestion that homosexuality should be counted as a civil right. Moreover, he insists upon the significance of sexual difference

---

25. Ibid.

26. Ibid., 116.

27. Cooper, "Why I Am Not a Postsecularist," 22–23. Cf. Milbank, *Theology and Social Order*, 380.

and is critical of liberal feminism. He also believes that the separation of sex and procreation is a state-capitalist program of bioethical tyranny.[28]

For me, returning to the "archive" of Luther's texts is a way to reread on the basis of current knowledge and new voices, rather than from some longing for what is in the past. It is a matter of reading these texts with new eyes, in an attempt to formulate a theology that resists the treatment of human beings as less than human. Women were long part of a group that had no say until, occasionally with the help of sympathetic men, they simply demanded one.

A number of theologians have highlighted certain groups of human beings who have been excluded on the basis of their bodies. Describing the church as Christ's wounded body in this context offers a way to restore human bodies. In this way queer theologians such as Althaus-Reid, Isherwood, and Loughlin are making visible and affirming different sexual orientations.

The fundamental question then is how the archives should be used and interpreted. Both creation and church can be interpreted conservatively as well as radically. My own starting point is a view of creation as dynamic and of the church as God's way of counteracting death and marginalization. While women throughout history have shouldered large parts of the church's work, men have assumed the role of interpreters and leaders. Today, growing numbers of women hold interpretative and leadership positions. Many of the early feminist theologians belonged to the Roman Catholic Church. Since they could not become priests, they chose instead to become theologians. In this interpretative role they have had an enormous influence upon the development of theology.[29] However, all people are part of life as it is lived, whether it is taken to be created or not. It is therefore important not to lose a creation theology perspective.

Atomism That Denies the Context of Human Life

My second battle line is drawn up against an atomism in which our era's much-vaunted individualism has run amok. Human beings always live in relationships. With themselves, with other people, and with their surroundings, what theology calls God's creation, the world, and

---

28. Cooper, "Why I Am Not a Postsecularist," 23.

29. Rosemary Radford Ruether, Elisabeth Schüssler Fiorenza, Elizabeth Johnson, and Ivone Gebara are prominent examples.

the cosmos. Martin Luther and his contemporaries took it for granted that they should see themselves from the perspective of eternity. In our era, human beings have become the measure of human beings. This is nothing new, of course, but is an axiom usually attributed to the Sophist philosopher Protagoras (ca. 481–420 BC). In the present, it is sometimes interpreted as saying that now nothing sets the limits for human beings. Climate threats and poverty crises affect the most vulnerable first. For the more privileged, the first reaction may be to feel a pang of conscience but, even more, an urge to escape before the calamity affects everyone. One of those escape routes is via the body, which increasingly absorbs our interest. We prioritize our own health. Amidst all this talk of individualism, a kind of collective individualism appears in which people striving for what is private and personal to them instead begin to imitate others, particularly celebrities.[30]

This is to be expected when the media, advertising, and commercial culture of our era show idealized bodies, apparently perfect, young, and toned, while rendering invisible those of the old, the sick, the poor, and the exploited as well as bodies that look different or are differently abled. In this study I am looking for another physicality from which to draw inspiration, one in which the body is not a problem to be managed through inner reflection but something able to deal with the cultural images that bombard us. In this way it should become natural to take care of our bodies, to see that they remain fit and healthy for as long as possible, but with a realism that also acknowledges the body's limits.

If the far-away Other risks becoming invisible and hence a non-person in the global structures currently at work, there is also a risk of privileged Westerners becoming non-persons to themselves. Brazilian-American theologian Vítor Westhelle, who works in Chicago and São Leopoldo, Brazil, describes this as an inability on the part of both individual and group to have a joint will.[31] This does not mean a lack of personal humanity, but that those who are made invisible cannot see the contours of their own existence, their true being.[32]

The insights of liberation theologians can help us here to see ourselves but also to identify comparable features in a movement such as the Reformation, which began precisely as a liberation movement.[33] For this

30. I am not, however, entering into the lively debate on the mimetic.
31. Westhelle, *Eschatology and Space*, 82.
32. Ibid.
33. Cf. Nahnfeldt, *Luthersk kallelse*. Elsewhere, however, I have also highlighted

very reason there are good grounds to reread some of Martin Luther's earliest texts.

The Periphery Moves

From early on, feminist theologians and philosophers criticized a Western canon in which women had largely been rendered invisible and portrayed as a threat to the divine. North American and French feminists such as Rosemary Radford Ruether, Julia Kristeva, and Luce Irigaray were succeeded by black womanists and Spanish-speaking *mujerista* theologians. They revealed how not only gender but skin color and cultural affiliation had been made invisible. Together with theologians from Latin America, Asia, and Africa, they mounted a challenge to Western academic theology. Liberation theology became a term for describing a theological production that until recently had been discredited within the conventional framework of academic theology but whose presence was now visible and even academically accepted. Westhelle points out that the various voices that emerge from contexts that are alien to the cradle of Constantinian Christianity do not speak in one voice. But all have experience of living at the margin and of balancing upon a knife-edge between system and power, habits and property relations, ecclesiological alliances and orthodoxies.[34] Johanna Gustafsson Lundberg has further shown how the right to interpret, hidden rules, and norms have been problematized from the perspective of what is seen as normal and what as knowledge and truth. Who decides what should be seen as normal? The power to construct the normal is one of the most profound expressions of power.[35] As a woman working with issues of global survival, it is natural to align myself with these intellectual movements.

The emergence of liberation theology and a postcolonial awareness, Westhelle argues, has led to the European worldview, religious and secular, becoming more decentralized and postcolonial.[36] If colonialism dominated and suppressed the Other, then postcolonialism has made

---

the fact that the Lutheran liberation movement went on to colonize thinking and territory in those countries where its intellectual legacy became dominant. The Reformation had many aspects. See Gerle, "Nationalism, Reformation and the Other," 140–78.

34. Westhelle, *Eschatology and Space*, 72–73.
35. Gustafsson Lundberg, "Feministiska perspektiv," 21.
36. Ibid., 75.

visible and authorized the Other. Postcolonialism therefore involves a departure from a particularist way of viewing the world from one's own perspective, as the universal goal or *telos* of all history. The very notion of a universal history emerged as a Western idea, not as a universal one, he observes.[37]

Postcolonialism additionally entails the crossing and transgressing of boundaries. At the same time as it affirms some of the values and achievements of the colonial world, it rejects others in a dynamic process. This is usually described as a hybridization since incompatible entities are brought together to produce something new: hybrids that have a unique character. Postcolonialism owes its unique character to *heteroglossia*, which involves a meeting between different linguistic fields that produces unexpected communicative effects.[38] The voice of the Other is regarded as equally legitimate as the *heteroglossia* of the dominant system. In other words, language is comprised of a co-existence between the present and the past, between different contemporary sociological groups, and between tendencies, schools, and trends.[39]

Powerful theological impulses are now coming from Africa, Asia, and Latin America. Within Christianity, it is now possible to speak of a pivoting away from Europe and the West towards other parts of the world with Christian traditions and movements that are connecting with precolonial traditions. While there is much here for theologians in the West to attend to, it is unfortunately also the case that many trends are characterized by anti-intellectualism and powerful patriarchal and authoritarian elements. Marking one's distance from the West is key, even if certain countries exhibit the influence of charismatic American missionary societies. At the same time, there are now many so-called poor, oppressed, and marginalized within academia, in both the North and the South.[40] It is thus no longer possible to talk with the same confidence about "the others." A global "we" is composed of many elements and incorporates not only diversity but also ambivalence and ambiguity.

Questions about body and sexuality, our views on desire, longing, and lust recur. Negotiations in the UN and between churches and religions are affected by this. Demands for equal rights for those who want

---

37. Ibid., 72–77.
38. Ibid., 77; cf. Bakhtin, *Dialogic Imagination*, 428.
39. Cf. Bakhtin, *Dialogic Imagination*, 291, 428.
40. Nadar, "Beyond the 'Ordinary Reader' and the 'Invisible Intellectual.'"

to live in same-sex relationships clash with patriarchal conceptions of marriage in which the man is seen as the natural leader. In many countries in Africa it is impossible to refer to a woman as the head of a family, even while it not infrequently is women who carry the entire burden of the family's survival.[41] There are strong reasons, then, for examining the underlying intellectual frameworks within which bodies are considered, treated, and experienced.

Among those voices can be found those who see themselves as the most threatened and most enlightened, possessors of what is true and just. For me, it was important to turn to my own tradition, namely, Lutheranism. Instead of analyzing and comparing Lutheran theologians, I have chosen to put Martin Luther and some of his texts into dialogue with contemporary theologians. I do so because I believe that he has meant a great deal for the Nordic countries, where some of the positive things for which he stood were not always implemented along with the Reformation. The impact of other things was correspondingly greater. Luther's influence has always been for both good and bad. To begin a conversation with his own texts is imperative, then, not least because most people toady have so little idea about what he wanted and how he thought.

The Challenge of *Eros* Theologians

It is five hundred years since Martin Luther nailed his theses to the church door in Wittenberg, an act that ushered in the Reformation. Despite the vast gap in time, language, and worldview, there are points of overlap with what is today called *eros* theology. It concerns a focus on relationships and shared life, on unsentimental caring combined with songs of praise and festivity. The above offers a reasonable summary of some of Luther's ideas, not least when he invokes the erotic language of the Song of Songs. He would agree that all human beings and all creation form part of the fabric of life and that our response to God's gifts should be festivity and caring. I am arguing, then, that Luther's sensualism and affirmation of life have points in common with contemporary *eros* theology, something that can be further elucidated in a critical dialogue.

---

41. Such a tension is well documented, for example, in developmental studies where women often carry the principal responsibility for their families. See, e.g., van Driel, *Poor and Powerful*, 19–21.

In order to offer a perspective on contemporary body worship and body loathing, this book examines views, both past and present, of sensuality, body, sexuality, and eroticism. This conversation between "the sensual Luther" and modern scholars takes place against the background of intellectual history. Every tradition needs its slave in the chariot whispering unpalatable truths about its own history. I have therefore also chosen to highlight contradictions and ambiguities. Such whispering is also a matter of revealing ambivalence, that space of ambiguity in which elements of light and dark mingle. This applies as much to the "triumphant chariots of systematic theology and the church"[42] as it does to the views and historiography of our secular or secularist[43] present.

However, my primary concern is not to focus on the drearier aspects but rather to identify sources of inspiration that are ethically defensible and relevant today. Luther criticized a spirituality that became private and non-political. He claimed that God's love disrupted human beings' preoccupation with themselves, opening them instead to the world in the shape of relationships and shared responsibility. But he idealized both marriage and sovereign power. Equality before God did not extend to the earthly realm. Luther's sexual revolution ossified into societal repression. A new reading of early texts can thus make a contribution to the development of new political applications. Luther used a gender-transgressing language in his nuptial mystery, emphasizing reciprocity and the independence of every human being.

By taking inspiration from contemporary *eros* theology, I want to challenge the Lutheran view that has contrasted different forms of love to each other. Those who emphasize curiosity, a longing for the Other, and community that calls into question unjust structures have an ally in Luther. My argument in this book is that the intimacy and reciprocity of Luther's nuptial mystery deserve to have a greater impact in politics, global as well as local.

42. Stenström, "Den irriterande rösten," 72.

43. Following Jürgen Habermas, I distinguish between secularization and secularism (Habermas, *Between Nationalism and Religion*). While secularization, according to José Casanova (Casanova, "Religion, Politics"; Casanova, *Public Religions*), denotes a separation of religion and the secular, the privatization of religion, and a waning interest in religion, secularism is an ideology that often comes with an aggressive, antireligious agenda. Cf. Gerle, *Farlig förenkling*, 39. Secularization can also entail a healthy measure of self-criticism and earthly responsibility, something that is found in Bonhoeffer. Both he and Gogarten made this distinction. See Persson, *Att tolka gud i dag*, 22–28.

4

A Woman Reads Origen, Augustine, Bernard, and Luther

Despite the growing 'body' of historical and philosophical writing on the body, sexuality, and theology, it is striking how often the actual physical body disappears from view. Today we speak of the material, akin to earlier trends that turned to the linguistic. Perhaps our era can be described in terms of the notion of "the materialist turn." This is not to say that the linguistic turn has disappeared but rather that there is a renewed interest in materiality and the body.[1] I have already highlighted the idea that human sexuality affects theology as well as the theory that views of the body affect all of society and how people live with each other. The everyday body was important for many of the great nineteenth-century theologians. But what did it look like during the early history of the church? How were the body and sexuality treated in relation to the spiritual? In this chapter, I consider some important moments in the intellectual history of Christianity.

Currently there is a revival of interest in the early Church Fathers and a desire for archaic traditions and ascesis. Neo-Augustinianism, the Desert Fathers, and pilgrimage mysticism are just a few of its signs.. In chapter 3, I warned of the risk of an idealizing nostalgia that obscures the gains we associate with enlightenment and modernity, such as human rights, equality, and democracy. The struggle for people's right to affirm their bodies, their sexual orientation, and their desire for intimacy conflicts with an ancient system of thought, which even today is invoked

---

1. Coole and Frost, *New Materialisms*.

in order to maintain lack of freedom and a culture of silence around the body and sexuality. Hoary arguments about will and intellect resurface here and are presented as if these two faculties are able to fully control the way we live as human beings. A patriarchy that gives precedence to the interests of heterosexual men can be found in all cultures. Women in large parts of the world are still regarded as drudges whose role is to make life easier for their families.

Within the cultural sphere of Christianity, ascetic and mystical traditions have sometimes created new opportunities for women and homosexuals. As often, however, they have contributed to the latter's marginalization and subordination. A preoccupation with the angelic, the life to come, has frequently been used to confer legitimacy upon male superiority because the virginal has been interpreted as masculine. On the other hand, a heavy emphasis upon creation has in certain periods led to an identification of "naturally ordained" roles for human beings. This has then served to grant divine legitimacy to hierarchies of men and women, hetero and homo. Before proceeding in the next chapter to tackle Luther's view of what was "natural" and good, I will sketch out in this chapter some background on the asceticism and angelic ideal of some of the early Church Fathers, an ideal that has had, and continues to have, considerable influence on Christian church traditions.

My point of departure is that life and interpretation are always ambiguous. Mere age does not in itself make something good and life affirming, any more than modernity does. Nonetheless, discovering and analyzing patterns of thought, something I have called *ideational figures* can enable us to search for the restorative. Historical knowledge can help to liberate the present.

Calling Polarities into Question

The thinkers who formed part of Sweden's so-called Luther Renaissance generally viewed the Reformation in contrast to earlier epochs. The Middle Ages represented a murky backdrop to the new era inaugurated by Luther in particular. One of the most famous representatives of this polarized perspective was Anders Nygren. His study *Eros and Agape* is still read and discussed in terms of its simple schema, which ascribes what is positive to *agape* and God's self-sacrificing love while according a negative role to *eros*. Eros was associated with human beings' striving towards the spiritual and away from the body. Human and divine were represented as opposites. These simple dichotomies are, however, problematic.[2]

There is a danger in drawing up overly simple polarities and emphasizing differences. Today, even some of the binary opposites of early feminist thought have been called into question. Grace M. Jantzen is an American philosopher of religion whose study of Christian mysticism, *Power, Gender and Christian Mysticism,* has shown that there is not merely one form of Christian mysticism but many. She has outlined a history of mysticism from a woman's perspective and claims that an opposition between masculine and feminine is a consistent feature throughout it. What is more, she claims that the gendering of language has served to marginalize women's experiences.[3] Her work, which is philosophy, has been criticized by medieval historian Caroline Walker Bynum for offering an excessively dualistic interpretation.

In my own reading of their respective studies as well as those of other scholars who have taken an interest in the body during the first centuries of the Christian era, I nonetheless see considerable areas of agreement. The early Church Fathers, who have often been accused of opposing body and soul, feminine and masculine, are actually quite heterogeneous. In the late medieval period, views on the body seem to have been even more complex. Among those ascetic movements that advocated sexual abstinence, too, there seem to have been different attitudes towards the body. There are therefore grounds for a study like the present one, which examines the body and sexuality, to return to some of these historical figures, particularly a Church Father like Augustine, who was a major influence on Martin Luther's theology.

It is well known that Martin Luther renounced asceticism's ideal of chastity and attacked the monastic ideal. But how did matters stand outside of ascetic circles? For early Christians, marriage and shared life were quite simply something that existed independently of their faith.[4] Although the Gospel entailed a radical reorientation of life, it did not require the rejection of marriage or the introduction of a new form of marriage. Nonetheless, a new direction gradually emerged, one that differentiated itself from both Jewish and Roman traditions. Not until the

---

2. See also chapter 7.

3. Jantzen, *Power, Gender and Christian Mysticism.* Her untimely death from cancer in 2008 prevented her continued participation in the debate.

4. Rubenson, "Äktenskapet i den tidiga kyrkan," 179–81.

ninth century, however, did a more uniform attitude towards Christian marriage emerge, and then only within the Latin Church.[5]

Nevertheless, for long periods sexuality seems to have been strictly disciplined, and there may well be grounds for asking which norms govern human beings' bodies and sexuality today. The reception history of the Reformation exhibits what Córdova Quero calls a "heteropatriarchal society."[6] Yet he sees this type of society as greatly predating the Reformation. We will come back to the question of whether this is not also something that defines many societies today, regardless of whether they are described as religious or secular.

For this study, whose aim is not to outline a history of sexuality but rather to examine the interplay between sexuality, views of life, theology, and society, I choose to present a philosophical background to Christianity that starts with the Church Fathers Origen and Augustine.

Creation, Matter, and Patriarchy

Attitudes to the body and sexuality are bound up with views of creation and of the value of the material and the earthly. Luther's commentaries on Genesis and creation give no evidence of either a nature-romanticizing approach or Marcion's second-century disavowing claim that creation was the work of a demiurge. Gösta Hallonsten notes that the early church operated in an environment in which "all religious movements gaining ground were characterized by ascetic ideals. Encratism, that is, the rejection of marriage and sexuality, was strong at that time, including among certain Jewish groups." This is reflected in the New Testament, as, for example, in Matt 19:12 and 1 Cor 7.[7] Hallonsten argues that the church was more positive than its closest competitors towards sexuality.[8]

Rejecting marriage was a way not only to suppress sensual pleasure but also to resist worldly occupations. Paul views celibacy as a higher form of Christian ethics since it provides greater opportunities for devoting oneself to a relationship with Christ. For women, argues Rosemary Radford Ruether, this brought with it the possibility of being liberated

---

5. Ibid.
6. Córdova Quero, "Friendship with Benefits," 34.
7. Hallonsten, "Sexualiteten och traditionen," 121.
8. Ibid.

from the tyranny of one's spouse, the master of the house.[9] Ruether contends that Paul completely accepted the notion held by the surrounding religious culture that patriarchal hierarchy was part of the order of nature. This hierarchy meant that slaves were subject to their masters, wives their husbands, and children their parents. Human beings' relationship to God was also hierarchical. Man was the normative likeness of God. When Paul argues in Gal 3:28 that baptism in Christ overcomes the division between man and woman, Jew and Greek, slave and freeman, a conflict emerges between subordination to the order of creation and eschatological emancipation. Woman is seen on the one hand as inferior in creation and, on the other, as liberated from the order of creation because she is already living in expectation of the new order.[10] Like other classical thinkers, Paul connects a shared physical relationship to marriage and mortality. Marriage thus made a woman socially unequal in her childraising role within a family headed by a man.[11] As Ruether argues, this conflict between eschatological, egalitarian Paulinism and patriarchal Paulinism continued throughout the first centuries. The fact that his letters to Timothy were included in the biblical canon shows that the patriarchal side was victorious.[12]

Irenaeus, who lived between approximately 130 and 200 BC, together with other anti-gnostic Fathers, defended marriage as something good that contained creation-theological themes. The fourth century saw the emergence of a synthesis between the patriarchal approach, which was for the family, and ascetic variants of Christianity, which were against the family.[13] Yet the struggles over approaches to the body and matter in the early Christian church cannot entirely be ignored if one wishes to try to understand Luther in relation to both his time and the intellectual background, which he alternately invokes and rejects.

Erotic Mysticism: An Opposition between Body and Spirit?

As is well known, early Christian mysticism is strongly influenced by Platonism. When the early Church Fathers conceptualize their mysticism,

9. Ruether, "Asceticism and Feminism," 235.

10. Ibid., 234.

11. Ibid., 235.

12. Ibid., 238. These letters are not usually viewed as having been authored by St. Paul.

13. Ibid., 241.

they "platonize"—to borrow Andrew Louth's term.[14] In Platonism's conceptual universe, human beings live in a changing world of sensual phenomena in which passing events and opinions exert an influence. But the soul belongs to a higher, truer world that is eternal and unchanging. In order to realize its affinity to this world, the soul must purify itself of the world, die to it, and live the life that it hopes to live after death. Such purification has two aspects, one moral and the other intellectual. Moral purification establishes the soul's transcendence over the body so that the latter ceases to be an obstacle. Intellectual purification trains the soul in abstract thought and frees it from dependency upon emotions so that it can become more Spartan but also more real, in the sense of eternal.[15]

According to Louth, the major difference with Christian mysticism is that it joins contemplation with action. Christian love is in fact Christ's love, which unites one with Christ and, through him, the other. Christian mysticism is thus ecclesial insofar as it is the fruit of participation in Christ's mystery, which is inseparable from the church's mysteries.[16] While the mystic of Platonic tradition is an individual, or at least a member of an intellectual elite, Christian mysticism cannot be separated from this relationship to the other. The relationship between bride and bridegroom in the Christian nuptial mystery is, Louth argues, both "singular and corporate," individual and collective, since every Christian is baptized into Christ's body at the same time as he or she remains an individual.[17]

In the next section, I will discuss particular themes within early Christian mysticism with which Luther aligns himself. I argue that he upholds certain aspects while distancing himself from others. I am interested above all in whether views of the body and sexuality change and how views of the body relate to different people's worth. My account will take up the work of various scholars who have all written about mysticism but who present their interpretations in different ways.

---

14. Louth, *Origins of the Christian Mystical Tradition*, 186.
15. Ibid., 188.
16. Ibid., 194.
17. Ibid., 195.

A Critical Reading of Origen

Origen (185–254 BC) was a Bible commentator and Christian philosopher from Alexandria. His teachers included Clement of Alexandria and the neo-platonic philosopher Ammonios Saccas. He pursued his studies in parallel with the celebrated pagan neo-platonic philosopher Plotinus, who also studied under Ammonios Saccas. In this sense Origen was not influenced primarily by Plotinus as is sometimes asserted. Rather, his thinking constitutes an originary, Christian branch on the tree of Platonism, one that can be characterized as a synthesis of Platonism and Christian faith.

Origen represents an allegorical mode of Bible commentary that has been enormously influential. Thanks to his commentaries on the Song of Songs, Origen is regarded as a prominent figure in the ongoing tradition of mysticism. "For Gregory of Nyssa and Ambrose of Alexandria as well as for Gregory the Great, Maximus the Confessor, and Bernard of Clairvaux, he was fundamental." In the history of Bible commentary, it is difficult to find an interpretation that cannot largely be traced back to Origen.[18] He wrote an extraordinary amount, yet the bulk of his writings have not survived. They were burned when he was declared a heretic.

Origen launched an erotic theme in the history of Christianity. The Song of Songs was the biblical foundation for this erotic mystery with deep roots in Jewish tradition.[19] The soul was conceived of as a bride and God as the bridegroom. The longed-for union with God was seen in terms of ecstasy and rapture. But what about the relationship between body and spirituality? Jantzen claims that this spirituality could only flourish when the physical senses were strictly disciplined.

The background to this perspective has been described by several scholars whose works are seen as classics in the field. Their number includes Andrew Louth, Peter Brown, and Bernard McGinn, whom Jantzen follows closely for her arguments. They all offer a similar account of the background to Origen's fascinating system of ideas or cosmology. Like other Platonists, Christians, and others, argues McGinn, Origen had difficulty explaining the nature of the Fall and, with it, the existence of evil.[20] How could there be such variety and difference between people?

---

18. Rubenson, "Himmelsk åtrå," 113.

19. Jantzen, *Power, Gender*, 90. Within the Jewish tradition this was seen as the relation between God and his people.

20. McGinn, *Foundations of Mysticism*, 114.

Taking his Platonic paradigm as a point of departure, he asked how these differences, which were observable in the material world, could have arisen.[21]

According to Peter Brown, Origen found the solution by imagining that every creature had chosen to be different. Every difference corresponded to an exact degree of distance from or proximity to an original, communal perfection. Human beings had originally been created as angelic spirits whose purpose was to devote themselves to perpetual contemplation of God's wisdom. What we now call the soul or subjectivity was the result of a subtle cooling of the glow of the original subject, the spirit.

The word *psyche*, Origen claimed, came from the word *psychos*, meaning cold. Compared with the hot and fiery spirit that blazed upwards, continually trying to merge back into God's original fire, the conscious subject was dull and insensible by virtue of its frigid lack of love. This universe, in which angels, humans, and demons occupied different levels, was characterized by an enormous impatience, an unceasing dissatisfaction or "divine discontent" at human beings' limitations.[22]

Whether angel, human, or demon, all beings had distanced themselves from God through their sin. Sin came from satisfaction with one's present situation instead of exposing oneself to God's love, which was an all-consuming fire. According to Origen, Christ was the only being whose deepest subject had not been chilled by inertia. Origen viewed the body as a limitation but also as an obstacle to be overcome. It should be seen as a "tent" rather than as a "house" or permanent abode.[23]

Yet the body was not evil. Origen regarded it as God's gift, which human beings had been given by a benign Creator. But the body was a limited good whose true purpose was to train the intellect to lift itself above it so as to gain an unrestricted glimpse of God.[24] As McGinn notes, he thus treated the body as something for the soul to overcome, a school, or an educational opportunity.[25]

Jantzen contends that this has consequences for human love. Origen, she proposes, viewed love of God, the spiritual bridegroom, as

21. Brown, *Body and Society*, 163.
22. Ibid.
23. Ibid., 163–64.
24. McGinn, *Foundations of Mysticism*, 114.
25. Ibid.; Jantzen, *Power, Gender*, 90.

making all other love highly suspect, particularly any kind of sexual love. At the start of his commentary on the Song of Songs, Origen "warns that anyone not practicing chastity ought not even to read the book."[26] He additionally declares: "For if he does not know how to listen to the names of love purely, and with chaste ears, he may twist everything he has heard from the inner man to the fleshly and outer man and be drawn away from the Spirit to the flesh."[27]

In this tradition, which has had enormous influence within Christianity, an erotic poetic language is used at the expense of human sexual relations, Jantzen argues. The language of passion is used while that of physical, sexual passion is rejected as every effort is made to channel all sexual desire towards God. Human sexuality is regarded as a distraction and as corrupt or something distasteful.[28] Since women have for centuries been associated with passion and sexuality, they are here considered as part of evil and as something to be avoided. Tertullian's phrase about woman being "the devil's gateway" is well known.[29] Yet no comparable expression is to be found in Origen. Even so, Jantzen argues that the price of eroticism, as a symbol of love for God during centuries of Christian spirituality, has been paid by denigrating actual physical, human sexuality and through a hatred and fear of women.

Virginity was viewed as a path to purity. According to Origen, the path to union with God lay through purification, enlightenment, and meditation.[30] Virginity, in solidarity with the virgin mother, is the bridge between heaven and earth.[31] Human beings' original state was considered to be virginal, in other words, angelic and masculine.

This perspective derives from the pre-Christian, Judaeo-Hellenic philosopher Philo. He considered Adam to be a perfectly asexual human being who encompassed both female and male. Adam thus had no sexual urges but was rather a perfect, androgynous, and virginal man. Sexuality came with woman. It led to the Fall. Since Adam was androgynous, he maintained a balance between reason and emotions. Creating Eve disturbed that balance. In this way, argued Philo, she caused the Fall.[32]

26. Jantzen, *Power, Gender*, 91.
27. Origen, *Exhortation to Martyrdom*, 218.
28. Jantzen, *Power, Gender*, 91.
29. See ibid., 47.
30. Ibid., 88.
31. Origen, *Contra Celsum*, 1.34–9; cf. Jantzen, *Power, Gender*, 90.
32. Aspegren, *Male Woman*, 14, 90–93.

Plato also connected femininity with sexuality and masculinity with virginity. In *Timaeus*, he describes how human beings were created in the same vessel that the Creator had used to mix the soul of the universe.[33] The Creator continued to stir what was left in it, but the remnants were now no longer so pure. The longer he stirred, the further from the divine his creation became. And since human nature was dual, "the more excellent of the two was that which would afterwards be called *man*."[34] A man who lived badly risked being restored upon his rebirth "into the nature of a woman."[35] But with the help of reason, a human being could be freed from "its turbulent and irrational part" and thereby return to "the first and best disposition."[36]

The break with the good, Aspegren argues, led to the division between male and female and was a part of the punishment.[37] The term *punishment* is questionable, however, because Plato does not presuppose a Fall. But, for Plato, divine love seldom has anything to do with femaleness since the latter is associated with matter, childbearing, and death. Love for another man, a love that does not lead to children, thus becomes preferable. The grown man who possesses higher reason does not follow his sexual desires for the beautiful body of either a women or a younger man. The spiritually fertile man instead seeks a grown man, who leads him away from corporeal beauty towards a love of beauty in itself.[38] On the other hand, Diotima in *The Symposium* praises procreation and childbearing and what is mortal in the immortal. Plato there describes intercourse between a man and a woman as something divine, and pregnancy and birth as something immortal in a moral being.[39] Plato's writings are not uniquivocal.

For a Neoplatonist like Origen, several of these philosophical frameworks operate in the background. The striving for virginity is a matter of turning away from the body's sexual desires and towards the eternal. Even though Origen, on the basis of his faith in God as Creator, affirms

33. Plato, *Timaeus*, 346.
34. Ibid.
35. Ibid., 347.
36. Ibid.
37. Aspegren, *Male Woman*, 14, 88; cf. Plato, *Symposium*, 62.
38. See, for instance, Pausanias's speech in Plato, *Symposium*; cf. Aspegren, *Male Woman*, 20.
39. Diotima's speech in Plato, *Symposium*, 208, 258; cf. Irigaray, *Ethics of Sexual Difference*, 26.

the material, his goal is the spiritual. For him, "knowing" meant partly sexual intercourse, partly intellectual vision. One had to choose. Adam knew God. He had a body in Paradise. Once he began to "know" Eve, his knowledge of God was undermined.[40] Rejecting his sexuality was thus a step towards the purification needed to attain enlightenment. Renouncing the world and its vanities became a part of the spiritual journey, a step towards enlightenment. Origen found scriptural support for these notions in the declaration in Ecclesiastes that all is vanity and transitory:

> Ecclesiastes . . . teaches, as we have said that everything visible and corporal is transitory and weak. And when the person who is eager for wisdom discovers that this is so, he will doubtless despise those things; and by renouncing, so to speak, the whole world, he will press on to the invisible and eternal teachings that are given to the spiritual senses in the Song of Songs through certain veiled figures of loves.[41]

The spiritual or mystical meaning of the text had its counterpart in the purification of the heart, which was to be achieved through strict control of the body. Origen saw the soul's journey as a quest for knowledge. While emotions formed part of it, they were directed towards God at the expense of every form of earthly love. This quest, notes Jantzen, was also largely reserved for men.[42]

Jantzen's reading has been criticized for being overly dualistic and for counterposing spirit and body, man and woman. Even so, her description closely resembles those of scholars such as McGinn and Brown. But let us consider other readings. One of the purposes of this book is to allow contrary interpretations to engage with each other.

A Sympathetic Reading of Origen

Samuel Rubenson, professor of Church History at Lund University, does not address those aspects that Jantzen and others regard as problematic. In his sympathetic reading, Origen proceeds from the idea that human

---

40. Jantzen, *Power, Gender*, 92. Origen claims in *Fragments on 1 Corinthians*, 29, 370, that it is wrong to believe that the body was made for intercourse. Rather, it was made as a "temple to the Lord" where the soul should act as "a priest serving before the Holy Spirit." In this way, Adam had a body in Paradise but did not "'know' Eve." See Brown, *Body and Society*, 175.

41. Origen, *Exhortation to Martyrdom*, 234.

42. Jantzen, *Power, Gender*, 92-93.

beings "are centred not upon themselves but in their movement outwards, in their relationship to what they are striving for. Their identity is to a large degree determined by what they desire, and desire, *eros*, is the expression of a longing to soothe their anxiety, to find wholeness and peace."[43] The Song of Songs depicts the apex of human beings' relation to God. It articulates a community, a respite, "in the song we sing together with the bridegroom when we reach our goal."[44] Rubenson additionally claims that it is a pedagogical text that guides us, and argues that "enlightenment and knowledge are not remote assertions but community, union." For Origen, loving is learning to know.[45] The intimate connection between love and knowledge is underscored by Origen in his commentaries on the Gospel of John when he refers to Gen 4:1. In his analysis of the Song of Songs, he applies the statement in Genesis that "Adam knew [*egno*] his wife Eve and she conceived" to human beings' knowledge of God and how such knowledge emerges from an intimate community.[46] Origen therefore warns against wrongly interpreting *eros* as an expression of fleshly desires.[47] Even in Rubenson's interpretation, then, we can detect the phenomenon highlighted by Jantzen, namely, a kind of competition between fleshly and spiritual love.

Contrary to Jantzen, however, Rubenson claims that Origen sees a connection between love for another person and for God. Instead of a polar opposition, he contends that Origen sees earthly love as an avenue to the divine. King Solomon, who was considered the author of the Song of Songs, treated love as central to being human. In his poem he exploits "its capacity to reflect and express something more, a capacity to transcend the ephemeral and the bodily, a capacity to be the word of God, to extol the love between God and human beings." Rubenson argues that for those "mature enough both to understand the language of love and to free themselves from a fixation with sexuality, the Song of Songs becomes a jewel, indeed, the crown jewel of the Scriptures." "Fixation with sexuality" is nonetheless something to be overcome. Rubenson describes it as a sign of maturity, but it is perhaps rather a question of different phases in a person's life.

43. Rubenson, "Himmelsk åtrå," 114.
44. Ibid., 115.
45. Ibid.
46. Ibid.
47. Ibid.

Rubenson observes that Origen criticizes love for the other as body if the focus is on bodily gratification.[48] At the same time, he claims that it is too simple to describe such a view of human beings as dualistic for counterposing the bodily and the spiritual. On the contrary, he emphasizes precisely this connection, that the body is not "just" body, that the soul cannot live without body.[49]

Rubenson instead reads Origen and Gregory of Nyssa as seeking to give meaning to the fact that human beings are in transit, that they are ephemeral, and that they cannot hold back time. The mystery of love, which is the fundamental driving force of existence and that which defies death, also includes "what is most fragile and most elusive."[50]

For Origen, according to Rubenson, there is ultimately only one kind of love. It can assume different forms. It can also be more or less pure. But "deep down, it is a divine gift intended to unite something that is divided. The essence of love includes a need to learn to know, to be known, to know one another, in both an intellectual and a more physical sense."[51] For Origen, Rubenson argues, love for God and love for your neighbor are virtually indistinguishable. "All human love, *eros*, is divine in nature." According to Origen, Rubenson adds, this is a consequence of human beings having been created in God's image.[52]

For Origen, a human being is not just a single earthly body but was created as two. One was created in God's image as described in Gen 1:26, while the other was formed from dust as described in Gen 2:7. Origen, following Paul (2 Cor 4:16), argues in his foreword to the Song of Songs that the outer person should be diminished and the inner one made anew every day.[53]

Human beings are both body and a spiritual being, then. Origen here articulates a general Christian perspective that may be found in several scriptural sources, particularly in John and the letters of Paul, to which Origen often makes reference. As Luther would many years later, he also speaks of how the inner and the outer person can only be separated conceptually, but "nonetheless such that an inner freedom and renewal

---

48. Ibid., 117.
49. Ibid., 127.
50. Ibid.
51. Rubenson, "Eros och Agape," 584.
52. Ibid., 591.
53. Origen, *Exhortation to Martyrdom*, 220.

must not be constrained by outward confinement and degeneration."[54] In Rubenson's reading of Origen, "our bodily experience" gives human beings "tools and expresses that which greatly exceeds this."[55]

Rubenson's reading of Origen thus posits a close connection between erotic human love and the divine. Origen's advice is not to worry too much about which term is used, *eros* or *agape*. Both refer to the same power.[56] At the same time, Origen argues that the Scriptures translated *eros* as *caritas* or *agape* in order to avoid reducing love to erotic desire or sexual gratification.[57] In his argument Origen refers not only to Jacob and Rebecca but also to Amnon's rape of his sister Tamar in 2 Samuel 13, which is translated as "affectionate love," *caritas* or *agape* instead of *eros*.[58] Yet when the Scriptures speak of loving wisdom, as in Prov 4:6 and 8, they use the word love, *eros*.[59] Love corresponds to *eros* or *amor*, while longing or desire is *cupido* or *epithumia*.

For Origen, Rubenson claims, *eros* and *agape* are not opposing terms for love or for a dualism between body and soul. Origen's shift from *agape* to *eros* "gives colour and flavour, a sensuality to talk of God's love." "It is the very intensity of human sexuality which makes sexual, erotic language, as expressed in the Song of Songs, the acme of his theological language."[60]

My point here, however, is that Rubenson avoids mentioning the fact that, for Origen, the material is something lower. This motif is highly evident in Origen's foreword to his commentary on the Song of Songs. In it, he describes love as the force that leads the soul from earth to the lofty heights of heaven.[61] A short while later, Origen writes that God's love cannot love anything material—anything that can be corrupted—since it is the source of incorruptibility.[62] The Latin translation of Origen uses

54. Rubenson, "Eros och Agape," 590.

55. Ibid.

56. Origen, *Exhortation to Martyrdom*, 225.

57. Ibid., 224f.

58. Women who, in relation to the story about Tamar, have been encouraged to share experiences of sexual assault or rape do not use terms such as *caritas*, *agape*, or "affectionate love"—a sign that this kind of reasoning lies very far from the bodily reality experienced by women.

59. Origen, *Exhortation to Martyrdom*, 224f.

60. Rubenson, "Eros och Agape," 591.

61. Origen, *Exhortation to Martyrdom*, 219.

62. Ibid., 226.

the word *caritas*, which corresponds to *agape* or "loving affection."[63] He further compares sowing in the flesh, or in the spirit, and argues that whoever bears the face of the earthly is governed by an earthly desire and love, while whoever bears a heavenly face is directed by heavenly desire and love.[64]

Angelic Love

Heaven is contrasted to the earthly. The material is something to free oneself from. As I see it, there are good reasons for reading Origen in order to make the most of his contributions to how different forms of love work together, not least within a Lutheran tradition that, on the basis of Nygren's opposition of *eros* and *agape*, often treats these concepts of love as entirely distinct.[65] Origen's poetic language is particular fascinating. But it is difficult to read him without noting that the angelic love that he seeks has implications for how material and earthly love is viewed. Can it ever be anything other than entirely fleshly?

This was in all likelihood wholly self-evident for Origen in light of previous thinkers such as Philo, and his Platonic background, and thus not something he saw any need to reflect upon. Louth argues that his spirituality is defined by joy. Unlike other mystics, he is a stranger to the cloud or the dark night of the soul. At every stage of Christian life, the soul sings.[66]

Another Church Father influenced by Plato was Augustine, who has come down to posterity as someone who meditated on life and the choices we make. He is sometimes described as a modern person.[67] Yet it is perhaps more precisely the case that he in some sense introduces categories that went on to influence later thinkers in a more philosophically subjectivist direction. He works with memory in a subjective way. As a result, we can recognize ourselves in his thoughts. Eva Österberg argues that he sees God as the source of friendship, something that transcends human

63. Translator's note to Origen, *Exhortation to Martyrdom*, 224.

64. Ibid., 223.

65. Nygren, *Agape and Eros*. See chapter 7 for a critique. For further discussion of various forms of love, see chapter 8 on *eros* theology.

66. Louth, *Origins of the Christian Mythical Tradition*, 55.

67. See, e.g., Scanlon, "Arendt's Augustine," 159. Scanlon holds that Augustine is often seen as the first modern human being at the same time as he appears in works ranging from Heidegger and Wittgenstein to Lyotard and Derrida.

limitations and has its roots in grace and compassion. She describes him as "a hypersensitive person with social vitality and an acute intellect. He is outgoing and gregarious while also being driven by an inner fear. He engages in ceaseless dialogue with God. It can seem contradictory. But through the paradoxes, I would argue, we nevertheless see an extraordinary harmoniousness."[68] A study of sensuality and Luther cannot bypass this giant, who was a particular influence on Martin Luther.

Augustine

Augustine of Hippo was born in what is now Algeria. He lived between 354 and 430 and is said to have had a great talent for friendship. Nonetheless, he appears to have lived his entire life in a struggle with his sexuality and bodily desires. Peter Brown describes how Augustine's mother Monica warned him against fornication but without offering him the relief that a respectable early Roman marriage would have provided. He was the only member of his family who was afforded the privilege of a good education. This was not to be disrupted by an early arranged marriage.[69] He was also influenced from an early age by Manichaeanism. This exacerbated the opposition between his own ad hoc sexuality and the idea of marriage. Indeed, according to the Manichaeans, sexuality and society were antithetical.[70]

Yet Augustine occupied a fairly peripheral position with regard to the Manichaeans, who therefore placed no great demands upon the young man. He no more wished to refrain from eating meat and having wealth than he wished to renounce sex. For more than ten years he lived with a concubine, a common arrangement at that time. When he came to Milan in his thirties in 384, he felt that it was time to decide how he wanted to live.[71] He was offered a wealthy spouse and his mother looked forward to it making him a good and powerful Catholic. Yet he saw it as a threat, to give up in the face of "the expectations of this world." Having enjoyed a sexual relationship for thirteen years, he describes in his *Confessions* how the power of habit holds him prisoner.[72]

68. Österberg, *Vänskap*, 119.
69. Brown, *Body and Society*, 390.
70. Ibid., 391.
71. Ibid., 392.
72. Ibid., 393; cf. Augustine, *Confesssiones*.

Reading Ambrose and the Neoplatonists had, however, made Augustine acquainted with the spirituality that Origen represented. By refraining from sexual pleasure of every kind, Augustine hopes to be able to grasp God's wisdom "in an utterly untroubled *gaze*, a most clean embrace, to see and to cling to Her naked, with no veil of bodily sensation in between."[73] Experience of spiritual joy made physical pleasure seem ephemeral. Even so, Brown argues, Augustine was afflicted by melancholy for the rest of his life following the "earthquake" that took place in his personal life with his conversion and baptism in 386. Sexual love remained a pale shadow of true pleasure, and he wished that he had grown up in seclusion.[74] Nonetheless, Augustine made new friends with whom he lived in community and chastity. This social life looked ahead to the monastery that he founded five years later after becoming a priest in Hippo.[75]

For Gregory of Nyssa, Ambrose, and Jerome, argues Brown, marriage, sexual intercourse, and Paradise were as irreconcilable as Paradise and death. Sexuality and death were a result of the Fall, when Adam and Eve had fallen from their angelic status and thereby become physical and mortal. For these Church Fathers, neither society nor marriage, sexuality nor sexual intercourse formed part of the original conception of humanity.[76] The angelic status of Paradise, Brown argues, glimmered upon the horizon of late antiquity like the angelic life of the desert.[77]

Augustine interpreted the first two chapters of the Bible differently from Origen and Gregory. In his Genesis commentaries, he did not describe Adam and Eve as originally sexless, angelic beings. For his entire life as a theologian, he wrote about Adam and Eve as human creatures equipped with the same bodies and sexual urges as us. This included sexual intercourse, childbearing, and childrearing.[78] Augustine argued that this also included a hierarchy. A woman was inferior to a man. It was also the man who had authority over their children.[79]

---

73. Brown, *Body and Society*, 394; cf. Augustine, *Soliloquies*.

74. Brown, *Body and Society*, 394.

75. Ibid., 395.

76. Ibid., 399. There are, however, other huge differences between these three theologians.

77. Ibid., 400.

78. Clark, *Augustine on Marriage and Sexuality*, 37n19. I refer below to the English translations from Latin in her book.

79. Augustine, *On Continence* 1.19, 2.13. In chapter 11 woman is described as a

Patristics scholar Kari Elisabeth Børresen nonetheless refers to Augustine as one of the feminist Church Fathers. One reason for this is that Augustine interpreted Gen 1:26–27b as God having created both man and woman in his image. He sees both genders as God's icon, image, and representative. This referred to the non-sexual soul's rational capacity, which was given to both men and women in creation. But this image did not include the sexual division of masculine/feminine that follows in verse 27b and the following verses, with their injunction to be fruitful and multiply.[80] In this context, according to Augustine, woman loses her portion of the trinitarian image. Even in Augustine, then, there are elements of a more angelic, "rational" primary state that disappears in conjunction with the command to be fruitful. Gender differentiation does not seem to affect men as severely, however.[81]

Interpretations of Creation and Three Different Views of Humanity according to Børresen

Two thousand years of church history have seen a gradual overcoming of the contradictions between a gender hierarchy interpreted as part of creation and an eschatological gender equality. According to Børresen, this came about by including woman fully in human beings' resemblance to the divine from the first moment of creation.[82] She describes the process as a series of stages, within which she identifies three distinct Christian anthropologies that in different ways have defined our views of men and women.

She situates the first of these in Paul, who in 1 Cor 11:7 excludes the possibility of woman having been created in God's image. By contrast, according to Gal 3:28, Col 3:10–11, and Eph 4:13, woman can actualize her resemblance to God by renouncing her sexuality and being incorporated into Christ's perfect masculinity. This line of argument is frequently discernible in those who emphasize gender equality in salvation but not in society. Women can thereby be seen as prophets and preachers and as the equals of men, but only if they renounce their sexuality.

---

helper. The man is supposed to rule, she to obey. See Clark, *Augustine on Marriage and Sexuality*, 37–39; cf. Brown, *Body and Society*, 400.

80. See Børresen, *From Patristics to Matristics*, 292.

81. Clark, *Augustine on Marriage and Sexuality*, 36n19.

82. Børresen, *The Image of God*.

The second model draws on Stoic and Platonic anthropology and can be found in the writings of the Graeco-Roman Church Fathers. In it, the human resemblance to the divine is redefined as a question of the rational capacity of the asexual soul, something that also exists in women. This exegesis was begun by Clement of Alexandria in the third century and further developed by Augustine in the fifth. Clement thereby becomes the link connecting Origen to Augustine. In this account, it becomes possible to see woman as God's image from the moment of creation, not merely in salvation. Yet this image does not include a woman's body, biology, or childbearing. This model became normative in medieval theology, argues Børresen, while the former lingers on in canon law.

Børresen identifies the third model in the writings of the northern European Church Mothers Hildegard von Bingen (d. 1179) and Julian of Norwich (d. 1416). They used feminine metaphors to refer to God and saw both women and men as created in God's image, precisely as female and male human beings. According to Børresen, this model became normative in twentieth-century Western Christianity, initially among Protestant exegetes and then in Catholic anthropology following the Second Vatican Council (1962–65), even as the second model lingered on in the Eastern Orthodox churches.[83]

The models are pedagogical. Although there appears to be a good deal of overlap, important points of divergence can be noted. Augustine, as we have seen, conceived of Adam and Eve as created man and woman. He also forcefully distanced himself from Hieronymus's negative view of marriage and sought to find a middle road. In *On the Good of Marriage* (*De bono Conjugali*) from 401, he defended both marriage and virginity within the church.[84] Both were social ways of living, one for having children, the other not. He also emphasized the sacramental bond between spouses, something that made marriage indissoluble on any grounds other than infidelity. In this he went further than Roman law, which allowed both spouses to initiate a divorce.[85]

However, for Augustine, procreation was the only legitimate purpose of sex. He therefore automatically excluded all other sexual activities, such as anal or oral sex but also sex between people of the same gender

---

83. Ibid., 292–93.
84. Clark, *Augustine on Marriage and Sexuality*, 6; Brown, *Body and Society*, 400.
85. Clark, *Augustine on Marriage and Sexuality*, 6.

since this could not result in children.⁸⁶ According to Werner Jeanrond, this meant that marriage was not a place for love but rather a framework for legitimizing shared life.⁸⁷ In *On the Good of Marriage*, Augustine argues that marital intercourse for the purposes of procreation should not give rise to feelings of guilt but that intercourse between spouses for the gratification of sexual desire occasions a venial sin (*venialis culpa*). Adultery or fornication, by contrast, involves a deadly sin. Augustine also claims that it is better to abstain entirely.⁸⁸

However, in his tract on chastity titled *On Continence*, probably authored sometime after 412, Augustine delivered a polemic against the Manichaeans and their sexual ethics. He argued that Manichaeanism proceeds from the view of bodies as something evil. Augustine did not mince his words, describing it as lunacy for the Manichaeans to ascribe some dreadful sinister quality to our flesh, as being "by nature evil." Instead he refers to the "true doctor" who, according to Eph 5:25–29, calls upon men to love their wives as they love their own flesh.⁸⁹ For Augustine, our views on marriage and chastity are bound up with our view of creation and our attitude towards the body and the material. In chapter 12 of the same text, he explains,

> The body is by nature certainly opposed to the soul, but it is not alien to the nature of man. The soul is not made up of the body, but man is made up of soul and body, and, surely, whom God sets free He sets free as a whole man. Whence the Saviour Himself assumed a whole human nature.⁹⁰

Augustine regards abstinence as something that should be justified by love for God and as a gift from God.⁹¹ For Augustine, however, marital intercourse is acceptable when for the purposes of procreation, even if abstinence is preferable. Beverley Clack argues that Augustine was haunted by a need to regain control of his penis. This, he believed, would have been possible in Paradise. Because of the Fall, however, man was no longer able to control his genitals through will or intellect. This was

---

86. Ibid., 5–6.
87. Jeanrond, "Kärlekens praxis," 228.
88. Clark, *Augustine on Marriage and Sexuality*, 48; cf. Augustine, *On the Good of Marriage* VI.6; cf. Jeanrond, "Kärlekens praxis," 228.
89. Clark, *Augustine on Marriage and Sexuality*, 33.
90. Ibid., 34.
91. Ibid.

seen as part of their punishment. As Clack observes, if sin is defined as disobedience, and the penis does not obey the intellect, it is not difficult to see how sexuality becomes identified with sin. She argues that all his life Augustine suffered from being unable to control spontaneous erections.[92] Clack argues that this is a decisive factor in how the spiritual and the sexual are placed in opposition to each other in his theology, whereby those who want to live a spiritual life must suppress their sexuality. This also explains the logic connecting sexuality, sin, and death.[93] The problem is one of disobedience. If the Fall had not occurred, Adam and Eve would have been able to continue loving and having children but without sexual desire.[94] Jeanrond contends that Augustine regarded the body as belonging to the outer, and that for Augustine there could be "no path to the inner through the outer. And the inner is human beings' highest ambition: the soul must live in the body and dominate it."[95] While he wanted to direct desire towards God as a way to avoid loss, he has been read in the Christian tradition as more directly connecting desire and sin.. As will be seen, Luther manifests a certain skepticism towards sexual desire even when extolling sexuality.

Jeanrond argues that Augustine's thoughts on marriage are part of his creation theology, his interpretation of the Fall and eschatology. They are not, however, part of his theology of love. Augustine does not see marriage as something specifically Christian and is aware that it has changed its form through the ages. Marriage for him exists in order to curb sexual desire. To be sure, he identifies three beneficial aspects of marriage, namely, friendship, fidelity, and sacrament.[96] By sacrament he means "something greater that what our feeble mortality can give rise to."[97] For Jeanrond, this constitutes yet another sign that Augustine's thoughts on marriage are connected to an awareness of human mortality.

Love is connected to God, however, and is the sum of the good, *summa bonum*. The framework is Platonic, but Augustine, unlike Plato, identifies love, *caritas*, with a personal God. While Plato claims that everyone loves the good, Augustine argues that everyone loves God, who

92. Clack, *Sex and Death*, 34; cf. Augustine, *Confessions* X, 30.
93. Clack, *Sex and Death*, 35.
94. Brown, *Body and Society*, 400.
95. Jeanrond, "Augustinus teologi om kärlek," 134.
96. Ibid., 131–33.
97. Augustine, *On the Good of Marriage* 7:7; cf. Jeanrond, "Augustinus teologi om kärlek," 131.

is love.⁹⁸ Moreover, Augustine distinguishes between true and false love, *amor*.⁹⁹ False love is facing the wrong direction, towards objects that frustrate its appetite, *appetitus*. Earthly love, which clings to the world and constitutes it, is *cupiditas*. Both these forms of love have appetite, desire, jointly. Augustine thus recommends loving while advising caution as to what to love.¹⁰⁰ The purpose of discipleship is to allow one's will to be shaped in such as a way as to raise itself above evil desires and to develop good desires.¹⁰¹ Augustine spoke of transferring one's love every day from temporal to eternal things, from sinful to intellectual, from bodily flesh to the spiritual.¹⁰²

Ola Sigurdson nonetheless argues that asceticism in classical antiquity was not based upon distancing oneself from the body as such. The idea of chastity that it advocated did not stem from some phobia about the body but was, rather, "integrated into a political context. Bodily asceticism was a way of breaking with societal discipline in antiquity."¹⁰³ Brown gives a startling account of how few people in antiquity lived to be fifty years old. The pressure on both young men and women to have children was intense.¹⁰⁴ Sexual desire was not viewed as a problem. Nor was it a problem if men wanted to caress and be caressed by other men. But severe condemnation was directed at any grown man who chose to perform a woman's role by allowing himself to be penetrated. No free man was exempt from the established hierarchy, which demanded that men exercise authority over women and slaves. The codes of the elite were imposed upon the entire public body.¹⁰⁵ At the same time, Clement of Alexandria (ca. 150-215) had learned from the Greek philosophers and Plato's *Symposium* that chastity offered a way to train the senses to resist the passions by instead seeking rational objects. Christians could go even further, argued Clement. Moses was able to control his body's

---

98. Jeanrond, "Augustinus teologi om kärlek," 136.
99. Arendt, *Love and Saint Augustine*.
100. Jeanrond, "Augustinus teologi om kärlek," 140.
101. Ibid., 132.
102. Augustine, *On the Holy Trinity*.
103. Sigurdson, "Kristna kroppar," 327.
104. Brown, *Body and Society*, 6, 30.
105. Ibid., 30.

needs for forty days, and through incarnation God had made the body capable of transformation.[106]

Since classical society was regarded as doomed, the ideal of virginity offered a way to challenge contemporary expectations and create alternative modes of life within monasteries and holy orders. Jantzen notes drily that at this time women's moral and religious duty beyond the convent involved dedicating themselves to the temporal and the sensual, namely, service and reproduction.[107] This is connected to what Hannah Arendt has already observed of women and slaves whose task was to sustain life and who were therefore not part of the free world. As the household was "born of necessity," they did not belong to the world of free men and their public space.[108] It is unsurprising that monastic life in these societies offered an attractive alternative. Many women, widows, and others allegedly made their way to Hieronymus in search of education.

Bodily exercises and practices here served to transform the body's desires from what Augustine called "the desire to dominate," *dominandi libido*, to "love of God," *amor Dei*.[109] Yet Sigurdson notes that this ideal was confined to an elite. While sexual abstinence provided an opportunity for unrestricted socializing with people with whom one was not related by blood, the celibacy ideal was to become a problematic legacy for the church given its association of sexual desire with sin.[110] The precise nature of these free monastic communities is also debatable. As will be seen, they were circumscribed by rigorous discipline and the oversight of church authorities.

Definitions Influenced by Power

Jantzen claims that Christian mysticism throughout history has been defined in a way that proceeds from specific conceptions of what is female and male. While it was assumed that men became more like themselves by denying bodily desires, the temporal, and the material, the reverse was true for a woman. She could also become more spiritual by renouncing her sexuality, disciplining her body, and, above all, minimizing her intake

---

106. Ibid., 31; cf. Clement, *Stromateis* 3.5.57.

107. Jantzen, *Power, Gender*, 74. Women in the age of Augustine were expected to give birth to at least five children. See Brown, *Body and Society*, 6.

108. Arendt, *Human Condition*, 30.

109. Sigurdson, "Kristna kroppar," 327.

110. Ibid. See the first of Børresen's models.

of food. In so doing, she became more spiritual and approached closer to God. At the same time, she became more like a man. The man, by contrast, became more manlike the more he renounced the bodily in his striving towards God. Hierarchical thinking about gender was reinforced by the definitions that one used.[111]

Jantzen writes from the perspective of a philosopher of religion. She has been criticized for her strong emphasis on the dualism between spirit and body, particularly by medieval historians, who argue that the opposition between spirit and body, God and human beings, man and woman, was more intricate. For example, Caroline Walker Bynum claims that during the Middle Ages the body was central to the practice of spiritual exercises. By contrast, she notes, gender differences between women and men, or, perhaps more precisely, gender stereotypes, played a more important role for men. Above all, women and men used gender-related images very differently. Male authors saw gender dichotomously, as opposites. Their point of departure was that masculinity as a concept was bound up with power, judgment, discipline, and rationality, while women were associated with weakness, charity, sexual desire, and unreason.[112]

In a society characterized by asymmetry between men and women, in which men had more power, men described themselves as women—that is, as lacking power, wealth, influence, and authority—when they wished to foreground their humility and renounce the world. Bernard of Clairvaux affirmed the value of mildness and gentleness when he wanted to demonstrate his spiritual superiority to other men, such as bishops and popes, his rivals for spiritual supremacy. At such moments, he described monks as women and bishops as men. Another spiritual leader, Francis of Assisi, not only married "Lady Poverty"; he was Madame Poverty.[113] Women, who were already seen as powerless, weak, and more bodily, instead chose to further emphasize these qualities. Vulnerability, illness, and bleeding became signs of their humanity, something that stood in opposition to the divine. But since God himself had become human, become flesh, this offered a way to unite oneself with Christ. They thus emphasized Jesus's humanity and his physical body.

111. There is not necessarily a contradiction between body and spirit, something that forms part of an ongoing discussion in this book. Here I refer to Jantzen's interpretation as a background.

112. Bynum, *Fragmentation and Redemption*, 175.

113. Ibid., 165.

This sometimes meant that Jesus was regarded not just as the object of love but quite literally as a lover. Catherine of Siena is a case in point. In a vision, she sees herself as married to Christ. Yet the ring she wears is made of skin—Christ's foreskin. Physical proximity to Christ and to his physical body signifies a bodily union. According to Bynum, female mystics regarded the use of images associated with the feminine gender, such as bride or mother and child, not as problematic but as entirely logical. In this way, they emphasized humanity, body, and incarnation and hence proximity to and union with Christ.[114]

Taking issue with Jantzen, Bynum argues that spiritual exercises made women not more masculine but more feminine.[115] However, there are texts from the early Christian period that suggest that both men and women imagined a woman as needing, in order to reach the divine, to suppress her femininity or develop it in the direction of masculinity because she was regarded as half of a man. Society in antiquity was androcentric. According to Kerstin Aspegren, this meant that men defined the parameters for women's activities.[116] In certain settings these limitations were profound, while in others there was greater freedom. Yet the man was always both benchmark and arbiter. A woman was always viewed in relation to the man. If she distinguished herself ethically, religiously, or intellectually, Aspegren argues, she was praised, not for being a woman, but for being a woman who had become more masculine.[117] Women's spiritual progress was viewed as a movement towards masculinity, rationality, and self-mastery. The angelic ideal of virginity was seen quite simply as something masculine, and a woman was viewed as half of a man.[118] Bynum argues that women in the later Middle Ages nonetheless seem to have rejected this line of thinking.[119] Yet women did not emphasize the specifically feminine or the differences between the sexes in the same way as men. They spoke instead of humanity. As women, they represented Christ's human side precisely through emphasizing the bodily and the vulnerable. Incarnation was important. God became flesh.[120] Men in-

---

114. Ibid., 173.
115. Ibid., 172f.
116. Aspegren, *Male Women*, 11.
117. Ibid.
118. Ibid.
119. Bynum, *Fragmentation and Redemption*, 178.
120. Ibid.,177.

voked the feminine when they wanted to present themselves as Christ-like. Religious conversion involved a reversal and a renunciation of the earthly world as progress and power. Instead, they embraced powerlessness, poverty, and weakness, all concepts associated with women. Men could thereby present themselves not only as without power or authority but also as irrational and lacking influence. If God was seen as masculine, then woman was instead treated as the natural image of what a powerful and successful man would become when he rejected the world.[121]

Yet men, Bynum points out, were seen as being like God in a way that women could never be. Women therefore had either to discard or disregard their femininity in order to elevate themselves to a level where they might encounter the divine. Pictorial representations from early Christianity suggest that this was how both women and men understood it.[122] Writings authored by men in the later Middle Ages similarly indicate that women's spiritual progress involved their becoming more masculine, that is, acquiring greater rationality and self-control. By contrast, women themselves seem to have rejected this perspective.[123] Aspegren, Bynum, and Jantzen all agree on the existence of a decisive gender hierarchy—an unsurprising but nonetheless noteworthy consensus given the nature of contemporary debates. When gender stereotypes are used, it happens on both sides, as part of a power game.

Inequality between men and women was intrinsic to the very notion of role reversal. The feminine was viewed as without power. For religious women, this might be seen as an asset. For them, it was more problematic that women were associated with irrationality and sexual desire. As far back as the early church, inequality between the genders had been constructed so as to associate men with divinity and rationality. This was contrasted with being human, physical, and woman. Women therefore had little to offer in any role reversal that involved abdicating power. Instead, they emphasized their humanness in a way that called the entire schema into question. They argued that humanity has no gender, only flesh, that is to say, is physical. By himself becoming flesh, the divine human, Jesus, reconciled the material that was seen as far removed from God. While a man was figuratively like God, a woman was literally

---

121. Ibid., 178.
122. Ibid.; cf. Børresen's first model.
123. Ibid., 178.

a human being.[124] For female mystics, then, incarnation became a means of asserting their humanity as divine.

This figurative language came about in an asymmetric society in which being male was an advantage. However, the use of feminine metaphors is not in itself a sign of feminist consciousness. To become like a man involved an elevation. Bynum claims that men in particular treated women and men differently. Women were usually seen as more physical, more body, and thus as worth less. Bynum is sometimes cited in rebuttals of Jantzen's reading. Her rigorous examination of late medieval spiritual writings in particular nuances our image of medieval mysticism, revealing an upheaval in gender stereotyping as well as in perceptions of the body's importance within ascetic piety. Yet both Bynum and Jantzen show how female mystics managed to navigate the prevailing system, often by exercising even stricter control over their bodies and sexuality, and, above all, by minimizing their food intake, something Jantzen calls "holy anorexia."[125] Women, one might say, upend the scale of values by emphasizing physicality. The result is a restitution and a road to salvation through identification with Christ's vulnerability.

Of particular interest to my line of inquiry is, not how much physicality can be found in holy orders since the twelfth century, but rather to what extent eroticism as realized concrete sexuality between people, was regarded as a rival to the erotic union between human beings and the divine.

Within the ascetic movements, the body and its erotic dimensions closely connected to community with Christ and union with God. Because of the conviction that eroticism inside the monasteries sometimes expressed itself in homoeroticism, many contemporary scholars are interested in the question of whether sexuality really was entirely suppressed and controlled. Córdova Quero is one of several scholars who want to disrupt the heteronormativity of history by demonstrating that sexuality had importance long before the term itself was invented. He shows that homoerotic love between monks occurred in the monasteries and even "with someone chosen especially."[126] For example, Aelred (ca. 1110–67), abbot of the Cistercian monastery at Rievaulx, writes in his *Theology of Friendship*,

124. Ibid., 179.

125. Jantzen, *Power, Gender*, 196, 208; Bynum, *Fragmentation and Redemption*, 175.

126. Córdova Quero, "Friendship with Benefits," 33.

> It is no mean consolation in this life to have someone with whom you can be united by an intimate attachment and the embrace of very holy love ... You may be so united to him and approach him so closely and so mingle your spirit with his that the two become one.[127]

While this can be interpreted in terms of the tradition of courtly love poetry, it could also be taken as evidence of the homoerotic that is foregrounded in Córdova Quuero's historiography, which shows that history can be used in many ways. This is interesting because theological outlooks exist in a synergy with lives and human bodies. The boundaries between different ways of living and different outlooks do not neatly demarcate different times or epochs, or distinct theological outlooks. Certain tendencies become apparent, however. My purpose in offering this background is to show that part of what our era takes for granted was not a given for the Reformation. It also serves to highlight that some of what we associate with the Reformation or the early modern period in fact has earlier roots. I will therefore continue my survey of the historical background.

Two Spiritual Paths: Eckhart and Bernard of Clairvaux via Dionysius the Areopagite and Thomas

A recurrent theme in mysticism concerns union with God, being made divine. For Jantzen, there were two routes to attaining this. One was an intellectual path, the other affective—the path of emotion. In her pedagogical survey of the history of mysticism, Jantzen describes each of them. She remarks that there is of course some overlap. But what is rarely mentioned is that neither path really has any space for women.[128] She puts Meister Eckhart in the intellectual tradition of mysticism.[129]

The second path, of affective love, is most commonly associated with Bernard of Clairvaux. He forms part of the tradition of erotic love. Perhaps surprisingly, this tradition also includes a spiritualizing that finds expression in different roles for women and men. An emphasis on intellect tended to marginalize women, who, since Aristotle, have been seen as wretched men and thus as both morally and intellectually inadequate.

---

127. Ibid., 44.
128. Jantzen, *Power, Gender*, 109.
129. Ibid.

Yet, Jantzen argues, the affective path's emphasis on love and will also came at the expense of ordinary human sexuality and thus of physical women.[130] In the following section, I summarize some of the perspectives that shaped these two paths, beginning with a description of the path initiated by Origen.

The Path of Contemplation or Knowledge

Origen developed an outlook that regarded the spiritual senses as existing in parallel to the physical senses.[131] As he saw it, the physical body and its sensations dulled the spiritual senses such that they became unresponsive. The path to purity, as already noted, therefore necessitated the strict disciplining of the physical senses so as to avoid dulling of the spiritual senses.[132] At the same time, bodily experiences can be a step on the road towards mystical experiences that nonetheless lie beyond the bodily realm.

Origen's tripartite path to union with God is founded on purification, contemplation, and enlightenment. It became known as the path of contemplation or the mystical path. It was adopted by other Church Fathers, perhaps most prominently by Gregory of Nyssa (c. 334–394) in his *Life of Moses*.[133]

This path remained prominent throughout the Middle Ages, Jantzen argues. Yet she claims that it gave priority to men because they were seen as identified with spirit and reason. For men, too, part of the price of this spirituality was a denial of the passions, something that created a widening gap between the genders. The body had to be controlled and suppressed. Since women were identified with the flesh, Jantzen argues, they needed in similar fashion to be controlled and suppressed, indeed, sometimes literally killed.[134]

American patrist Virginia Burrus points out that while martyrdom for men often took the form of a figurative and metaphorical transformation from death to life, martyrdom for women involved, as a path to life,

---

130. Ibid., 87.

131. Origen, *Exhortation to Martyrdom*, 222–23; cf. Louth, *Origins of the Christian Mystical Tradition*, 66.

132. Jantzen, *Power, Gender*, 90.

133. Gregory of Nyssa, *The Life of Moses*.

134. Jantzen, *Power, Gender*, 94–95.

physical and often literal death.¹³⁵ She has highlighted the intricate interplay between gender and sexuality in the writings of the early Church Fathers. In a polemic with Radical Orthodoxy theologians, she argues that there is an intimate connection between orthodoxy and heresy: "Whether we read the representation of heresy as negation or (as I would prefer) as mimicry, it must be admitted that orthodox discourse thereby addresses a number of real problems." She claims that it has to do with "the practice of theology itself" where an ongoing theological production is justified by a view whereby

> doctrine—represented as divinely granted revelation transmitted via apostolic succession—is presumed to be both fully accessible and fully unchanging. The need to refute heresy supplies such justification, allowing doctrine to break out of its self-consigned stasis by providing the church fathers both the pretext and cover for their own immensely innovative theologizing.

However, she continues,

> the temporality of orthodoxy must bend and split in order both to accommodate and to repress the historicity, and thus the inventiveness of theology. Christian truth is by definition prior, in terms of the orthodox script: it always already *is*. It is however also necessary by the terms of that same script that the heretics see it first, albeit through distorting lenses: the negation or perversion of orthodox truth by heretics is understood to *precede* its doctrinal articulation by the orthodox fathers.

She concludes,

> in practice orthodoxy and heresy must always be spoken in the same breath, at the same time: paradoxically there is no orthodoxy without heresy, no confession without negation, no original without mimicry. This "paradox," of course, begins to undo the claims of orthodoxy, even as it also sustains them by supplying endless grist for the heresiological mill.¹³⁶

---

135. Burrus, *Sex Lives of Saints*, 56, 455.
136. Burrus, "Radical Orthodoxy," 36.

The Angelic Ideal as Horizon and Goal

British theologian Sarah Coakley often invokes and praises the aesthetic tradition and the Greek Church Fathers. Clayton Crocket sees the adherents of Radical Orthodoxy as drawing on postmodern critique while steering clear of its nihilistic conclusions.[137] Instead, they evince an ambition to reinstate a Christian point of departure and a transcendent God.[138] They are often keen to articulate the first truth. In an article from 2002, Coakley makes a fascinating comparison between Gregory of Nyssa and Judith Butler with regard to the concept of gender fluidity. According to Coakley, both seek to move beyond the binary models of gender that remains culturally normative even today. They both want to find a transformative path through them:

> Whereas in Butler, however, this escape is effected by punctiliar subversive acts of "performativity," in Gregory it represents a life-long ascetical programme, a purification and redirection of *eros* towards the divine, a final withdrawal from the whirligig of marriage, child-rearing, the quest for social status and financial security.[139]

Coakley observes that Gregory was married while young and wrote about the tragic death of a child. But, unlike Augustine, he was not racked by guilt or fear about his sexuality. Instead, Coakley argues, his spirituality was characterized by a gradual "progressive ascent" and freeing of the intellect, something that is evoked in *Life of Moses* "by analogy with the procreative act." She points out that Gregory argues in the introduction to his commentaries on the Song of Songs that the transition from the bodily to the spiritual cannot be realized through suppressing fears of bodily love. He hopes that his commentaries will be "a guide for the more fleshly minded, since the wisdom hidden [in the Song of Songs] leads to a spiritual state of the soul."[140]

Coakley follows Bynum's reading of the eschatological body as being, for Gregory, a body that is continually changing. While the body is "labile and changing" in this life, it is "on its way to continuous change

---

137. Crockett, *Secular Theology*.
138. Carlsson, *Theology beyond Representation*, 18.
139. Coakley, "Eschatological Body," 162.
140. Gregory of Nyssa, *Commentary on the Song of Songs* 35, quoted in Coakley, "Eschatological Body," 162.

into incorruptibility in the next."[141] As Virginia Burrus ironically observes, when Coakley takes up Judith Butler and her ideas about gender fluidity, she seems to be arguing that Gregory already knew everything Butler does, and more.[142] On the basis of Gen 1:27 and Gal 3:28, Gregory held that human beings had originally been created "non-sexed (that is, non-genitalized)." It was only just prior to the Fall that "'man' was distinguished from 'woman.'" For this reason, human beings will again be "de-genitalized" at the end of time and "receive that angelic status that was our lot originally." Unlike Augustine in *The City of God*, he does not believe that people will recognize each other in heaven as women and men.[143]

This angelic ideal is not only found in the writings of the early Greek Church Fathers. As we have seen, it also reemerges, explicitly or otherwise, in contemporary debate among theologians close to the Radical Orthodoxy movement. Exactly how this ideal understands those seen as the most material—slaves, women, and others—is thus no trivial matter. Nor is the issue of whether people seek to be more angelic and genderless or more human.

Dionysius the Areopagite

The history of mysticism can hardly be sketched out, even in bold strokes, without mentioning Dionysius. Though the most influential author of the Middle Ages, his name is today unknown. He was in the habit of referring to himself as belonging to the apostolic era and as being closely connected with Paul and his Areopagus sermon. He was thereafter often known as Dionysius the Areopagite or Pseudo-Dionysius. Martin Luther referred to him as "this Dionysius, whoever he was."[144]

Dionysius argued that the "poetic force [of the Song of Songs] contains the basis for a mystical experience, the glimpse of a loved one, and, indeed, a loving contact that occurs in an encounter beyond time and space." Rubenson foregrounds this perspective in his reading of Dionysius the Areopagite. He claims that the latter's theology includes the notion that we can detect divine love through the human:

141. Ibid., 163.
142. Burrus, "Queer Father," 160.
143. Ibid., 163; cf. Børresen, *From Patristics to Matristics*.
144. Jantzen, *Power, Gender*, 95–96.

> Just as a lovers' tryst involves undressing, so, too, does heavenly desire. Getting to know and getting close to presuppose a set of clothes that protects and conceals while also hinting at what lies beneath. For Dionysius, the language and the liturgy, the space of the church and the sacrament, all constitute this set of clothes, this meeting-place.[145]

Yet for Pseudo-Dionysius, argues Rubenson, language is a way to talk, not about, but with God. The words involve not a description but a confession. However, this theology needs the symbolism encountered in the liturgy, in the rite, "of the mysteries revealed in deeds and matter."[146] It includes performative elements. Just as words do something new when they are spoken (as when lovers whisper to each other), so, too, is something achieved by the use of these material things.[147]

Pseudo-Dionysius likely lived in Syria in the late fifth century. His origins may be obscure, Grace Jantzen argues, but there can be little doubt as to his enormous influence on medieval thought, particularly upon what counted as mysticism.[148] He was especially interested in questions of church hierarchy and its intrinsic authority, which he saw as closely tied to the mystical. Dionysius, who coined the word *hierarchy*, emphasized the importance of secrecy with regard to the divine mysteries. For instance, Jantzen observes, he argued that what he wrote should not be taught to those on the outside, the uninitiated. She notes that he begins his treatise *The Ecclesiastical Hierarchy* as follows:

> Most sacred of sacred sons: Our hierarchy consists of an inspired, divine, and divinely worked understanding, activity, and perfection. With the aid of the transcendent and most sacred scriptures, I must demonstrate this to those who have been initiated in the sacrament of the sacred mystagogy by our hierarchy's mysteries and traditions.[149]

That the Bible contained symbols and hidden truths was taken to mean that these must be kept inaccessible for the unconsecrated. Knowledge was not for everyone.[150] As he saw it, the church's hierarchy had a paral-

145. Rubenson, "Eros och Agape," 594.
146. Ibid., 593.
147. Ibid.
148. Jantzen, *Power, Gender*, 96.
149. Ibid.
150. Ibid., 96–98.

lel in that of the angels. Questioning the church's structure thus became equivalent to questioning God's creation.

This spiritual system was a way to return to God from sin and a fallen world. And yet, Jantzen claims, the system was neither innocent nor neutral as regards its distribution of power. It was a perspective that invested enormous authority in bishops and priests. Women, she adds, were wholly absent.[151] In Dionysius's thought, the mystical was extended to include not only the hidden meaning of the Scriptures but all of God's mystery in the church and in the Bible. It is a "theology of mysticism," encompassing all that God has revealed and administered by the ecclesiological authorities. They both interpret the Scriptures and administer the sacrament. Rosemary Radford Ruether argues that the clericalization of asceticism changed its psychology. Instead of constituting a radical ethics that dissolves worldly authority and liberates women to act with spiritual authority, sexual abstinence was tied to magical conceptions of the sacredness of the sacramental priesthood. The holy and the secular were divided into two spheres. The one included celibate priests, the other sexual laypeople, with women forming the quintessence of the non-sacral or something that contaminated the holy.[152]

Much of Dionysius's thinking about angels and created beings was influenced by Platonism. The divine was seen as perfect. It could also be seen as a movement outwards that, like the sun's rays, creates life in everything that exists. Yet these things can also be drawn upwards by divine attraction and thereby return to God.[153]

For Platonic thinking, only like can recognize like. This means that only a pure heart can see God. Knowing God by being united with God involves a transformation that makes it possible to use reflexive language. To know God is to be known by God. To be united with God in some sense involves being incorporated in the divine, to be transfigured. Jantzen observes that, for Origen and for much of the mystical tradition, it is a matter of becoming God or being united with God. Origen refers to how Moses's face shone when he saw God's glory: "So the mind, purified and passing beyond everything material, so that it perfects its contemplation of God, is made divine in what it contemplates."[154] This is the project

---

151. Ibid., 99.
152. Ruether, "Asceticism and Feminism," 242.
153. Jantzen, *Power, Gender*, 98.
154. See Louth, *Origins of the Christian Mystical Tradition*, 71.

of knowledge, the path of intellect. Intellect is driven by sexual desire and is transformed through love. It is thus neither a vocation nor a calculating rationality. But it is not the body or emotion that has the capacity to be transformed into the knowledge of God that leads to union with the divine, to transfiguration.[155]

When intellect has gone the whole way, however, it comes to the end of the road and becomes the path of negation. Passing through every stage of greater enlightenment on the path towards God, the mind at last attains an enlightenment so dazzling as to be indistinguishable from divine darkness. Knowing is then transformed into not-knowing, something that is beyond but never beneath knowledge. This is the path of mysticism: the mind's gradual enlightenment through negations until it reaches the hidden things of God and is thrown into the truly mystical darkness of not-knowing. This wordless state beyond language entails ecstasy, from the Greek *ekstasis*, literally standing outside of oneself.[156]

Thomas Aquinas was deeply influenced by Dionysius, whose ideas he learned from Albert the Great, his teacher (ca. 1200–1280). Thomas used these ideas in developing his negative theology, which thereby exerted considerable influence in the high Middle Ages as well as on perhaps the best known medieval mystic, Meister Eckhart.[157]

Meister Eckhart

The Dominican priest, teacher, and mystic Meister Eckhart (ca. 1260–1328) is one of the most famous figures within mysticism. He, too, argued that union with God could be realized through a number of meditative steps by which the soul would be liberated from the bodily. He regarded food, drink, and sensual comfort as things that tied the soul to the body and the earthly, to which the soul is a stranger. One means of liberating the body was penance.[158] Eckhart had considerable influence on late-medieval mystics such as Johann Tauler (ca. 1300–1361) and a lay movement that emphasized prayer and abstention from all worldly pleasures in favor of exercising virtue. This movement, *Devotio moderna*, in turn

---

155. Jantzen, *Power, Gender*, 94.
156. Ibid., 105–6.
157. Ibid., 110.
158. Meister Eckhart, *A Modern Translation*, 123.

inspired the best known book of the fifteenth century, *De imitatio Christo* by Thomas à Kempis (1379/1380–1471).[159]

Meister Eckhart also preached to unlearned women. When this was criticized, he defended himself by saying that if no one were to teach those who hitherto had not been taught, no one would learn anything. Like Augustine and Thomas before him, he argued that spiritually women were created in God's image. However, this did not contradict the fact that their primary task was to serve men, particularly as regards the need for procreation.[160] Woman symbolized sensuality, and the Fall took place because Adam yielded to Eve and her fruit, as described in Genesis 3.

As such, he confirms the relation between sexual desire and sin that Augustine established. The view of the Church Fathers and the Middle Ages, that women were more sensual and men more rational and intellectual, continues and is passed on. When he develops his own kind of intellectual mysticism, it therefore automatically takes on a gendered aspect, since sexuality, sinful sexual desire, and original sin are associated with the woman's physicality. However, Jantzen notes, Meister Eckhart even more often associates women with inferior intellect. The superior intellect is always figuratively masculine, while sensuality is feminine. In his commentaries on the Fall, the serpent represents sensuality, Eve, and the inferior intellect, Adam the superior. These are traditional patterns according to which the woman is passive and more material while the man is described as spiritual and active.[161]

Eckhart's intention, however, is not to discuss differences between men and women. While passivity is most often used to denote something of less value, he also talks in a sermon about the Son as passive, because he was born, and the Father as active. The Son is thus wisdom, the mother within whom the man is to rest and to live happily.[162] The inferior intellect, which is metaphorically feminine in Eckhart's metaphorical schema, is what binds us to the world, to our bodies, and to each other. This is something that the divine spark in a human soul, which knows God and is one with God, wishes to separate itself from.[163]

159. See Cortright, "'Poor Maggot-Sack That I Am,'" 50f.
160. Jantzen, *Power, Gender*, 112.
161. Ibid., 114–15.
162. Ibid., 116. This imagery in which the man has his rest and home in his mother, the woman, the passive one, is also prominent in Emmanuel Levinas's writings. See Young, *On Female Body Experience*. I develop this line of argument further in Gerle, "Mot ömsesidighetens," 301–2.
163. Jantzen, *Power, Gender*, 120–22.

Jantzen claims that Eckhart's mysticism, which contains numerous misogynistic metaphors, is more than metaphorically traditional. It proceeds from an entire worldview. God, nature, and the spiritual serve to keep the woman in a subordinate position. According to the Platonic ascetic ideal, physicality and outer knowledge are to be transcended. It is something from which the mind ought increasingly to detach itself.[164]

In her study Jantzen shows that it was difficult for women within this system to be counted as mystics or as spiritual beings, let alone as spiritual leaders. For my own inquiry into the body and sexuality and their relation to how God and the spiritual is understood, it raises additional questions beyond those relating to views of gender, namely, whether affirmation of the material, the sensual, and the bodily can create new forms of spirituality. We will have reasons for returning to this issue in due course.

The Path of Love

If, as Jantzen suggests, Eckhart and the path of intellectual knowledge reveals, in its language and thinking, an innate contempt for the feminine and the material, one might reasonably assume that the other strand within mysticism, which emphasizes emotion and will, would be more open to the feminine and the sensual. This path, which is principally associated with Bernard of Clairvaux, is usually described as the affective path—the path of love. Like Luther, Bernard is known as a theologian of love. His affective mysticism lies closer to Augustine's emphasis on love.[165] It is about the heart, rather than the intellect. If God, for Eckhart and, before him, for Dionysius, is being and knowledge, for Bernard he is charity, *caritas*. This, Jantzen argues, stands in sharp contrast to the speculative tradition. Progress is a question of increasing, not one's knowledge, but one's love. It was a matter of training one's humility and penitence, and thereby one's love.[166]

It is not that Bernard scorns knowledge, simply that love is fundamental. Love is the most profound influence upon human beings and for this reason can effect a process of moral transformation and perfection, something that can reconcile human beings and all of the personality

---

164. Ibid., 122.
165. Ibid., 123.
166. Ibid., 124–25.

disorders entailed by sin. The goal, even for him, is to become one with God. Thus he writes in *On Loving God*, "When a feeling of this kind is experienced, the soul, drunk with divine love, forgetful of self, and seeming to be a broken vessel, goes completely into God, and cleaving to God becomes one spirit with him . . ."[167] Bernard also uses an erotic language. His sermons are filled with longing for the presence of the Other and for sexual union and gratification. And yet, as Jantzen observes, this emphasis upon erotic love in his writing is everywhere accompanied by a flat denial of its having any connection to the body. There is no place in his sermons for a passionate, physical, and sexual love that is good beneficial, and welcome. Instead, he views human physicality and sexuality as barriers to God's spiritual love.[168]

According to Jantzen, female mystics during the high medieval period did not recognize this opposition. Their sexual language is explicit and carries no warnings against literal interpretation. Instead, they describe their authors' direct, charged, and passionate encounters with Christ. The thirteenth-century writer Mechthild of Magdeburg is a case in point. She recounts part of her mystical tryst as follows:

> The Most beloved goes toward the Most Beautiful in the hidden chambers of the invisible Deity. There she finds the couch and the pleasure of Love, and God awaiting her in a superhuman fashion. This is what Our Lord says:—Stay, Lady Soul.—What is your wish, Lord?—That you should be naked.—Lord how can this happen to me?—Lady Soul, you are so "co-natured" in Me that nothing can be interposed between you and Me . . . your noble desire and your insatiable hunger . . . I shall satisfy eternally with My infinite superabundance.[169]

Eroticism here does not seem to be an allegory of the spiritual. Rather, it is a way to get to know God: "It is precisely through actual eroticism that lessons of God are to be learned." Jantzen argues that the same holds for a number of medieval women authors. She cites Gertrude the Great of Helfta, Catherine of Siena, Beatrice of Nazareth, and, much later, Teresa of Ávila.[170]

---

167. Quoted in ibid., 125.
168. Ibid., 128–29.
169. Quoted in ibid., 133.
170. Ibid., 134.

Within the monastic world, however, all women were physically subordinate to men. They were kept apart and enclosed. Only with the permission of a man could they temporarily leave their seclusion. For Jantzen, this was a consequence of the threat posed by women to the spiritualization within both these spiritual paths. Women constituted a physical temptation for men. Yet women were also a threat to the ecclesiastical structures since they made mysticism accessible, beyond the religious orders, to ordinary pious women and men. Such women were therefore often charged with so-called "free-spirited" heresy or with being witches.[171]

The Reformation did not bring about any immediate improvements on this point.[172] But female mystics were pioneers of a spirituality that could flourish outside the convent and holy orders, a legacy that the Reformation could invoke. That the Reformation led to a closing of the spiritual paths that the convent had offered to women is an issue worth wrestling with.

The opposing of spirituality to sexuality often goes hand in hand with an emphasis upon difference and polarity between men and women. Within the practices of monastic piety these roles sometimes seem to have been overturned in favor of an affirmation of gender-transgressing elements. Yet this did not pose a serious challenge to the hierarchical structures. As both Bynum and Jantzen show, the disruption of gender roles often involved a protest against clerical and ecclesiastical hierarchies.[173] This did not go unpunished, however, but brought the explicit condemnation of the church authorities. Strong women in orders were especially vulnerable.[174]

From an early stage, it was evident that views on women and men were different. Virginia Burrus, who has analyzed early Christian hagiographies, has shown how virginal martyrs were able to transform their passivity at the prospect of torture and violence into a mode of active

---

171. Ibid., 204.

172. On the issue of witch hunts, Luther's views lay close to those of the fifteenth-century Roman Catholic Church. One of the first to try to cast doubt upon the witch hunts was Johann Wier, who sought in his *De præstigiis dæmonum* (1563) to show that witches were the more or less innocent victims of an obsession with the devil, and that much of what was regarded as sorcery was fraud or optical illusion. That accusations of witchcraft and heresy continued to be leveled at women after the Reformation has been well established by previous studies and does not need further discussion here.

173. Jantzen, *Power, Gender*; Bynum, *Jesus as Mother*.

174. Jantzen, *Power, Gender*, 204.

resistance. By not merely refusing to resist martyrdom but actively desiring it, they transformed gender roles in such a way that the accused woman gained power over the soldier who was to execute her. Her martyrdom was thereby constructed as an ascetic praxis. Inferiority was transformed into resistance.[175]

In her reading of Hieronymus's account of the death of the accused adulteress in Epistle 1, Burrus claims, however, that he sexualizes the woman's death. To have any meaning for a woman, death must be literal, whereas the death described in other narratives—that of men—is merely symbolic:

> Martyrdom is thus a metaphorical affair for the man, whose Life is thereby prolonged, extended through the repetitions of sublimation into a truly lengthy hagiographic text. Life for the woman, on the other hand, must emerge through (the recounting of) her actual death, if it is to exist at all. Indeed, she becomes visible in the marks of death, as her history is incised in her flesh.[176]

Burrus also shows how, in Ambrose's story of Agnes, longing for an executioner's sword is portrayed as a shameless desire to become a bride of Christ.[177] Women might be able to turn resistance to torture into a great deed, yet the stories passed down to us are of women literally and concretely dying.

The eroticism advocated by the women of the convent involved an erotic union with Christ. As will be seen in the next chapter, Luther also likens the relationship between God and the soul to a nuptial union. At the same time, he does not associate this community with a rejection of human beings' shared sexuality. We will return to the question of whether this can be considered a signpost to divine experience. Before God, both

---

175. Burrus, *Sex Lives of Saints*, 55: "He [the executioner] succeeds only because she now *desires* death. Indeed, here as in other ancient Christian accounts of torture and resistance, the plot pivots on the subject's consent: the perverse extravagance of her passivity is the source of her power. Martyrdom is thereby construed as an ascetic practice, and submission is converted to defiance, subverting the fraudulent script of 'self-betrayal' insinuated by the ritual of forced confession and further underwritten by the body's betrayal in pain. Reclaiming her voice (not least through the eloquent performance of the 'noble silence' of bodily endurance by which pain itself is betrayed), the woman gives witness not only to her own faith but also to the injustice of the torturer's tyranny."

176. Ibid., 56.

177. Ibid., 53.

woman and man are equal, at once sinners and saved, as whole beings of spirit, soul, and body.

In our own time, too, it is sometimes possible to glimpse a hierarchy in which the spiritual and the angelic count for more than the bodily, with which woman is often conflated. This constitutes a problem for egalitarian societies, less because it conflicts with contemporary attitudes than because of the risks it entails for those viewed as feminine, that is to say, not merely women but also non-macho men. The association of woman and nature as things to be investigated and mastered has also had devastating consequences for attitudes towards ecology. The mystics Origen and Gregory of Nyssa should thus be read more freely today and detached from their contemporary emphasis upon women's inferiority.

The Language and Images of Tradition in New Contexts

This background, which I have evoked with the help of Jantzen, Bynum, Burrus, Louth, and others, reveals at times contradictory views of the relationship between body and soul. From the vantage point of the present, it is not surprising that a woman is not seen as equal to a man. For many, it is an anachronism that needs no pointing out. Yet it remains difficult for women to be seen as spiritual leaders or as artistic, intellectual, or creative. It is therefore important to expose some of the roots of these notions and attitudes. My summary has shown that very different kinds of readings are possible. The societies of antiquity were characterized by the subordination of women. Nevertheless, this should not prevent women today from reading and allowing themselves to be inspired by great thinkers, even if they in many respects shared their era's views on femininity and masculinity. Origen, Augustine, Gregory, and Luther were complex personalities. It is vital that we recognize that all of them were in different ways influenced by contemporary ideas and relationships, philosophical as well as economic. Far from viewing them as having articulated timeless truths, we should see them as representatives of creative people theologizing in their own historical moment.

For my own purposes, it is significant that Luther in a number of regards adopts aspects not only of the early churches but also of medieval piety. He uses elements from the language of tradition but sometimes in a new way. For the present study of sensuality and of the body's significance for ethics, it is interesting to note that Luther applies the same (or similar) images of bodily love between people as he does for the love between God and the soul. At the same time as he affirms its spiritual interpretation, he thus brings this figurative language back to its original earthly context, one in which he celebrates sexuality and intimacy between earthly, physical bodies. It is possible to trace the influence of the nuptial mystery of tradition in several of Luther's texts.

In his sermons on the Song of Songs, Bernard of Clairvaux describes the relationship between the Word and the soul as a love relationship between a bridal couple:

> No sweeter names can be found to embody that sweet interflow of affections between the Word and the soul, than the bridegroom and bride. Between these all things are equally shared, there are no selfish reservations, nothing that causes division. They share the same inheritance, the same table, the same home, the same marriage-bed, they are flesh and each other's flesh . . . Therefore if a love relationship is the special and outstanding characteristic of the bride and groom, it is not unfitting to call the soul that loves God a bride.[178]

Bernard compares the relation of God and soul to that of a bridal couple. So, too, does Luther in *On the Freedom of a Christian* (1520), in which he describes what has come to be known as "the blessed exchange" between Christ, the groom, and the soul, the bride. In this text, then, he invokes the language of tradition at the same time as he deploys it in a new way.

More striking still is the fact that he applies the same metaphors in wholly different contexts. Bernard's formulations about the bridal couple as sharing everything—bed, table, home, and inheritance—make a revolutionary reappearance in Luther's 1531 Wedding Sermon. In it, Luther refers to the shared life of the human bride and groom by means of near-identical formulations. Thus he writes:

> that the classical doctors rightly preached that marriage was necessary because of children, loyalty, and love. But the physical advantages are also something precious and have justly been proclaimed the greatest virtue of marriage, namely that spouses can rely upon one another and confidently entrust to each other everything they own on this earth because it is as secure in the other's possession as in their own.[179]

---

178. Bernard of Clairvaux, *On the Songs of Songs* 7.2, quoted in Jantzen, *Power, Gender*, 127.

179. WA 34 I, 52:5–9, "Eine Hochzeitpredigt über den Spruch Hebr 13, 4" (1531); trans. Stephen Donovan.

The instrumental view of marriage as merely a means for procreation and children is conspicuously absent here. Instead, Luther eulogizes the physical advantages, and, in the same breath, the trust, that allow spouses to be at home with each other.[180] It is not so much a possibility for a man to find solace in the woman as of their being able to be at home with each other. Physical advantages can mean a lot. A common bed, a shared home, and responsibilities. And yet it would not be unreasonable to suggest that Luther is here also referring to a physical proximity, the sexual desire and intimacy of the bodies. Sexuality and sexual desire are, just like everything else, grounded in the ambiguity of life; they can be used to dominate and rule over another person as easily as they can be a source of joy and closeness.

An intertextual reading thus reveals new dimensions to Martin Luther. He does not break with the centuries-old view of women as having lesser worth and being associated with sexual desire, passion, and irrationality. That which is self-evident, society's view of a man as superior to a woman, is not called into question. However, for what Luther views as sinful—absorption within oneself, *incurvatio in se ipse*—there is no gender difference. More importantly, he and, to a greater extent, other reformers initiate another perspective. It proceeds from a conviction that everyone is equal before God because one's relationship to God is not a question of efforts by the individual. The body does not thereby become, through mortification and control, a vehicle for drawing closer to God, a way of achieving divine union. Instead, the body, sensuality, and eroticism are viewed in an earthly context, as things given by God in his continual process of creation.

180. Ibid.

5

The Movement of the Senses: Towards the Everyday

Literary scholars often emphasize the reader's independence with regard to both text and author. The various readings of Origen in the previous chapter show that in the capacity of reader one can interpret texts in quite different ways. This depends in part upon what one is looking for or what one wants to examine, but also upon the fact that both sender's and receiver's signatures are unique. Every interpretation involves a way of relating to the text. A different theological perspective not infrequently produces a different interpretation. In the present study I wish to problematize a number of binary opposites, such as spiritual and material, masculine and feminine, profane and sacred, and I have made a reading of the texts accordingly. Our own era is characterized by a yearning for the truly ancient or archaic and its ascetic practices. It also includes hedonistic trends. Sensual pleasure and instant gratification are becoming another way to escape an ambiguous present. Looking to Luther for support and introducing some of his ideas into contemporary ethical-theological discussions offers one way to put things into perspective. It also provides an opportunity for revising the Lutheran tradition in a late modern moment that can at times seem post-Christian. In the first part of this chapter, I discuss some of Luther's theological themes. In the latter part of the chapter, I present a more systematic summary of his views on the body.

Reading Luther against Luther

Luther, the Reformer, is either relatively unknown or associated with austerity and duty. In this chapter I highlight those overlooked or unknown dimensions of his thought that relate to sensuality, sexuality, eroticism, gender, and desire. This will involve foregrounding his colorful mode of expression, but also those more intimate feelings which are much less visible in his systematic and theological writings. Luther had his front, battles where he was intensively engaged. One was to affirm the power of grace, as a gift that is given freely, against a meritocratic ethos that he sought to dismantle. Because this was so central to his theology, it can seem as though he entirely dismisses the idea of our own potential and capacity for love. Yet this is an over-interpretation, and perhaps even a distortion. What he stresses is that human beings in their inadequacy cannot stand the zeal of righteousness of God, which is like a burning fire. *Coram Deo*, in relation to God, you can only trust the gift of love, grace. When it comes to one's relationship to other human beings, *coram hominibus*, and to the world, *coram mundo*, Luther has great confidence in human beings. In this world, human beings are able to see the image of God in other human beings, whether believers or not. They are also capable of doing good. Luther describes this as the second righteousness, that is to say, in relation to other people and creation at large.[1] But it is God's love in Christ that makes human beings virtuous before God. Luther describes this as an embrace.[2] This alien justice is a gift that disrupts people's fixation with themselves and thereby makes them receptive to the divine presence in the here and now. Love creates abundance, joy, and freedom. God does not need to be appeased. His love is a gift. Luther argued that the right response was praise and gratitude. Now everyone's energy might be directed towards their fellow humans.

Seeing people as equal before God did not, however, remove the unequal structures that existed in society and the family. Luther regarded asymmetry in the relation between master and matron, master and servants, and parents and children as not merely given but essential. Relationships were mutual but hardly egalitarian. While Luther took the radical view that all people were equal before God, they had still to live their lives on earth in hierarchical relationships.

---

1. Luther, WA 2; cf. LW 31 "Sermo de duplici iustitia" (1519).
2. See also chapter 6.

This study has as its specific focus the way that we view the body, the senses, and sexuality. Can the Lutheran tradition make a constructive contribution, or does it mainly represent attitudes that we ought to get rid of? Theology has long colluded in the perpetuation of notions of woman's inferiority by regarding her as guilty of bringing sin into the world.[3] This kind of subordination theology has often been used to legitimize violence within relationships. It is therefore highly dubious.[4] As will be seen, there exist very different ways of interpreting the various creation narratives.

Martin Luther's writings on women and on married life are ambivalent. Claims for women as the weaker sex sit alongside statements that emphasize strength in a way that unsettles traditional gender roles, not least in his correspondence with his wife Katharina.[5] Luther had a positive view of sexuality and the body within the collaborative work of everyday life, and he emphasized the partnership between woman and man.

The reformers did not regard eroticism, sexuality, or the body as paths to God. But—and this is crucial—none of them constituted any kind of obstacle. Nor did the earthly vocation stand in the way of a relationship with God. Instead, we glimpse the notion that God is behind every good thing in life, even sexuality.[6] However, Luther inherits from Augustine an ambivalence that reveals itself in his descriptions of sexual desire. Perhaps it is bound up with the melancholy that resulted from Augustine's specifically having connected sexuality to original sin and its transference across generations. Luther writes that while the power to procreate remains, it is submerged and overwhelmed by sexual desire. The latter is described as leprosy, scarcely more than a bestial urge.[7] Since Luther, unlike Augustine, did not believe that women or men could deny their sexuality or sexual desires, marriage was a salvation, a *remedium ad peccatum*.[8] Demanding celibacy, according to Luther, led to double standards and immorality.

Perhaps it was his own experience of a powerful sexual urge that could not easily be controlled. Perhaps it was a fear of not being able to

3. Børresen, *From Patristiscs to Matristics*; Ruether, *Sexism and God-Talk*; also Gerle, *Mänskliga rättigheter*.

4. Bóasdottir, *Violence, Power, and Justice*.

5. Stolt, *Luther själv*, 180–92.

6. Ibid.

7. WA 42, 79–80; cf. LW, 2, 16–17 "Genesisvorlesung" (1535–38).

8. WA 42, 88, "Genesisvorlesung" (1535–45).

handle the liberatory forces unleashed by the Reformation that created a need in Luther and his successors to channel sexuality into maritally regulated forms. In marriage, mutual trust and intimacy could grow. Another, equally plausible interpretation is that the prevailing patriarchal structures of the time found their way into Luther's pronouncements on society. What is interesting, however, is less the way in which he mirrors contemporary values than how he calls them into question.[9]

Although Danish theologian N. F. S. Grundtvig would later claim that what was good in creation endured after the Fall, Luther was more pessimistic and often underscored the consequences of the Fall. While he consistently affirmed the material conditions of created life, he was torn as to how to interpret them. At the same time as they were God's gift, and thus something good, the Fall meant that they also involved toil and duty, and sometimes suffering.

The Conditions for Human Life

Augustine read the third chapter of the Bible, Genesis 3, as a description of the conditions for human life.[10] Like all interpreters of the creation narratives, Luther revises these conditions. He does so from a masculine perspective and the experience of his own sexuality. But he broadens his perspective to include women's experiences. Even so, he does this from the standpoint of a man, as when he describes women as endowed with desire and a "natural" longing to live with a man and have children.[11] In his commentaries on Genesis, he laments not only men's duty to provide support but also the pain that women endure in childbirth. He interprets both pain and burdensome responsibility as a consequence of the Fall. For Luther, the perils and pains of childbirth, like the endless work of feeding and caring for one's progeny, are signs of the tremendous power of original sin.[12] For those theologians who, following Irenaeus, regard the restoration, restitution, and growth of a fallen creation as part of

---

9. See, e.g., WA Br 3, 327–28 (no. 766), "Luther an drei Klosterjungfrauen" (1524).

10. Westhelle, *Eschatology and Space*, 24. Arendt, who wrote her dissertation on the notion of love in Augustine, used this notion in particular. See Arendt, *The Human Condition*.

11. As we will see in chapter 8, his views on what was natural were strongly influenced by his time.

12. WA 42, "Genesisvorlesung"; cf. LW, 2.

salvation, it is therefore important to work for painless childbirths and to assist parents in various ways in the discharge of their responsibilities. Even desire is seen as something God-given and as a part of creation. It is necessary for the continuation of one's bloodline. But Luther's attitude is ambivalent. As he sees it, the damage caused by the Fall makes sexual desire more bestial and brutal.[13] According to Luther, however, since sexual desire is necessary for the continuation of one's bloodline, God conceals its shortcomings under the mantle of his grace.[14] Here, too, he was perhaps influenced by Augustine, who conceived of intercourse between Adam and Eve in Paradise as taking place without sexual desire and in a controlled fashion. But, unlike Augustine, Luther does not link sin to sexuality. His own view is clearly more positive. In an open letter on marriage in 1528, he claims that Christ, as God's creating Word, is also present in sexual desire: "And it is God's word by which the seed in a person's body becomes fruit and the ruttish, natural attraction to woman is created and maintained. Nor can this be hindered by promises or regulations. For it is the word and deed of God."[15] One of the conditions for human life is living in community. Those who wish to live alone should not call themselves people, says Luther. They must demonstrate that they are either angels or spirits.[16] For Luther, intellectual control, even if possible, is not entirely a good thing, since good and evil intersect throughout our entire life, both body and soul. A person must be seen in their entirety.[17] Luther radicalizes sin, which he interprets as a turning away from God, from Life; in whatever form it takes, it represents a fixation with oneself. Paradoxically, this radicalization of sin makes it a precondition that every aspect of human experience be liberated, even sexual pleasure.

---

13. WA 42, 79–80; cf. LW, 2, 16–17.

14. WA 49; cf. LW 51 "Predigten," no. 803 (1540–45) [33] "Sonst im Ehestand geschicht, da decket Gott den Himel uber." See also Karant-Nunn, "Masculinity of Martin Luther," 172.

15. WA 18, 275, "Christliche Schrift an W. Reißenbusch, sich in den ehelichen Stand zu begeben" (1528). "Und dis ist das wort Gottes, durch wilchs krafft ynn des menschen leib samen zur frucht, und die bruenstige, natuerliche neigung zum weib geschaffen und erhalten wirt. Wilchs widder mit geluebden noch mit gesetzen mag verhindert werden, Denn es ist Gottes wort und werck. Wer aber yha einsam sein will, der thue den namen 'mensch' weg, und beweise odder schaffs, das er ein Engel odder geist" (26–29); trans. Stephen Donovan.

16. Ibid.

17. Hägglund, *De Homine*; Hägglund, *Arvet från reformationen*, 76.

For Luther, however, the conditions for human life always remain defined by rupture, what is often traditionally described as Christian realism. Neither desire nor sexuality can therefore be seen only as something good; rather they are gifts which after the Fall, in a postlapsarian world, can be used for evil or selfish ends.[18] The ambivalence of life permeates all things, not just the body but also the intellect.[19] Elizabeth Stuart and Adrian Thatcher make a distinction between desire and lust; the former is associated with longing, the latter is demanding and possessive and treats the other as an object.[20] Luther alludes to this tendency—to make the other into an object for the gratification of one's own needs—using the concept of self-absorption, *incurvatus in se ipse*. Hence, desire ought therefore to be connected, not solely to the vulnerability and ambivalence of life, but to life and the yearning for relationship. This view is shared by a number of scholars today.[21]

As I have written above, medieval historian Caroline Bynum has shown how the body occupies an important place in medieval spirituality. She has thereby called into question those interpretations that would counterpose body and spirit. Philosopher of religion. Grace Jantzen, however, argues in her study of the history of mysticism that Origen's use of the erotic language in the Song of Songs had the effect of spiritualizing this tradition at the expense of physical love.[22] Spiritualization had its price. In its neoplatonic emphasis, the tradition that he inaugurated served to subordinate the material to the spiritual, to treat the intellect as superior to the body, and, since women were associated more with the body than the spirit, to subordinate women to men.

The interesting question for the present study is whether Luther effected a break in this process of spiritualization and whether that in turn influenced spirituality and how sanctification was understood. My view is that this is unquestionably what happened.

---

18. WA 43, 451, 559, cf. LW 5, 1–386, "Genesisvorlesung" (1538–42).
19. WA 39 I, 175:9–10, "Die Disputation de homine"; cf. LW, 34, 133–44 (1536).
20. Stuart and Thatcher, *People of Passion*, 215.
21. This will be further developed in relation to eros theology in chapter 8. What is traditionally called original sin, or to be *incurvatus in se*, is tied to one's entire life rather than to sexuality in particular. One can also talk about original grace or blessedness.
22. Jantzen, *Power, Gender*.

Luther's Language Is Closely Connected to the Body

Luther uses a great deal of physical, sensual imagery when describing divine love.[23] He often compares the living word to poetry and music, something that physically touches and changes body and senses in one and the same moment. Listening to music, playing, and singing were, for Luther, a means of dispelling doubt and despondency. The living word had the same power.

What did this entail for his view of the body? One might perhaps say that the body becomes important in the present moment. The body is no longer a means of transformation, to guarantee eternal life. Instead, it is directed towards the earthly, natural, ordinary life—not the afterlife. The project of becoming divine, of being united with God, does not disappear. But this process of becoming divine is described as a gift from God that simultaneously redeems us and clothes us in a body that God will make immortal.[24] The emphasis of *eros* spirituality upon a yearning that cannot be satisfied, as we will see in the next chapter, is replaced by a loving embrace.

The German Luther scholar Oswald Bayer claims that Luther interprets this gift from the perspective of Horace's celebrated notion of seizing the moment, *carpe diem*.[25] Luther talks about time as something that is coming to me, but also about everything having its time.[26] In the case of the most important, union with God—or, in the more reformist formulation, being redeemed and forgiven—Luther often calls upon his readers to seize the moment. Although this moment cannot be created by people, they can be receptive to it. In his table talk, he refers to the moment as something that calls to you, inviting you to grab hold of its hair.[27]

When Luther talks of seizing the moment and the opportunity, therefore, what he has in mind is being receptive to God's grace. However, he frequently alternates between referring to divine love and referring to the gifts that God provides through other people. Though not a part of salvation, they are nonetheless an expression of God's love. According to Oswald Bayer, Luther thereby proposes that theology is

23. Anttila, "The Innocent Pleasure."
24. See chapter 6.
25. See Bayer, referring to Horace, *Odes* 1.11.8, in *Martin Luther's Theology*, 23.
26. WA 20, 1–203, cf. LW 1, 1–187, "Vorlesung über den Prediger Salomo" (1526).
27. Bayer, *Martin Luther's Theology*, 23.

more reminiscent of wisdom, *sapientia*, than of science, *scientia*. He also spoke of an experiential knowledge, *sapientia experimentalis*.[28] Luther insists that knowledge of God, indeed, knowing God himself, is revealed through time—not outside of time through abstract principles, but through a teaching that belongs to history and experience.[29] He does not counterpose the spiritual senses to the physical. It is always a case of both/and, at the same time, *simul*. Despite his praise for reason in this life as something "almost divine,"[30] he is brutal in his criticism of the intellect's capacity to understand eternal life and to attain knowledge of God and the self.[31] Reason can be wholly misleading and can make one look for God in places where he does not permit himself to be understood. On this issue, Bayer argues, Luther is extremely critical of scholasticism's intellectual theologians. He is scornful of them, claiming that if they were to ascend to heaven and look around they would find no one there. For Christ is to be found in the infant's crib and the mother's lap. For this reason, they would fall backwards and break their necks.[32]

At the same time, Luther describes theology as an infinite wisdom because it can never be fully understood. It is an experience that people cannot control or design. Such experience is often connected to their having gone through something.[33] This presents a stark contrast to Platonic thought, something also found in Aristotelian metaphysics, for which seeing something beneath one's own status involves a belittling of oneself. For them, the most purely divine activities are seeing and reflecting upon oneself, things Luther sharply condemns. "The Primeval being sees (only) himself. If he were to look outside of himself he would see the suffering of the world. At this point he (namely Aristotle) negates God without saying a word."[34] In his perfection, Aristotle's God sees nothing beyond himself, Luther argues. In so doing, he neither loves nor suffers. But for Luther this is not a complete but a miserable being, *ens*

---

28. Ibid., 30; WA 9, 98:21 "Zu Taulers Predigten" (1516).
29. Bayer, *Martin Luther's Theology*, 31.
30. WA 39 I, 175:9f.; cf. LW 34:137 "Die Disputation de homine" (1536).
31. Bayer, *Martin Luther's Theology*, 33.
32. WA 9:406, 17-20 "Predigten Luthers" (1519-21); cf. Bayer, *Martin Luther's Theology*, 33f.
33. WA 40 III, 63:17f.; cf. LW 26:4-12, "In epistolam S. Paulus ad Galatas Commentarius" (1531-35); Bayer, *Martin Luther's Theology*, 43.
34. WA TR 1, 57:44, "Tischreden" (no. 135); cf. Bayer, *Martin Luther's Theology*, 32.

miserrimum.³⁵ For Luther, it is extremely important that people acquire knowledge of God within time and history, not through speculation. It is in the midst of variability and vulnerability, in the heart of historical events, that closeness to the divine is to be found.

Meditation and Sanctification for Luther

Meditation, as Luther sees it, is an interaction with what has been written and what is heard.³⁶ It is something that happens not merely in one's heart but also externally. By using one's voice, evaluating, working, reading, and listening again to the Word without growing weary, all of the senses are activated.³⁷ Here Luther not only recommends that which lies within, but speaks of the early church's practice of reading and praying aloud as a way to avoid becoming trapped within oneself and indulging in navel-gazing.³⁸ Luther wanted to find a third way so as to dismantle the dualism of theory and practice, *via contemplativa* and *via activa*.³⁹ Luther's third way, *via passiva*, is a path that people choose not of their own accord but rather endure. One becomes a theologian by living, not by knowing, reading, or speculating. Righteousness is received passively.⁴⁰ It is, argued Luther in his lectures on the Letter to the Galatians, someone else at work inside of us, namely God. This is not something that the world can grasp.⁴¹ Luther's claim that human beings come to know God through life's suffering is part of his polemic against speculative late-medieval scholasticism.

This emphasis upon toil and suffering fits well with certain interpretations of Luther that cast him as a melancholic figure. Not infrequently, the claim is advanced that he saw to it that life became dreary and burdensome, whereas the opposite is in fact the case, that he sought relief and encouragement. For him, part of being human was to accept that

---

35. WA TR 1, 73:32, "Tischreden" (no. 155).
36. Bayer, *Martin Luther's Theology*, 35.
37. WA 50, 659:22–35; cf. LW 34, 279–88, "Vorrede zum 1 Bande der Wittenberger Ausgabe der Deutschen Schriften" (1539).
38. Bayer, *Martin Luther's Theology*, 35.
39. WA 5, 85, 1–5, "Operationes in Psalmos" (1519–21).
40. Bayer, *Martin Luther's Theology*, 43.
41. WA 40 I, 41:2–7; cf. LW 26:4–12. "In epistolam S.Paulus ad Galatas Commentarius" (1531–35).

life entailed hardship. Often what mattered was to endure and to see the good even in things not of one's own choosing. On this point his thinking stands close to Nietzsche's notion of being able to love one's fate, *amor fati*.[42] For Luther, life brings a need for consolation. This consolation has a rich significance for Luther. It is about giving and receiving positive energy and encouragement. Today we would call it coaching. It is an encouragement that is often given in the midst of life's hardships through other people and their bodies, through all of the senses.

On earth, the body exists for our own comfort, desire, and joy as well as for those of our fellows. The body thereby ceases to be a problem. Luther describes the fact that humans are sexual beings as something natural, akin to their need for food and drink.[43] He refers to the physical union between spouses as a gift. And in his 1522 treatise on marriage he describes how the word of God interprets this relationship and thereby opens your eyes to what married life creates—eyes that see it as a blessing. Wife, woman, child: all are gifts, something undeserved.[44] Natural reason regards married life as a problem, but Luther ironizes against the clever people and how they think:

> Alas, must I rock the baby, wash its diapers, make its bed, smell its stench, stay up nights with it, take care of it when it cries, heal its rashes and sores, and on top of that care for my wife, provide for her, labor at my trade, take care of this and take care of that, do this and do that, endure this and endure that, and whatever else of bitterness and drudgery married life involves? What, should I make such a prisoner of myself? O you poor, wretched fellow, have you taken a wife? Fie, fie upon such wretchedness and bitterness! It is better to remain free and lead a peaceful, carefree life; I will become a priest or a nun and compel my children to do likewise . . .[45]

Against this natural reason, Luther claims that the Christian faith, through the spirit, makes all of these insignificant, unpleasant, and mean tasks seem made of gold and precious metals. He extols "the child through my body" as something that pleases God. He describes himself as unworthy to rock the infant, wash its nappies, or take care of its mother, and asks

---

42. On the notion of *amor fati* in Nietzsche, see, e.g., Ulfers and Cohen, "Nietzsche's Amor Fati."

43. WA Br 3, 327–28 (no. 766), "Luther an drei Klosterjungfrauen" (1524).

44. WA 10 II, 295:16–296:11; cf. LW 45:39–49, "Vom ehelichen Leben" (1522).

45. Ibid.

himself how he could have become worthy of all this, having no merits, and exclaims that neither frost nor scorching heat nor any amount of drudgery can wear him down since he is convinced that all this work is pleasing to God.[46]

Luther goes on to encourage wives to see this as their true vocation. Here, too, he seems to be referring not to any capacity for reason but rather to a bodily vocation to be a mother.[47] Women's and men's duties are interpreted within essentialist categories that define what is appropriate to each sex. The patriarchal worldview is abundantly evident. The man is the protector.

For the present study, the interesting point is that Luther values simple, disdained, everyday chores. In the classical period these were viewed as of less value, not least because they were performed in the home by women and slaves. Hannah Arendt argues that because these two groups worked together in the home, they were connected by their shared responsibility for all domestic duties. "The driving force was life itself." She holds that "the labor of the man to provide nourishment and the labor of woman in giving birth, were subject to the same urgency of life." As the household was "born of necessity" they did not belong to the world of free men and their public space.[48] For Luther, these bodily defined functions acquire value. They become a form of worship. This is related to the look of faith and the explanation for life provided by the word of God. Luther thus values that which today is often regarded as part of the profane and the everyday. He describes it as a form of worship. He transgresses and dissolves the traditional boundaries between profane and sacred, and does not associate the sacred with particular areas, people, offices, or duties. In Luther's theology and view of life, remarks Cecilia Nahnhfeldt, there no longer exists a division between sacred and profane modes of living the Christian life; rather, every Christian life or vocation that is not sinful is truly holy. Holiness inheres in the midst of creation, which is to say in the midst of the everyday.[49]

Given the background to the spiritual traditions, which I presented in the previous chapter, this constitutes a revolution in the view of bodily life and the physical senses. Diapers and unpleasant odors become

---

46. Ibid.
47. Ibid.
48. Arendt, *Human Condition*, 30.
49. Nahnfeldt, *Luthersk kallelse*.

recurrent analogies for Luther in his descriptions of God as a mother. God loves humanity despite its sin and imperfection, just as a mother loves her children. Luther compares the act of love in changing an evil-smelling nappy to the way that God remains undeterred by the stench of sin: "A mother's love is far stronger than a child's feces and sores. So, too, is God's love for us far stronger than our filth. Despite being sinners we neither lose our childlikeness because of our impurity nor fall from grace on account of our sins."[50] This is just one of many examples of how Luther derives theological insights into God's love from every day, often bodily, sensual experiences.

But are the body and its experiences a path to God? Are the physical intimacy and tenderness between spouses that he describes as a gift and, in words inspired by the traditional formulations relating to the marital mystery, also a way to reach God? Luther's letters and sermons, and especially his table talk, sometimes give this impression.[51] He unquestionably sees them as a sign of God's gifts in life, as experiences through which the hidden God, as if behind a mask, reveals his goodness and solicitude

For Luther, one's relationship to God is defined by gifts and grace, forgiveness and childlikeness. But he also views the earthly life as a gift in which our fellow humans, food, drink, and home as well as physical intimacy are things to be received in trust, to be preserved and managed. Childlikeness and forgiveness before God produce a surplus, an intepretative screen that is required when the needs of one's fellow human beings become demands. But one's fellow human beings and daily life are defined not only by demands but also by gifts. Music, food, children, sexuality, all are gifts from God. It is obvious that Luther sees God as present in the earthly, sensual, and bodily aspects of people's lives. In the here and now. He often emphasizes that God, far from distancing himself from his creation, but is a continual creative force in the life journey of every single person. God is endlessly creating "new people, children being born, new trees, animals, fish in the sea, and birds in the air." This process of sustaining and creating anew, Luther argues, will continue until the last days. He

---

50. WA TR 1, 189 (no. 437) "Tischreden" (1530–35); Stolt, *Luther själv*, 200.

51. Luther writes, "liege oft meiner Käthen an der Seiten, et est tamen mulier digna amari," WA TR 1, 210 (no. 476) "Tischreden" (1530–35). Stolt quotes Luther in *Luther själv*, "I love my Kätha," "Ich hab meinen Kätha lieb," 185f. He also uses words taken from Prov 31:11: "The heart of her husband doth safely trust in her."

THE MOVEMENT OF THE SENSES: TOWARDS THE EVERYDAY

goes on to compare God the Father, Son, and Holy Ghost to a shoemaker and a tailor. Unlike them, God cannot withdraw when the work is done.[52]

As theologian Charles L. Cortright observes, Luther thus regards creation as something taking place throughout history. Creation is not allegorical, as in Augustine.[53] Moses, Luther argues in the introduction to his commentaries on Genesis, wishes to teach us something about, not allegorical beings, but actual creations in a visible world that can be understood by means of our senses.[54] Cortright contends that Luther here distances himself from the allegorical, speculative view held by several of the Church Fathers. Instead, Luther stresses the real and the concrete. Human beings are trapped, not in time, as Augustine holds, but by sin, an emptiness from which only God can liberate, by continually creating anew.[55]

God's love is thus not tainted by anything human or bodily. It is extended to us precisely in and through the material and physical.[56] Since it is a question of receiving gifts in trust, however, the efforts made by human beings are pushed aside. Luther rejects the attempt to find union with God through asceticism or bodily control. Even when, following the marital mystery tradition describing the meeting with God in erotic imagery, his focus lies not on the act of seeking or suspension; instead, he describes the union of Christ and the believer as an embrace. He emphasizes the encounter here and now, the gift rather than the longing. The love is made complete and reaches a climax. Like lovers returning to each other and being reunited, the soul and Christ seek each other out in order to repeat their meeting and union. Christ's embrace liberates the human being and thus sets her or him free to nurture human sexuality and pleasure too.

The preceding chapter sketched out the background to the ascetic ideal. Although the ascetic way of life was an ideal for the Church Fathers Origen and Augustine, who viewed it as a higher form of the Christian life, Luther claims that ordinary life is far more important. People do not need to perform special religious acts in order to come nearer to God.

---

52. WA 46, 558–62; cf. LW 22, 1–530 "Auslegung des ersten und zweiten Kapitels Johannis" (1537–38).

53. Cortright, "'Poor Maggot-Sack That I Am.'"

54. WA 42, 4f.; cf. LW 1, "Vorlesungen über 1. Mose" (1538–42); cf. Cortright, "'Poor Maggot-Sack That I Am,'" 69.

55. Cortright, "'Poor Maggot-Sack That I Am,'" 71.

56. This also influences Luther's view on Holy Communion.

Such acts risk becoming self-imposed. Luther instead argues that God is present in the everyday and through the words of restitution, words that must continually be heard anew. Our fellow human beings need good deeds. God does not need them. As will be seen, this has consequences for how Luther views the body.

Luther here breaks with scholasticism, which, according to Björn Vikström, "formulated doctrines and speculative intellectual systems by means of logic and rhetoric."[57] Advocates for the Catholic Church argued that "the educational system presided over by the pope possessed the competence and authority to determine which interpretations belonged to the true Christian tradition."[58] Merely by insisting that the text of the Bible was clear and unambiguous, Luther thus rejected the view that interpretations needed the authorization of a church synod or pope. Instead of the allegorical mode of interpretation represented by Origen, Luther claimed that different texts should be judged upon how they promoted Christ. However, what Luther regarded as the literal meaning does not always coincide with the views of scholars working in a historical tradition today.[59] When Luther breaks with the scholastic tradition, he also affiliates himself with earlier traditions and the intimate language of the marital mystery. But he does something radically new with it.

In the next section of this chapter I review Luther's views on the body, sensuality, sexuality, gender, and eroticism, before discussing the powerful influence of the family and marriage as institutions upon Lutheran theology.

Luther's Views on the Body

Luther imagines people as bipartite with regard to the quality of their love and tripartite with regard to their natural composition. In his discussions of spiritual division, *caro* (carnality) and *spiritus* (spirit) are closely aligned. Carnal life is governed by *concupiscence*, desire or craving, while the spiritual life is governed by love of God. These constitute two feelings or affects of human life. But carnality and spirit correspond, not to body and soul or other parts of a person, but rather to what drives people and the quality of their actions. A person can thus be wholly carnal—that is,

57. Vikström, *Den skapande läsaren*, 15.
58. Ibid.
59. Ibid.

someone who does not believe or have trust—or wholly spiritualHere Luther closely follows Augustine, who spoke of turning one's senses towards the divine every day. Hope, for Augustine, is "to be liberated from the desire to rule in favor of the possibility of a love that is capable of loving without owning."[60] This vision is evoked in *The City of God* as a time "when we shall enjoy each other's beauty without any lust."[61] Augustine takes our carnal beauty as a given. It forms part of the balance and proportion that exist between our various parts, something that will be even more apparent in our heavenly bodies. Humans will be able to take pleasure in this beauty without debauchery for all time. Our efforts should be devoted as much as possible to achieving a desire that is "purified of all greed and that is capable of taking pleasure in human beauty without wishing to possess it, i.e. by looking with a so-called erotic gaze."[62] This is to some extent already possible now, for example, with regard to the beauty of creation.[63]

The concept of desire is important in contemporary theology. Here, too, a distinction is drawn between different forms of desire. As we will see in chapter 8, Jan-Olav Henriksen, for example, writes of an opening and a closing desire. Luther evinces a profound pessimism about people's capacity to govern their desire, however. Instead, he emphasizes the gift, love, as something that can change the direction of desire.

For Luther, the tripartite division between *spiritus* (soul), *anima* (spirit), and *corpus/caro* (body/flesh) represents a division that originates in human nature and the human constitution. He views spirit as preeminent, passively capable of remaining in contact with the divine, the infinite and eternal. Reason is a quality of the soul. Reason is, however, incapable of understanding the invisible and incomprehensible although it can use concepts and imagery taken from the visible realm. Finally, the flesh is the body and its parts whose deeds enact that which both spirit and soul long for and desire.[64] But it is the whole person—body, soul, and spirit—that is encompassed by God's love. Good and evil affect all of its parts.

---

60. Sigurdson, *Heavenly Bodies*, 586.
61. Augustine, *City of God*, XXII, xxiv (Green, 335).
62. Sigurdson, *Heavenly Bodies*, 586.
63. Ibid., 587; cf. Augustine, *City of God*, XXII, xxiv (Green, 335).
64. WA 7, 550–51; cf. LW 21, 302–4; "Das Magnificat verdeutschet und ausgelegt" (1521).

Luther views a human being as a totality, *totus homo*, who is entirely in either a fallen state or a state of faith. This prospect can be described as Luther's *totus-perspektiv*.[65] In the words of Bengt Hägglund,

> The conventional dualism, between soul and body, reason and sensuality, higher and lower forces of the soul, is replaced on the theological level by a holistic description of the person. The unavoidable dualism, the struggle between good and evil, is not equated with different parts or principles of life but with the entire direction of life that someone chooses and their submission to the authority of God or the devil.[66]

Viewed from this perspective, a human being can be said as a totality to be either sinful or redeemed. However, the line does not run between body and soul since a human being is a totality. The body exists as a creation of God. It cannot be regarded as good or evil in and of itself but forms part of the larger whole constituted by a person. Luther does not differentiate between flesh, soul, and spirit.[67] He is critical of the interpretation Hieronymous takes from Origenes, that the spirit is viewed as confined to reason.[68] In his critique of the scholastics, Luther claims: "They would have it that only the soul and its nobler parts are subject to grace . . . while in actual fact all of a person is flesh and all of a person is spirit, flesh to the degree that he hates God's law and spirit to the degree that he loves it.[69] Flesh and spirit should thus not be seen as separate. Luther draws an analogy with the dawn, which is neither night nor day but both, albeit "more day since it is turning away from the darkness of night."[70] For this reason, according to Luther, asceticism does not make a person better. Mortifying the body is not a path to piety. On the contrary, Luther celebrates physical pleasure. As we will see, he is able to describe the pleasures of the body as a means of driving out evil, or the devil.

The body constitutes a battlefield on which reason and consciousness contend with the other senses. But it is not, as with a particular medieval monastic tradition or with the health cult of our own era, a vehicle

---

65. Hägglund, *De Homine*; Hägglund, *Arvet från reformationen*, 76.

66. Hägglund, *Arvet från reformationen*, 76.

67. WA 2, 585f.; cf. LW 27, 151–410; "In epistolam Pauli" (1519).

68. Hägglund, *Arvet från reformationen*, 79.

69. WA 2, 415; cf. LW 31, 307–25, "Resolutiones super propositionibus Lipsiae disputatis" (1519).

70. Hägglund, *Arvet från reformationen*, 80.

for salvation. The physicality that Luther appears to advocate bears no relation to the bodily transformation as described by medieval historian Caroline Bynum and invoked by Sarah Coakley.[71] Within the Lutheran tradition, the body is understood, rather, in terms of being used as a tool for the sake of life. Gustaf Wingren describes how our bodies are worn out in working for our fellow human beings, just as the ear of wheat dies:

> Life is death. Life is a way to die. There is an old saying about the ear of wheat that lives exactly when it dies, a New Testament saying with many meanings but also a saying that is still readily understood by the farmer today. Nothing in life is truly meaningful if it does not entail my being in some sense being used. Death on one's deathbed is merely a special instance of this meaningful attrition.[72]

Physicality of this kind does not consider the young, beautiful, and well-toned body as something desirable in itself. Rather, Luther's train of thought is distinguished by its strict realism. This may be due to the fact that vulnerability was a continual presence in his everyday life. We have testimony to his profound grief at the death of his fourteen-year-old daughter Elizabeth in 1528.[73] He describes the experience and his feelings, the pain it caused him.[74] Luther did not have to look for the vulnerability of the body: suffering and death were palpably present in everyday life.

For Luther, the incarnation of vulnerability, God as human being, in flesh, was part of his interpretative screen. The body is beset by disease, pain, and death. In the work of caring for others, Luther encourages people to be a Christ to their fellow human beings. When this becomes painful, it requires us to carry a cross just as Christ did. In precisely this everyday toil, there takes place a sanctification that need not be sought for through special deeds. Hence, everyday life emerges "as the principal arena of spiritual exercise."[75] For Luther, the suffering Christ is a continual presence and comfort, not least in everyday life, in what is physical and ordinary. The very notion of presence is crucial.

---

71. See Bynum, *Christian Materiality*, 252f.
72. Wingren, "Livets mening."
73. Stolt, *Luther själv*, 198.
74. WA TR 1, 104 (no. 250).
75. Johannesson, *Helgelsens filosofi*, 174.

It is thus not only in the bread and wine of the mass that Christ is present but in the everyday, in one's fellow human beings. Also, the shared meal of the large household is a comfort and a bulwark against evil, against despair and distrust, or what Luther calls the devil's temptations.

For Luther, everyday life becomes a means of understanding God theologically. The pleasure given by children brings a new discovery. After becoming a father himself, he often returns to the image of God as loving and sensitive.[76] He insists, as phenomenologist and feminist theologians were to much later, that one's own experiences should be taken seriously. The body thus represents, not merely toil and vulnerability, but also joy. It is an integral part of reproduction, work, vulnerability, suffering, and death. But it also gives joy and pleasure. The body experiences festivities of food, wine, and friends. It feels erotic desire and sexual pleasure. What characterizes Luther's view of this is that he sees the individual as an entirety.

Sensuality

In Luther's writings, the sensual is visible in his appreciation of food, wine, and beer. Joy at his physical intimacy with Katharina is apparent in his table talks, where he refers to how he often lies beside his dear Kätchen.[77] He holds that the physical advantages of married life create trust.[78] As we saw at the end of the last chapter, Luther uses almost exactly the same formulation as Bernard of Clairvaux does when he describes the relationship between God and the believer. This is no coincidence. The erotic language of nuptial imagery forms part of his arsenal. Luther understood human love, including that of two lovers, as related to the divine.

According to sociologist Zygmunt Bauman, however, we live today in an era that views relationships as a contract that can be dissolved at any moment.[79] In this light, Luther's trust can seem dubious. And yet Luther believed that human love could never be more than a pale reflection of the perfect, divine love. What is more, he connects trust to physical proximity. It is not a matter of some Platonic, idealized love at a distance but

---

76. Stolt, *Luther själv*, 198–202; see also Luther, WA TR 1, 250, "Tischreden" (1533).
77. WA TR 1, 210 (no. 476) "Tischreden" (1533).
78. WA 34 I, 52:5–9, "Eine Hochzeitpredigt" (1531).
79. Bauman, *Postmodern Ethics*, 106.

rather of common ownership and responsibility. What he invokes can also be a carnal, physical experience. The figurative language of the Song of Songs is not applicable solely to the relationship between God and the soul, but also to human beings who love each other. This is an example of how Luther's own experience, his sexuality, affects his theology. Luther makes use of the imagery of the marital mystery in order to express his own experiences. There is, then, a reflexive relationship between the language of tradition and the experiences of the body.

The bodily senses, indeed, even sensual desire, are also visible in Luther's writings when he discusses having company at table and conversing with friends. When the devil tempts you, Luther's advice is to seek out a jolly group and company. Tell jokes and sing, he urges the reader. Force yourself to eat and drink, even if food has no taste for you. Fasting, as he sees it, is the worst remedy. On one occasion, according to Bainton's account, he gives three pieces of advice about how to overcome despair: believe in Christ; become horribly bad, that is, angry; and fall in love with a woman. In addition, he recommends music, something the devil cannot tolerate because he cannot bear joy.[80] And yet this chapter from Luther's table talk, where he advises the despondent to alleviate their melancholy by dancing and by thinking about beautiful girls, was censored as early as 1566 in the first edition of his *Tichsreden* (*Table Talk*). Birgit Stolt argues that from the very start one can see "an editorial elision of ordinary tangible *joie de vivre* in favour of ascetic piety." In her translation, Luther's Latin text reads as follows: "When you are afflicted by depression or despair or some other torment of conscience, you must eat, drink, and seek out company. If you can take joy in thinking about girls, you should do so."[81] In Aufaber's translation, this becomes instead: "If anyone is tormented by gloominess, despair, or other trials and has a worm gnawing at his conscience, he should first and foremost seek consolation in God's words; thereafter, he should eat and drink, and seek the company and conversation of god-fearing and Christian people. Then things will go better with him."[82]

Birgit Stolt's new readings and translations of Luther's texts have shown how the Lutheran tradition from early on sought to erase the practical and concrete advice that Luther gives. She also points out the

---

80. Bainton, *Luther*, 323; cf. Stolt, "*Laßt uns fröhlich springen!*"
81. Stolt, *Luther själv*, 18, 45.
82. Ibid., 46.

close connection between *intellectus* and *affectus* in Luther's thought. "Thoughts produce feelings and vice versa, and often the greatest emphasis is placed on affect."[83] Body and sensuality, then, form part of a whole. Neither consciousness nor body is given priority.[84] Discernible here is a point of intersection with how embodied phenomenology regards the reflexive relationship of body and consciousness.

While several decades of popular accounts have served to highlight the severe aspects of Luther's thought, there also exists another narrative, one that has been passed down over the centuries, not least in the vicarage tradition. Love is concrete, carnal. It is about physical care. Luther continually comes back to how the baker rises early so that others may eat fresh, newly baked bread.[85] His recurrent examples are of making life good for others, like the baker and the tailor, or the mother who gets up in the middle of the night to comfort her child or change its nappy.

The message of the Reformation was received in an era with very different economic institutions from today. Biological knowledge was also quite different. A woman at that time had no means of protecting herself from unwanted pregnancy.

The concept "sexuality" has no sixteenth-century counterpart and appears nowhere in Luther's writings. It is a modern concept, which was not used before at least the eighteenth century.[86] Even so, it is quite obvious that Luther regarded sexuality as something natural for both women and men. Abstinence should not be promoted. Virginity and chastity, which had hitherto been ideals within the mystical tradition, were dismissed.

The Reformation was accompanied by a celebration of everyday life as something good. To be a mother, a baker, a tailor, or a maid was viewed as a vocation every bit as important, if not more so, than being a monk or a nun.[87] This also entailed a rehabilitation of human sexuality. The sexual relationship of a man and a woman was described as something good and natural.[88]

83. Ibid., 10.

84. Compare Tuner, who holds that we read images that create our interpretation and our mind: *The Literary Mind*.

85. Such actions belong to the economic sphere, but Luther also refers to the soldier and executioner in the political domain as being tools of God.

86. Smith, "Premodern Sexualities," 318.

87. WA 32, 296f.; cf. LW 51, 209–18, "Wochenpredigten über Matth. 5–7" (1530–32).

88. WA BR 3, 327–28 (no. 766) (1524).

On this point the former Augustinian monk parted company with the Church Father Augustine, who held that marriage and immorality should not be seen as "two evils, of which one is worse," but that marriage and abstinence are two goods, of which one is better.[89] While Augustine viewed monastic life as the better alternative, this was not even an option for Luther but, rather, something he dismissed as unnatural and a self-infliction.[90] However, the difference between the position of Augustine and Luther should not be exaggerated. For Luther, too, desire and a longing for children are what prompt him to advocate the married state. After he himself had married, he has a more sensitive tone, presenting physical intimacy as something good in itself that produces trust and reciprocity. It is now no longer just a question of having children, even if this remains essential.

But Luther recommends marriage above all because it is a part of "natural" life, in contrast to the self-imposed good works of the monastery. Marriage is a worldly, external thing, subordinate to reason.[91] Luther does not consider it a sacrament. But it is a Christian "art to hold one's husband or wife very dear, so that the one endures the other's faults and various passing afflictions."[92]

At the same time, Luther interprets sexuality, not only as it relates to creation, but also in relation to the Fall.[93] Finnish theologian Sini Mikkola argues that the Fall is as important as creation for Luther's understanding of sexuality. It was the Fall that made Adam and Eva aware of their nakedness. From this emerged sexual attraction and an evil and shameful lust within them.[94] She observes that Luther understood this desire as having been translated across the generations. He accused his contemporaries of being driven by the same lust as that of Adam and Eve.[95] Before the Fall, intercourse had taken place without desire, whereas lust was now a defining feature of human behaviour. On this point Luther follows Augustine, who believed that "had the Fall not happened Adam and Eve

---

89. Augustine, *On the Good of Marriage* VIII.8; cf. Jeanrond, "Kärlekens praxis," 228.

90. See chapter 4.

91. WA 32, 352:29f., "Wochenpredigten über Matth. 5–7" (1530–32).

92. WA 32, 274, 7f., "Predigten des Jahres 1530" (no. 33); cf. Hägglund, *Arvet från reformationen*, 141.

93. Mikkola, "Gendered Sexuality."

94. Ibid.

95. WA 24, 90–91, "In Genesis Declamationes" (1527).

would have continued loving each other and would have had children in paradise, but this would have happened without desire."[96]

Mikkola points out that Luther proceeded from the premise that human beings lived in a postlapsarian world in which sexual desire could lead to various forms of sexual sins. She mentions lechery (*hurerey*), adultery (*ehebruch*), and secret sins (*stummen sund*).[97] As we have seen in Marie Lindstedt Cronberg's historical studies, *hurerey* in seventeenth-century Sweden meant lechery, whoring, or fornication, even premarital sex.[98] In Luther's 1522 treatise on marriage, secret sins refer to masturbation and homosexuality.[99] All these types of sexual sins ought to be prevented since they led to social and spiritual problems. As already noted, in practice this meant that marriage became the only way to affirm one's sexuality if one wished to live as a decent and upright citizen.[100]

That giving birth to children is the lens through which Luther views sexuality becomes apparent in his contemptuous descriptions of eunuchs. These are described as pitiable since, because of their violation, they cannot live a normal life as a man. They appear to be exceptions. However, they retained a sexual desire that they were unable to exercise. Since it was impossible for them to gratify their urges, according to Luther, they became obsessed with women, feeling an evil desire that drove them to continually seek women's company. Worse still, in his view, they had become feminine (*gantz weybissch*),[101] something he clearly regarded as negative in this context.[102]

Luther's treatise on marriage defines the sexes on the basis of their reproductive capacity. Men who lacked the capacity to become fathers were, as he saw it, not worth much.[103] An upright man who took a wife whom he was unable to make pregnant was advised to ensure that she had children through someone else. If the husband did not arrange it, the wife, possibly in secret, should ensure that she became pregnant by

---

96. See Brown, *Body and Society*, 400, where he makes this reference to Augustine, *The City of God*; cf. Clack, *Sex and Death*, 34. Also cf. chapter 4.
97. Mikkola, "Gendered Sexuality."
98. Cronberg, *Synd och skam*, 62.
99. WA 10 II, 299–300; cf. LW 45:75–129, "Vom ehelichen Leben" (1522).
100. Mikkola, "Gendered Sexuality"; Cronberg, *Synd och skam*.
101. WA 10 II, 279; cf. LW 45:75–129, "Vom ehelichen Leben" (1522).
102. Mikkola, "Gendered Sexuality."
103. WA 10 II, 275–304; cf. LW 45:75–129, "Vom ehelichen Leben" (1522).

someone else so as to redeem both her own and her husband's honor.[104] Disdain for or incomprehension of the impotent and the childless are thus combined with a hefty dose of pragmatism. Prudishness is noticeably absent. Luther also discreetly accepted the bigamy of Philip of Hesse, a Reformation patron who had taken a fancy to a new woman.[105] This can be interpreted as double standards and an accommodation to power but, equally, it can be seen as a consequence of Luther's way of reading the Bible. Whenever he was able to find biblical support for an idea—here, the Old Testament account of Jacob and his two wives—it became possible. What is more, it should perhaps be seen as showing that, despite everything, he sees human beings first and foremost as men.

Sexuality and the Critique of Monasteries

Luther's view of sexuality was connected to his critique of the monasteries. There, Luther argued, monks and nuns sought to live in defiance of their physical nature. He saw this as doomed to failure.[106] Gustaf Wingren argues that if one wishes

> to meet Luther on this anti-gnostic, ancient Church terrain, one should not read his settling of scores with the regiment of papal churches but study instead his polemics against monastery life, monastic vows, and celibacy. Sexual intercourse between a man and a woman is an act that God wants and an act through which God creates. It is not the case that God has been a creator and now is nothing more; no, he is Creator today. And the act of creation in sexual intercourse leads directly into the suckling and caring of the child.[107]

Human beings, in the act of sexual intercourse as of nursing, are seen as God's co-creators. A number of points of interest emerge from Luther's critique of monastery life. In his letter *To Several Nuns*, which I have mentionend several times, he writes from Wittenberg on August 6, 1524, that if they did not freely choose the convent, if their compliance was forced, now was the time to call upon their friends and ask for help in escaping. If parents and friends were not prepared to help, they should

---

104. Ibid. See also M. Farley, "Sexual Ethics," 6.
105. Grisar, *Martin Luther*, 515f.
106. WA 10 II, 277; cf. LW 45:75–129, "Vom ehelichen Leben" (1522).
107. Wingren, *Öppenhet och egenart*, 101.

try to engage the help of other good people "regardless of whether your parents become angry, die, or make a recovery."[108]

It is striking that Luther, who so often preached obedience and submission to parents and other authorities, in this context urges nuns to defy their parents' will where necessary. Putting one's daughters into a convent, even against their will, was at this time a common way for those in the upper classes to relieve themselves of the responsibility to provide for their children. Luther counters this by asserting the nuns' right to choose freely. They were within their rights to defy their parents even if the latter should grow angry or die as a consequence. Luther strongly emphasizes personal freedom and individual choice.

The second reason why nuns were within their rights to abandon their convent vows involved the flesh. Luther invoked nature, which in this context meant the body and sexuality. Human beings were not created to live in celibacy. On the contrary.[109] Just as food, drink, sleep, and rest had been created by God and formed part of natural life, so, too, did sexuality. It was nothing to be ashamed of: "Though womenfolk are ashamed to admit to this, nevertheless Scripture and experience show that among many thousands there is not a one to whom God has given to remain in pure chastity."[110] Luther goes so far as to claim that women have no control over themselves, something more typically attributed to men:

> God has made her body to be with man, to bear children and to raise them as the words of Genesis 1:1 clearly state, as is evident by the members of the body ordered by God Himself. Therefore food and drink, sleep and wakefulness have all been created by God. Thus He has also ordered man and woman to be in marital union. Suffice it to say that no one needs to be ashamed over how God has made and created him...[111]

Martin Luther argued, then, that neither women nor men should be ashamed of their sexual urges. God had made them thus.

---

108. Luther, WA BR 3, 327–28, (no. 766), "Luther an drei Klosterjungfrauen" (1524); trans. Erika Bullmann Flores.

109. Ibid.

110. Ibid.

111. Ibid. Johanna Gustafsson in *Kyrka och kön* shows how Lutheran sexual ethics, even in the 1950s and 1960s, assumes that it is the man who is unable to control his sexuality.

In the reflexive interpretation I have chosen to make, Luther's pronouncements do not constitute the answer to what is good or evil, right or wrong. From the viewpoint of our own era, we note immediately that Dr. Martin here devalues woman despite earlier in the same letter having presented her as an independent, active agent. She is portrayed as lacking control over herself, and her sexuality exists only in order to be with a man and to give birth to and raise children, all in accordance with the first chapter of the Bible. Woman's divinely ordained purpose is limited to being a wife and a mother. The independence, intellectual and spiritual, offered by the convent disappears in Luther's interpretation. Nor are men depicted as any more able to suppress their sexuality. Luther sees both men and women as sensual and sexual beings. The idea that they cannot curb or control their sexuality may have something to do with the double standards that Luther had observed at first hand. However, it is a notion that easily leads to the excusing of sexual behavior, without respect for the other. Sexuality is an important driving force in life. Yet this insight need not lead to a disavowal of responsibility.

As Lyndal Roper has pointed out, Luther's reference to special states—that the space of life is limited for many women, particularly in their involvement in the domestic sphere—is bound up with the demand that a woman be subordinate to a man, her husband.[112] At the same time, woman's role as a spiritual nurse involves recognition of the need for women's education. In practice, this gave women the possibility of exerting a considerable influence within the household. However, married women clearly had a higher status than unmarried women, even if there was a place for everyone within the framework of the large household. Moreover, only heterosexuality was regarded as natural.

While physical relations between men and women were seen as natural, celibacy was not something to be encouraged. From the viewpoint of this almost deterministic reading, voluntary celibacy or abstinence for Luther was understood as something so unusual as to be considered unnatural. Unlike Augustine, who champions celibacy and marriage as two good alternatives, Luther argues that the former is "unnatural." The reader is reminded of the common perception in our own era that sexuality must necessarily be lived; not merely a human right, it is also expected of anyone who wishes to be seen as normal. Might this be part of a biologizing tendency, in which anything that is understood

---

112. Roper, *Holy Household*, 2.

as natural becomes norm-creating, in an almost deterministic fashion? Even many contemporary cultures seem to lack a vision of diversity that encompasses voluntary celibacy.

While our era has broadened its understanding of what constitutes normal sexuality, such that it now includes sex between two men or two women, there may be reason to ask whether contemporary notions of what is natural can also accommodate the right to live alone. In the Lutheran tradition, marriage became normative, consigning many people to a state of exclusion. Even in debates today the word "natural" is used to refer to the nuclear family of mum, dad, child. But now it is not primarily a Lutheran argument. In the UN, the Vatican has for decades formed alliances with conservative Muslim states, laying claim to the definition of the word "family" and excluding not only families with homosexual spouses or parents but also the considerably broader familial configurations that occur in large parts of the world.[113] Theological notions of what can be deemed natural thus affect cultures and laws as they relate to sexuality and gender. Establishing theology- or religion-free zones is a poor solution, especially in a global perspective. Instead, the issue becomes which theology and which interpretations should be allowed to prevail.

Sex

Luther views human beings as gendered and as having divinely created needs for sexual relations. He presents procreation as something natural and good. This shapes his understanding of gender such that the sterile man, no less than the infertile woman, is granted inferior status. Virginity and celibacy are presented as unnatural, something that should be the exception. Luther breaks here with the ascetic traditions.

Luther's notions of biology and what was natural were interpreted within a framework in which he saw every person as created in the image of God. However, men possessed a stronger aura than women, just as the sun shines more brightly than the moon.[114] In his 1523 commentary on Genesis 2, he claims that Adam, in consequence of his masculine nature,

---

113. Definition of the family is a contested area for the UN. See Gerle, "Various Interpretations."

114. In his commentaries on Genesis, Luther follows the tradition of speaking about man as sun and woman as moon. The man is more *imago Dei* than woman. "Quare imago Dei, ad quam Adam fuit conditus, fuit res longe praestantissima et nobilissima." WA 42, 46, "Genesisvorlesung" (1535–45).

was more rational than Eve. As woman, she was the weaker sex through whom Satan had more easily gained access.[115] Luther considers himself to be reading literally, even when he incorporates traditional interpretations and his own perspectives into his narratives. As Else Marie Wiberg Pedersen observes, in the case of his views of men and women, it is particularly apparent that his commentaries on Genesis reflect the exegetical tradition that goes back to Augustine.[116]

Luther nonetheless portrays both woman and man as created in God's image; thus far he follows Augustine. Yet, in salvation woman and man are also equal before God. This is a break with tradition. However, Luther does not connect this equality before God to a demand that woman should renounce her biology and sexuality. On the contrary, it is precisely as a biological woman that she achieves salvation. He underscores her role as wife and mother. As we have seen, he also uses images taken from women's everyday lives in order to describe God. Everyday experiences shape the imagery he uses, as they would for phenomenologists of a later era. He sees women's solicitude and tenderness towards their children and uses them as the basis for comparisons with the essence of God. This is connected with the issue raised in the introduction, that God encounters human beings in and through the material. Everyday experiences give an intimation of the divine.

Luther was clearly influenced by the bridal metaphorics. One's relation to Christ involves gender-transgressing images and disruption of gender roles. Yet this openness is absent from Luther's treatise on marriage, which instead confines men and women within traditional categories and relations of dominance/subordination. Here, too, one can detect the influence of Augustine as well as of Luther's contemporaries.

Luther thus held traditional as well as sixteenth-century notions that are far removed from the claim of modern LGBTQ movements, backed by contemporary research, that there are more than two sexes. Luther quite simply imagined woman as a weaker version of man. This way of understanding gender difference persisted until the end of the eighteenth century.[117] Only then did philosophers, scientists, and others begin to conceive of a more "qualitative difference between women and men."[118]

---

115. Ibid.; WA 14, 129–30, "Predigten über das erste Buch Mose" (1523–24).
116. Wiberg Pedersen, "Bad Anthropology and Good Theology?," 191–201.
117. Laqueur, *Making Sex*.
118. Sigurdson, *Heavenly Bodies*, 343–44.

Hence, according to Laqueur premodern anatomy, following this notion of gradual difference was thus capable of depicting a woman's sexual organs as deformed male organs. The "pictorial representation of the body was (and is) also socially conditioned."[119] Prior to the seventeenth century, the body was a sociological, not an ontological, category.[120]

A contemporary Lutheran ethics must proceed from new knowledge. This means that creation cannot be interpreted as something static and past. Nor should the narratives of Adam and Eve be taken to imply that the only polarity between human beings exists between masculine and feminine, or that a gender hierarchy ought to be applied to man and woman.[121] While reproduction may be a duty for some, it is not for all. People realize different ambitions and vocations. There are many ways to share the responsibility to care for all life.

Nor are structures and institutions fixed once and for all.[122] Just as relations develop, so, too, are structures reshaped in tandem with technology, economics, and culture. My argument here is that Luther's Christ mystery and the gender mobility within it should inspire a greater diversity of relations, genders, and intimate relationships.

Desire and Luther's View of Eroticism

Desire is presented ambivalently in Luther's writings. It is in this aspect that postlapsarian humanity most closely resembles the animals.[123] Sometimes he complains about it. Before the Fall, even "the breeding of offspring was associated with the highest respect and wisdom, indeed, with God's own knowledge! Now the flesh is so overwhelmed by the leprosy of desire that the body, to be frank, becomes bestial in the act of procreation and cannot beget in the knowledge of God."[124] As Mikkola observes, Luther typically refers to sexual desire with the formulation *schendliche lust*, evil or shameful lust. He uses words such as *kutzeln* (*kitzel* in modern German), meaning titillate, to describe desire. Within the framework of a phenomenological reading, then, it can be said that he

119. Ibid., 343
120. Laqueur, *Making Sex*, 8; cf. Sigurdson, *Heavenly Bodies*, 344
121. See also Gerle, *Mänskliga rättigheter*, chapter 1.
122. See Granténs, *Utanför Paradiset*.
123. WA 42, 53–54; cf. LW 1:28, "Genesisvorlesung" (1535–45).
124. Ibid.

describes desire in a highly physical way. Unlike Origen, however, Luther does not argue that human beings lose knowledge of God when the man first has knowledge of Eve (i.e., sleeps with her).

I have chosen to read different texts alongside each other, not only texts from Luther's pen but also texts that appeared much later. In this particular context, it is interesting to make a comparison with Kierkegaard. While he lived in a Danish Lutheran culture, he is usually regarded as a precursor of existentialism. According to Danish theologian Pia Søltoft, Kierkegaard interprets erotic desire and sensuality as signs that love as a phenomenon always expresses itself physically.[125] He sees love, as a pre-reflexive form, as dreaming or seeking desire. It is experienced as an anxiety that comes from within and directs itself towards the world but without properly knowing what it is directed towards.[126] This is a sign that the body wishes to relate to the world before it is even aware. Kierkegaard likens love to the feelers of an insect, something by means of which we apprehend the other at the same time as we confer upon that other his or her lovableness.[127] Kierkegaard describes the desire to touch the other as a gift. Someone who is touched from without by tenderness and desire becomes lovable. This is an experience common to all humanity.

Kierkegaard, who himself chose to live alone, argues that Christianity imported sexuality as an independent urge. In *Begrebet Angest* (*The Concept of Anxiety*) from 1844 he argues that sexuality awakens as an urge at that moment when humanity became mythologically conscious of gender difference, even if sexuality has self-evidently been present prior to this experience. At that point, according to Pia Søltoft, anxiety is also awoken. Anxiety and desire are two sides of "the same sweet anxiety in man's inner being."[128]

Kierkegaard thus connects the experience of gender differentiation to something that occurs in association with the insight into good and evil. According to myth, this came via the Tree of Knowledge. It can thus be interpreted as an awakening, a leap into freedom rather than a fall.[129] Kierkegaard asks himself whether sexuality's conscious awakening means that one should equate sexuality with sin. No, he argues, it is not quite

125. Søltoft, "Kaerlighed og krop," 142.
126. Ibid., 138, 142.
127. Ibid.
128. Søltoft, "Kaerlighed og krop," 138 (my translation).
129. This is one Jewish interpretation that also was suggested by Church of Sweden archbishop Antje Jackelén in a radio program broadcast on June 25, 2014.

that simple. A kind of innocence operates in the unconscious, immediate desire that is experienced psychologically as an anxiety about the void. Sexuality is anchored in desire, and there is nothing to be done about it. Any such attempt, according to Kierkegaard, will lead to dissimulation.[130] He regards sexuality as the ultimate apex of physicality, a point at which humans find themselves between body and soul. Kierkegaard struggles with the relationship between consciousness and sexuality. The problem he identifies is that sexual pleasure puts consciousness out of the running. At that point desire becomes the governing principle. According to Søltoft, it is here that the problem arises for Kierkegaard, who wishes to claim that the spirit is unifying in relation to the soul and the body. That is, sexuality eludes consciousness.[131]

Even in Kierkegaard's writings, then, we find arguments that continue the tradition we encountered in Augustine and that can partly account for his ambivalence towards desire. For Augustine exhibits a powerful yearning for control. He longs for a time when the body "will be in every way subject to the spirit." Then it "will not be an animal body, but a spiritual body, having indeed the substance of the flesh, but without any fleshly corruption."[132] If sin is defined as disobedience, one can understand the connection Augustine makes between sexuality and sin.[133]

Augustine imagined that human beings, despite the dramatic weakening of their will caused by the Fall, might increasingly direct their desires and urges towards the divine. Luther shared this yearning but was more pessimistic about the possibility of success. He seems not to have wanted to insist that the soul should control the body. But he is concerned that people cannot think of God during sexual intercourse.[134]

For Luther, the outer can be a path to the inner. This idea was foreign to Augustine. According to Luther, as we have seen, the body's sensual joy can be a means to put the devil to flight, since the devil hates joy. The outer affects the inner, and vice versa. In Luther's writings, this does not become a competition between spiritual and physical. It is our habit of being turned inwards on ourselves that must be disrupted. It is easy to imagine that Luther, were he alive today, would criticize spiritual as well as physical self-absorption.

130. Søltoft, "Kaerlighed og krop," 138-39.
131. Ibid., 139.
132. Augustine, *City of God*, 22.25 (Green, 339).
133. Clack, *Sex and Death*, 34.
134. See also chapter 10.

Luther's Realism

Luther's faith in the possibility of controlling body and soul through the spirit seems weaker than Augustine's. For him, the only way out was to give oneself up as a whole person to Christ's mercy and love. Luther's pessimism, or realism, about the preconditions for existence led him to criticize all claims to have created zones free of sin. This was not possible, whether in a monastery, church, or society. He was therefore doubtful about all institutions controlled by clerical authorities and clergymen, thus challenging theocracy. They were no more able to exclude sin's fixation with its own concerns and, accordingly, no better equipped to manage worldly affairs than anyone else. Yet this critique resulted in his insufficiently critical acceptance of the institutions of profane society—in his day, the rule of the sovereign.

According to his theology, however, good and evil directly intersected in all spheres, as spiritual and worldly dominions. He explores quite different contradictions than those of Origen and Neoplatonism, for example, which saw the spiritual as superior to the material. Yet the fact that Luther employed a vocabulary in which evil is described as carnal and good as spiritual has not exactly facilitated an understanding of his dialectical thinking, one in which the body and the material are seen as gifts from God and, simultaneously, as everything else that is involved in the cosmic battle between good and evil. For this very reason it is important to emphasize that Luther views both body and matter as something good, both in the case of caring for one's fellow humans and as a place for encountering God. As an extension of these ideas, it also seems reasonable to interpret eroticism and desire as bearing a trace of the divine.

For Luther, there is no division between private and public, or between God and the world, something that modern thought imagines as self-evident and innocent. Luther saw the whole world as belonging to God but drawn into a struggle between God and the devil.[135] His conception of the world had no place for a secular realm separate from the religious one. Nonetheless, he regarded many everyday institutions in this world as God's spheres of promise for a good life and as a bulwark and protection against evil. While the task of the church, *ecclesia*, was to encourage, comfort, protect, and forgive, that of the sovereign—what we

---

135. In "Lutheran Theology as a Resource," I analyze several different interpretations of the so-called Two Realms doctrine, which aims to avoid theocracy as well as Christocracy, while still viewing the world as the world of God.

today see as the political realm, *politia*—was to maintain order, law, and justice. The family, *oeconomia*, represented the realm that provides most of what is good in life. It offers a highly physical and bodily community, a roof over one's head, food, drink, rest, fellowship in work, joy, intimacy, and closeness. Many of God's gifts that Luther itemizes in his commentary on the first article of the Creed on God as Creator—"clothing and food, house and home" and "all that I need for the sustaining of life"—are, as he sees it, specifically connected to the family, *oeconomia*.[136]

Family, Marriage, and Economics

In Luther's day, the family, the home, and the large household were a crucial institution that represented *oeconomia*, a far larger community than what we today designate the nuclear family. This was a space for reproduction but also for the production of commodities and services. It represented survival and, optimally, surplus. Here women were crucial. Luther's wife, Katharina von Bora, managed a large household for her husband and children as well as student lodgers. It could at times swell to twenty-five people. She would have had good use for her experience of the large household of the convent. The convent, which represented another kind of economy for people's lives, was outlawed in the territories of the Reformation. Now the large household and the family would become the economic sphere that assumed responsibility for production. It collaborated closely with the guilds. As historian Lyndal Roper has shown, the guilds drew for their ideological and gendered structure upon the Reformation's talk of a partnership between husband and wife with the man as its head.[137]

Katharina's lodging house and brewery provided the economic basis that made it possible for Martin Luther to work as an author, poet, biblical theologian, and reformer. Birgit Stolt points out that one of the reasons why Katharina was not always portrayed positively in Luther's table talks may be that she saw to it that she received payment for her activities.[138] In other words, the fact that Katharina was in charge of the finances did not automatically give her higher status, as would seem to be the case when the masculine gender is united with economic responsibility.

---

136. See Luther, Small Catechism.
137. Roper, *The Holy Household*.
138. Stolt, *Luther själv*, 185f.

Lutheran societies primarily connected sexuality to reproduction, following a tradition going back to Augustine. But the fellowship and the special intimacy that sexuality creates is also involved. The focus lay on marriage as the place for sexual relations between men and women. Sexual relations outside of marriage were condemned. Social norms dictated that a sexual relationship should lead to marriage.[139] Historian Eva Österberg notes that infidelity was judged particularly harshly in post-Reformation Scandinavia. She contends that during the period ca. 1570–1850, people's lives were governed by a strict code of sexual morality that was imposed with the church's help. Neither the Middle Ages nor the twentieth century enforced restrictions upon marriage in so strict a fashion. The impact upon women's lives was especially pronounced.[140] Österberg argues that a "theologization of punishment" took place, which revealed itself in two ways: in part, by focusing upon "sexuality as the Great Sin"; in part, by "the church supplementing the temporal punishment with a shaming punishment." This might involve sitting on a so-called "shaming stool" in a church or being denied Holy Communion.[141]

When the state, pursuing its interest in disciplining the population and giving moral instruction, incorporated parts of the Ten Commandments into national laws, Mosaic Law acquired a direct relevance for legislation. Both pre- and extramarital sexual relations were regarded as a breach of the seventh commandment. During the era of Lutheran orthodoxy, men and women were judged equally severely.[142] Historian Marie Lindstedt Cronberg argues that there was a "common interest by the emergent nation-state and the Reformed church in disciplining their citizens." They joined forces in a struggle against disorder, immorality, and disobedience to the injunctions of both God and king.[143]

Against this dismal background, it is easy to understand the hatred felt towards conformist Lutheran society and the feeling that secularization brought with it freedom, not least for women. We are well rid of the symbiosis of church and state that existed during the orthodoxy of the seventeenth century and long after, during which time they jointly disciplined the population. Ecclesiastical historian Sinikka Neuhaus

---

139. Cronberg, *Synd och skam*, 35, 104, 204f.
140. Österberg, *Folk förr*, 62.
141. Ibid., 163.
142. Cronberg, *Synd och skam*, 54f.
143. Ibid., 56.

nonetheless describes the advent of the Reformation a century earlier as a time when court rulings in Malmö paid a new kind of attention to evangelical freedom and grace in connection with divorce cases.[144]

There are thus grounds for connecting to discussions of the uses of history and acknowledging that it is important to allow a range of accounts to be heard. Sometimes the liberating insights of a fledgling movement are lost to history, something that makes it important to return to those early texts. Even so, my intention is neither to idealize nor to demonize either the past or the Lutheran tradition, but rather to tease out ambivalences and contradictory interpretations.

Polarity and Hierarchy between the Sexes

In the Lutheran tradition, the polarity between man and woman is described as complementary.

The hierarchy between the sexes was unquestioned. Both were regarded as created in God's image. Men and women were equal before God. However, this did not alter the hierarchical structure of society. The Aristotelian notion that woman was a mute (i.e., incomplete) man prevailed for a long time. It persisted as late as the nineteenth century, when, for example, August Strindberg could still imagine a woman's uterus as merely a vessel for a man's child prior to delivery. The biological knowledge of our own era quite simply did not exist at this time.[145] There has, however, never been any doubt about which gender was most important. Indeed, to this day a surreptitious ranking can often be discerned whenever the issue of complementarity arises.

A guiding light of this study is the intimate connection between sexuality, body, theology, and politics that have been identified by contemporary scholars and examined here in previous chapters. Such a perspective makes it necessary to call attention to the fact that heteropatriarchal practices enjoyed considerable privileges in Lutheran societies. The upgrading of marriage did not lead to a questioning of traditional gender hierarchies. For Luther, this was not the important question. It may also have resulted from the influence of Scandinavian peasant

---

144. Neuhaus, *Reformation och erkännande*.
145. Laqueur, *Making Sex*.

society and from the German burghers' implementation of Reformation theology and views on partnership between man and woman.[146]

And yet the institutions and conditions surrounding the family and marriage have varied greatly during different historical periods. Today these conditions are being continually renegotiated—questioned as well as celebrated—even as they are being steadily changed, not least by economic and technological factors. That frameworks and content have not always been identical serves as an important reminder, especially for Lutheran ethics, which has not infrequently tended to idealize the marriage between Martin Luther and Katharina von Bora.

Shifting Views of Marriage and Praxis

Throughout its entire history, Christianity's understanding of what constitutes a marriage has shifted and been shaped by contemporary society. We have already seen evidence of this. Samuel Rubenson demonstrates convincingly that notions of marriage have varied during the course of history.[147] In a historical survey of the first centuries of Christianity, he claims that early Christians followed the customs of the time. Quite simply, marriage was something that existed independently of their faith. It was not until the sixth century before a specifically Christian view of marriage was formulated.

Rubenson argues that the early churches conceived of marriage differently. There are no indications that they saw marriage as anything other than a secular institution.[148] Only at the end of the fourth century did marriage begin to be interpreted as something subject to divine law, and even then only in Western Christianity. The laws and regulations on how marriage should be entered into and regulated, which the Christian emperors implemented in the fifth and sixth centuries, were not applied to the lower classes. Another century passed before marriage was also administered in relation to those regarded as unfree.[149] For the church, the problem lay in the fact that one "on the one hand lived in a culture and a legal system in which marriage was a privilege, and other forms

---

146. Roper, *The Holy Household*.
147. Rubensson, "Äktenskapet i den tidiga kyrkan."
148. Ibid.
149. Ibid., 194–97.

of cohabitation were fully accepted but clearly differentiated from marriage, while on the other hand holding fundamental beliefs that, strictly speaking, did not accommodate such doubleness."[150] For the Jewish and Roman traditions, it was self-evident that "the legal requirements for men and women differed." Even the New Testament texts draw a "clear distinction between the requirements for a man and for a woman in the case of divorce and remarriage." For example, Matthew 19 allows the possibility for a man to divorce his wife and remarry in the event of adultery. Christianity gradually introduced a new approach, on two counts. First, it argued that women and men had to follow the same law. Second, it began to question whether marriage could be dissolved at all.[151]

Divorce was no simple matter for the Reformation. Both Luther and Calvin were opposed to it.[152] Even so, the Reformation made it possible to get a divorce. However, it required special reasons, and the decision was taken by the municipal court. Valid reasons included infidelity, impotence, or abandonment of one's spouse.[153]

Self-absorption, Not Sensuality, Is the Threat to Life

By way of summary, it can be said that Luther's assertion of everyday life and affirmation of sensuality, sexuality, and the body transformed those countries and territories where the Reformation took place. The ascetic ideal of a path to God was rejected. It reorganized societies in the countries affected by Luther and other reformers and can still be detected in their hidden cultural legacies. The sexuality it championed was once again connected to reproduction and the family, albeit with an emphasis upon both community and sensuality. Traditional conceptions of gender extended their influence and came to be widely viewed as natural. Luther describes man as a stronger reflection of God. Despite their theological equality, the sexes continued to be organized hierarchically in both the family and society. On the basis of his interpretation of the creation narratives, Luther can thus be described as heteronormative.

At the same time, the basic theological insight that all people are created in the image of God was deepened. All people, sinners and

---

150. Ibid., 196.
151. Ibid., 200f.
152. M. Farley, "Sexual Ethics," 64.
153. Neuhaus, *Reformation och erkännande*, 235–41.

redeemed, were also equal before God. Life, including its physical, material, and carnal dimensions, was considered a gift to be received and administered in trust. For what Luther regards as sin, self-absorption, *incurvatio in se ipse*, there is no gender difference. Nor does he hold out any hope of creating pure, sin-free zones. Our intellect, like our body, is engaged in the struggle between good and evil, just as the economic, political, and ecclesiastical realms are. We can conclude this chapter, then, by stating that Luther views the body and the physical senses as part of a whole human being. Self-absorption, not sensuality, is the threat. On the contrary, it is through our senses that love, the divine is revealed. In the following chapter we will see that Luther, even as he defends traditional interpretations of gender, relies upon formulations that disrupt gender boundaries.

6

Commercial Transaction or Loving Embrace?

Given its emphasis upon life as divinely ordained, it is only natural that the Lutheran tradition should take contemporary issues as its starting point. In this study the contemporary world will be seen to challenge Martin Luther just as much as he challenges some of our own notions. The aim of this study, to discuss sensuality, the body, and theology in a Lutheran tradition, may result in a critique of both traditional Lutheran interpretations and contemporary emphases.

His dialectical thinking, with its deep strains of contemporaneity, *both/and* instead of *either/or*, contradiction, and ambivalence, makes Luther surprisingly relevant to our own late modernity. Renewed attention to his texts promises to highlight their dimensions of intertextuality and heteroglossia by showing how they engage with a complex fabric of contemporary and earlier discourses in his own culture.[1] This may, in turn, encourage readers to question attempts to impose interpretative uniformity on them.

In this chapter, I draw on elements in Luther's metaphorics in order to deconstruct traditional oppositions that have long influenced our views on the divine and the human. My starting point is the image of a marriage that Martin Luther, following tradition, uses to describe the

---

1. See Kristeva, *Desire in Language*. The concepts *intertextuality* and *heteroglossia* are replacing that of intersubjectivity. They point towards the dialogical, which, in contrast to the monological, understands texts within a web where they relate to, discuss polemically, or build upon other texts, including the texts of others. See Bakhtin, *The Dialogical Imagination*, on "the 'dialogic' and the 'monologic' work of literature."

relationship between Christ and the believer in his treatise *On the Freedom of a Christian* and elsewhere. But is he not reinforcing traditional gender stereotypes by describing the groom as active and virtuous and the bride as passive, receptive, and wicked? Without according prescriptive authority to Martin Luther or his writings as to what can be deemed reasonable and liberating for a relational Lutheran theology in late modernity, I wish to join other scholars in mulling over this metaphor. My hypothesis is that the image of a marriage and a marital bed contains elements that are less dichotomously gender-stereotyped than the post-Lutheran tradition has often been claimed. In this chapter I reconsider a number of alternative interpretations. While some aspects of this metaphorical language are alien to our own moment, others have the potential to serve as building blocks in the search for a relational theology. Perhaps some of the elements of the overarching metaphors and images of loving, reciprocal relations invoked by Luther can provide inspiration today. My aim is constructive. For this reason I wish to let Luther's ideas about the equality of human beings before God contribute to the discussion of human beings' relation to each other. In this way, even the worldly orders can be influenced.

One obvious perspective is that how we refer to God affects our view of humankind. It follows, then, that a relational theology will become an instrument on the path towards a relational ethics. My aim is to let Luther's view of Christ's mystery and his views of humanity's relation to God, *coram deo*, influence his ethics, that is to say, human beings' relation to others, *coram hominibus*. *Ecclesia reformata semper reformanda*[2] underscores the necessity of continual reformation and reinterpretation. I therefore wish to let elements of his own theology challenge the worldly conditions affecting relations between human beings.

Expressive Metaphors

Martin Luther was a Bible translator and commentator. In his writings and sermons he continually returned to images and metaphors taken from the Bible. His affective style is closely linked to powerful images. These metaphors are key to understanding his thought. In this chapter I

---

2. Luther discussed *coram deo* and *coram mundo*. The notions *coram hominibus* and *ecclesia reformata semper reformanda* are mainly connected to John Calvin and the Reformed tradition but are also relevant in the Lutheran tradition. Comparison of these traditions is not part of this study.

therefore discuss Martin Luther's use of the image of a married couple to describe the relationship between Christ and the believer. For Luther, this is a description of the Christian's oneness with Christ. Yet this union is evoked less in spiritual terms than by means of erotic images and formulations. In the Latin edition of *On the Freedom of a Christian*, he uses the word *copula* (copulate)[3]; in the German, he uses the word *brunst* (rut).

As we saw in chapter 4, Luther belongs to an exegetical tradition that derives from Origen and Bernard of Clairvaux, who interpret the Song of Solomon as a metaphor for the love between Christ and the believer. Subsequent commentators have argued that this song should not be interpreted in spiritual terms but rather be seen as a description of devoted worldly eroticism and sexuality.[4] God is barely mentioned. Rather, prominence is given to humanity in all its physical splendor.[5] The poem may have been authored by a woman. It has sometimes been said to lack patriarchal elements and to deal, not with binary complementarity between man and woman, but rather with subversive desire. Other scholars have highlighted its idealization of the masculine king, the warrior, who can be glimpsed among the images. Phyllis Trible contends that the poem seeks to reconcile a love story that has been warped.[6] For long periods, however, the Song of Solomon has primarily been interpreted in an allegorical and spiritualized way. Luther was a Bible commentator and translated the Bible from the original Hebrew and Greek. This meant that he sought biblical authority for opinions when polemicizing against contemporary phenomena. He claimed to read literally and thereby to restore an original that had been misrepresented by latter-day commentators. Naturally, his interpretations were often colored by contemporary factors, by the tradition from which he hailed, and, not least, by his polemical intentions. Although he was critical of the allegorical method of interpretation, he himself used the marital trope from the Song of Solomon metaphorically, as an image of the love between the king and his people, when he wanted to defend political authority and, following tradition, as an image of the love between Christ and the believer. When he invoked the marital mystery—that is, nuptial imagery—in his treatise

---

3. WA 7; cf. LW 31 "Von der Freiheit" (1520).
4. Jeanrond, "Kärlekens praxis," 230.
5. Stuart and Thatcher, *People of Passion*, 204–6.
6. Trible, *Rhetoric of Sexuality*, 144.

On the Freedom of a Christian, it was just one of several examples. Such metaphorical usage is also discernible in his sermons..

Understanding Martin Luther in relation to sixteenth-century attitudes towards gender and relationships is not easy, however. Although he sees both women and men as created in God's image, he writes that woman appears to be a little different, with special limbs and "a much weaker nature."[7] Although Eve was an extraordinary creation and like Adam in her godlikeness, she was nevertheless a woman. Luther compares man to the sun and woman to the moon in order to claim that woman is unlike man in nobility and prestige.[8] Eve is described thus:

> Although Eve was a most extraordinary creature similar to Adam so far as the image of God is concerned, that is, in justice, wisdom, and happiness, she was nevertheless a woman. For as the sun is more excellent than the moon (although the moon, too, is a very excellent body), so the woman, although she was a most beautiful work of God, nevertheless was not the equal of the male in glory and prestige. However, here Moses puts the two sexes together and says that God created male and female in order to indicate that Eve, too, was made by God as a partaker of the divine image and of the divine similitude, likewise of the rule over everything. Thus even today the woman is the partaker of the future life.[9]

Luther emphasizes, then, that man and woman are both created in God's image and with equal value before God. This was not a given in Luther's day.

At the same time, he retains the gender hierarchy by comparing man to the sun and woman to the moon. In the post-Augustinian tradition, the order of creation, in which Eve, according to Genesis 2, was created from Adam, has been used to justify man's superiority. This perspective has been reinforced by a harmonizing reading of the two different creation narratives that introduce the first two chapters in the Bible. The younger of the two, which occurs in Genesis 1, draws its imagery from a coastal setting in which the waters of chaos represent the threat. In this poetic narrative, humanity is created last, as male and female beings, in God's image. The second narrative, which begins in Genesis 2, verse 4b, is set in an arid desert landscape in which water represents a sign of

7. WA 42, 51, 52; cf. LW 1, 27 "Genesisvorlesung" (1535–45).
8. Ibid.
9. Ibid.

life, not a threat. Here, the first human being is created from earth and therefore called "an earth creature." The second human being is created from his side, usually translated as his rib. A second human being who is similar yet also dissimilar was necessary in order to dispel the loneliness that animals had not succeeded in remedying. Although these magnificent stories foreground human beings' need for other humans beings to counter their existential isolation, traditional theological interpretations narrow-mindedly accentuate the polarity between man and woman, as something necessary for the sake of propagation, not as something good in itself or as a means of fostering tenderness, solidarity, and reciprocity. Additionally, there has been a strong emphasis upon Adam's having been created first and as therefore having greater value. As I have noted in my book *Mänskliga rättigheter för Guds skull*, it might mischievously be argued that this could as easily be interpreted as saying that the first human being was merely a sketch for a more finished artwork in creation.[10]

That Eve was created from the man's rib—from Adam, not earth—also seemed to Luther to accord greater value to the man.[11] Luther read the Bible in a precritical way. According to his reading of Genesis 1, creation took place in six days and concluded with the creation of human beings. However, according to Genesis 2, animals were created even earlier. This seems not to have troubled his line of argument, conventional at that time, for which the sequence of creation as given in Genesis 2 was significant for the story of Adam and Eve. They were also regarded as actual historical figures. On this point, Luther departed from Origen's reading, which refers to creation in two stages, as an inner and an outer human person, with Genesis 2 describing the creation of the outer and Genesis 1 as describing the inner.[12]

Luther additionally argues that because of the Fall it was no longer possible to know what woman had been like. This view of woman was fairly self-evident in Luther's time. In Luther's writings, however, this is not presented as something that makes her different before God or in her relation to God. However, for Luther, this equality before God does not remove the gender hierarchy evident in everyday life. In the household, the wife was seen as a partner who had a common interest in children and property. She might thus hold a strong position even as she was seen

10. Gerle, *Mänskliga rättigheter*, 17–19.
11. Ibid. A historical-critical reading of the Bible that we today use did not exist in Luther's time. Instead, the Bible was read in what might be called a pre-critical way.
12. See chapter 4.

as subordinate to her husband. It was he who governed the household. This emphasis upon everyday vocation and the duties it entailed eventually led, however, to an upgrading of the status of women's traditional activities.[13]

In Luther's reading of Genesis can be discerned Augustine's ideas about fertility being part of God's creation. Woman is therefore viewed primarily as a mother. What emerges is a traditional conception of essential difference, one long taken as axiomatic. Women and men were seen as having different purposes. When Luther talks and writes about the relationship between people in marriage and in society, therefore, he is reflecting a model of domination and subordination that was widespread at the time. This inflects his description of the household estate, *oeconomia/familia*, as well as of *politia*. Before God all are the same. Even within the family man and woman belong to the same estate. Moreover, they are *simul iustus et peccator*, that is, sinners and righteous at the same time. This held true in each of the three spheres that he theorized about, that is to say, also within *ecclesia*, the church.[14] For Luther, the doctrine of the estates was a way to break with a hierarchy in which the church, *ecclesia*, held the power. Luther often emphasizes the importance of *oeconomia/familia* for maintaining God's creation.

Although Luther floated the idea of a general priesthood in which every person would be a Christ to his fellow humans in the drudgery of everyday life, this did not dissolve the strict divisions that existed between different vocations. In the Lutheran reception history, the strict division between what applies before God, *coram Deo*, and what applies with regard to people or to the world, *coram hominibus* or *corum mundo*, not infrequently served to legitimate the prevailing order. This has served to protect unequal temporal orders from being challenged even as it has emphasized people's responsibility towards one another and the world.

13. See also Gerle, "Var dags," where I argue that the value of ordinary life and thus women was restored through the emphasis placed by early Christianity and the Reformation on the equal value of all human beings, as well as through their challenging of the primacy of the political sphere.

14. The model of different estates derives from Aristotelian ethics and is not an invention of Luther. Yet they are connected to his social ethics. Brian Brock claims that "the orders indicate the steady states set up by the divine promises and in which truly human life can exist. In these terms, to act or think as if we are gods is to obscure the divine address, and so to introduce a decaying interference into the states of activity in which human fullness of life exists" ("Why the Estates?," 20, 179). Following this precept, I have described them as "spheres of promise" in Gerle, *Luther som utmaning*; Gerle, *Mänskliga rättigheter*.

Ambiguous Images

During the Reformation major changes took place that affected society, argues John Witte Jr., legal historian and director of a research institute for law and religion at Emory University. He takes issue with the views advanced by the great twentieth-century German sociologist Ernst Troeltsch, namely, that Lutheranism was merely a theological movement without political or legal consequences. According to Troeltsch, the medieval legal traditions lived on after the Reformation. Drawing on examples from late sixteenth-century Germany, however, Witte shows that Reformation theology had clear consequences for how the care of the poor and charitable organizations was organized.[15] Witte points out that the Reformation led to new regulations for healthcare and education. These would no longer be subject to canon law, and thus under the church's jurisdiction, but would now be seen as part of the responsibility of the Christian community. The church would therefore no longer be an institution responsible for charity. In the first instance this would be the responsibility of the family, but the Reformation also saw the introduction of local municipal welfare institutions. These were administered by local judges or by the local community and were aimed at the genuinely poor and needy. As a bare minimum, food, clothing, and lodging would be provided to the poor and needy in times of war, plague, and catastrophe. Their funds were comprised by church donations and confiscated property. These coffers would eventually be supplemented by local taxes and individual donations. Witte claims that these legal reforms have their origin in Lutheran theology's emphasis upon the general clergy and the notion that God is active in both the church and the world.[16] According to Witte, the religious revolution thus had sweeping legal and political consequences.

This was far from always a good thing for people, however. For example, when the Catholic church's healthcare institutions disappeared in the wake of the Reformation, standards of hygiene dropped catastrophically. Moreover, "tinkers" or "gypsies" were singled out as "wastrels" and "idlers" or "useless" people. Suspicion of those without fixed abode was widespread for a long time. Luther's criticism of mendicant (or begging) friars such as the Franciscans and the Dominicans too easily lent itself to criticism of those who could not earn their living through work. Parish

15. Witte, *Law and Protestantism*, 21–24.
16. Ibid., 21f.

communities were not interested in taking care of those of the poor who could not maintain themselves, a view that has not entirely disappeared.

Many structures were for a long time interpreted in terms of the doctrine of the estates and were regarded as divinely ordained, sometimes as necessary ordinances established after the Fall as a means of protecting human life. The German theologian Thielecke, however, saw marriage and family not as a "necessary ordinance" but as divinely created.[17] People's roles within the different estates—or spheres of promise, as I prefer to call them—were not usually seen as static, however. They changed during the course of a life and were related to age, wisdom, and strength. According to Thielecke, however, the relationship between man and woman, between parents and children, had certain fundamental features that did not change. To view the relation between man and woman as divinely ordained, and as having a strong element of domination and subordination, was to choose an interpretation that followed Augustine in locating gender hierarchy within creation itself. This interpretation, as we have seen, was not the only one adopted by the early Church Fathers. But interpretations that trace a gender hierarchy back to the creation narratives have not been consigned to history, unfortunately, and are still offered to this day by conservative groups.

Interpretations in Doubt

Within Lutheran tradition, however, there have always been other readings that claim that specific regulations and external forms should not be seen as divinely ordained or originating in creation. On this view the Bible should be considered not as a rulebook for regulations but as a love letter. The priesthood, the vocation to be a servant of the Word, *Verbi Divini Minister* (VDM), and to administer the sacrament, should thus be seen as determined not by gender but by a mandate from the Word. It took time before this interpretation, which has a close affinity with Lutheran liberation theology, established itself in Lutheran churches. For a long time the impetus of a Roman Catholic view of the office, which

17. Other estates, such as the state, economy, law, and culture, were not to be seen as created orders, according to Thielecke, but rather as estates to protect human beings against evil in the postlapsarian era. They are estates against destitution and hardship to protect life after the Fall. For Thielecke, however, marriage and the family are founded on divine will in creation, before the Fall. See Thielecke, *Theologische Ethik*, 335f. See also Grenholm, *Tro, moral och uddlös politik*.

linked the priesthood to the masculine gender, went hand in hand with so-called literalist readings that cited Paul's statement that women in a congregation should remain silent. These are two quite different lines of argument. Both reflect traditional attitudes towards masculinity and femininity, rather than fundamental insights of the Reformation.[18] In similar fashion, there was a considerable passage of time before the view that different people had differing value was challenged. For a long time slavery and the subjugation of black people were defended by reference to the Bible's accounts of Shem, Ham, and Japheth, Noah's three sons, or by reference to the confusion of tongues and the division of the world's various peoples according to the account of the Tower of Babel.[19] New interpretations of what a Lutheran ethics should include are continually emerging. Today Luther's Christ mystery can provide inspiration for tenderness, warmth, and respect for different relations between people.

Martin Luther's views on man and woman are more ambivalent than his position on the question of salvation, points out Else Marie Wiberg Pedersen. She claims that his "good theology" is not fully expressed in his anthropology.[20] As she presents it, these can easily be differentiated. If one instead starts from the premise that how we talk about God affects how we talk about humanity, then Luther's theology, that is to say, his view of humanity in relation to God, should be able to challenge his notions, characteristic of the time, about human relationships. Luther claimed that all people are the same before God, but not in relation to each other. Within each of the estates every person has different tasks. These should not be seen as static, however, but rather as assigned in an organic fashion. For Luther, as I have already indicated, this included hierarchical interpretations of how people ought to relate to each other. This idea also included a self-evident ranking of the genders, which Luther never seriously questioned. Luther thus seems unafraid to describe woman as different in nature. His essentialist interpretation, as so often in contemporary essentialist thinking, incorporates an image of woman as essentially other, in practice often subordinate to man.

---

18. WA 7; cf. LW 31 "Von der Freiheit" (1520); M. Lindström, *Bibeln och bekännelsen.*

19. Gustaf Wingren often mentioned these examples of how it took time before Christians started to challenge the hierarchical models inspired by the gospels. See Wingren, *Växling och kontinuitet.*

20. Wiberg Pedersen, "Bad Anthropology and Good Theology?," 191-201.

Today, flexibility and fluidity of gender are emphasized. Relations within the family and society are very different from in Luther's day. Desire and sexuality are not merely linked to procreation but seen as a driving force for creativity and for tenderness and intimacy.

As I see it, Luther's distinction between what applies before God and what applies in relation to human beings and the world should today be challenged by his own sense of the Christ mystery. He himself transgresses this boundary.

Christ as Bride/Groom—a Hybrid

In his early treatise *On the Freedom of a Christian* from 1520, Martin Luther writes about the relationship between the Christian and Christ as a relationship between bride and bridegroom.[21] Everything they possess they hold jointly, the good and the bad alike. This figure has been criticized by feminist theologians for its gender stereotyping. The Christian is described as a passive and receptive bride while Christ is described as the one who gives. In this fortunate exchange, in which Christ takes away the person's sin, death, and damnation, giving in return mercy, life, and salvation, all the negative qualities are associated with the bride and all the positive with the groom.

Superficially, this account of an exchange emphasizes the forensic, legal aspect of righteousness. The human being is acquitted and declared innocent before God. The bride takes what belongs to the groom and the groom what belongs to the bride. However, American theologian Kathryn A. Kleinhans argues that this language, which evokes a commercial transaction, illustrates for Luther a reality that is fundamentally relational. Faith unites the believer with Christ.[22] It even contains erotic elements that find expression in the metaphors used and in the powerful intimacy they articulate.

Kleinhans discusses several ways of interpreting Christ as bride/groom. Her article appears in an anthology of writings by contemporary American Lutheran theologians. Kleinhans's contribution, which I will return to, is interesting for this study because she is attempting to formulate a Lutheran and feminist relational Christology. She shares this aim with Else Marie Wiberg Pedersen, a Danish theologian at Aarhus

21. WA 7, 12–38; cf. LW 31:351, "Von der Freiheit" (1520).
22. Kleinhans, "Christ as Bride/Groom," 128.

University, who has also studied Luther's use of language in both his Latin and German writings. She, too, shows that Luther's description of Christ as a bridegroom has gender-transgressing qualities. These slippages and mixed metaphors can be used against those who seek to cling to polarized notions about what it means to be a bride or a bridegroom. These are elements that extend the tradition further by making it available to the contemporary emphases provided by gender-transgressing and queer theologies.

Both of these feminist theologians, one from the United States and one from Denmark, are in the present chapter presented as contributing to a relational interpretation of marital metaphorics in Luther. While Kleinhans stresses what is new in Luther, Wiberg Pedersen has shown that Luther as well, on many important issues, continues an older mystical tradition. Wiberg Pedersen highlights not only his further developments but also how he connects with the medieval tradition. Kleinhans emphasizes what is pioneering in his thought. At the same time, she also reads Luther in relation to the language developed at the Fourth Ecumenical Council (the Council of Chalcedon, AD 451), which declared that Christ has two natures in one person. Wiberg Pedersen has shown that Martin Luther's play upon the image of a bride and groom drew inspiration from Bernard of Clairvaux, a mystic who lived four hundred years earlier. Luther invokes his theology of love.[23] This is a sign that he is choosing what he is taking from his tradition and what he is excluding. In similar fashion, those today who would revise or mediate traditions operate according to more or less conscious choices. Luther thus engages in a kind of intertextuality, aligning himself with some themes while remaining silent about or polemicizing against others.[24]

Wiberg Pedersen shows in her study of Bernard of Clairvaux how he echoes the opening verses of the Song of Solomon when describing the church: "For your love is more delightful than wine. / Pleasing is the fragrance of your perfumes..." Bernard reproduces the Vulgate, which is even more concrete: "For thy breasts are better than wine, / Smelling sweet of the best ointments." These words are applied to both Christ and the bride, the soul and the church.[25] Initially Bernard attributes the breasts to

---

23. Wiberg Pedersen, "This Is Not about Sex?," 15–25.

24. This is abundantly clear from Luther's lectures on Genesis, in which he often polemicizes against other interpretations of creation, such as the Stoic, the Aristotelian, and various rabbinical interpretations.

25. Wiberg Pedersen, *Bernhard af Clairvaux*, 110.

the bridegroom, Christ. They then represent patience with the sinner and kindness towards the repentant. They are signs of Christ's mercy. Bernard also exhorts his monks to suckle at these breasts rather than the wounds of the crucified man. He, Christ, himself wishes to be a mother to you his son.[26] The crucified man is thus likened to a mother and the bridegroom given breasts from which Christ's mercy flows like a mother's milk to the child.[27] The image of the breasts, argues Wiberg Pedersen, underscores the fact that Christ is a source of love, a *fons pietatis*, or a motherly source, a *fons materni*, whence milk flows to his bride in a loving kiss that is also constituted and established by Christ's mercy.[28]

Bernard's choice of idiom was inspired by Anselm, who called Christ a mother. According to Wiberg Pedersen, the big difference between Anselm and Bernard is their theological framework. For Anselm, salvation is reconciliation in a court of law, while Bernard sees salvation as union in a loving embrace, a kiss, a marital bed. While Anselm, with his images of honor and righteousness, delivers a classically forensic doctrine of reconciliation, Bernard, with his images of the marital bed, is preoccupied with the reciprocal and nourishing love between God and human beings (and their fellow humans).[29] Wiberg Pedersen therefore contends that Martin Luther had derived considerable inspiration from Bernard, not least his erotic imagery.

The question in this context is what influences and implications all this might have for the search for a relational theology today. Two aspects stand out, even at this early stage. One is that maternal feeling and attentiveness need not be associated with the feminine gender exclusively. The other is that the relation between being giving and being receiving can shift.

Kleinhans claims that a number of difficulties associated with the marital metaphorics are closely linked to the tendency to see Christ as a model and example. For a Christian, there is a significant difference between "becoming like" Jesus, as imitative readings propose, and being "with" Jesus in an intimate, almost organic union.[30] Kleinhans cites the Finnish critique of a one-dimensional forensic interpretation of justification, arguing that talk of oneness with Christ, what is also described as

26. Ibid.
27. Ibid., 110–11.
28. Ibid., 111.
29. Ibid., 90.
30. Kleinhans, "Christ as Bride/Groom," 126.

actual presence or Christ's real presence, is something that clearly shows that justification also has a real effect on the believer, namely, renewal.[31] What emerges here is yet another aspect, namely, that the relation as presence and movement in itself creates something new.

Kleinhans sees this as a resource for feminist thought and highlights such ideas within early Christianity. In 325 the First Council of Nicaea emphasized Christ's identity with God by means of the term *homoousios*, meaning of one and the same substance, of the same being. This concept was taken a step further in 451 in Chalcedon, where it was stressed that Christ is one with God and with humanity. The two natures were described as relational. Christ is *homoousios* with the Father and with us. The christological claim is not that Jesus is "like" God and "like" a human being but that Jesus is wholly God and wholly human. This entails a relation of identification.[32] It is an intimate, unique, and indissoluble union. Despite this, every person remains distinct. The optimal identity for a Christian is "not that I *become like* my spouse. It's that I be *one with* my spouse."[33] This means that intimacy, as an inspiration for ethics in close relations, is not synonymous with the kind of symbiosis in which one individual's ego disappears and is absorbed by another's. Even in an intimate union both partners should be able to remain distinct.

Kleinhans investigates four aspects of how Luther uses the image of a marriage: (1) the difference between Luther's use of marital metaphorics and its late-medieval use; (2) the union's transformative nature; (3) the union's unique character; and (4) reciprocity and the perfect sharing that the union results in.[34]

The Difference between Luther's Use of Marital Metaphorics and Its Late-Medieval Use

The metaphor of a marriage to describe the relation between Christ and the believer primarily appears in the biblical texts. In the later Middle Ages this image was in fairly common use among both female and male mystics. These mystics sought to achieve union with the divine. In its

31. Ibid.

32. Ibid.

33. Kleinhans draws a parallel here to the distinction between *homoousios* ("one" or "the same") and the rejected Arian *homoiousios* ("similar"). Kleinhans, "Christ as Bride/Groom," 133.

34. I here follow Kleinhans, "Christ as Bride/Groom," 128–32.

classical form, this mystical ascent comprised three stages: purification, enlightenment, and union. For some mystics, union with the divine was experienced as a vision of a marriage to Christ. Against this background, Luther's use of marital metaphorics stands out as conspicuously different.

First, Luther views such a union as an effect of faith. It is not the culmination of disciplined human effort. Luther changed the *de facto* direction of the process. He describes the bridegroom as someone who spontaneously pursues the person as his bride, not the other way round.[35]

Second, since sinners are justified by faith alone it is not necessary to distance oneself from one's sinful state in order to experience union with the divine. The believer enters into marriage just as he or she is. Purification is a result of union with God, not its precondition.

Third, medieval mystics usually emphasize the physical union with Christ in his suffering. Luther instead describes the marital union as a happy and joyful interchange. It is a union with Christ in his victory over sin, death, and damnation. Luther here does something new with the marital metaphors, argues Kleinhans.[36]

The Transformative Nature of the Union

When Luther uses the image of a marriage, he rejects the active striving that was a common feature of medieval mysticism; yet the image is not entirely passive. To see the relation as one in which the bride is wholly dependent upon the bridegroom is no less problematic than an understanding that emphasizes that it is necessary for human beings to struggle or suffer in order to become like Jesus. In his sermon "On Two Kinds of Righteousness" Luther offers a more general marital metaphor that emphasizes personal sympathy. Only with the sympathy of the loved one and the explicit yes can the marriage be consummated: "Through the first righteousness arises the voice of the bridegroom, who says to the soul. 'I am yours,' but through the second comes the voice of the bride who answers, 'I am yours.' Then the marriage is consummated, it becomes strong and complete in accordance with the Song of Solomon (2:16): My beloved is mine and I am his."[37]

35. WA 40 II, 581–84; cf. LW 12:279, "Praelectio in psalmum 45" (1532–33); cf. Kleinhans, "Christ as Bride/Groom," 128.

36. Kleinhans, "Christ as Bride/Groom," 129. She makes a Lutheran reading and emphasizes how Luther differentiates himself from medieval theology.

37. WA 2, 145–52; cf. LW 31:300 "Sermo de duplici iustitia" (1519).

Marriage does not deny the bride's individuality. It presupposes it. Marital union requires more than an exchange of wedding gifts. It is intimate. And it is through its intimacy and sensual presence that the union is transformative and lifechanging.[38] As previously noted, this kind of union and intimacy involves the partners remaining independent subjects who freely join with the other under no kind of duress, manipulation, or fear.

In Luther's treatise *On the Freedom of a Christian*, argues Danish theologian Bo Kristian Holm, it is significant that the image of the married couple is used both symmetrically and asymmetrically.[39] While the bride's passivity is foregrounded in Luther's early lecture on the Letter to the Romans, the bride here is in fact active and gives herself voluntarily. It is put even more starkly in the original *Sermo de duplici iustita*, in which the bride answers Christ: I am yours!

Philologist Anne Carson has proposed that *eros* can be seen as bittersweet and as living off desire, never achieving satisfaction.[40] In Luther's use of the marital metaphor, what might be called a de-eroticization takes place since he emphasizes not a desire for union but an actually realized union between God and humanity.

The accent is on the embrace. Paradoxically, this very de-eroticization puts an end to the competition between love for God and love for another person. The marital metaphor is linked to faith. In this way, as will be seen in the following chapter, love can be set free. Earthly love will no longer be a rival to one's relationship to God.

When Luther uses the imagery of the Song of Solomon, it is not necessarily a matter of the relationship between soul and Christ or between man and woman. In his interpretation of the Song of Solomon from circa 1531, he states explicitly that it concerns neither of the above, but politics.[41]

---

38. Kleinhans, "Christ as Bride/Groom," 129.
39. Holm, *Gabe und Geben*.
40. Carson, *Eros the Bittersweet*.
41. WA 31 II, 537:6–8; cf. LW 15, 189–264 "Einleitung zur Vorlesung über das Hohelied" (1531). See also Holm, "Dynamic Tensions"; cf. Gutmann, *Über Liebe und Herrschaft*, 179f.

The Unique Character of the Union

Where traditional Christology, according to Mary Daly,[42] has functioned as a means of ascribing all divine status to men, Luther chooses to emphasize the uniqueness of Jesus Christ. This also leads to a unique relationship between Christ and the Christian. Luther warns against "turning Christ into Moses" by focusing more on Christ as exemplar than as gift.[43] Luther used marital metaphorics in order to criticize the medieval church hierarchy. In so doing, he joined a long tradition in which intimacy emerged as a reaction formation when the church hierarchy becomes too powerful. At such moments counter-movements appeared in the monasteries, where the abbot, for example, could be described as a mother.[44]

Luther warns against "false bridegrooms" and scolds those church potentates who falsely present themselves as bridegrooms and appropriate Christ's rightful position. This is a recurrent theme in Luther's writing. In biblical commentaries, theological tracts, and polemical treatises, Luther returns repeatedly to the critique of all claims by the church as an institution to be a representative of Christ. Thus he writes in his 1527 lecture on the Epistle to Titus, "No one is allowed to be both a husband and a bridegroom, except Christ alone, as John 3:29 says."[45] In a sermon on the Gospel of St. John he puts it even more forcefully: "In their writings the popes claimed that they were the bridegrooms of the Christian Church and that the bishops were the bridegrooms of their dioceses. In reality they were panders!"[46] Popes and bishops cannot play the role of Christ by wearing the mantle of the bridegroom, any more than other men can.[47]

When Luther uses the metaphor of the bride, Kleinhans claims, he deliberately rejects androcentric generalizations.[48] In her view, every Christian's unique relation to Christ can be used not merely to chal-

---

42. Daly, *Beyond God the Father*, 19; also Ruether, *Sexism and God-Talk*.

43. WA 10 I 1, 8–18; cf. LW 35:123 "Ein klein unterricht"; "A Brief Instruction" (1522).

44. Bynum, "Jesus as Mother and Abbot as Mother."

45. WA 25, 17–18; cf. LW 29:18 "Vorlesung über die Briefe an Titus und Philemon" (1527). Kleinhans, "Christ as Bride/Groom," 130.

46. WA 47, 156:16 1; "Auslegung des dritten und vierten Kapitels Johannis"; cf. LW 22:440 "Sermon on St. John" no. 40, (1537–38); Kleinhans, "Christ as Bride/Groom," 130.

47. This is also an argument against connecting ordination with the male sex alone.

48. Kleinhans, "Christ as Bride/Groom," 130.

lenge androcentrism and patriarchy but to question and challenge the glorification of suffering.

The classic view of suffering in the history of Christianity is not that it is something praiseworthy in itself, but rather that Christ's suffering is unique. When Christians suffer, it has nothing to do with following some commandment to suffer; rather, it is an almost organic consequence of union with Christ.[49]

This, too, represents a building block for a relational ethics. Every relationship can involve sharing in the other person's suffering. However, it cannot be something one seeks and that the relationship in itself should create. In Luther's writings, there is a strongly life-affirming attitude that sees suffering as neither good nor desirable. Instead, he celebrates the sensual for its capacity to give joy and to drive away despair.

Reciprocity and the Complete Sharing That the Union Brings About

Criticism of the marital metaphorics of Luther's *On the Freedom of a Christian* (1520) tends to focus upon how the bride is described as passive and her qualities as wholly negative. Even if Luther, as I pointed out above, is talking about human beings, this still has some relevance for matters before the happy exchange. In the marital union, however, the relation is described as considerably more equal. The bride is now not merely a nominal beneficiary of her husband's wealth and status. She assumes full responsible authority for their now joint household. Luther uses legal figures such as common property: "The bride and bridegroom hold everything in common . . . She is a part of his body and carries the keys by her side."[50] Luther sees human marriage as an incomplete reflection of the union with Christ. For Kleinhans, Luther's own marriage, though hardly equal by the standards of our time, gives a hint as to how he understands the joint authority that the believer shares with Christ.[51] Whether this marriage was characterized by more reciprocity than was typical for the sixteenth century is, however, debatable.[52]

As noted earlier, Luther's opinion of women was characterized by ambiguity. On the one hand, he shared the view, common at the time,

---

49. Ibid., 130-31.
50. "Auslegung," WA 47, 164; cf. LW 22:450 (1538-40); my translation.
51. Kleinhans, "Christ as Bride/Groom," 131.
52. See, for example, Stjerna, *Women and the Reformation*.

that a wife should obey her husband. On the other hand, he referred to his wife Katharina both lovingly and with great respect. That he called her *Herr Käthe* must be seen in relation to its context of a time when men had higher status. Kleinhans points out that when Luther translates Gen 2:28, he does not use a belittling term, such as the term "helpmate" that commonly figures in English translations. The German word Luther uses is *Maennin*, a feminine form of the word *Man*. This word becomes his German equivalent for the Hebrew wordplay on *ish* and *ishah* to describe the duality of the first human couple. Nor, as Kleinhans notes, does he use a possessive pronoun. She is not her husband's helper or his woman.[53] The word *ishah* can mean "a worthy adversary" or "finding yourself facing someone" and could therefore be roughly translated as "equivalence."[54]

The keys that Kleinhans provides for making a non-patriarchal interpretation of the marital metaphor in Luther's writings hinge upon not focusing solely upon the exchange as an isolated transaction but as an intimate, transformative love relationship. The aim of a marriage is not to become like one's spouse but to be with one's partner. It is about presence. What is more, the benefits of living in this relationship constitute a gift to both partners equally. This precept represents a contribution to a relational ethic with reciprocal qualities. The gift in the relationship is not furnished by one party alone. Both are drawn to each other by a desire for what the other has to give, for something different, challenging, and transformative. Both are responsible for more than each other, also for the relationship as such.

To this can be added something emphasized by Wiberg Pedersen, namely, the fact that neither the New Testament nor the Confessions, including the Augsburg Confession, describe Christ as a man (*aner*, *vir* or *Mann*). Their emphasis lies rather upon the relationship between God and the human being who is precisely identified as a human, as flesh (*antropos/sarx*, *homo*, or *Mensch*), something that is rendered invisible by the English term "Man" to designate humanity.[55] She claims that Luther's sustained engagement resulted from the question of salvation, which turned on the relationship between God and humanity, not relations between the sexes or between people at large. Yet, there is also the rhythm

---

53. Kleinhans, "Christ as Bride/Groom," 132.

54. In Gerle, "Kön, genus och religion." I am referring to various interpretations of *ishah* as antidote or someone standing up to something (ibid., 69f.).

55. Wiberg Pedersen, "One Body in Christ?," 59–82.

of love where divine love is effecting human relations.[56] In a series of lectures on Isaiah, Luther also describes the believer as a bridegroom and Christ as a bride: "Thus all of us who believe are by faith bridegrooms and priests, something the world does not see but faith accepts."[57] Reflecting upon the image of the mother in Isaiah 66:9, he assigns to Christ a double identity: "I am both Bridegroom and Bride. I can beget and give birth, and I can give others the power of begetting."[58] Here, too, Luther's playing upon images and metaphors can be seen to make a contribution to contemporary discussions of shared life, parenthood, and other kinds of family configurations. In our time, when same-sex marriage is becoming more common, the focus can be shifted from the gender of the two partners to the intimacy and the unique and full sharing of marriage.

For those seeking a relational theology that addresses the way people live with each other in the everyday world, Luther's redemptive theological interpretation offers both a challenge and an inspiration.

Concluding Reflections

Both Kleinhans and Wiberg Pedersen argue that the image of Christ as bride/bridegroom provides a resource for a relational theology. Wiberg Pedersen emphasizes, as we have seen, that Luther avoids using a gender-specific term when he refers to the relationship between God and human beings, the focus of his theological engagement. The individual is described as *antropos/sarx*, *homo*, or *Mensch*. When Luther describes Christ as both bride and bridegroom, it is as a hybrid form that also appears in the writings of Bernard of Clairvaux. She shows how the marital metaphorics developed four centuries earlier by the latter are preoccupied with a reciprocal and sensual love between God and humanity in which hybrid forms also have a place.[59] Luther thus affiliates himself with an earlier mystic whom both Wiberg Pedersen and Luther designate a theologian of love. At the same time, she points out that Luther and the tradition he invokes put the emphasis upon the relationship between God and human beings, not on the relationship between the sexes. However, my own argument is that Luther's Christ mystery, which emphasizes the

56. Ibid.
57. WA 31 II, 525-26, "Vorlesung über Jesajas"; cf. LW 17:342 (1527-30); Kleinhans, "Christ as Bride/Groom," 133.
58. Ibid.
59. Wiberg Pedersen, *Bernhard af Clairvaux*, 90.

intimate love between Christ and the believer, can serve as a challenge and an inspiration for shared relationships between individuals. Luther himself uses the formulation of marital mystery in his wedding sermon of 1531, in which he emphasizes physical presence and the sharing of everything.

The metaphor of Christ as bride/groom shows that motherly feelings and affection can be given by both men and women as well as that relations alternate between being giving and receiving. In such reciprocity, the relationship in itself becomes innovative. At the same time, the separate parties are not erased as individuals. They remain distinct, even within the intimate relationship and in relation to each other. There is a counterbalance here to the devotion that gives up everything and thereby risks becoming self-destructive. This strand of thinking in Luther resonates with the feminist critique of an *agape* love that does not include reciprocity. Glorification of subordination or suffering forms no part of an intimate relationship between either Christ and the believer or between people. What is more, it is not only one partner who gives. Both are drawn to each other by a desire for what the other has to give, for something different, challenging, and transformative.

The justification that Luther finds in his Christ relationship becomes as strong as a loving embrace, an ever-present haven. A presence in the middle of life. Luther seems to have had a somewhat harsh, but realistic, insight that love so perfect can never fully be found in earthly love.[60] This latter remains but a pale reflection of Christ's perfect love, which can nonetheless inspire earthly love. Divine love can also serve as a bulwark against the group pressures of the present moment, which sometimes lead to a herd mentality in which many people, notwithstanding all their talk of individualism, charge in the same direction. A person who has encountered love and been seen and understood profoundly has greater opportunities for managing anxieties about not being sufficient, not belonging, or not being good enough.

The ideal love to which Anthony Giddens alludes in his discussion of "the pure relationship," which really comprises love without ethics, is wholly alien to Luther. This is partly because the ideal is not attainable in this life, which is characterized by rupture and ambiguity, and partly because love is indissolubly bound up with reciprocity and tenderness. The result is a growing skepticism towards the pursuit of perfection, or belief in the pure relationship, something that has caused what Zygmunt

---

60. Kleinhans, "Christ as Bride/Groom," 131.

Bauman calls "floatation of love" in which one abandons a relationship if it fails to provide all that one is looking for.[61]

However, when reading Luther's commentaries on Genesis alongside his marital metaphors it is hard to dispel the view that man is a shining sun and woman, like the moon, his paler reflection. The gender-transgressing imagery does not prevent the masculine gender more often being used in connection with the divine. If there is an important insight to be taken from Luther's ideas about the necessary imperfection of earthly love, there is also reason today to question his gender-defined interpretations of what and who are presented as radiant.

Kleinhans intentionally uses the hybrid form bride/groom in order to emphasize that, for Luther, gender is not the point. This hybrid term partly avoids an either/or dichotomy and partly a tendency to wholly exclude gender as something irrelevant. Kleinhans claims, on the contrary, that all Christians relate to Christ in his particularity, trusting that the relationship will embrace but also reach beyond our gendered existences.

For a Lutheran theology and ethics that seeks to relate to contemporary scientific insights into human identity, Kleinhans's reading of Luther's marital metaphorics is inspirational. Thanks to Wiberg Pedersen's historical studies, we are able to trace the strands of an earlier tradition that Luther chose to invoke. Both call into question the strict gender divisions that, according to Roper, came to define German civic life after the Reformation. In contrast to how the reception of his ideas in Nordic peasant society led to women being rendered invisible, Luther's own texts, and his life, offer evidence of a playfulness that disrupts the division of human beings, metaphorical and actual, on the basis of sex and behavioral stereotypes. Like Radical Orthodoxy, contemporary queer thinking emphasizes a Christ above and beyond gender.[62] This can be used as a critique of those traditional interpretations in which God and humanity, woman and man, are seen as each other's opposites. Instead, his playful language can encourage the valuing of hybridity over essentialist and categorical notions of gender. Not even the much decried gender metaphorics of *On the Freedom of a Christian* reveals itself, in Kleinhans's reading, to be as gender stereotyped as can seem at first glance. Her reading paves the way for a multiplicity of intimate relations.

61. Giddens, *Transformation of Intimacy*, 58, 61; Bauman, *Postmodern Ethics*, 106.

62. Althaus-Reid, "Queer I Stand"; Coakley, "Introduction"; Burrus, "Radical Orthodoxy," 38.

Skepticism has additionally been leveled at the usual, often moralizing interpretation of Jesus as a model to be imitated. Instead, emphasis is placed upon the relationship as a transformative loving relationship. Luther's euphoric description of the joyful exchange contains elements of emotional release and spiritual breakthrough as powerful as an orgasm. Perhaps the best way to understand his metaphorical language is in relation to how Luther conceived of a righteous God who could not disregard the reality of sin and who therefore appeared as a judge demanding recompense. In St. Anselm's doctrine of atonement, this leads to a demand for sacrifice, a line of thought that deeply affected Luther. In Luther's Christ mystery, in which Christ is described as a bride/groom, there emerges a different image of the divine. The court of law has been replaced by a marital bed. The passing of judgement has been transformed into a loving embrace. Instead of a calculated commercial transaction, there appears a metaphor characterized by mutual love, erotic desire, and devotion, a love and a presence that take seriously the reality of the other. This mode of relating to other people has consequences that stretch far beyond the intimate relationship.

Today, we would use the term *embracing* as a keyword to designate such a relationship. Notions such as embracing, accepting, recognizing, and including have other connotations than conversion, persuasion, or "churchification" or loyalty to church. While a segment of contemporary political theology and Radical Orthodoxy seems to want to fix a particular Christian identity, at the risk of essentializing inherited religious forms, gender patterns and boundaries, the word *embracing* opens up the possibility for new forms of religious expression and a respectful meeting with that which is different. It may also include the reciprocity that *eros* theologians are trying to highlight in the relationship between God and human beings.

7

Eros as Poisoned Chalice, Medicine, or Everyday Body? *Eros* and *Agape* in a New Light

Friedrich Nietzsche claims that "Christianity gave Eros poison to drink; he did not die of it, certainly, but degenerated to Vice."[1] Can the same be said today, when eroticism and sexuality are regarded as something entirely natural, nay, often necessary for a healthy life? Nietzsche's challenge remains an important point of reference.

The Reformation caused a renegotiation of contemporary attitudes towards the body, sensuality, and sexuality. The present moment is also posing new challenges to how sexuality and gender are viewed. For several of the last century's great Swedish theologians, such as Nathan Söderblom, Anders Nygren, and Gustaf Wingren, the real focus lay on the everyday body of work, labor, and pleasure. In this chapter I will be discussing the everyday body in the light of this renewed interest in erotic mysticism and asceticism.

The Materialist Turn

Just as the unitary subject has been called into question in our time, so too has any simple dualism of spiritual and material been challenged. Today we speak of "the materialist turn."[2] This has also affected our views on *eros* spirituality. The turn towards bodies and the material has

1. Nietzsche, *Beyond Good and Evil*, §168 (71).
2. Coole and Frost, *New Materialisms*.

prompted several scholars to call into question a dualistic interpretation that counterposes body and soul. The monastic pietism of the late medieval period has been described as especially fixated upon the body.[3] When the Hebrew belief in creation meets the Hellenist world, the early church theologians stimulate new interest. The Platonic world of ideas and its different stages and angelic ideal is attractive to some, while others are instead inspired by the anti-gnostic Fathers' struggle for a faith that celebrates all creation as coming from God, not merely the soul or the spiritual.

Scandinavian Creation Theology as a Horizon

Contemporary theological discussions proceed from new knowledge that shows a strong connection with tradition. By contrast, several twentieth-century Scandinavian theologians stressed that the Reformation represented a break with late-medieval thought and practice. They constitute a background against which I wish to position myself in a dialogue with contemporary scholars and theological trends. There is a perspective here that must be dealt with but also insights worth preserving. In the introduction to this study I mentioned Gustaf Wingren's dynamic view of creation as something continually in progress. This view of creation, with its powerful strain of Trinitarianism, presents an alternative to a static and hierarchical view of creation that emphasizes domination and subordination between men and women as well as between different peoples.

There is nothing new about taking seriously the body and its senses. Celebration of the body was emphatically advocated by Irenaeus. It also constituted an important element in the thinking of the Danish priest, poet, theologian, and popular educator N. F. S. Grundtvig (1783–1872) and the Lund theologian Gustaf Wingren (1910–2000), who particularly emphasized the everyday body. In his study *Luther och melankoli* theologian and archbishop Nathan Söderblom (1866–1931) has examined many of the aspects of Luther's ideas that interest me in the present study. Söderblom cites countless examples of Luther's often burlesque sense of humor. Humor seems to have come to him quite naturally, a way of looking at the world and one's self that went beyond all pompous dissimulation. Söderblom writes of "the rumble of laughter and the risqué joke" that "fizzes with good spirits but can also have a severity verging

---

3. Bynum, *Christian Materiality*; Bynum, *Resurrection of the Body*.

on scorn."[4] Citing a wider range of primary materials than I have used, Söderblom finds in Luther's writings an everyday physicality.

Contributions from theologians such as Söderblom and later Wingren, including their readings of Luther, are largely absent from current theological discussions. In recent years, however, they have been the focus of renewed attention.[5] They differ from contemporary theologians, however, in referring to sensuality and physicality instead of lust, eroticism, or desire. Lust, music, pleasure, intercourse, song, and wine are regarded as comforts amidst the trials and tribulations of life. After theology, according to Söderblom, Luther accords a place of honor in life to work, intellectual reflection, and, not least, music. Just like theology, it makes for a joyful heart.[6] Söderblom connects these experiences to the everyday. Work can also be seen as a comfort and help, not merely as a necessary evil or interpreted within some general notion of vocation. "To discover God's wonders in the most ordinary things, things everyone has seen and done countless times—that was Jesus's art," argues Söderblom. He claims that "humor's gaze rested kindly and warmly upon labor, even upon the most unpleasant and insignificant chores."[7]

Absent, however, is the focus on the church as a body that one finds in the writings of Sarah Coakley and Graham Ward, among others. When Söderblom or Wingren refer to the body's vulnerability, they have in mind not Jesus's vulnerable and abused body in some figurative ecclesiological sense, but ordinary concrete bodies. As they see it, there is a relationship to the divine right there. However, they lived and worked in a very different society, in which everyone had some kind of knowledge of Christian faith, knowledge that not infrequently needed to be challenged. Interpretation was therefore important.

For Söderblom, the goal was to broaden the horizons, including for other people's *way of believing*. It was part of his peace work, which resulted, among other things, in the great ecumenical World Conference of Life and Work held in Stockholm in 1925. In 1930, Söderblom received the Nobel Peace Prize for his ecumenical work. He was controversial, but as archbishop also a unifying figure, not only for Sweden but for European Christianity.

4. Söderblom, *Luther och melankoli*, 164.
5. Kristensson Uggla, *Becoming Human*.
6. Söderblom, *Luther och melankoli*, 165; WA, Br 1727.
7. Söderblom, *Luther och melankoli*, 62.

Gustaf Wingren, by contrast, was a pugnacious personality throughout his life. At his inaugural professorial lecture in 1951 he wasted no time in launching an attack on the Lund School of Theology in which he had been trained, in particular his predecessor Anders Nygren, whose method Wingren claimed was unhistorical. In his 1954 book *Teologiens metodfråga* (translated as *Theology in Conflict* [1958]), he fiercely attacked Nygren's method.[8] In his biography of Wingren, Bengt Kristensson Uggla describes this moment under the heading "The Apostasy."[9] He contends that Wingren had a problematic relation to the church throughout his life and that he was a "fiery critic of the church," something he also saw as part of his scholarly mission.[10] Wingren often used his studies of Luther as well as the Bible in order to criticize the church. While Söderblom saw the bishop as a unifying figure, Wingren was critical of apostolic succession, which he described as a late Anglican invention, a wretched and poorly substantiated theory that had been used against the flourishing free-church movement in nineteenth-century England. His ideal was Denmark, rather, whose bishops deliberately broke with the line of succession.[11] In 1974, Wingren resigned from the clergy in protest against the opponents to women becoming priests. Wingren refused to allow his interest in the church and clerical office to deflect his interest from "the rather colorless members of the congregation, those who live their everyday life of death and resurrection."[12] For Wingren, ordination was far less important than baptism.[13]

It is often easier for contemporary theologians to identify with Söderblom and his engagement with ecumenism than with the polemical Wingren, for whom, like Luther, all questions hinge upon the Word with a capital W, a word that requires groundbreaking reinterpretation in order to be relevant in the present day. Wingren was wholly uninterested in the outward regulations of the church.[14] These had only one task, to fulfill the mission that Christ had given the church, which he sometimes also spoke of as a body. When interest in clerical office and the church as

8. See Kristensson Uggla, *Becoming Human*, 52f.
9. Ibid., 48.
10. Ibid., 303.
11. Ibid., 319.
12. Ibid., 324. The quote is from "Begreppet lekman," 186, an article by Wingren.
13. Kristensson Uggla, *Becoming Human*, 324.
14. Ibid., 324f.

a body becomes increasingly evident, it is easier to turn to theologians in the Anglo-Catholic tradition. This holds particularly true of those who long to refer to the church with a capital C.

Earlier I mentioned Sarah Coakley and Graham Ward as examples of more church-oriented theologians. Ward emphasizes a relation to God in which, he writes, "I am found in God most myself, my sexual, gendered and gendering self—but I have to be taught what it means to be such a self by the Christ who draws me into a relationship with him."[15] Ward then quickly proceeds to discuss the church as a body, as an organism, as a social organization that affirms people as bodies, as queer, homo, hetero in a community without boundaries. In so doing he contributes to the churchification of the body that I here wish to separate myself from. In this context, Scandinavian creation theology, with its interest in everyday bodies, becomes an important affiliation. Where is the relation to God that Gustaf Wingren, following Irenaeus, contended was given with life? With a more creation-theological point of departure, one's own and one's shared life are a mystery and a gift. While this interpretation of life is deepened through encountering Christ and, in the best case, the church, it does not appear then for the first time. One's relation to God comes with life, not through the church, claims Wingren. The church's role is to heal us, to make us human again. Wingren acutely observes that the first centuries of church history show a lack of interest in "the religious components of the surrounding culture. It is the *irreligious* human life that is a *life in God*. A child grows up, begins to recognize that which evokes fear, smiles with joy at some things, bursts into tears at others—this is a life in God. And so is *everyone's* life."[16]

Wingren frequently returns to Irenaeus, whom he follows in arguing that it is a matter of becoming human, "in accordance with the first decree for creation."[17] On this reading, Luther wanted to "give the worldly occupations a place of honor as the only truly 'spiritual' places for a Christian's life."[18] To live like a Christian, according to Wingren, was thus not primarily a religious life but a human life.[19] *Recapitulatio*, for Irenaeus, meant to become human again. It is connected to growth

15. Ward, "On the Politics of Embodiment," 72.

16. Wingren, *Människa och kristen*, 63; cf. Wingren, *Man and the Incarnation*.

17. Wingren, *Man and the Incarnation*, 201; cf. Kristensson Uggla, *Becoming Human*, 162.

18. Wingren, *Öppenhet och egenart*, 13.

19. Wingren, *Människa och kristen*, 65.

and healing, also for the world, as all of creation is groaning as in labor (Rom 7:22).

This dynamic creation faith, which is associated, both in Sweden and internationally, with the Lund theologian Gustaf Wingren, is once again being read and published.[20] The tradition of Irenaeus that was continued by Grundtvig and Wingren remains important. Language and its idioms change and with them our forms of address. But keeping the bodily and the spiritual together is essential for me, just as it is to take as a starting point the idea of a creation in continual process, one in which the grand narratives of creation, atonement, and perfection are kept together.

This perspective is to be found in a new reading of Luther. New philosophical perspectives, which have called into question modernity's antitheses between inner and outer, spiritual and material, nonetheless bring new challenges.

Between Sexual Phobia and Erotic Elements of Tradition

While the church and Christianity have often been accused of fomenting sexual phobia and assuming the role of defender of chastity, the Christian tradition also includes some powerfully erotic elements. The relation between Christ and the believer is not infrequently described in sexual and erotic language. Patrologists and medieval scholars, from Virginia Burrus to Caroline Walker Bynum, have drawn attention to this language and foregrounded the body's significance within monastic piety.[21] In the process the *eros* spirituality that in the Protestant tradition has often been interpreted as humanity's efforts to move beyond the body, from the material and worldly to the divine, has acquired new dimensions. Late-medieval ascetic exercises in particular related to the body's transformation and reshaping as a path to union with God.[22] In contrast to previous scholarship, these researchers draw attention to how the body in monastic piety was not regarded as an obstacle but as an instrument for union with the divine.

---

20. See Wingren, *Man and the Incarnation*; Wingren, *Creation and Law*; Kristensson Uggla, *Becoming Human*.

21. Burrus, *Begotten Not Made*; Burrus, *The Sex Lives of Saints;* Bynum, *Jesus as Mother*.

22. Bynum, *Fragmentation and Redemption*.

The distinguished medieval historian Caroline Walker Bynum, who has written primarily on female mysticism and physicality, believes that our own era's distinction between spirit and body was unknown in the medieval period. At that time it was expected that both body and soul would be resurrected at the end of time. These ideas were characterized by what Bynum calls an "extreme literalism and materialism" that strongly emphasized a continuity between the earthly body and the resurrected body. She interprets this as a fear of losing one's self by losing one's body.[23] Bynum claims that the West's attitudes to the body and personality must be seen in the context of great changes in how matter was viewed. She therefore proposes a new way of tackling questions relating to material culture and religious praxis.[24] For her part, she is investigating the relationship between the body and the ego through terms such as preservation through change, hybridization, and transformation.

A number of scholars are building on her scholarship, which argues that female mystics in particular emphasized incarnation. The bodily, which was often associated with women, thereby become something positive, since God himself had become flesh. Bernard of Clairvaux, for example, represented himself as a woman when he wanted to stress humility in contrast to the ambitious and power-hungry popes and bishops of his time.

Religious Orders, Gender Transgressing, and the Versatility of Sexuality

A number of writings by mystics also seem to indicate that friendships with erotic and sexual aspects occurred within the monastic world.[25] In certain periods homoeroticism appears to have been more accepted. In the early medieval era it seems to have been tolerated but not, however, by the late medieval. The decree issued by the Fourth Lateran Council of 1215 marks a clear turning point that had been prepared by earlier writings such as Peter Damian's *Liber Gomorrhianus* (ca. 1048–54). In it, homoeroticism is designated a sin against nature and associated with Sodom and Gomorrah.[26]

23. Ibid.
24. Ibid.; Bynum, *Christian Materiality*.
25. Córdova Quero, "Friendship with Benefits," 32.
26. Ibid., 39f.

Martin Hugo Córdova Quero makes a gender-crossing interpretation. He claims that the ascetic's celibate way of life made it possible for women and men to reject traditional gender roles in society and construct other support systems. The literature of the fourth and fifth centuries shows that seeking "the angelic path" offered the only opportunity, for women in particular, to transcend their assigned roles. Only then could they find alternative forms for male and female relationships outside of marriage.[27] Not infrequently was the heteropatriarchal ideal of angelic love changed into homoerotic love.[28]

Queer scholars such as Marcella Althaus-Reid and Lisa Isherwood contend that there is an intimate connection between sexuality and theology, a connection that is becoming political. Today there is reason to ask whether the Reformation did not in fact start a sexual revolution that is still ongoing. Marcella Althaus-Reid, a Latin American scholar, claims that every theology is a sexual theology. The question is how it can be disrupted and questioned. In order to disrupt, she argues, it has to admit the instability of sexuality. The problem with heterosexuality, which she sees as a quite reasonable alternative, is that it is an ideology, a domineering worldview, which functions as a way of grasping reality: "To say that theology is and always has been a reflection rooted in sexual practices means that there is an epistemology which sacralizes sexual exchanges and regulations by a circle of permanent reconfigurations of the sacred, based on heterosexuality's symbolic structures and value systems."[29] Marcella Althaus-Reid argues, then, that theological praxis comes not from heaven but rather from theology's bedroom—or closet. She contends that not only is there an important theological element in the formation of heterosexual ideologies in the history of the churches, but that these contribute to the shaping of theological praxis in itself. While heterosexual ideologies go hand in hand with economic, political, and specific cultural understandings and interpretations that emphasize ethnicity or skin colors as limitations, queer theology consists of loosely connected alliances between sexual dissidents. For this very reason they are able to make space for new ideas and ways for us to relate to one another.[30] For Althaus-Reid, queer theology can therefore offer alternatives. Relations

---

27. Ibid., 34.
28. Ibid.
29. Althaus-Reid, "Queer I Stand," 106.
30. Ibid.

that build upon mutual understanding represent something new both for the church and in relation to God. They challenge hierarchical and autocratic ways of organizing people. On the basis of different theories of sexual knowledge, it is possible to look for new ways to understand not only what salvation and liberation can mean but also alternative church structures. She points out that feminist theologians have already discovered that desire, which is the material expression of longing, is a place from which to develop a bodily theology.[31]

The West beyond Chastity and Marriage

The West has, in practice, long accepted serial polygamy, that is, a series of monogamous relations that succeed each other. Lifelong heterosexual marriage is thereby being called into question by another practice, but also as an ideal. For a long time most Protestant churches have performed marriages and blessings for divorcees. Since 2009 homosexuals have been able to marry in Sweden, including in church. A powerful identification with marriage as the form for union, though not shared by everyone, was a recurrent feature of the debate that preceded this decision.[32] Jon Davies offers a summary of the framework for sexuality in the West that reveals its widening scope: "Virginity is no longer an issue. Heterosexuality has no monopoly. Marriage is on the way out. The divorce rate, which is at a historically high level, seems to be levelling off only because people no longer bother to get married. Marriage has lost both its sexual and procreational monopoly."[33] As well as becoming an object of desire for new groups, marriage has lost its status as a monopoly. Polyamorous and homoerotic relationships now take place in the open and demand respect. Heteronormativity has long been questioned by gender scholars and feminist theologians and more recently by queer theorists such as Marcella Althaus-Reid, Lisa Isherwood, and Gerald Loughlin.[34] Current practices and demands for different kinds of relationships are posing new challenges not only for a Roman Catholic sacramental view of marriage but also for a broad Lutheran tradition, modeled on Martin Luther and Katharina von Bora, that has focused on the family and mar-

---

31. Ibid., 108.
32. See Lindfelt and Gustafsson Lundberg, *Uppdrag samliv*.
33. Davies, "Sex These Days," 26.
34. Althaus-Reid and Isherwood, *The Sexual Theologian*.

riage. Although Jon Davies views the ideal of chastity as belonging to the past, some of the more influential movements in contemporary society are promoting virginity, chastity, and asceticism. Within each of these debates, then, new interpretations and renegotiations of relationships, eroticism, sexuality, and the body are taking place. It is, one might say, a clash between differing claims for the human body.

Ancient Truths Scrutinized Anew

Phenomenologists proceed from the body as a phenomenon. Historians have partly emphasized the body's importance within monastic piety, partly problematized the assumption that the Reformation entailed an improvement for all bodies, for example, for women and homosexuals. In other words, a number of the assumptions informing earlier Lutheran scholarship have been called into question.[35] As a result it has become urgent to ask new questions of Martin Luther, who is typically seen as one of the most important reformers and a giant of the European tradition. He was not alone, naturally, but part of a wider movement. His influence can be attributed, in part, to his prolific output.[36] The theological traditions with which he aligned himself, and which he was to lambaste, nonetheless indicate that in many regards he was daring to think in a new way.

Erotic spirituality, in which the relationship between God and the soul is described using images from the Song of Solomon, had a profound influence on Western Christianity via Origen and other early Church Fathers. Anders Nygren has described *eros* as a part of the Greek worldview, one that contrasted sharply with the Hebrew. According to Nygren, Luther revived this early Christian perspective by emphasizing *agape* and self-giving love. Nygren's habit of polarizing, as will be seen, has been the object of sharp criticism. The claim that abstracted conceptual figures can be treated as characteristic for entire intellectual traditions is regarded as essentialist and overly inflexible. Wingren was one of the first to identify the lack of history in this method.

Luther, too, made use of the erotic language in the Song of Solomon. He does so both when referring to the relation between Christ and the believer, and when referring to the relation between man and

---

35. Bynum, *Christian Materiality*; Roper, *The Holy Household*; Althaus-Reid, "Queer I Stand."

36. Stjerna, *Women and the Reformation*; Lindberg, *The European Reformations*.

woman, but also when discussing the relationship between a king and his people. He thus aligns himself with the bridal mystery. But he uses these metaphors in a new way. Unlike traditional *eros* spirituality, it is not the case that the soul, after various stages of longing and purification, finally achieves union with God. For Luther, the union of the marital bed takes place in an instant, in what is usually described as the blessed exchange.[37] As we saw in the previous chapter, the order is reversed so that it is the bridegroom, Christ, who seduces the bride—that is, the soul—not the other way around. Here and there Luther also juggles with metaphors of gender and expresses himself by means of a queer formulation—bride of Christ. He here invokes a set of terms that are prominent in the writings of Bernard.[38] Writing in the fifteenth-century, the female mystic Julian of Norwich also argued that God could equally well be described as a mother as a father, and that Jesus resembled a mother in his wisdom, tenderness, and love.[39] Luther can therefore be said both to build on and break with this tradition.

Eros and *Agape* Again

In the Lutheran tradition *agape* has been associated with Jesus's words on the Cross. Just as Jesus sacrificed his life on the cross, so should we in our everyday lives offer something of ourselves through self-giving love. In this context, *eros* theology becomes a challenge by calling into question the clear-cut opposition between different forms of love as well as between spiritual and material, man and woman. Seeing oneself as valuable has been particularly important for women. Whether one puts the emphasis on opposition or connection has implications not only for one's view of the body but also for the material in general, that is, land and sea, air and water. *Eros* theology here provides a resource by which to view the individual as part of all creation, without hierarchies or dualisms. This challenge has especially affected the opposition for which Anders Nygren became world-famous. Eros theology challenges, then, traditional Lutheran ethics, particularly those that have emphasized hierarchical, existing orders.

---

37. WA 7, 32; cf. LW 31, "Von der Freiheit" (1520).
38. Wiberg Pedersen, *Bernhard af Clairvaux*.
39. Bynum, *Jesus as Mother*.

Researchers from various camps have criticized Nygren's notion that cultures and motifs are essentialist and homogeneous and can be identified by their underlying forms. One early critic, as we have seen, was Gustaf Wingren.

Wingren, who was Nygren's favorite student, criticized his method for being unhistorical.[40] The concept of ideas being above history, as without history and reaching beyond their immediate context, was misleading. One might say that Nygren's method, in his exclusion of history, became disembodied, even though Nygren invoked the anti-gnostics' struggle for the body as God's creation and a part of creation. Moreover, Wingren argues that "if Luther, according to Nygren, represents the purest and clearest expression of the concept of *agape*, then it is nonetheless remarkable that the works of Luther are rife with contexts in which *nomos*, *eros*, and *agape* intertwine and are actually closely associated with one another."[41]

Wingren's critique was based on this perspective, a "systematic attack on the three most important theologians of the day: Anders Nygren, Karl Barth, and Rudolf Bultmann." Two basic motifs "stand in juxtaposition against this unconditional love: *nomos* (the law), which represents the legal piety of Judaism, and *eros* (desire), which represents the metaphysical longing and striving characteristic of Hellenism and later Catholicism."[42] To separate the motives was therefore not only unhistorical but also not in line with Luther.

At this point can be discerned a connecting link to contemporary *eros* theologians who have sought to examine *eros* as a resource, not a threat, and to yoke its power to curiosity, creativity, and the joy of discovery, indeed, to life itself.[43] American theologian Catherine Keller argues that different forms of love affect, shift, and interact with each other.[44]

In the following part of this chapter I analyze Anders Nygren's well-known opposition between different kinds of love. I then briefly consider the discussion of deification, *theosis*, and sanctification from the perspective of those scholars influenced by Tuomo Mannermaa who

---

40. Wingren, *Theology in Conflict*; Kristensson Uggla, *Becoming Human*, 53.
41. Kristensson Uggla, *Becoming Human*, 53.
42. Ibid.
43. See also chapter 8.
44. Keller, "Afterword: A Theology of Eros, After Transfiguring Passion."

are sometimes called the Finnish School; this is a theme to which I will return later in the book.

Nygren's Opposition between *Eros* and *Agape* Re-examined

When discussing the opposition between different forms of love, it is impossible to avoid returning to Anders Nygren and his world-famous study *Agape and Eros*.[45] In this book Nygren, more than anyone else, advocated an opposition between a pure, divine, and self-denying love, and a selfish love that serves itself. In *Agape and Eros* these two loves are contrasted with each other in a way that has been challenged by later scholars. Nonetheless, the book has influenced not only how we view love and the body but also the relationship between divine and human love. To this day many people read Luther in terms of Nygren's oppositional pairings.

The attempt to construct a system in which *eros* and *agape* stand as polar opposites is still being debated, and not only in Sweden.[46] *Agape* is represented as a comprehensive metaphor for the Christian notion of love throughout the ages. Self-denying love, which does not serve itself, is the emblem of God's love. In opposition to it stands *eros*, human love.

Nygren describes *agape* and *eros* as two opposed fundamental motives, one Platonic, and one Christian, belonging to "two entirely separate spiritual worlds" without "any direct correspondence and commensurability."[47] For Nygren, these "two independent historical conceptions"[48] are in constant opposition. Many have questioned Nygren's exclusive interpretation of *agape*.[49] Colin Grant, a close adherent of Nygren's theories, summarized these criticisms thus: "Pleasure, Plurality, and Patriarchy have caught up with the distinctive Christian understanding of love. Emphasis on the uniqueness of agape is questioned today because this understanding neglects more immediate physical, erotic love, obscures the mutual love of friendship, and perpetuates the male sense of

---

45. Nygren, *Agape and Eros*.
46. Parts of the following appeared in Gerle, "Mot ömsesidighetens."
47. Nygren, *Agape and Eros*, 30–31.
48. Ibid., 33.
49. D'Arcy, *The Mind and Heart of Love*; Outka, *Agape: An Ethical Analysis*; Heyward, *Touching Our Strength*, to mention but a few.

hierarchical superiority."⁵⁰ A reappraisal of these theories was begun by Paul Tillich and developed in a more sustained and constructive manner by several feminist theologians and philosophers. In the first volume of his *Systematic Theology* Tillich provides definitions of some of his key concepts. *Philia* is considered an expression for a movement in which like is drawn to like. Love such as *eros* is described as a movement from something that is inferior in power and meaning towards something that is higher.⁵¹ While *philia* and *eros* are both driven by longing and are dependent upon attraction and rejection, passion and sympathy, *agape* by contrast is unconditional and universal. *Agape* applies to everyone, while *philia* and *eros* are more limited and ambiguous.⁵² Although Tillich differentiates *agape* as something divine that supersedes other forms of love, he believes that it would be wrong to demonize any of the latter. "Lower" or "higher" forms of love, including *eros* and *agape*, can be seen as expressions of the same ontological "striving for union." Otherwise our love for God remains incomprehensible. If *eros* and *agape* cannot act together in people's lives, *agape* for God becomes impossible. Hence, Alexander C. Irwin claims that the project of reconciling *eros* and *agape* therefore becomes a priority for Tillich and something to which he continually returns.⁵³

American theologian Sallie McFague is one of many theologians who has further developed these concepts in order to move beyond the kind of polarization that characterizes Anders Nygren's work. As McFague observes, there is a long theological tradition that emphasizes that all of reality is connected, including God and the world.⁵⁴ This monistic tradition can be seen in the Gospel of John and has its roots in wisdom literature. A dualist mode of thought, by contrast, emphasizes the distance between God and the world that has been caused by sin. It views salvation theologically as redemption for humanity's insubordination, something that enables God and humanity to be reconciled. In monistic thought, salvation becomes more cosmological, a restoration of all reality to harmonious synergy.⁵⁵

50. Grant, "For the Love of God," 3.
51. Tillich, *Systematic Theology*, 1:280; cf. Irwin, *Eros Toward the World*, 8–9
52. Tillich, *Systematic Theology*, 1:280.
53. Irwin, *Eros Toward the World*, 10.
54. McFague, *Models of God*, 72, 93.
55. McFague finds this tradition in many theologians, such as Irenaeus, Augustine, Schleiermacher, Hegel, Teilhard de Chardin, Rahner, Tillich, process theologians, and

Dualism stresses the distance between God and humanity. Western thought is strongly characterized by dualism and has often portrayed salvation as if it were a matter of individuals being saved. A more monistic way of thinking entails the notion that the power that gives us life, our existence, loves us and the world "deeply and passionately, by the power whose love pulses through the universe."[56] In accordance with Paul Tillich's precept that the foundation of being is maternal love, which both gives life to everything and strives for reunion, *agape* love here acquires a second, more reciprocal, meaning. As will be seen, similar ideas can be discerned in Luther's writings.

Anti-modernism and the Logic of Oppositions

Nygren was an early representative of what we would today describe as anti-modernism. In contrast to liberal theology's efforts to find something in common with the culture around it, Nygren sought out what was uniquely Christian. The self-giving love that was incarnated in Jesus and that led to the Cross and the Resurrection became the litmus test for what was genuinely Christian. This was regarded as radically different to the efforts of the surrounding culture. *Agape* was placed in opposition to, or rather above, *eros*. Nygren aligned himself with the early church's struggle against gnosticism and its *eros* thinking. Humanity's striving and longing for the divine was unimportant. The key thing was God's activity and self-giving love. Incarnation, the belief that God became body and human flesh, became a line of demarcation against the liberal theology of the day. For Nygren, the shocking element of the Christian message was essential. He strongly emphasized belief in bodily resurrection and showed a special liking for the expression *resurrection of the flesh*. The metaphor of the grain of wheat that dies, like belief in bodily resurrection, were things liberal theology had difficulty accepting. It can thus be read as a reaction to contemporary liberal theology, which chose to downplay the shocking element in the Christian message. It has sometimes been claimed that Karl Barth and neo-orthodoxy found it difficult to gain ground in Sweden because Nygren had already drawn up a battle line against liberal theology. In the realm of ideas he sought to establish a protected zone for theology, clearly distinct from the social

---

some feminist theologians (ibid., 93).

56. Ibid., 144.

sciences. Catharina Stenqvist points out that Nygren eventually aligned himself with Wittgenstein's later theories on different language games. These ideas gave him the tools with which to differentiate between his roles as philosopher and theologian and to defend radical particularity, a strand of Lund School theology carried on within the framework of Luther scholarship.[57]

Although Nygren's defense of the idea of Christian love was triggered by his perception of liberal theology as a threat, his own theology meant that he also limited himself in a number of regards. The polarization of *eros* and *agape* rejected human striving as expressed in all other religions, but also the *eros* thinking that had, via Augustine, become part of Roman Catholic theology. The idea of *agape* as a "pure" Christian love was revived, according to Nygren, by Martin Luther. As with identity politics in later eras, his point of departure was a need to defend his own tradition.[58]

Nygren's interpretation of *eros* and *agape* plays upon the powerful oppositions between divine/human, self-giving/self-seeking, and active/passive. The consequence is that *agape*—that is, the divine, self-giving, and active—is assigned all value, while that which lies on the other side, *eros* and human striving, becomes classified as passive and as something that derives its value from God. At best, it can be receptive.

Casting the relationship between God and humanity in terms of domination and subordination may be part of our wonder at creation, in which the Creator is seen as greater, superior, and radically different to the created. Hierarchical thinking may, however, emphasize distance instead of mutual dependence, proximity, and pleasurable communion. Piety risks becoming synonymous with fear of the Almighty instead of that wonder which is conveyed by the English word *awe*. This has long been the case in the Lutheran tradition, too, not least for the masses. The link between a demanding God and the authority of the state was embodied in the church's controlling function. In Sweden, for example, catechistic knowledge, church attendance, and the taking of communion were preconditions for being considered a full citizen well into the twentieth century. Piety in the form of wonder at the grandeur of life and creation had to exist alongside the church of a uniform society.

57. Stenqvist, "Nygrens dilemma," 123–34.
58. A big difference is, however, that Lutheran theology had been hegemonic in Scandinavia but began to be questioned in Nygren's time. Other movements based on identities such as black, queer, or women emerged from below.

The distancing and separation of God and humanity, in which God was represented as a severe master and humanity as an obedient servant, affected both women and men. For some men, however, it was possible to identify oneself with a role in which God was viewed as a patron or as a father.

The polarized schema used by Nygren fits a patriarchal pattern: it is not gender neutral. The human qualities of being passive or of primarily seeking privacy have traditionally been ascribed to women. Men have been represented as more capable of using reason to see beyond their own interests and passions and to identify an altruistic and common good.[59] A number of subtly gendered factors warrant consideration here. Even if they were not intentional, and possibly even wholly unconscious, it is perhaps no coincidence that it has often been men in powerful positions who have discussed *agape* while expecting women, children, and less powerful men to enact it in self-denying fashion.[60]

For Nygren, everything attributed to human beings loses its intrinsic value since the latter are contrasted with God, upon whom all value is conferred. This polarization ensures that the hierarchical relationship between God and humanity becomes dominant. Rather than discussing human beings' similarity to God or what it is that unites them, Nygren chooses that which differentiates them.[61] Since Nygren goes on to reject all efforts from below in favor of self-giving from above, the consequences for the human, and particularly "the feminine," are severe.[62] In Nygren's account, the Song of Solomon's erotic poetry about the amorous encounter between woman and man, which has also been interpreted metaphorically as love between God and humanity, feels very distant.

The Asymmetry of Patriarchy and Paternalism

Itemizing differences is often accompanied by ranking. Continual calling attention to difference can therefore also become part of the logic of difference that ensures the devaluing of what the Other represents.

---

59. See, for example, Pateman, *The Disorder of Women*.

60. In her book *Luthersk kallelse* Nahnfeldt shows how vocation has been interpreted and misused.

61. See Nygren, *Agape and Eros*, 402.

62. For me, the concepts of female and male have nothing to do with essentialist views about something being naturally female or male. For the most part, I consider female or male attributes to be socially and historically constructed.

When diversity gives way to the identification of differences, and polarity is presented as something stable and biologically grounded, there almost always emerge hierarchies, whether of skin color, ethnicity, or gender.

In our era and our cultural sphere, hierarchical thinking about domination and subordination has lost the positive valuation it once had. Emergent democratic movements question not only the King of God's grace but also the static relations of domination and subordination between human beings. The concept of the autonomous, self-governing citizen replaced the view of human beings as obedient subjects. This notion of equality had a profound influence. Contract ethicists imagined the social body as a union of free contract-forming citizens. The fact that such free citizens were, in practice, invariably men became increasingly apparent.

In our time the notion of equality that underpins contractualism has thus been subjected to scathing criticism. It has not done justice to the diversity among people and their real differences. Enlightenment philosophy's belief in people's sameness evolved into the demand that everyone in the entire world be like people in the West. The white man, who controlled everything with his brain, became an ideal to which everyone, including women, should aspire.

Foregrounding disparity and difference has therefore become a way to clarify that equal worth included diversity and multiplicity. And yet there is a risk that this emphasis upon asymmetry, difference, and diversity may help to confer legitimacy upon the increasingly brutal differences in the relations to power, influence, status, and money that are part of the world of late capitalism. Any discussion of asymmetry and difference that does not also discuss the difference that emerges from inequity, among groups and within groups, will easily become a way to disguise injustice. Just as the notion of race has been used to single out an array of different "races" while whiteness and its ties to power have remained invisible, so, too, does our era's focus upon ethnicity run the risk of cloaking that which is presented as "the normal"—that is, Western or white. "Normal" thereby imperceptibly becomes *normalizing*.

In Anders Nygren's writings, God is presented as radically independent and exalted. God does not need humanity, it is humanity that needs God. It is in this way that many men, though far from all, in the history of the church have chosen to represent God, as independent in his autonomous glory. They thereby create for themselves an ideal image through which they can deny their dependence upon other human beings. Just as the relation between woman and man is in danger of being objectified and becoming manipulative, so, too, is there a corresponding danger for the relationship between God and humanity. When independence is emphasized, there emerges a problematic perspective on both God and man.[63]

The Hebrew texts are characterized by very different images of God. The exegete Fredrik Lindström claims that "the God we encounter in *most* Bible texts is not all-powerful, omniscient, omnipresent, unchanging, exalted above pain and suffering, and so forth."[64] Images of the divine such as these, which often stress unchangeability and independence, are rather the result of theologians having applied concepts such as *apatheia*—that is, exaltation above pain and suffering—to the Bible texts. These contexts have been developed within Greek philosophical metaphysics and are a poor description of the Bible's dynamic image of the divine. In the latter, God's perfection inheres in his capacity to change in accordance with the divine plan and in relation to a changing world, rather than in unchangeableness and *apatheia*.

Nygren's emphasis on *agape* and divine love has not only resulted in humanity being described as without value. It also has consequences for ethics. No one but God can love in the right way. And when God loves human beings, it is not because the latter is valuable but in spite of the fact that they are not. This attitude risks making ethics, and relations between people, more passive. If love cannot find nourishment in desire, longing, and feeling for the other, it risks becoming weak and spiritually impoverished. In this event love will not be seen in relation to friendship, in which one looks for the other as such and acts on the other's behalf.

When transcendence becomes the principal thing, there is a danger of the concrete individual disappearing. He or she is, strictly speaking, no longer needed. Not for God, at least. The passionately adoring, even jealous, divine image that is a feature of the Yahwistic tradition, which is carried on by Christians as part of their Hebrew inheritance, is replaced with an exalted, Platonic, divine image. God needs no one.[65] It is an im-

---

63. Stenqvist, "Nygrens dilemma," 123, 134, shows the difference between Nygren the philosopher and Nygren the theologian. His philosophical thinking is not allowed to influence his own subject, its psychology and historicity, while faith is situated in both. He thereby keeps science and faith apart.

64. F. Lindström, "Guds långa näsa."

65. The dualism between Platonic and Hebrew that I am suggesting here is not significantly connected to notions such as giving or being. While Jean-Luc Marion

age seemingly shaped by the masculine dream of autonomy. The dream of an idol takes over, a powerful self-portrait in which vulnerability has been suppressed.

This image differs markedly from the Hebrew prophets' view of life. Hosea's God, who never stops loving his unfaithful wife, is a vulnerable God. Perhaps also oppressive, like someone who refuses to let go. But not independent! And Hosea's image of God as loving someone who is continually unfaithful is something to which Martin Luther repeatedly returns.[66]

In Nygren's thought, separateness serves to conceal this image of God as vulnerable. Reciprocity in the form of giving and taking thereby becomes more difficult. For this reason I regard it as important to foreground more of the biblical, dynamic, passionate, and tender qualities in God. *Eros*, *agape*, and *philia* can then be seen in an interaction that emphasizes reciprocity and a striving for equitable relations instead of patriarchal asymmetry. It is not a matter of either/or but of a more productive interplay. Such a theology has implications for how we view humanity and ethics, and reaches in the direction of a theology of mutuality that encompasses all living things.

Anders Nygren makes a point of the fact that divine *agape* love is extended towards that which has no value. Paul Tillich emphasizes that *eros* seeks union with something that is a bearer of values because of the values embodied by that person, object, group, or idea.[67] At the same time, Tillich contends that "Agape unites the lover and the beloved because of the image of fulfilment which God has of both."[68] *Eros* and *agape* meet. We love the other person in God by means of the love that God evokes in us. *Agape* is here described as "a type of love which seeks the other because of the ultimate unity of being with being within the divine ground," not presented against a backdrop of the yawning gap between divine and human, as Nygren has it.[69] McFague interprets *agape* as the life-giving power of creation in a mother or father who loves their creation and

---

has tried to describe God in terms of giving and *agape* rather than being, in order to get away from the dualism between Hellenistic and Hebrew, my aim is rather to escape a purely vertical view on the giving of God that excludes any human activity and response. See also Webb, *The Gifting of God*.

66. WA 7, 26, 4-12; 7, 55, 25-7; cf. LW 31 "Von der Freiheit" (1520).
67. Irwin, *Eros Toward the World*, 6.
68. Tillich, *Systematic Theology*, 1:280; cf. Irwin, *Eros Toward the World*, 6.
69. Tillich, *Systematic Theology*, 1:280-81.

seeks to be united with it. Instead of emphasizing the unjustified, unselfish, and independent in God, McFague makes possible an interpretation of *agape* as mutual love and a desire for wholeness. This may be a way to dissolve the rigid opposition between *eros* and *agape*.

Power as Sharing

When the boundaries between different forms of love are relaxed, love does not become a one-way mode of communication. It becomes relational, reciprocal. For the interpretations I have just outlined, this is an important step towards liberating love from the negative dimensions of power. Mutual love means that neither partner can hold the other in their grasp and assert an advantage by invoking their "stronger" or "purer" love. Power is instead shared, relational. Love is not exploited in order to maintain the subordination of women. Nor is woman given the opportunity to keep men and children close through feelings of guilt. My vision is to free *agape* both from unnecessary domination and subjugation and from the distancing of God from humanity, and humans from each other, in order to avoid oppression and deadlock and to enable new dynamics.

Reciprocity is, in fact, more than strict justice or similarity within a concretizing mode of thought. *Eros* is not static but a relational movement, a way to share power in such a way that everyone who enters into a relation is emboldened to gradually become the person they really are—a whole person.[70] When reciprocity permeates relations, women will be able to see other women as human beings worthy of respect and allow themselves to be inspired by them. Men will be able to look up to women, and vice versa, in a dynamic profusion.

Reciprocity between God and humanity is also very remote from the logic of exchange that often constructs self-evident norms in our own era. It is, rather, a question of a relationship characterized by giving. In my view, a theology of reciprocity that views even *eros* and *philia* as divine forces will be capable of interpreting the superabundance, giving, and experience of love as something that unites God and humanity. Instead of the great distance between God's love and human love that is a defining feature of Nygren's thought, the relationship between God and humanity can be defined by that which unites and binds them together. There is also space for humanity's love for God to be something more

---

70. Irwin, *Eros Toward the World*, 191.

than a dutiful response. Love for God and love for one's fellow human and all creation belong together.

Agape, Eros, and Philia

In Sallie McFague's figurative terminology, different forms of love denote different ethical dimensions, such as justice (*agape*), healing (*eros*), and companionship (*philia*). For a theology of reciprocity, justice entails a questioning of the various forms of subordination theology that are to be found in the history of the church.

Finding a theology that does not polarize *eros* and *agape* is one phase in the work of justice and healing. If agape leads to reciprocity and justice between different kinds of people in the world, then *eros* presents itself as an impassioned striving for healing in the world. It is a longing that draws strength from the conviction that God created a world that is good, with an abundance of different kinds of people interacting with each other. In this *eros*, a longing for healing, there is an intuitive sense that all of creation is living in the "hope that the creation itself will be liberated from its bondage to decay" (Rom 8:20–21).

Philia encourages and allows us to sense God's presence at our side, like a friend who challenges and invites us to be God's collaborator and co-creator. In each of these three forms of love, the boundary between the immanent and the transcendent is dissolved. In love, God, who beyond all conception and any words loves this material world, can be apprehended as concrete and present. A longing for infinity does not preclude interaction with the other as a concrete fellow human being, near and tangible. The infinity contained within every person, as an image of the divine, makes it even more important to meet him or her as a concrete person, here and now, in reciprocity.

Without entirely accepting Origen's Platonic apparatus of stages, hierarchies, and different levels between the orders of angels, humans, and demons, it is reasonable to criticize Nygren's project of differentiation. As a number of scholars have shown, separateness is often gendered.[71] Where the boundary for Nygren runs between *eros* and *agape*, Kant distinguishes between the rational, which for him is masculine, and the

---

71. Hirdman, *Genus*; cf. Gerle, "Mot ömsesidighetens."

passionate, which is associated with desire, and with women and people of color.[72]

Church historian Samuel Rubenson argues that Anders Nygren found *eros* difficult, not merely because he saw it as the opposite of *agape* but because he had difficulty in affirming qualities common to all humanity, indeed, even the notion that human beings were created in God's image.[73] In Greek, he argues, *agape* is a weaker word for love, however. It roughly means appreciate, prefer. But when Jewish scholars translated the Old Testament, they avoided the term *eros* because it was the name of one of the Greek gods.[74] For Nygren, however, *eros* came to represent humanity's striving for God, while agape represented God's self-giving love.

Today there are grounds for reading Luther in a way that takes on board this critique of Nygren, rather than reading Luther and the Protestant tradition from Nygren's perspective.[75] Unlike Nygren, Luther had no difficulty in connecting with qualities common to all humanity. Theologian Werner Jeanrond is right that when Protestant theologians have defended *agape* love, it has been as a defense against people's claim to be able to approach God by means of their own will or by following their own wishes and desires. Jeanrond sees this as an important aspect of the critique of "mystics in all traditions for their longing to achieve a union or affinity with the divine in mutual love."[76] But, as we saw in chapter 6, there are also strong elements of mysticism in Luther. However, Luther views communion with God, union, not as the result of one's own efforts, but as a gift. Whether human beings' capacity to love is a part of the gift of creation is a question to which we will return. The notion that the love we give to our fellows is unaffected or unsullied by what is human accords badly with the imagery used by Luther.

My background survey of twentieth-century Lutheran theology has focused on Nygren, Wingren, and Tillich. Today, there are many who would associate themselves with what is somewhat simplistically called the Finnish School. In the following section, I briefly consider these

---

72. Schott, *Feminist Interpretations of Immanuel Kant*; Shell, *The Embodiment of Reason*.

73. Rubenson, "Himmelsk åtrå," 590.

74. Ibid., 589. Louth also claims that *eros* and *agape* are basically the same word (*Origins of the Christian Mystical Tradition*, 65).

75. Jeanrond's reading of Luther's view on love also seems to have been influenced by Nygren. See, e.g., Jeanrond, "Kärlekens praxis," 230.

76. Ibid.

Finnish reinterpretations in the wake of Mannermaa. Where Gustaf Wingren and Sallie McFague in their different ways foreground how God works through people, Mannermaa inquires into the nature of divine union and deification or *theosis*. The issue thereby once again becomes more narrowly focused on Christ.

Finnish Interpretations of *Theosis*

The issue of whether humans can become deified is a sensitive one for many Lutheran theologians who wish to uphold the idea of humanity receiving God's love through grace. Tuomo Mannermaa has another point of departure, which may have something to do with the ecumenical dialogue with the orthodox in Finland. He seeks to show that Christ truly is and must be present in the believer. This becomes an objection to the view of justification as purely forensic, as an outward absolution. When believers receive justification by faith, it also includes their reception of God's sanctity.[77]

Luther often holds up Christ as an everyday example, inspiration, and model. But there is only one Christ, growls Luther. He thereby criticizes the claim made by popes and bishops that they were Christ's representatives.[78] Popes and bishops cannot assume the bridegroom's role as Christ any more than other men can.

Christ, his life and service, are to be seen as models, particularly in everyday life. For Luther, however, being a Christ to one's fellow human beings means, not taking Christ's place, but, rather, giving comfort and support in precisely the way Christ did—as a fellow human being. This is not a matter of identification but of an intimate and close relation to Christ, who provides the strength to be a human being in everyday life. For Luther, Christ is a model, naturally, but above all a gift.

But does justification by faith as a gift lead to a permanent sanctification or should it rather be seen as a point of contact that in every instant of proximity creates union? A strictly forensic view would argue that justification is exclusively a question of an outward absolution of guilt. This would in turn lead to freedom with regard to God, thereby

77. See, for example, Jocic, "Tron är aldrig allena," 16–17.

78. In a sermon on the Gospel of John, Luther says, "In their writings the popes claimed that they were bridegrooms of the Christian Church and that the bishops were the bridegrooms of their dioceses. In reality, they were panders!" Cf. Kleinhans, "Christ as Bride/Groom," 130.

releasing energy to be used for one's fellow humans. However, Mannermaa and his followers adhere more closely to the idea of a divine presence that extends everywhere. Gustaf Wingren would sometimes refer to divine presence as infectious.

Luther opposed the notion that grace infuses an extra dimension into people. He firmly rejects the idea, also found in Roman theology, of an additional, permanent nature. People cannot be anything other than people. Yet they are summoned to be exactly that, people, to restore their humanity. This means that we are summoned to become like Christ, *simultudo*. Luther sees Christ, in other words, as the perfect human being. He is described as the second Adam, someone without sin. At the same time, Adam is the name for a human being or, more precisely, an earthly being.[79] To become like Christ, then, means quite simply becoming human. It is about returning to health. In the tradition deriving from Irenaeus, this is called *recapitulatio*, restoration and growth.

Before God, says Luther, we cannot itemize our merits. But divine proximity is infectious and changes us, body and soul. "Faith creates godliness, not in God's own substance, but in us."[80] This influence is also physical, he argues. More than just an aspect of the verbal, the Holy Spirit changes flesh, the body's limbs and senses. These changes introduce a new sense, a new will, new senses, and new physical actions.[81] Loving God, according to the Finnish theologian Anttila, does not mean abandoning lower things to strive towards God above. By contrast, Anttila claims that "loving God means to receive God's endless and continuous goodness in the visible world. To love the creation does not obstruct but advance the love of God, because the creation reveals the essence of God as self-giving love."[82] This new creation, as I see it, has very little to do with the old catalogues of sins, or with being reborn, but rather with a new framework, a new interpretation of life that ever and anew disrupts our self-absorption. It is about a transforming embrace.

---

79. Trible, *God and the Rhetoric of Sexuality*, 90. Luther, WA 40 I, 360:24–25, cf. LW 26, 1–461, "In Epistolam S. Pauli ad Galatas Commentarius" (1531–35).

80. Ibid. (my translation).

81. Luther, WA 40 I, 178–79, cf. LW 26, 1–461, "In Epistolam S. Pauli ad Galatas Commentarius" (1531–35).

82. Anttila, "Innocent Pleasure," 161. He also comments in footnote 612, "*Forma* in Luther and in medieval philosophy is the 'actual reality' of a thing, opposed to its *materia*. Thus, when Luther calls the righteousness of faith *formalis iustitia*, it does not mean 'formal' but 'real' righteousness." Cf. Mannermaa, *Christ Present in Faith*, 23–30.

The Christ Mystery Directs Our Gaze upon the Gifts of Creation and Re-establishes Desire

Luther's Christ mystery reveals a way beyond the two alternatives of seeing justification as purely forensic—an outward absolution—or as receiving the sanctity of God that deifies. Everyday life is not merely subject to laws and constraints but can also be interpreted as desire and play. In his Large Catechism, Luther describes this as if the heart could dance and overflow: "Should a heart not dance and overflow with joy as it goes about its work, doing what it has been enjoined, such that it might be said: Look, this is better than all holiness of the Cartusian monks, even if they fast until death and pray uninterruptedly on their knees."[83] For Luther, the connection between prayer and work, or the certainty of vocation, gave meaning and joy to everyday drudgery.[84] The monastic orders' motto *ora et labora* also held true for the laity. The curse of work that is described in Genesis 3 as a consequence of the Fall is lifted by Christ and his deed of atonement. When Adam and Eve planted and tended the Garden of Eden, it was free and without pressure. It was not intended as a way to become righteous before God, argues Luther in his 1520 treatise *On the Freedom of a Christian*.[85] The paradox is that human beings are both free and enslaved. Before God, humans are free. At the same time, they are tied to their fellow humans. All of the commandments presuppose freedom and liberation: "Only people who are free can bind themselves with responsibility towards other people. The enslaved person is not free to serve."[86]

Joy at being freed releases energy and desire. The bridal mystery's role-reversal and emphasis upon unity and affinity in a playful, pleasurable dance is an inspiration for everyday, physical life. Amid the drudgery and ambiguity can be glimpsed the harmonious state that, argued Luther, had existed before the Fall. Adam and Eve had worked as if in a dance, playfully working and loving each other as free people. Righteousness was not a static state to enter into, however, but something that was continually given anew, in the embrace.[87]

---

83. WA 30 I, 149, "Deutsch Cathechismus" (1529).

84. Stolt, *Luther själv*, 35. See also Wingren, *Luther frigiven*.

85. WA 7, 12–38; cf. LW 31, "Von der Freiheit" (1520).

86. Brandby-Cöster, "Sökvägar och ledtrådar," 60–61.

87. Other classical metaphors for this are to die every day and to be resurrected in baptism. Just as we need additional showers, the old human being needs constantly

Luther's metaphors for describing the love between Christ and the believer do not present this relationship as one-sided, either. Christ is presented by turns as pursuing and pursued. According to one of Luther's sermons on the Gospel of John, there can be no union between bride and bridegroom without the response of both. Reciprocity and trust are necessary for the relationship.[88]

The devotion and reciprocity that characterize the relationship between Christ and the believer reappear when Luther describes the good relationship between husband and wife in his 1531 wedding sermon.[89]

As already noted in chapter 4, the formulations used by Luther in his wedding sermon to describe the trust and affinity between spouses are almost linguistically identical to those used by Bernard of Clairvaux with regard to Christ and the soul. I contend that he thereby removes the clear distinctions between what applies *coram Deo* and *coram mundo* or *coram hominibus*. Luther stressed that human righteousness is insufficient for God. At that point human beings need to be arrayed in divine grace. In the earthly sphere, by contrast, human beings can perform both just and good deeds within what is known as civic justice, *iustitia civilis*. When these fail, they seek recourse in Christ's mercy. The distinction between what is required for God and for this world was important in order to affirm the idea that salvation is a gift and not the result of human efforts or merits. But Christ's love also opens the door to a worldly vocation, *coram mundo*, and a relationship to one's fellow human being, *coram hominibus*. *Eros* theology's emphasis upon vulnerability, reciprocity, and longing as key elements in both divine and human love can here be seen as an important component in a Lutheran argument. The traditional opposition between *eros* and *agape* is challenged. Images of a vulnerable God can enable new ideals for both women and men. It is a question of reconciling the principal narratives.

Incorporeal Lutheranism or an Unambiguously Ordinary Body

Here and there we catch glimpses of Lutheran ideas as part of a hidden cultural heritage. But where is the body? Bodily, physical expressions of

---

to be renewed, cleansed and restored.

88. See chapter 6.

89. WA 34 I, 52:5–9, "Eine Hochzeitpredigt" (Sermon on a Marriage) (1531).

faith have become so familiar that they are hardly noticed. Many theologians today claim that what is Lutheran has been rendered invisible by emphasizing commonalities. One might reverse this claim, however, and echo Gustaf Wingren's claim that a relation to God comes with life itself. In trying to emphasize that what is specifically Christian is radically different, one naturally looks for its distinguishing features. So, too, did Nygren and many in his wake. It is unquestionably the case that when belief in God comes to be regarded as a special interest, it becomes more difficult to sustain belief in life as created and good, as always threatened by death and destruction yet continually preserved. Ola Sigurdson argues that this process of rendering invisible has been strengthened by the way in which the religious has come to be seen as something private. The worldly and the spiritual, like the public and the private, have been counterposed to each other. Faith is separated from politics, just as "rationality and feeling, activity and passivity, soul and body, masculinity and femininity" are set against each other.[90]

Moreover, the Lutheran tradition is often said to have emphasized an inner closeness to God, one connected to experiences in one's heart and thoughts in one's brain. In the Orthodox and Roman-Catholic churches, the faithful kiss icons, images of saints, and statues; they light candles and incense, genuflect, make the sign of the cross, and dip their fingers in holy water when entering the church. In an evangelical-Lutheran church one might conceivably slip in and light a candle, listen to a choral or organ concert, take part in a service. Is religiosity incorporeal, then? Many people would like to see more ritual, more bodily expressions.

However, my view is that many bodily expressions of faith, responsibility, and community in the social body have their roots in Lutheran concepts and that they represent the everyday body as I have here been discussing it. But we do not associate it with a religious interpretation of life since the religious part has been stripped away. At the same time as we develop rituals, it is important not to close our eyes to this. Perhaps it is a matter of cultural blindness. A Lutheran legacy in Reformed areas has affected the organization of society, not least its educational institutions. The focus on universal literacy was a contribution from the Reformation as was the notion of equality before God. Then as now, theological thinking and church praxis connected with philosophical, cultural, and scientific discussions.

90. Sigurdson, "Kristna kroppar," 353.

Traditions encompass narratives, customs, rites, texts, and values, conscious and unconscious, which form into clusters. Making visible the different components in this cluster involves making a valuation. Some parts are affirmed, while others move steadily toward the periphery, perhaps to be ultimately rejected.

In many countries churches are highly visible. In architecture the church lives and has a powerful physical presence. Whether it also lives in people's hearts and acts is harder to determine. But lighting candles, listening to music, singing, playing, and taking in words of justice is considerably more physical and sensual than we sometimes imagine. Skin, eyes, ears are involved. What is more, Lutheran spirituality gains hope from an interpretation of life that helps people to see things they encounter in their everyday lives as a divine greeting. Things such as the gaze of friendship, a hand stroking a cheek, the longing and meeting in love. Yet in life they also meet destruction, everything that breaks down friendship, love, trust, and relationships. *Philia*, *eros*, and *agape* are threatened by obstructive desire, by fear and greed, and fixation upon what is one's own. For this reason, according to Lutheran ethics, we need the law, *nomos*, to protect and foster the good. These different concepts, which for far too long have been contrasted with each other, can also be interpreted as a pleasurable dance for protecting life and opening the way to health.

If the everyday body is made visible by this theological interpretation, the expression of faith and trust through bodies becomes considerably more present, spiritually and bodily. This is the indispensible insight provided by Scandinavian creation theology.

The early secularization theorists argued that religion would become increasingly private and invisible. Their predictions have not come to pass, however. Across the world, religion is becoming increasingly visible in the public sphere. It is thus no coincidence that these theories have been revised.[91] But it is not always in specifically religious terms that faith and trust find expression. Sometimes it serves to drive people against one another. From the perspective of creation theology, it is important to make visible not just specifically religious actions but those common to all human beings, which express and create faith and trust.

The longing for work and context, somewhere I belong, is connected both to *eros* and *agape*. *Eros* then becomes a longing for community, and *agape* a wish to live in solidarity with others. Both these forms of

---

91. See, e.g., Casanova, "Religion, Politics and Gender Equality."

love are threatened by an atomizing individualism that looks to its own interest alone.[92] Luther would have spoken of people as absorbed with themselves. That this creates anxiety was for him self-evident. Today this is something many psychologists encounter in their conversations with children and young people.

From Burden to Pleasurable Dance

In this chapter I have partly foregrounded the everyday body and life as it is given, something Scandinavian creation theology has particularly underscored, partly made a critical examination of the polarizing of different forms of love. In the next chapter I will present what is called *eros* theology. This theological direction strives to talk about love in a new way, without sharp oppositions. *Eros* is seen as a creative force.

In this language there may also be points of overlap with Luther's affective qualities. For Luther, ethics do not emerge from new knowledge or via intellectual speculation. It is a matter of freedom, a freedom that comes from the experience of love. Like music entering the body and doing something to it, the experience of love involves a transformation. The embrace creates something fresh and new.

Instead of seeing lust, or desire, as a burden, *eros* theology affirms lust, desire, and passion as a longing for life, healing, and justice.

---

92. See, e.g., Bauman, *Community*.

8

Eros Theology Challenges Traditional Lutheran Binary Opposites

A number of contemporary theologians have emphasized the concept of love as a fundamental driving force for human beings and for the universe. They argue that something has gone wrong in traditional theology, which has often described human sexual desire as something negative and menacing, closely associated with sin.[1] Instead, they wish to describe sexual desire as a "redemptive force connected to the enlivening and enlightening experience of grace."[2] F. LeRon Shults notes that most people do not see theology as something seductive. Rather, theology is associated with an ostensibly blatant obsession with regulating. Sexual desire then appears as something that should be suppressed, restricted, and controlled.[3] The introduction to *Saving Desire* describes a project that instead seeks to rescue the concept of sexual desire "from its imprisonment within repressive, individualistic, and rationalistic categories as well as emphasizing the power of the phenomenon of desire for engendering human flourishing in relation to God."[4] The theologians present themselves by claiming that they are united by a passion for pursuing theology. They see theological research as "powerfully and positively seductive—even erotic."[5] Shults states that "experiences of seduction feel

1. Shults, "Introduction: Saving Desire?," vii.
2. Ibid.
3. Ibid.
4. Ibid.
5. Ibid.

dangerous as well as delightful." He holds that "attending to desire—even in academic contexts—intensifies both our fear of vulnerability and our hope for intimacy."[6] He continues: "Theology is interested in the origin, condition, and goal of desiring, in the infinite ground of the human experience of being-interested. What could be more interesting than tending to that ultimate reality in which all things live and move and have their attraction?"[7]

Several chapters in this book have dealt with the erotic language of the marital mystery. For Luther, as an Augustinian monk, this was well known. He continued to make use of this language but, as we have seen, in new contexts. He stressed that love was an embrace that creates something new in the present moment. In accordance with the language of mysticism, he also used gender-transgressing metaphors, such as that the bride and bridegroom alternately seduce each other. Yet not even in these contexts did he refer specifically to *eros*. Does this mean that he had no understanding of *eros* as a creative force? Or did he just use other terms? In this chapter I wish to describe some of the fundamental concepts in *eros* theology and discuss them in relation to Luther and Lutheran theology.

Eros as the Original Force of Creation

I have certain themes in mind when using the term *eros theology* in this study, such as viewing *eros* as a driving force that in its longing, curiosity, and desire for the other creates relations and contexts. Freud described *eros* as a creative force that establishes "ever greater entities."[8] He defines *eros* as the unifying force that preserves all life.[9] This notion, which Herbert Marcuse develops in his civilizational critique *Eros and Civilization*, resurfaces in the work of theologians such as Rita Nakashima Brock and Catherine Keller. In Christian theology the theme is bound up with the idea of God's assumption of human form—incarnation. As Jan-Olav Henriksen observes, this is also a question of taking seriously the fact that we as human beings are firmly grounded in our "incarnal mode of

---

6. Ibid.
7. Ibid.
8. Freud, *Outline of Psychoanalysis*, 26.
9. Freud, *Ego and the Id*, 88; Freud, *Civilization and Its Discontents*, 102.

being" and are thus carnal beings.[10] My own view is that *eros* theology's goal of creating new visions of social life in both the smaller and the larger world, by drawing on theories of vulnerability, relationality, and longing, makes a constructive contribution. *Eros* theologians are united by their efforts to emphasize the positive aspect of desire. While desire in Christian theology often has been connected with "lack, deficiency, loss, transgression, and guilt," many people want to "stress its potential relation to fullness, being, gift, creativity, and joy."[11] In dialogue with Luther and his texts, they form both a contrast and a challenge.

In this chapter, I intend to allow contemporary theological voices to be heard alongside Luther's. By adopting the perspective of *eros* theology on questions of social life, sensuality, eroticism, and politics, I want to get closer to Luther's underlying thinking. My aim is to investigate whether this encounter with contemporary *eros* theology can make a contribution to the issue of how we can live as spiritual, bodily, sexual beings in a politically responsible fashion. This working method is inspired by my conviction that historicity and context are indispensable components of all interpretation.

Relation and Curiosity Instead of Opposites or Similarity

In the present era, then, *eros* theology has emphasized *eros* as longing, sexual desire, and curiosity towards the other. The keywords are relation and reciprocity, not just between God and humanity and between human beings, but also in relation to the cosmos. *Eros* theology has underscored not only human beings' longing for the other, for transcendence, for God, but also God's longing for humanity. Relation is one of the keywords.[12]

Erotic feeling means that relations transcend the binary of hetero/homosexuality as well as the idea that relation equals identity, as here given poetic formulation by the American feminist theologian Carter Heyward:

> In the beginning is the relation, not sameness. In the beginning is tension and turbulence, not easy peace. In the beginning, our erotic power moves us to touch, not to take over; transform,

---

10. Henriksen, "Desire," 5.
11. Shults, "Introduction: Saving Desire?," viii.
12. See, for example, Heyward, *Saving Jesus*; R. N. Brock, *Journeys by Heart*; Camnerin, *Försoningens mellanrum*.

not subsume. We are empowered by a longing not to blur the contours of differences, but rather to reach through the particularities of who we are toward our common strength, our shared vulnerability, and our relational pleasure.[13]

Heyward emphasizes turbulence and the longing to touch without taking over or assuming possession of. In turn, Graham Ward points to the boundlessness of eroticism, arguing that the erotic is immense in relation to sexuality. This gives an intimation of its relatedness to God's *caritas*, which is God's own activity:

> It is not that our longing to understand Jesus Christ, to embrace and be embraced by that body which is given so completely for us, negates the sexual. The sexual is the very mark of embodiment itself; a mode of intense relation such that the body experiences itself as such. But desire reorders the sexual as a deeper mystery of embodiment unfolds. Divine embodiment moves us to affirm our own embodiment in a new way—as a temple of the Spirit to use the Pauline term, as holy, as graced, as transcending our understanding. The gendered relations as set up by the erotic affectivity within which the enquiry into the body of Jesus Christ takes place are queered. For they render unstable the categories of sexual difference that might attempt to describe those relations or the performance of the enquirer with respect to the gendered body of Jesus Christ. It is not that gender disappears. Gender is not transcended. It is rather rendered part of a more profound mystery; the mystery of relation itself between God and human beings.[14]

Eros as Redemptive Transformation

Many theologians today are asking what role eroticism can play in a redemptive transformation of the human subject, indeed, of the cosmos itself. On the other hand, as, for example, the American patristics scholar Virginia Burrus wonders, "how does *eros* infuse theological practice and transfigure doctrinal tropes?"[15] Instead of following the well-trodden path of moralizing about sex and eroticism, a number of scholars are breaking with Nygren in order to explore the unknown terrain of theo-

13. Heyward, *Saving Jesus*, 100.
14. Ward, "On the Politics of Embodiment," 72.
15. Burrus, "Introduction," xiii.

logical eroticism. In a contribution to an anthology on *eros* theology, Burrus argues that this involves disrupting the disciplinary boundaries of theology in favor of "the mutual seduction of disciplines—theology, philosophy, scripture, history—at multiple sites charged by desire at once bodily, spiritual, intellectual, and political."[16] *Eros* theology seeks to find new avenues through which attraction, love, and sexual desire can express themselves, but also to challenge conventional interpretations of these concepts. Needless to say, this involves some element of risk, above all for the theological subject, by opening the possibility for *eros* to commit various kinds of infringements and transgressions. Once transgressed, however, boundaries can reveal themselves as "places of emerging possibilities." Burrus claims that it takes discipline "to its limits in a stretch towards transcendence" but she also asks "what kind of transcendence is imagined or hoped for?"[17]

She further thinks that a reader of Nygren's historical study might wonder whether *agape* "does not require an overflow of eros in order to reopen its congested channels" or to "shatter its repressive defense. Is the posited distinction between agape and eros, as well as between carnal and sublimated eros, not in itself in need of interrogation."[18] Nygren's critique rests not only upon his conviction that syncretism is something bad but also upon the premise that the two concepts were originally distinct and denoted purely cultural features which could be identified as "motifs." The fact that most theologians have not viewed them as such ought instead to inspire a continued evaluation of the relation between bodily and spiritual, passive and active, ascending and descending, human and divine love. Questions that have been important for many centuries will return.

Eros, Agape, and *Nomos* Return

To write about love and eroticism in a Lutheran tradition is to recall the Greek concepts of love, *eros* and *agape*. Perhaps they also eventually call for a discussion of the law, *nomos*. Martin Luther's theology is usually read as an *agape* theology. As we saw in the previous chapter, this view has been promoted by theologians such as Anders Nygren. Thanks to

16. Ibid., xii.
17. Ibid., xiii.
18. Ibid., xiiiff.

Luther's strong emphasis on the cross and self-giving love, *agape* has moved center-stage. Jesus's life and death imply both atonement and an ethical standard. As Christ gave his life for us, so should we give life to one another in the everyday. This is not always pleasurable but involves carrying a cross as Christ did. In practice, the ethical ideal of self-giving love has often focused on women. Perhaps women have had a tendency to take this message to heart more than men. One can speculate about the possible reasons. Women's empathy, their feeling for children and family, and their subordinated position are frequently cited as explanations. Whatever the reason, feminists have subjected cross theology to comprehensive critique.[19]

At the same time, the concept of *agape* has also been questioned on the grounds of its association with narrow-mindedness and a domineering power that only ever gives or influences, never receives.[20] *Eros* theology, by contrast, has been linked to the concept of *eros*. While *agape* has been seen as a love from above—masculine, universal, and impartial but given on conditions as to its reception—*eros* has been presented as longing and searching. In this way *eros* has been interpreted as a force that creates relation in its desire for the other, for the new. Close reading reveals, however, that *eros* theology wishes not to replace *agape* with *eros* but to move beyond the antagonisms between these concepts. But *eros* theology, too, has met some criticism. One such criticism is that *eros* theology is too individualistic.

Eros as Expressing Contemporary Individualism and Pleasure?

British sociologist of religion Linda Woodhead observes that in the past Christian sexual ethics sought to distance considerations of sexuality and love from an individualistic context to one that included two parties. Within *eros* theology, an effort has been made to situate sexuality within a broader context by asserting that *eros* provides an underpinning for a renewed political vision and the struggle to realize it.[21] Eros is described as a force that not only overwhelms the individual or forces people together;

---

19. Guðmundsdóttir, *Meeting God on the Cross.*

20. Keller, "Is That All?," 20. "The *spirit* in which a gift is offered (to a woman in particular) effects an indelible theological event."

21. Woodhead, "Sex in a Wider Context," 105.

it is also a force that generates a new vision of a reciprocal and coherent society and that releases the energies necessary to resist the forces of oppression. Eros, it is argued, breaks down the boundaries between private and public, private and political.[22] Woodhead contends that *eros* theology, despite this, risks creating a situation in which the individual's unforced erotic pleasure occupies center stage: "For is not the *eros* which it sees as foundational to new relationships, new society, and a new religion, an *eros* that is still basically the freely willed pleasure of the individual?"[23] She quotes Carter Heyward, who identifies orgasm as an apogee, the climax of our capacity for momentary experience of ecstasy, a possibility for joining the self and the other with sexuality and other dimensions of life.[24] Woodhead argues that *eros* theology accepts the underlying conditions for modern individualism by treating the experience of orgasm as fundamental—the only thing sufficiently powerful to provide a basis for relation, society, and religion. The latter cannot stand on its own legs but must be verified and ontologized by *eros*. In *eros* theology, even God is reduced to erotic experience, what Heyward calls "the power in mutual relation."[25]

Woodhead is claiming, then, that *eros* theology, far from challenging contemporary conceptions of sexuality and eroticism, runs the risk of canonizing them. *Eros* theology wishes to establish new forms of just relations and community on the basis of erotic experience. As a contrast, she identifies traditional religion, which, even before Foucault, considered sexuality in a wider context, as a product of social and cultural institutions. Woodhead claims that *eros* theology talks about individual and state but has no interest in the forms of community that exist in between, such as church, family, and marriage.[26] It is possible that this critique derives from the fact that her own research has been primarily concerned with different forms of community in society, that is to say, precisely those hybrid forms that exist between state and individual.

Woodhead's critique is directed towards *eros* theology's earlier publications. Subsequent developments within *eros* theology, however, seem to have moved away from the early individualism that Woodhead

22. Ibid.
23. Ibid.
24. Ibid.; Heyward, *Touching Our Strength*, 33.
25. Woodhead, "Sex in a Wider Context," 105; Heyward, *Touching Our Strength*, 188.
26. Woodhead, "Sex in a Wider Context," 106.

criticizes. Virginia Burrus, for example, speaks of the need to confirm the sanctity of love as both incarnated and transcendent, sensual and spiritual, filled with suffering and joy. She argues that it can encompass, while not limiting itself to, biological reproduction or marriage as an institution. At the same time, it does not allow itself to be reduced to the modern cult of orgasms.[27] What we see here, then, is a dissociation from the focus on *eros* as merely equivalent to individual pleasure.

My hope is that the aspects raised by *eros* theology can contribute to new interpretations of how we ought to live with each other as carnal, spiritual, sexual beings, not only in intimate relations but in a world that, on the one hand, is regarded as shrinking in time and space and as becoming increasingly aware of its mutual dependence, and, on the other hand, seems to be devoting itself to various forms of escape into what is ultimately private experience. In the dialogue between contemporary *eros* theologians and Lutheran texts as well as intellectual figures, certain traditional notions are being challenged. Certain ideas within *eros* theology may even reveal themselves to be closely aligned with traditional Lutheran concepts but formulated in a new language.

Sexual Ethics from a New Perspective

Sexuality and marital ethics have long operated in a universe predicated on the experiences of men. When women engaged with this field, it was often from the point of view of justice.[28] The lack of reciprocity and sensitivity that has led to women's becoming invisible and subordinate, at times even taking an openly violent form, has meant that many feminist ethicists have chosen to focus in particular upon the issue of justice between women and men.

However, with a strong focus on ethics as justice comes the danger that the desire and joy in erotic, sexual attraction disappears. According to American theologian Catherine Keller, if one takes the view of feminist ethicists and theologians such as Rita Nakashima Brock, who sees *eros* as the driving force in the universe and moves away from an apathetic conception of God towards *eros* as "the energy of incarnate love,"[29] then

---

27. Burrus, *Sex Lives of Saints*, 1–2.

28. See, for example, Bóasdottir, *Violence, Power, and Justice*. In theological terms, the law has been central, implying regulation and control.

29. R. N. Brock, *Journeys by Heart*, 49.

eros becomes more than merely a divine element or a metaphor for the universe. Like Brock, Keller is a process theologian who did her doctoral work at Claremont under the supervision of John Cobb Jr. Keller argues that in the cosmology influenced by Whitehead and process theology, *eros* becomes something that takes me "into the heart of the matter where I become world, there where the world itself is becoming, where the event 'passes into its future.'" As a response to Susan Griffin's expression that it is in love we surrender our uniqueness and become world, Keller claims that it is in my "singularity that I become world." She continues: "My difference is the self-differentiation of the world. And the Eros calls it forth."[30]

She claims that "this feminist Eros desires a world whose beauty is steeped in justice."[31] There is a risk that "ethics becomes cloyingly anthropocentric, abstracting justice from its planetary flesh and obligation. Ethics dries out without *eros*," claims Keller.[32] At the same time, it is not possible to avoid the tension between ethics and *eros*, especially for ethicists who are looking for justice in the realm of sexuality. Liberated from ethics, *eros* will "stimulate the ravishing violations that belong to a social structure of dominance and submission, which will strangle *eros* itself."[33] Ironically enough, an anti-erotic ethics risks having the same result. An inability to differentiate sexual justice from sexual oppression blocks the energies of social transformation, argues Keller.[34] It undermines the *eros* that drives cultures, namely, aesthetics.

Discernible here is an important theme in Keller's writing: *eros* as a reconstructive social force in both the private and the political spheres. As I read her, Keller is arguing that *eros* and ethics must be kept together as law, *nomos*, but without losing *eros* and its creative aspect, the aesthetic. But can *eros* challenge our own era's focus on the individual, something Woodhead warns us about, and contribute to a reciprocity not only for two people but for a vision of society founded on relationality? Translated into Lutheran: Can *eros* in theology help us to see that we all belong to a greater narrative than our own?

30. Keller, "Afterword," 372.
31. Ibid.
32. Ibid.
33. Ibid.
34. Ibid.

Competing Loves and Sanctity as Erotic Art

With the advent of Martin Luther and the Reformation, self-giving love seems to have come back into favor. The earthly everyday life became the locus of spirituality. It is there that my fellow human being needs my love. This was inspired by God's self-giving love and grace, by *agape*.

But what happened to *eros*? Did sexual desire, *eros*, and everyday intimacy all disappear? Or was there also a place for *eros* spirituality? *Agape* became an ideal worth invoking. Within cross theology, *agape* was cherished. Women in particular seemed to have a vocation to give their lives for others.[35] Critics of monastic isolation and *eros* spirituality emphasized the greater value of everyday, physical, concrete life. For a study of sensuality, body, and eroticism, it is easy to follow in these well-trodden paths.

Anders Nygren's separation of *eros* and *agape* has undoubtedly had a great influence on the Lutheran tradition.[36] The international scholarship on *eros* and *agape* continues to refer almost without exception to Nygren.[37] Today we know that the different designations for love correspond to different translations, not radically different forms of love. What is more, Nygren's sharp distinction is being criticized for its lack of flexibility and historicity and for being organized within a hierarchical system. It is highly doubtful whether this division of *eros* and *agape* faithfully reflects Martin Luther's own way of thinking. Even if it does, it is not necessarily relevant today. My own point of departure is that the challenges raised by a changed image of God, one that emphasizes not distance and hierarchy but nearness and reciprocity, means that the ideal for intimate human relations is changing.

Virginia Burrus suggests in *The Sex Lives of Saints* that "sanctity can be restyled as an erotic art, that the holy Life carries us to the extremities of human desire, that (conversely) 'erotic experience is possibly close to sanctity.'"[38] Burrus admits that these are "queer notions, seductive insinuations, even downright perverse proposals." However, she holds that the stories of saints who "steadfastly reject both the comforts and the confinement of conventional roles and relationships" can help us "discover

---

35. Guðmundsdóttir, *Meeting God on the Cross*.

36. One finds this interpretation in *A Theology of Love*, where Jeanrond asserts that Luther meant that only God can love, not human beings.

37. A fact also noted by Woodhead, "Sex in a Wider Context," 104.

38. Burrus, *Sex Lives of Saints*, 1, also referring to Georges Bataille.

not only evidence of historic transformation of desire but also testimony to the transformative power of eros."[39]

It is therefore difficult to adopt even the Reformation's well-known critique of monastic life's *eros* spirituality. By contrast, one could perhaps say that the Reformation served to bring the ethos of monastic life, an *agape* life, into the space of the everyday.[40] And yet a self-giving love that fails to problematize power relations runs considerable risks, regardless of gender. Matters have not been helped by the fact that the interpretation and practice of Luther's ideas and theology have taken place within a patriarchal, anthropomorphic worldview. However, there is much to suggest that Martin Luther himself held a more complex view of eroticism and sexuality. Sexual desire and joy play a big roll. *Eros* is an important and "natural" component in the order of creation. Christology has both egalitarian and self-giving dimensions that involve the abandonment of privileges.[41] There are good reasons, then, for taking a more complex view of *eros* and *agape* than the polarized interpretation pioneered by Nygren. As we have seen, Woodhead also problematizes talk of desire and *eros*, and warns about a perspective that can become far too narrowly individualistic. Late modernity emphasizes the reflexivity, ambiguity, and complexity of life and its interpretations. In my view, this also holds true for discussions of *eros* and *agape*.

Eros Theology as Contemporary Challenge

Contemporary *eros* theology places a greater emphasis upon *eros* than *agape*. Even so, its main aim is to call into question any strict division between *eros* and *agape*, human and divine, or immanent and transcendent. A strict division between human and divine, *eros* and *agape*, has also been criticized for not being gender neutral, indeed, for helping to maintain a traditional gender order in which women are expected to be passive on the one hand while actively living out a self-giving love on the other hand. Keller and a number of feminist ethicists and theologians have shown how an asymmetrical gender order has resulted in women being badly treated.[42]

39. Ibid., 2.
40. Stolt, *Luther själv*.
41. hooks, *All about Love*.
42. Keller, "Afterword"; Bóasdottir, *Violence, Power, and Justice*; Guðmundsdóttir, *Meeting God on the Cross*.

Both Brock and Keller received their theological training in process theology, and in their writings they have integrated the ideas of Alfred North Whitehead and John Cobb Jr. with feminist and postcolonial theory. In relation to her reconstruction of creation and divine power, Keller asks whether this may "suggest a third way for love itself: neither the eros rendered dissolute by loveless sexual conquests, nor the moralistic 'love' that knows no holy eros?"[43] Women, but also all those not accommodated within the framework of heteronormativity, have throughout history suffered badly at the hands of both extremes. In some countries living as a homosexual is punishable by death, and women often pay a high price if they question a gender order in which men are granted more power and freedom of choice.

Homosociality still constitutes a discreet form of rule that often retains power precisely by remaining invisible. The concept of homosociality should not be confused with homosexuality; rather, it denotes the way in which so long as men are regarded as the norm and as more valuable, a majority of men will choose to surround themselves with other men. In so doing they can validate their own importance in a way denied to women, who are generally regarded as of inferior status.[44] Laws and ethical guidelines notwithstanding, decision are not infrequently made within a framework or structure chosen by influential men.[45] What is more, when homosociality between men is strong, most women will choose to seek validation from men. Masculinity is associated with power, in effect. It is felt to be natural and self-evident. It therefore demands considerable autonomy and empowerment to call such a system into question. *Eros* theology here represents a resource.

Contemporary *eros* theology sheds new light on Lutheran theology, calling into question traditional dualisms between God and human beings, man and women, and between different forms of love. In the process, it contributes to the discussion of the presence of sensuality and of how we can live as spiritual, carnal, sexual beings. Responsibility, sexual desire, and mutuality then appear in new varieties. How we talk about God is bound up with how we see ourselves and the cosmos.

43. Keller, *On the Mystery*, 93.
44. Holmberg, *Det kallas manshat*, 93.
45. If gender is an important criterion, the same can be said about color of skin, ethnicity, and, increasingly, religion too, where nonreligiosity more and more is seen as the "normal" in many Western countries. "Intersectionality" is a notion intended to denote how many different criteria overlap to marginalize or exclude.

In her doctoral dissertation, theologian Sofia Camnerin has analyzed the image of God and view of atonement in the writings of Rita Nakashima Brock and Daphne Hampson. Brock, she argues, challenges a theistic image of God. By emphasizing the divine as relation, she finds herself advocating an immanent conception of God with some potential for transcendence. Camnerin describes Brock's image of God as horizontal since it concerns the relation between people, not between God and people.[46] Daphne Hampson, she argues, leaves more space for transcendence and her image of God is accordingly described as vertical.[47] Camnerin wants to create a synthesis of Brock and Hampson, that is, a concept of God that is both transcendent and relational:

> The transcendence which Hampson ascribes to the subject could challenge Brock's more horizontal theology. God can be represented as both incarnate and present in relations, but also simultaneously more than that. The emphasis which Brock places on relations could challenge Hampson's more impersonal image of God. Taken together, this could produce a concept of God that is both horizontal and vertical. The divine fellowship might be described as the transcendence of communal life.[48]

As we have already seen, Catherine Keller has a cosmic vision with repercussions for people's relations both to each other and to the cosmos. She also interprets Brock in this light. One might perhaps say that she has progressed further along the path advocated by Camnerin. I will therefore offer a more detailed account of some of Keller's ideas about creating and relation.

Eros as Driving Force of Creation

For process theology the "becoming moment, the 'actual occasion,' is key to the cosmos."[49] Creation is connected with becoming. This becoming is the real, actual now or moment. At this point a characteristic element of *eros* theology appears, namely, the now as creating. We will return to this emphasis on presence in the next chapter.

---

46. Camnerin, *Försoningens mellanrum*, 167.
47. Ibid.
48. Ibid., 167–68.
49. Keller, *On the Mystery*, 99.

A foundational concept in *eros* theology is that *eros* and creation are connected. Process theology speaks of two aspects of divine activity in the world: God's creating love and God's love as sympathy.[50] Creative love can also be described as desire, longing, or passion. Whitehead spoke of "the Eros of the Universe" as having a cosmic appetite to create, become, long for, or desire beauty and the intensity of experience. This divine *eros* is felt in every being as "the 'initial aim'—or the 'lure.'" It tempts us into becoming, into realizing possibilities for greater beauty and intensity in our lives. Sympathy's love, on the other hand, can be called divine agape. While *eros* attracts, tempts, and invites, *agape* replies to what we have become; "in com/passion it feels our feelings: it is the *reception*."[51] *Agape* is reception, claims Keller. This is worth noting in view of the fact that *agape* is routinely described as giving.

Eros is connected with life, its origin and development. It is the attractive force that draws out life and is the basis for all relation. It is also the divine force that invites and encourages the other to choose, to respond freely. To use the language of process theology, it involves tempting or enticing created beings, individually and collectively, to self-realization. Keller often makes use of a division within a word in order to visualize the word's history and force us to look more carefully:

> The power of God, if it is a response-able power, *empowers* the other—to respond. In their freedom. God's will is indeed God's will! But the term *will* derives from *voluntas*, from which also comes "voluntary," which means not control but desire. What God *wants*. That wanting, that desiring, has a decisive element, limiting in advance what is possible for this universe.[52]

This will is nonetheless not the same as causation, Keller points out, but rather a qualitatively different kind of power. This power appears weak when domination is the ideal.[53] Yet the image of a power that "is perfected in weakness" seeks to express and make comprehensible the difficult alternative to coercive superiority.[54]

50. Cobb and Griffin, *Process Theology*.

51. Keller, *On the Mystery*, 99.

52. Ibid., 89. See chapter 6 for a comparison with how Luther refers to the bridegroom as being the one to seek out the bride.

53. Ibid., 90.

54. Gregersen holds in that what he labels "deep incarnation," that God becoming human is a way to enter the condition of creation and evolution. "God's incarnation means that God's *logos* not only has assumed human form but has become unified with the world of material." Gregersen, "Dybdeinkarnationen", 260 (my translation).

Meditating on this, Keller puts her readers in a situation in which they feel themselves here and now. In her text she interpellates readers directly:

> You are reading right now, embedded in a web of relations that are more or less chosen, awkward edgy or warm, heavy with a past that also includes the theological perspectives that are still competing for your attention.

You emerge—now—in a dense collective of nature and nurture, turbulent with memories, anxieties and hopes. Still, here, now, you feel your lungs opening, drawing breath, air shared by all the breathers near and far breathing the same air as those near you, those whose feelings you sense, breathing with all creatures, sealed in an ozone layer enveloping our rich atmosphere, swirling gracefully amidst the choreography of the planet, turning amidst the galaxies; there you are.[55]
This elemental quantity of relations, forcefields of creation, impacts this instant so forcefully that they can almost feel how they connect you, there, now with me, here and there.

In what she calls a guided meditation, Keller challenges the reader to see this instant as a wave in the water of creation, a water of becoming in which, at the same time, you become yourself and the collective transforms itself into a divided created life, an "emergence of our shared creaturely life."[56] That is now. In this you gather yourself by remembering and recreating earlier becomings and by anticipating the future. Outside of this instant, both the past and the future remain abstractions.[57]

Keller continues her meditation by linking this instant to the water of creation, a wave of becoming that is simultaneously you becoming yourself and the collective origin of our divided created life, since our cosmic relations are the result of an infinite profundity that lacks the personal relationship to what we call love, or God. And yet this infinity, what might be called God's own profundity, is the creative womb of all that exists, something Whitehead called "creativity." The infinite enters into relations with the spiritual beings that can be glimpsed on the surface of the unfathomable deep:

> That infinity enters into relations with the finite beings surfacing on the face of the deep: we creatures, called forth amidst the

---

55. Keller, *On the Mystery*, 99.
56. Ibid.
57. Ibid.

> swirling choreography of it All. Called forth, born—natured, nurtured—at every moment. That call, that invitation is the creative Eros: the amorous desire of God for life, and more life. Life not for the sake of my life alone but for the sake of the evolving network of relations in which my life is worth living—*worthyscipe*, lived as an act of worship.[58]

According to *eros* theology, this longing for life is something that unites God and human beings. One could say that God tempts and teases forth his creation. In her writings, Keller has also questioned the notion that God creates out of nothing, *ex nihilo*. Instead, drawing on chaos theory, she has interpreted Gen 1:2 as a collaboration between materiality and the divine wind.[59]

Emphasizing creation as a great web that draws each of us into a larger narrative than our own is a way of thinking that lies close to Luther's even after emphasizing the distance between God and human beings. As Luther sees it, God's longing for humanity is like the bridegroom's longing for the bride.[60] In one of his table talks, Luther speaks lyrically of how animals, trees, and plants are created for each other and lean upon each other in longing and desire. Just as God created man and woman for each other, he argues that all creation is gendered and filled with sexual desire. But he sees this as a magnification of marriage, a model that extends to stones and corals.[61] For Luther, erotic attraction between the sexes was a sign of God's longing for life, in which humanity becomes God's co-creator. Eroticism, but also the present moment, like presence and longing for life, are thus related to Martin Luther's emphasis upon God as continually creating things anew. These ideas bear a strong affinity to those we encountered in Swedish creation theologian Gustaf Wingren, who follows Ienaeus in claiming that human beings, merely by breathing, live in a relation to God.

It is also in the present moment that the ethical demand reaches us as human needs. But is *eros* theology's description of *eros* too idealistic? Evolutionary theorists are today showing how new creation is driven by more than just sexual desire and longing. The struggle for survival is not only sweet.

58. Ibid., 100.
59. Keller, *Face of the Deep*.
60. See chapter 6.
61. WA TR 1, 560 (1530–35) "Tischreden" (no. 1133); cf. WA TR 1, 4, "Tischreden" (no. 7) 1530–35.

The Interplay of *Eros* and *Agape*

Eroticism is one of the forces that make life continue. Like all life, it is threatened by destruction, by being ruled by narrow self-interest. However, one cannot replace *eros* with self-giving *agape*. Both forms of love must live in reciprocity. *Agape* can be made whole by means of what Keller calls "amatory oscillations" between separate expressions of love. Different forms of love must continually challenge and inspire each other. *Eros* stands for longing and desire for "something more, for an other in excess of the self," argues Keller. *Eros* may drive "greed or invitation," while *agape* "may express either domination or welcome. But if they fluctuate back and forth, like "complementary flows or gestures of love," then desire can grow into generosity and the gift become increasingly inviting.[62] Perhaps it is time to return to one word for love, which today encompasses many nuances and is becoming something of a rebus. However, different words can also elucidate the dance, the tension, and the various connotations.

As we have seen, divine activity is also described as God's creating love. This love is also described as response.[63] These are two different forms of divine relation, Keller argues, but their movements are spiritually indistinguishable and exist in a continual interaction. She views this dual conception of love as a constructive alternative to omnipotence, where neither "passion nor com/passion," temptation, vocation, or reception constrain us.[64]

Theologian Mario Costa likewise interprets *eros* and *agape* as different Christian concepts for love that interacts. Christ as gift shows both, he argues.[65] On the one hand, God's erotic love for his creation appears as a longing to reconcile the world to itself. This love produces Christ, who carries out this reconciliation and thereby manifests God's *eros*. God's erotic love for his creation not only wants, it gives. In its longing for reconciliation, God's love is shown to be *agape*, giving itself. In Christ, *eros* and *agape* are so close that they cannot be separated. As a consequence, an intimacy is established between divine *eros* and *agape* as well as between God and the world.[66]

---

62. Keller, "Afterword," 373–74.
63. Cobb and Griffin, *Process Theology*.
64. Keller, *On the Mystery*, 99.
65. Costa, "For the Love of God," 59.
66. Ibid.

Different Fronts

Martin Luther had different struggles. His eagerness to reform the church to which he belonged developed into a resistance struggle in which he asserted a view of ordinary life that ran directly counter to that of the monastery. This also involved a critique of monastic *eros* theology as humanity's striving towards the divine and transcendent. When incorporated into meritocratic thinking, this became something reprehensible. For Luther, the key thing was to emphasize the gift of grace. The gift of God's love, as he saw it, was free flowing in our divinely given, created lives and in forgiveness, rehabilitation. As we saw in chapter 6, he described this as a loving embrace.

In this regard the issue thus becomes whether the emphasis on *eros* in Luther's struggle came to be associated so strongly with monastic spirituality that it fell into disrepute after the Reformation. Must *eros* necessarily be connected with lack and craving, or with finding one's own merits? Or was it the case that *eros* could be accommodated within everyday love? Luther's longing for Käthe recurs in his letters and he speaks often of his longing for Christ. Yet his focus is on presence, the here and now. Birgit Stolt argues that the experience of God's love and the gift of atonement left its mark on the everyday and on our collective social life.[67] She claims that, for Luther, it is the connection between faith and certainty of one's vocation that eases labor and makes it joyful.[68] In his Large Catechism, Luther writes about the joy of work.[69]

Luther speaks of the heart's superabundance. This denotes a basic theological precept that forms part of the Reformation critique. Daily, ordinary life becomes more important than any self-imposed, specifically religious acts intended to impress God and other Christians. Such acts are not needed. God loves you as you are. That is a gift. Our response is an unbounded joy, which also reaches some of our fellow human beings. These latter need to encounter God's love and solicitude through you. There is no question that even if this can be regarded as an ideal that often remains unrealized amid the trials of everyday life, it represents a theological attitude. God does not need your good deeds, but your fellow human beings do. These sometimes need to be elicited by structures,

---

67. Stolt, *Luther själv*, 34–37.

68. Ibid., 35.

69. WA 30 I, 149, "Deutsch Catechismus" (1529). See the previous chapter, page 177, for the full quotation.

regulations, and commandments, but are often induced by means of love. They are bound up with God's gift of grace, which, by disrupting our fixation with ourselves, liberates us to love each other. Earthly love between people, in other words, is not in competition with divine love.[70] Sensuality thereby becomes present in the everyday and in earthly love. It is not continually drawn towards the divine but makes the divine gaze interpret life here in relation to cosmic presence.

Even so, the question of *eros* cannot be put to one side. Just as people turn to others in sexual desire, for their own sake not for others', so too do they search for God in their hearts for its own sake, sighing and praying for help but also in order to express joy and songs of praise. That God also yearns for and seeks humanity is something Luther often emphasizes. And this mutual, loving embrace gives new strength. Responsibility and guilt, which follow upon being human, are countered by the forgiveness and fresh start offered by the Gospels. The unceasing requirement to show sensitivity towards our fellow human beings can feel oppressive and become a source of despair. For Luther, this is something that drives people to seek forgiveness and new courage from Christ. At times, however, the Lutheran tradition has so strongly emphasized the fact that God meets us unconditionally in all our vulnerability that revealing one's failings has almost come to seem a merit. In this respect, alternating between *eros* and *agape* can be healthy. As we saw in chapter 6, union with Christ is a union in joy. In our everyday lives, too, we find grace in unexpected experiences of goodness, often through other people. Our fellow human beings make demands from us in the everyday. But other people are not there merely as demands, laws, *nomos*, but also for joy. In the transcriptions of Luther's table talk, it is evident that other people give sexual pleasure and joy, company and comfort. The boundaries between *eros*, *agape*, and *nomos* are no more hard and fast than those between the gifts God provides through the creation and Christ. Nor must a yearning for one's fellow human beings, or for the divine, be interpreted as stemming from a lack, but rather as a way of escaping despair and turning one's face towards life, towards the good, towards superabundance.

---

70. His sermon at a wedding is just one example. WA 34 I, 52:5–9, "Eine Hochzeitpredigt" (1531).

God in the Everyday

In the everyday, then, we meet other people but also the divine. There is a direct relation to God here, not merely in church. The demands of our fellow human beings can feel oppressive. But our fellow human beings are also a source of joy, even when they need me, perhaps even for that very reason. The hidden and the revealed exist at the same time. Humans encounter God's gifts in the form of material things such as food, drink, and other people. The divine here intrudes as something far more concrete, not as something disembodied and hereafter, transcendent, but in and through the material. For Luther, God's gifts are there all the time. Present but not self-evident, things to marvel at. In his Small Catechism, Luther highlights precisely this everydayness in order to explain that God has created heaven and earth: "I believe that God has made me and all creatures, given me body and soul, eyes, ears, my reason, and all my limbs and senses, and that he still takes care of his creation. He also provides for me richly every day by giving me clothes and food, house and home, and all that I need to maintain life."[71] Faith helps us to identify all this as gifts and as part of God's providence. As we saw in chapter 5, Luther describes how ordinary people moan about the effort of having children, whereas the perspective given by faith is of a joy and a gift from God.[72]

Through faith, then, divinely ordained life gains a significance that confers meaning, joy, and gratitude. For Luther, it is unthinkable that this gift might not exist in the absence of such an interpretation. God's gifts exist regardless of everything. To receive them spontaneously and directly is a part of trust, faith. Such trust can even scare the devil away, argues Luther. But the prospect given by faith awakens joy.

Dr. Martin mixes the earthly, the carnal, the sensual and the divine. He interprets physical proximity as , something underestimated by earlier traditions. Trusting each other and entrusting to each other all that we have on this earth is mentioned in the same sentence as "the physical benefits."[73] Spouses are here presented as living in a mutual intimacy and trust that creates reliance. To imagine creation without love is therefore to oversimplify. To see creation filled with love is made possible by the

---

71. WA 30 I, 292, "Der Kleine Katechismus" (1529).

72. WA 10 II, 295–96, "Vom ehelichen Leben" (1522).

73. WA 34 I, 52:5–9, "Eine Hochzeitpredigt" (1531). For the whole quotation, see chapter 4.

perspective conferred by faith. It deepens our joy in the gift, but also our responsibility.

Obligation and Grace in Overall Interaction

For Martin Luther, the notion that God worked with two hands, through law and gospel, did not involve a division. It was a way to express the fact that God worked in different ways, against death and destruction, for life and redemption. The different estates, of *familia/oekonomia*, *ecclesia*, and *politia* can thus be seen as spheres of promise.[74] Within these areas, God works to redeem and liberate. Law and gospel, obligation but also redemption, are everywhere. Obligations elicit good deeds. Grace, mercy, and forgiveness cause them to flow. Each of us, Luther argued, lives in a tension between law and gospel, obligation and redemption.[75] But for the church and its representatives, it can be tempting to care only about one's own sphere—that is, the ecclesiastical—instead of demanding that God's promise of justice and mercy should be a guiding star in every area of life. However, the belief that God is at work everywhere, together with human beings, is a reminder that the church does not always take precedence when it comes to showing justice and mercy. The initiative can as easily come from the realm of politics. The tenet of *eros* theology that divine love is a vision for society and the world can potentially be seen as another way of expressing similar ideas.[76]

As Mikael Lindfelt observes, when reading Luther today it must be borne in mind that his world was very different. The sixteenth century was a special kind of unitary culture in which "a shared religion was a self-evident precondition for the representation of reality." The so often misunderstood two-kingdoms doctrine should therefore be understood dialectically, as a way of talking about how God works simultaneously in different ways. It starts from the premise, not that society's legislative or

---

74. B. Brock, "Why the Estates?"; Ulrich, "Grammar of Lutheran Ethics," 29; cf. Witte, *Law and Protestantism*, 93. Witte holds that these three regimes are equal in relation to God and each other. Luther called them *in ordo economicus, ordo politicus och ordo ecclesiasticus* (WA 242). I have used the notion of "spheres of promise" elsewhere. See, for example, Gerle, "Eros, Ethics, and Politics"; Gerle, "Var dags."

75. See Luther's comments on the sacrament of Baptism, fourth article, WA 30 I, 308-13, "Der Kleine Catechismus" (1529).

76. If Luther invokes Aristotle when talking about the estates, *eros* theology is often said to have been inspired by Plato.

peacekeeping function can be separate from God, but that God works in different ways in his worldly and spiritual dominions. "In other words, a society that is secular or that holds a neutral philosophy of life was unthinkable. All reality was God's reality."[77] The modern conception of a secular sphere within our world is therefore a later historical construction, argues Lindfelt.[78]

Mikael Lindfelt contends that Luther, by affirming marriage over monastic life, wished above all to emphasize that God's creative activity cannot be limited to any particular sphere of life; instead, "God is everywhere and continually creating anew, especially in marriage."[79] In this line of argument, however, the idea emerges of love as a gift that needs protection because of the destructiveness both of life and of human beings. Marriage is thus seen as a protection for love, but also as a regulation that compels us to care for our neighbors.

Good regulations are needed as a defense against people's egocentricity and unwillingness to take responsibility. But in our delight at our neighbors, love breaks through. Gustaf Wingren illustrates this dialectic in his book *Luthers lära om kallelsen* (*Luther's Doctrine of Vocation*):

> Delight at one's neighbour, that is love's breakthrough.... There is no more delightful or lovable creature on earth than one's neighbor. Love does not think about doing good deeds, for it takes delight in people, and when something good is done to one's fellow human being, it is not as a deed of love but, on the contrary, merely as a reaching for gifts. Love *must* never do anything good. It *may* do it. And on earth "with its trees and grass" is also to be found our human vocation. Whoever has the Holy Spirit, he can, *inter alia*, signal this by managing the affairs of his vocation in faith and in joy. When someone joyfully directs his efforts towards earthly tasks—helping neighbours precisely when they need it, managing their vocation—then God's or Christ's love is at work; then the Spirit is near. Discovering love is thus the same as discovering one's neighbour and one's vocation as something one can inhabit with joy in the heart. Our own love is thus a thing of no interest. We are interested in our neighbours and in our vocation.[80]

77. Lindfelt, "Olof Sundbys," 256.
78. Ibid.
79. Ibid., 269.
80. Wingren, *Luthers lära om kallelsen*, 52–53 (my emphasis).

Gustaf Wingren here describes a freedom that Christian faith provides in the everyday. It is a freedom that breaks up self-absorption such that it becomes almost invisible. But are we driven by joy and sexual desire? The relationship between love and law can be seen dialectically, as contemporary, yet the concepts of *eros* and *agape* are not mentioned. However, Wingren's strong emphasis upon our fellow humans, as a joy, is closely aligned with the ideas I have summarized above, about *eros* as a longing for and curiosity about the other.

The Lutheran tradition comes very near to reading *eros* as urge, sexual desire, and selfishness, and hence as something threatening. It is not that simple, however. Sexual desire and longing for the other are also the origins of community and the preconditions for life and procreation. Every walk of life is governed by a dialectic between what is required, what lays claim to people, and what simply gives, freely and unconstrainedly. These are trains of thought that in our own era have been particularly developed by *eros* theology. In earlier chapters I have argued that Luther's discussion of eroticism has elements of both *eros* and *agape*—and *nomos*. A connective thread that I am following in this study is, however, his strong affirmation of sensual presence.

Freedom That Triggers Sexual Desire

Human beings are free before God. Joy at this releases energy and sexual desire. For Luther, the role reversing of the bridal mystery and its emphasis upon unity and sympathy in a playful, joyful dance is an inspiration for everyday, physical life. As we have seen, Luther also used images and metaphors from the intimate bridal mystery to evoke the relation between man and woman. The intensity and reciprocity that characterizes the relationship between Christ and the believer in *On the Freedom of a Christian* is something that reappears when Luther describes the good relation between husband and wife..[81]

Reciprocity and trust have thus been a part of the conceptualization of the ideal Lutheran marriage. By contrast, the Lutheran tradition has hesitated to accept a role reversal in which the initiative is taken by not just one of the parties. It has interpreted earthly love as belonging primarily to the creation.[82] Life after the Fall is viewed with ambivalence,

---

81. WA 34 I, 52:5–9, "Eine Hochzeitpredigt" (1531).
82. As noted in chapter 4, this was also Augustine's interpretation.

as both good and evil. For this reason, law is needed, as a defense against evil.

The emphasis upon order and preservation has, however, as I have already pointed out, been questioned from a perspective of *creatio continua*.[83] In the imagery Luther uses to describe the love between Christ and the believer, the relation is presented as anything but static. In his treatise *On the Freedom of a Christian* from 1520, Christ is alternately seducer and seduced. According to his sermon on the Gospel of John, no union of bride and bridegroom can occur without the response of each. Reciprocity and trust are necessary for the relation.[84]

He often dissolves the sharp distinction between what constitutes *coram Deo* and *coram hominibus*. For Luther and those who came after him, this distinction was important in order to defend the notion that salvation is a gift, not the result of human exertions or merits. But Christ's love has significance for the relation between people, *coram hominibus* and in relation to the world, *coram mundo*. In both instances, however, he assigns a dominating role to agape. Love was often interpreted from above, as a gift. It was thus man, as the stronger partner, who was capable of giving life. In a patriarchal system, God is presented above all as father, ruler, and king, something that creates contradictory ideals. Vulnerability and a longing for the other were accorded very little space. *Eros* theology's emphasis upon vulnerability, reciprocity, and longing as important components of divine and human love was therefore an important contribution to a Lutheran discussion in which traditional oppositions between *eros* and *agape* were being challenged. The image of a vulnerable God can inspire new ideals for both women and men.

Eros Theology and Luther

Is there any common ground between *eros* theology and Luther? Recent scholarship has called into question the strict dualism between *eros* and *agape*, claiming that it is rather a question of one single love or of different elements within love that are variously emphasized on different occasions.[85] My argument is that this notion is already present in Luther's writings.

83. For a summary, see chapter 2.
84. See chapter 6.
85. See chapters 4 and 6.

When speaking of the relation between God and the soul, Luther uses the imagery of a wedding but goes his own way by rejecting people's own efforts and merits. Instead, he invokes the prophet Hosea, who compares God's love to the love of a cuckold, who continues to love despite having been betrayed. This is the background for Luther's description in *On the Freedom of a Christian* of the blessed exchange as an instantaneous union, a loving embrace in which both parties give themselves to each other. Marriage cannot be completed without the sympathy of both. The entity which Luther describes using the mystical imagery of the Song of Solomon concerns a mutual relation. The criticized interpretation of *agape* as a one-sided gift thus seems not to accord with Luther's own imagery. Instead, he emphasizes the expectation of sympathy.

Catherine Keller claims that in its original context God's gift is offered neither in a unilateral purity nor as a manipulative egoism but in a spirit of radical reciprocity that is colored by expectancy:

> In its *ur*-context this gift—the gift of God—is offered neither in unilateral purity nor manipulative egotism but in a spirit of radical reciprocity. And this asymmetrical reciprocity is colored, indeed charged, by expectancy. *Expectancy*, however, should not be identified with *demand*, as for repayment or countergift, in kind or at least in gratitude. Much can be expected that can precisely *not* be demanded. Expectancy may comprise *hope* rather than debt.[86]

A hope that never gives up is something different from a guilt accompanied by demands for repayment or countergift.

The focus on bodily expressions of faith and praxis advocated by ecofeminist theology, for example, may be a contemporary response to and development of Luther's thought and practice.[87] It may also be a way to do full justice to a currently neglected aspect of incarnational theology, namely, the idea that faith to a far greater extent is connected to this life.[88] If *eros* theology wishes to draw the political consequences of these ideas of relationality and longing for the other, Luther's affective theology can be a source of inspiration for our own moment, a presence but also an openness to the unexpected, for reciprocity, for the gift, and for generosity towards the other.

---

86. Keller, "Is That All?," 20.
87. See, for example, Jansdotter, "Makten och måltiden."
88. Grenholm, "Makt under inkarnationens villkor," 29f.

Body and *Eros* Theology as Lens

In this study have I have chosen to focus on Luther's view of sensuality, body, and sexuality in dialogue with contemporary scholars. *Eros* theologians have questioned traditional Western oppositions between spiritual and material, masculine and feminine, and divine and human. Naturally, these binary opposites are different in kind, yet they have functioned in the tradition as a designation for what is important and unimportant. On this issue Martin Luther seems, at least in part, to have parted company with contemporary thinkers. In conversation with a number of contemporary scholars, it seems as though the old oppositions between different forms of love serve rather to obscure than to contribute to an understanding of the meaning of love, eroticism, and relation.

At an early stage, *eros* was associated with *Amor*, the god of love, and therefore became a difficult concept for Christian theologians to use. At the same time, as we have seen, there flourished an *eros* spirituality, particularly in the monasteries, which strove for union with the divine. For Anders Nygren, this was one of the reasons for so radically opposing *agape* to *eros*. While *eros* strove upwards, towards God, *agape* was concerned with God's self-giving love. For a Lutheran theology that wishes to defend the notion of salvation as a gift, this became important. But the polarization of *eros* and *agape*, as we have seen, had other, negative consequences.

Where Augustine, writing in the wake of Plotinus sought to keep body and soul separate, or at least within a hierarchy, Luther sets out humanity's likeness to God, *imago dei*, from a holistic perspective, *totus homo*.[89] This holistic perspective can help us to move beyond the traditional oppositions.

Eros Opens Up—Not Merely for Togetherness

The core of *eros* theology is word as relation. The term does not designate merely togetherness or sexual relations, as Woodhead claims, even if this can serve as a starting point. There is a risk of privatization. At the same time, however, there is a continual effort to identify cosmic and ecological connections. Carter Heyward describes God as desire, as a longing

---

89. Hägglund, *De Homine*; WA 39 I, 174–80, "Die disputation de homine" (1536); cf. LW 39:1, 108.

for justice and compassion, solidarity, and friendship: "God *as* the desire for justice and compassion, solidarity and friendship."[90] In chapter 4 we glimpsed the Platonic idea that like can only be recognized by like. *Eros* theology, by contrast, emphasizes the longing to discover what is different, even foreign. It paves the way for something new and indeterminate that is simultaneously understood to be something good.[91] Henriksen argues that desire can contribute to strengthening individualistic qualities by permitting us to fall back upon ourselves and our own self-preoccupation. At the same time, and unlike Woodhead, he contends that this longing can help to conquer the unrelentingly individualistic understanding of humanity that is so dominant in modernity. Invoking natural theology, he argues that this can be interpreted as saying that God gave human beings an insatiable desire for good in order to make it possible for us to enjoy creation more fully and lastingly. Quite simply, we cannot break off our relation to good, but are continually pushed back to this longing.

Henriksen distinguishes between opening and closing desires. Sexual desire exists prior to our conscious choices and wishes. There is thus a pre-subjective element in sexual desire, which means that it originally lies beyond our control and is deeply rooted in a development-oriented experience. Henriksen interprets this theologically as a double gift, in which sexual desire and subjectivity function in a dialectical relationship to each other because human beings in their current stage of development also have the possibility of distancing themselves from some of their desires. Fundamental desires are related to appetite—that is, biological and psychological needs for security, food, warmth, sex, and sexual desire. On another level, there exists a desire that emerges from a conscious and reflexive consciousness made possible by evolution. According to Henriksen, these latter have more to do with our wishes than our needs. These desires are "emerging out of human life as a socially and culturally constituted world." They may therefore open up to the world rather than close off.[92] In this context, he also argues, certain ascetic practices can be seen, not as a way to subdue or suppress desire, but as a way to focus and intensify certain desires above others.[93] However, theol-

---

90. Heyward, *Saving Jesus*, 22 (emphasis in original).
91. Henriksen, "Desire," 1.
92. Ibid., 5–8.
93. Ibid., 8.

ogy cannot ignore the primary role of sexual desire for human beings in becoming an ego, a subject, both for themselves and for others. At this point the danger of exploitation emerges. It is here that Henriksen finds the pathological forms of self-sacrifice that express an utter contempt for one's own needs.[94]

Henriksen further claims that sexual desire can make the other "a means for my gratification of immediate needs" and appears then as "closing." It can, however, also appear as "desire for the other's desire for me, and for my desire of being somewhat for her." Such a situation is far more open and makes both "appear as subjects." The first case is an example of closing desire, the latter of opening desire. Another example of opening desire is art, closely connected to curiosity and creativity, a desire presupposing "reflexive consciousness." It is thus more likely to emerge in a "nature/culture context of exploration."[95]

As feminist theologians have shown, the asymmetry between human beings must be taken seriously. In my view, it is therefore also important to consider which wishes and which longings one makes oneself receptive to. For what or for whose sake? Lutheran realism warns against blind faith in reason and intellect. Ascetic practices or special spiritual exercises are no more able to disrupt people's fixation with their own concerns. Although *eros* theology challenges and inspires us to look after, but also to look beyond, our own needs, I believe it is important not to lose sight of the *totus homo* perspective. On this view, it is not a question of cultivating one aspect of ourselves—often the so-called spiritual side—at the expense of the bodily aspect, but rather of discovering that the divine is also to be found in what is material: to let our self-preoccupation be exploded by a love that makes itself receptive to the other and the world.

Eros Theology's Image of God

Eros theology can also be described in terms of its image of God. This refers not to obligation so much as to process, to seeing God as a friend who tempts us out of ourselves. There would seem to be a contradiction here with all the talk of law, duty, and obedience, talk that is associated with a realism that takes evil seriously. Does *eros* theology take evil

---

94. Ibid., 10. We will return to the question of idealizing self-sacrifice and victimhood in chapter 10.

95. Ibid., 9.

seriously? My view is that there are strong formulations in *eros* theology about human greed and selfishness that involves confronting evil at close quarters. Its strategy for combating evil is substantially different, however. This is part of a consequence of the vast passage of time and our own era's calling into question both patriarchy and hierarchies. Luther held that structures and regulations were necessary in order to both compel and induce good. He therefore emphasized obedience to the prince, the master, the husband, or the father, seeing this as a way to protect life. *Eros* theology, by contrast, rejects patriarchy, constraints, and hierarchies, which it instead views as a part of evil. Rather, it emphasizes reciprocity and a love that encourages good. Trust is fragile but relational. As we have seen, however, contemporary Lutheran ethics does not interpret regulation as something static or hierarchical and profoundly questions patriarchal interpretations. As we saw in chapter 6, there are elements of Luther's love mystery that lie closer to *eros* theology's emphasis on reciprocity and response. Luther is contradictory.

Within *eros* theology there is a recurrent critique of a society in which consumerism has been given unlimited freedom to shape and direct human beings' desires. Wendy Farley argues that *eros* theology offers an antidote to consumer society's obsession with individual, instantaneous gratification. Perhaps, she contends, it may also help us understand motherhood in a more realistic and humane fashion.[96]

Farley also refers to Luther, who long ago proposed that divine love comes to us as grace, and that human beings do not have the power to turn God against us. The erotic language of the bridal mystery is not about a sovereign decision-maker who imposes his will upon others.[97]

Even when applied within political theory, the concept of the decision-maker cannot be said to stand above or outside of the state.[98] Rather, it is a matter of a political authority that forms part of the political entity while also being somehow more than it. Paulina Ochoa Espejo points out that panentheism shares some views with classical democratic theory in which the "citizens are held to be both citizens and subjects at the same time." She summarizes, "Citizens are decision-makers *beyond*

---

96. W. Farley, "Beguiled by Beauty," 129.

97. Ibid., 128.

98. Carl Schmitt's thinking about the political sovereign is difficult to combine with *eros* theology or nuptial imagery. See Schmitt, *The Concept of the Political*.

the polity as part of the popular sovereign, but as subjects they *are* the polity."[99]

In comparable fashion, the fundamentally panentheistic worldview of process theology means that one can see the divine in the sensual and material without equating them, as one would do within a purely immanent system. Instead, the divine is understood as both a creator and a life-giving force behind the universe, as both immanent and transcendent. The divine is simultaneously encompassed by and exceeds the earthly. God does not entirely contain the world, but God is bigger. Thinking and speaking about God in a panentheistic fashion lends support to democratic politics rather than inflexible sovereigns.

God's creating love conveys *logos*, the wisdom, *sofia*, that wishes to be incarnated in the world, Keller argues. Not merely once but everywhere and for all time.[100] *Logos* encompasses everything. At the same time as he is present in all creation, he is also distinct "in being from the universe and present in all things . . ." Keller goes on: "In this classical panentheistic vision, the divine will for all creatures seeks embodiment in every wave of becoming. This is God-in-love: *willing* in the original sense of the world—wanting, desiring, urging."[101] Keller points out that there is no formal doctrine of omnipotence in the Bible. Rather, it is a later abstraction to indicate that God decides everything that happens. She asks rhetorically how the unique, brilliant ethics of the Hebrew Bible could have come about if you as an individual or a people were not responsible for your actions, but everything were decided by an omnipotent providence. Instead, we encounter narratives about complicated relations with a divinity with many names, one who cannot be reduced to absolute power. "The Almighty" is even a faulty translation of "El Shaddai—the Breasted One."[102] Nevertheless, the image of the "infinite mother" can often be glimpsed when Shaddai is invoked. Then it is a question of fertility and fecundity. The name of God can be translated in a great many ways, as breast, mountain, and spirit, to name just a few. The trace of God as the "infinite mother" was subsequently erased by the Hebrews. But a later canon could not entirely erase the memory of her as having "the blessings

---

99. Ochoa Espejo, "Does Political Theology Entail Decisionism?," 725–43. Cf. Keller, *Cloud of the Impossible*, 260.

100. Keller, *On the Mystery*, 100.

101. Ibid.

102. Ibid., 74.

of breasts and womb."[103] As we saw in previous chapters, the images of breasts and suckling recur in the Christian bridal mystery, not least in the writings of Bernard of Clairvaux.[104]

Keller argues, however, that the Hebrew awareness, rather than divine determinism, was a matter of "the process of divine call and human response-ability . . . a relationship of asymmetrical and yet reciprocal *trust*worthiness already narrated in the creation from the *tehom*, the infinite deep that calls to our own deepest realities."[105] To talk of an asymmetric relation, divine calls, and human replies, reciprocal and trusting in their infinite appeal to our deepest realities, is another way of talking about divine and human. In it, how we respond to our vocation is connected to our capacities and responsibilities. Within a Lutheran context, this can be formulated as saying that liberation is a precondition for responsibility. Despite this, Keller argues, the lure of heathen fatalism remained, that is to say, the idea that everything that happens is the will of the gods or fate. This notion was so appealing that it crept into monotheism, she proposes, arguing that when the Only One seemed to emerge as a merciless, all-powerful dictator, there was no longer any way out. Yet calls for a way intersperse the Hebrew texts. An indicator of the power of biblical honesty, they can be heard in the cries of Job and that of the psalmist, "My God, why have you forsaken me?"[106]

We thus encounter here a divine image that is vulnerable and near, and that gives life, sexual desire, and superabundance. When Luther emphasizes the gift and describes love as an embrace, it is possible to detect archetypal images that have not disappeared from the canon, of a sensual presence in relation to both the divine and between human beings. While this is not its only trace in Luther's writings, nor what post-Reformation Sweden has emphasized, it is perhaps something that can become a healthy challenge for Lutheran theology today.

103. Ibid.
104. See Wiberg Pedersen, *Bernhard af Clairvaux*.
105. Keller, *On the Mystery*, 74.
106. Ibid.

9

Body, Sexuality, and Institutions: Roads to Salvation, Disciplining, or Presence and Gift?

Martin Luther lived in a time of historic rupture. This involved a sexual revolution and led to an emphasis on everyday life as the locus of piety. The sensuality that can be glimpsed, among other places, in the erotic language of the female mystics was suppressed by the Reformation. Sensuality was instead tied to everyday life and its physicality, to food, sexuality, and children. This can be interpreted as sensuality moving into everyday life. Instead of the bittersweet yearning of an *eros* that lives on longing and deferral, the emphasis is placed upon a material, bodily presence in everyday life—something that will be the focus of the present chapter. As we saw in chapter 6, the bridal embrace can have gender-transgressing qualities. And yet the emphasis lies on the present and on the gift, a presence without exertion.

The previous chapter showed that contemporary *eros* theologians do not interpret *eros* as a lack, but as a longing for community and justice. The divine is contained within the earthly while simultaneously going beyond. Can anything of this perspective be found in Luther's writings? In this chapter, I present the critique of a theology and a view of knowledge in which symbols and concepts become something that point beyond reality, such that the present is emptied of divine presence. This view of reality is challenged by Luther, who argues that God is always encountered in and through concrete matter.

Scholars today argue that one of the Reformation's driving forces can be traced back to a dearth of sexuality.[1] A key factor in Luther's critique of the trade in indulgences was the question of what kind of religion made it easier for rich people to find salvation through the purchase of absolution for sins.[2] He may have been seeking a theological reformation rather than a societal revolution, but material distress, destitution, and suffering were all contributing factors in the Reformation that he initiated.[3] Despite its great temporal remove, Luther's existential, theological convictions ask important questions of an age in which achievement is often a condition for political and cultural presence and human community. In this chapter, accordingly, I wish to bring into my analysis this important discussion of presence and representation. Luther's insistence upon presence and the encounter with God in the midst of our rupture represents a contribution to this discussion, I argue. This interpretation of life has consequences for what we regard as spiritual.

The Body in a Field of Tension between Appearance and Future

The present moment, just as in Luther's time, exhibits tensions between body, sexuality, economics, and cultural notions. My point of departure is that notions of gender and sexuality, like what we call *nature*, are bound up with theology, technology, and economics. Where Luther's thinking was informed by a theological context in which he viewed God as creator of the world and as giver and preserver of life, our own era's theology, in the sense of view of life or ideology, is largely defined by a modernist view of knowledge, body, and technology. Control, choice, and self-realization are the watchwords of our time.[4] "Eternal life" is attained through chil-

---

1. See, for example, Plummer, *From Priest's Whore to Pastor's Wife*.

2. Cöster, *Kyrkans historia och historiens kyrka*, 104–14, esp. 107. He points out that many of the ninety-five theses can be read as a critique of greed. For example, thesis 28 reads, "Certum est, nummo in cistam tinniente augeri questum et avariciam posse: suffragium autem ecclesie est in arbitrio dei solius.—Gewiß, sobald das Geld im Kasten klingt, können Gewinn und Habgier wachsen, aber die Fürbitte der Kirche steht allein auf dem Willen Gottes."

3. Luther's decision to distance himself from the peasants' uprising and, after having sought to mediate between lords and peasants, to encourage the lords to crush the revolt, is well established.

4. See the value studies of Inglehart et al., *Human Values*.

dren, sexuality, and a strong body.[5] At this intersection Luther presents a challenge to the present moment, just as the new knowledge and values of our era illuminate and challenge him.

While the body has during certain periods been understood as a vehicle for eternal salvation, it is today viewed as a means of conquering the world, not merely the people whom one is physically close to but also via the Internet. The body is also an instrument of reproduction. To continue living through one's children has in every age served as a way to ensure a kind of continued existence or eternal life. And thus it is today also. There is, then, a "need for salvation" that can be exploited in a system of global trade made possible by new technology. When bodies become commodities, along with paid surrogate mothers, the trade in organs, or the sex trade, they pose a challenge to theological notions of integrity and human worth. New questions arise in our glocal society in which local needs are satisfied on a global, unequal market.[6] Technology, economics, and global communications have made possible a reproductive industry capable of coming up with "the right kind of egg" that researchers in this industry need along with healthy sperm.[7] People's longing for children can in this way be satisfied by an industry that risks exploiting the poverty of others. Technology, economics, and biology thus affect our conceptions and create new ethical attitudes. Movements such as transhumanism imagine that new technology will give human beings the means to live far longer.[8]

In an intertextual conversation, I have principally engaged Martin Luther and contemporary scholars, partly in order to let the present and the past challenge one another equally but also in order to search for mental connections. In chapter 4, I described how the body during certain periods was understood as something to successively liberate oneself from, but during other periods was central to the attaining of salvation and eternal life. Today, the body is once again the focus of efforts to achieve health, well being, and longevity. New technology has created new possibilities, and needs, for reproduction and life-prolonging

---

5. My perspective and thus my language are, as I have pointed out earlier, consciously theological.

6. See, for example, S. Lundin, *Organs for Sale*. The notion *glocal* implies that the local is related to the global.

7. S. Lundin, *Guldägget*.

8. These and other movements are not the focus of this study. For a critique, see, for example, Schweiker, "Against the Seductions of Transhumanism."

treatment of the body. Technology has also made it possible to improve and change one's body for cosmetic purposes, for example by enlarging lips and breasts. Sometimes the technology becomes almost an imperative. What can be done must be done. In her book *Mumieland*, Sara Tuss Efrik writes about brothel madams, bodily control, and illegal methods of rejuvenation. "I can relate to the attempt to conquer the world through one's body," she says in an interview, and goes on, "but also to vulnerability in a completely ruthless world. I hung onto my Barbie dolls during my teens at the same time as I underwent a tough coming of age. I both played with dolls and made myself into an available doll."[9] Transformation of the body in order to achieve communion with God and eternal life were during certain periods important elements of monastic piety. Today, our own cult of health and demands for beauty and satisfactory sex can seem like secular paths to salvation by keeping the body "alive, youthful" as long as possible.[10] Once again, the body has become a means to an end.

The body, like our knowledge, thus occupies a field of tension between technology, biology, and economics, which is in turn shaped by theological and philosophical ideas about human beings as bodies. There is an intersectionality here in which different perspectives operate together. The body's presence, or perhaps absence, today challenges both philosophy and theology. "The new materialist turn" is an expression of this renewed interest in the body and substance.

Presence or Representation?

After Immanuel Kant, it became customary to view theology as able to treat only what words and actions represent, never reality as such. According to Kant, consciousness cannot imagine the total or the eternal but merely remains conscious of its own inability.[11] As a result of this perspective, theology began to proceed from the premise that an absent reality can only be represented indirectly in the present, for example by means of words, images, music, and art. Theologian Petra Carlsson claims that in this model of representation, substance can be about as absent as

9. Gustavsson, "Min bok."

10. Coakley, "Eschatological Body," 155.

11. ". . . it can never be anything more than a negative presentation—but still it expands the soul." Kant, *Critique of Judgment*, 29.

divine reality.¹² In my view, both the physical body and the divine are at risk of disappearing from view.

Modern thought includes the notion that the universal is representative of everyone, of totality. What is other is seen as particular and valid only for a few. The universal and the particular have often been presented as opposites. Today, we talk instead about how the universal is always related to the particular, the question being how. A key aspect of critical theory concerns asking questions about what we regard as universal or particular. The question then becomes what is particular or universal for whom.¹³ As we saw in the introduction, Latin American theologians have noted that the idea of the universal arose in the West. It therefore cannot be fully dissociated from the West's global dominance and tendency to regard its own values as universal. Even if one asserts a faith in universal values, as I do, the question remains: who decides what is regarded as universal and representative for everyone? Whose voices are heard and are able to exert an influence? Feminist theologians have pointed out that for long periods of history, not merely humanity but even God has been represented by man. This has led postcolonial and feminist theologians to wonder how, for example, that which differentiates women can be represented by this generically male God. The questions they ask proceed from concrete, physical premises. Did He ever suffer the pains of childbirth? Was He ever raped? Petra Carlsson, for example, asks how women's desire for reconciliation is reflected in the larger narrative.¹⁴

Sociologist and economic historian Diana Mulinari argues that there is a fundamental strength in Immanuel Kant's moral-philosophical argument about what is common and shared. At the same time, she points out that feelings or a particular skin color seem to Kant to be in conflict with what makes us human, namely, reason. She claims that, for Kant, the emotional, when not, like his racism, suppressed, is equally in opposition to the human ability to be an active, rational subject.¹⁵ Kant appears to imagine that it is possible to exclude from philosophy everything that does not seem to make us human, or that it is logical to view certain people as of lesser worth. Africa, women, and children are at the same time fundamental to his moral philosophy, in which they are included as

12. Carlsson, *Theology beyond Representation*, 15.
13. See, for example, MacIntyre, *Whose Justice?* for an early awareness of this.
14. Carlsson, *Theology beyond Representation*, 16.
15. Mulinari, "Ett postkolonialt feminististk samtal," 208; cf. Schott, *Feminist Interpretations*.

imagined arenas and bodies. Mulinari therefore asks whether his racism (and sexism) weaken his basic argument. Not necessarily, she argues. But it reveals a "tension between talk of the human and the universal on the one hand, and on the other the embodiment of the universal in a limited (white and male) worldview: a worldview founded upon the systematic construction of different groups as the other."[16]

The body challenges theological thinking around representation. Where is presence? How can it be understood, and by whom? Descartes's ideas about the primacy of reason have long been challenged. By reading Luther in relation to this challenge, I hope to make a contribution to this issue that raises more questions than I can answer. But it is a way to start a conversation. Luther not infrequently invoked "the natural," not least in relation to bodily needs. He lived with a sensual, bodily presence that also influenced his theological ideas. But what does the relationship between representation and presence look like? His fundamental question, "How am I to find a merciful God?," is metaphysical. His "discovery" that there is a merciful God can be compared to an embrace, one that had lasting consequences for how he envisaged the material. Presence in the midst of the worldly became a recurrent feature. In the following section, I discuss presence in dialogue with a number of contemporary scholars.

Presence—Absence—Representation

The German theologian Martin Wendte argues that Luther turns to the body long before this becomes a trend. One of Wendte's essays takes as its starting point Heidegger's description of the West as technological. It incorporates dualisms between word and body, spirit and nature, and "a loss of presence."[17] According to Wendte, Heidegger argues that technology affects our entire conception of reality, such that everything appears to us as means to an end. All reality, including the individual's body, is regarded as raw material, a resource to be used and shaped by human creatures. We no longer describe reality through technology and science, he argues; we produce it. With the help of biotechnology, human beings can take all living entities, including their own bodies, as material, "a stock (*Bestand*) for future improvement." In this way nature becomes a

---

16. Mulinari, "Ett postkolonialt feminististk samtal," 209.

17. Wendte, "'This is My Body,'" 90. In what follows I take up some of the main ideas in this essay.

product of cultural activity.[18] This is in itself nothing new, I argue, but reiterates the view that time and space are being forced together in our own era. As a result, there are a dwindling number of barriers to an "all-encompassing domination" in which nature disappears.[19]

Wendte describes our bodies in terms of three aspects. First, we are our bodies. By breathing, feeling, and thinking, we are connected to our bodily sensations and activities, which give a holistic dimension to all bodily and mental activities. Second, we *have* bodies. They are a part of the material world "out there" and can accordingly be treated thus, for example as objects of desire. Third, our bodies are products of cultural activities. They are constructed from discourses and lifestyles in which fashion and tattooing, but also discussions of gender, play a part.

Wendte contends that the Internet in particular is of great importance for these second and third aspects of our bodies. There is a large market dedicated to the gratification of every bodily need. There we can consume everything, including that notorious word which begins with "s" and ends with "ex." In this way, the Net involves new paths to freedom in which one can experiment with different genders such as "cross and trans-gender 'reality.'"[20] But the new freedom made available by the Internet is a non-physical freedom, argues Wendte. It is disconnected from the body, from flesh. A new gnosticism is thus lurking just around the corner.[21] My view here is that Wendte himself risks winding up in the old dualisms between body and consciousness. Moreover, many contacts that take place via the Net result in real, concrete meetings between people. Despite this, I believe that there is much to be said for his basic analysis that our present moment can be described as a massive shift from "a culture of presence" to a "culture of representation."

While the late-medieval and Reformation eras had a pre-understanding of reality in terms of presence, that of late modernity characterizes it in terms of representation. According to Wendte, the principal symbol of a culture of presence is the Eucharist, while the most important for a culture of representation is the media. For the former, the body is central to our relation to the world; for the latter, it is consciousness, the mind. For the former, knowledge is something revealed and made

18. Ibid., 91.
19. Ibid., 91f.
20. Ibid., 92f.
21. Ibid., 93.

manifest. For the latter, knowledge is produced. In a culture of presence, the body is integrated into the rhythm of the world. In a culture of representation, human beings change the world. For the former, space is central; for the latter, time.[22] Technology provides new opportunities for action while also reducing our ways of being. This technological domination entails a loss of presence, a loss of real, surprising presence, argues Wendte, following Heidegger. This loss involves a muteness in our relation to things around us, a muteness at the resistance offered by things in their own materiality and worth. It also involves a forgetfulness towards the insight that all things are given to us. Instead, things are taken to be abstract presence, as "stock." The loss of presence entails a marginalizing of non-technological thinking and ways of life, a loss of ourselves as physical, bodily beings and thereby a blindness to vulnerability.

Like the so-called bodily turn, theology's attempt to see reality not as raw material but as a gift involves a resistance. According to Wendte, this emphasis upon body and presence is something we find in Luther. Luther's ontology is characterized by the notion of giving and by life as gift. Luther is a highly "promising author" when it comes to the bodily turn before the latter became a trend. He is thus a "fascinating defender" of presence long before the loss of that very presence in the modern era, argues Wendte. What is more, Luther claims that the gift is given in bodily form. The physical word is thus part of the contents of the gift. As Wendte sees it, Luther's way of mediating between words and representation makes the Eucharist a locus of resistance to technology's all-invading tendency.[23]

Luther understands creation, atonement, and perfection as a tripartite giving from a trinitarian God. creation is one of God's gifts, but it is a gift that is given in a form in which body and word unite. The Eucharist does not constitute a special or different way for God to act towards humanity. Rather, it is "a concentrated form of the way in which God always acts with regard to us."[24] Its content, concrete grace, has an inner connection to the physical, bodily form, in which the form is also a part of the content. The material is part of God's way of communicating with us. It is "a vehicle of the devine."[25] The world's objects communicate with us in

22. Ibid., 93f.
23. Ibid., 95.
24. Ibid., 97 (my translation).
25. According to Luther, the devil has neither flesh nor bone. WA 23, 261, 36; cf. Wendte, "'This is My Body,'" 99n32.

the same way. Creation speaks to us. For Luther, creation in its materiality is very benign.[26] Wendte points out that Luther insists that we always encounter God in and through creation and warns against those who say that the flesh is of no help.[27] Turn it upside down instead, and say: "God without flesh is of no help." Luther's anthropology views the human being as a whole, a unity of body and soul. God's words help us to see the world in a new light and to act on that basis.[28]

Just as heaven is not to be found in some special place up above, but can just as easily be down here when a relation between God and humanity and between people is established, argues Luther, so, too, does this mean that when you put God before me, you must also put the human being there. For they have become one single person.[29] Wendte concludes his essay by claiming that the Eucharist is a sign that the fundamental nature of reality is a matter, not of desiring power, but of giving. This giving adopts benign materiality as its medium. In the Eucharist, God himself promises to be present. At the same time, Wendte claims, he changes our hearts by limiting our desire for power.[30]

Frederick Christian Bauerschmidt is a Roman Catholic theologian at Loyola University. Following the insights of postmodern philosophy, he is also suspicious of the notion of representation to be found in modern thought. Modernity in fact undermined faith, leading to the discovery of a "reality deficit" in all representations of reality.[31] As Kant understood, the Enlightenment created a fundamental pessimism about human beings' capacity to produce any kind of adequate image or account of the sublime.[32] From such a perspective, this reality cannot be represented at all.

Bauerschmidt is searching nonetheless for a way to present the sacred by means of the temporary and historical. Yet postmodern thought, he argues, is characterized by a Nietzschean irony that parodies the modern faith in the existence of a reality outside of representation—that is, beyond words, images, music, and poetry. However, according to

26. WA 23, 351:5–18; cf. LW 43, "Ob man vor dem Sterben fliehen möge" (1527).
27. WA 25, 107, 4–5; cf. Wendte, "'This is My Body,'" 99.
28. Wendte, "'This is My Body,'" 99, where this quotation of Luther's is also mentioned.
29. Ibid., 101; WA 26, 333:6–11; cf. LW 37, "Vom Abendmahl Christi" (1528).
30. Ibid., 103f.
31. Bauerschmidt, "Aestetics," 205.
32. Ibid., 203.

Bauerschmidt, the Christian challenge to theology beyond representation has its roots in the Jewish ban on images. The belief that God became human, the invisible incarnated in Jesus Christ, extends beyond modernity's suspiciousness but without postmodernism's irony.[33] It is not an ironic, distanced attitude towards the world, but a path to real presence. The cross, the tomb, and the road to Emmaus are place of negation, of loss. At the same time, claims Bauerschmidt, it is precisely as particularities that these events take us beyond the mere negation of meaning, to an abundance of meaning. He argues that "in the cross we are presented with a God, who is present even in godlessness, and in the resurrection we are promised that godlessness shall not have the last word."[34] According to Bauerschmidt, then, God is present even in the death of God.

Both Wendte's and Bauerschmidt's theological analyses lead them to the mass. Christ's body is there. God's presence is there. Like several others who belong to or are close to Radical Orthodoxy, they focus on the church and the mass. In this churchification, there is a risk that ordinary human bodies in the context of everyday life disappear from view.

In sharp contrast, the physical human being is the starting point for that radical theology that is usually known as Death of God theology. What one finds in it is a powerful critique of the notion of God as a transcendent God, divorced from human beings, bodily suffering, and passion. This theological tendency emphasizes instead the lived experiences of people. For example, the idea of a God in heavenly glory, far removed from a world that has experienced the Holocaust, becomes unbearable for a German theologian such as Dorothee Sölle (1929–2003).[35] However, according to Petra Carlsson, Sölle interprets representation in a way that opens onto new theological avenues.[36] For Sölle, the notion that the living Jesus is replaced by Christ in the Resurrection leads to a separation of God from the suffering world. She does not wish to encourage a line of thought in which an all-powerful god is imagined as having suffered once and for all, and, having conquered the world, as now merely observing earthly suffering at a distance.

For Sölle, "representative Christ" is something else. He plays the part of God in a world in which God is dead. His representation is neither

---

33. Ibid., 205.
34. Ibid., 210.
35. Sölle, *Christ the Representative.*
36. Carlsson, *Theology beyond Representation,* 15.

powerful nor eternal, argues Sölle, but exists in the world as a temporary representative for God, as a provisional but continuing incarnation, as a powerless advocate who plays the part of God.[37] Christ as representative remains in the "not yet" of the anguish and impotence of the cross, Carlsson explains.[38]

Carlsson argues that both Sölle and Bauerschmidt emphasize God's presence. But Sölle claims that in a world of suffering and oppression, there must be an opportunity for complaining and calling into question. She believes that this is possible because Christ on the cross is present as a temporary representative. However, according to Petra Carlsson's interpretation, Bauerschmidt's idea of a presence beyond suspicion obscures the fact of suffering.[39]

What does Martin Luther have to say about this? As Wendte observes, Luther argues that Christ is truly present in the Holy Communion, the Eucharist. But what does this presence look like outside of the mass? Does Luther imagine a divine presence in the body, sexuality, and eroticism as well, or is all that separate from the divine? The vulnerable, tired, suffering body becomes for Luther a reminder of Christ. Luther's theology of the cross is closely tied up with his intense experience of the world as having been violated by the Evil One. Suffering, violence, and death are the consequences of this destruction. Against this, God is continually creating new life, healing, and restoring. Whether consciously or not, human beings form part of this act of creating and redeeming. The strong, desiring, receptive, and giving body is compared with God's creating words. It is God's words that create lust and attraction, making "the seed in a human body become fruit." This is not, Luther argues, something that can be disciplined or "obstructed by means of promises or regulations. For these are God's words and deeds."[40]

Luther's attack on asceticism's disciplining is evident. It forms part of his strong emphasis that it is God who acts, while human beings receive life and salvation as an undeserved gift. This continues for all of one's life. Sarah Coakley, a contemporary advocate of asceticism, talks about how contemplative or charismatic prayer in particular can open the way to the

---

37. Sölle, *Christ the Representative*, 200.

38. Carlsson, *Theology beyond Representation*, 17.

39. Ibid., 19.

40. WA 18, 275, "Christliche Schrift an W. Reitzenbusch, sich in den ehelichen Stand zu begeben" (1525). The view that a woman's uterus was as important as sperm did not exist at this time.

Holy Spirit and the mystery of the Trinity. In such prayer, human beings become conscious of their inability to pray and to allow God to be God.[41] For Luther, it is rather life in itself that helps people to discover their inability and blindness to God. That it is the Holy Spirit who prays in us strikes him as self-evident. But he broadens the notion of God's actions to apply to all of life. It is God who works through the estates, those different arenas in which people's bodies are required for the fulfilment of God's actions: "A vocation is a 'station' which is by nature helpful to others. And this is not confined to an occupation, but includes being a mother or father, son or daughter. What is important is to avoid a station that is not good, not if the heart is sinful."[42] As Gustaf Wingren argues in his reading of Luther, these actions occur independently of people's hearts or any inner re-creation.

And yet Christ's presence is a comfort in suffering. But suffering is nothing to seek out or strive for. In joy, everything good reminds us of God's gifts, given through other people's bodies, within which God remains concealed. People's bodies and desires are part of God's own creating and divine presence.

Ideas about representation and presence raise new questions about familiar issues. In what follows I therefore examine modernity's desire to discipline the body.

The Modern Disciplining of the Body

On the basis of contemporary historical studies and new knowledge of the body and sexuality, it is possible to describe Lutheran societies as ideologically hetero-patriarchal. But our discussion of presence and representation means that we can also catch a glimpse of the modern "disciplining of the body," to use the terminology of Michel Foucault.[43] Theologian Ola Sigurdson summarizes that the "modern discipline of the body aims to generate an effective body rather than a virtuous or sensual body."[44] Its ideology was not about strengthening the "individual's control over the body." Rather, the goal was to increase "society's 'use' of the

---

41. Coakley, *God, Sexuality*, 55.
42. Wingren, *Luther on Vocation*, 4.
43. Foucault, *History of Sexuality*; cf. Foucault, *Discipline and Punish*, 135–69.
44. Sigurdson, *Heavenly Bodies*, 334.

body."⁴⁵ Sigurdson claims that the body does not exist independently of institutions but is dependent upon its environment and lives in interplay with the latter. The body is always implicated in institutions and "woven into a larger context of practices and discourses that fight for its attention and form its desire."⁴⁶

The nation-state has to a large extent taken over the control of sexuality from the church.⁴⁷ Just as we receive advice from the Department of Health on what we should eat and how much, so, too, is there an official ideology in which the church and theology no longer constitute providers of ideology. In his study of the history of sexuality, Foucault claims that confession made sexuality a concern of the church. The church in question here is French and Roman Catholic. Had Foucault studied Protestant societies, he might have seen other patterns. Historical scholars have emphasized that firm control over people's sex lives was exercised jointly by both state and church after the Reformation, as, for example, in Sweden.⁴⁸ Sarah Coakley notes that even contemporary biblicist, fundamentalist, and conservative theologians, particularly the anti-gay lobby, view modern heterosexuality as stipulated and regulated by the Bible.⁴⁹ At the same time, it may be noted that Foucault's thesis, that disciplining of the body and sexual life has in modernity passed to the state and various authorities, is correct. Sex must now be not merely assessed, but administrated. It is thereby becoming a matter for the authorities.⁵⁰ These are to determine which sex can be assigned to a newborn child, the consequences of a possible sex change, and the opportunities for forming a family, for example, by means of adoption.

And yet there is also an ongoing debate over how much influence the state should have. The authorities and legislation determine which sexuality should be protected and promoted—via legal support for particular forms of cohabitation and via tax breaks, inheritance rights, and parental leave entitlements. A juridification of ethics can be discerned in demands that consent to intercourse should be introduced into legislation relating to rape. While this may seem self-evident on an ethical level,

45. Ibid.
46. Ibid., 336.
47. Ibid., 436.
48. See, for example, Österberg, *Folk förr*, 162.
49. Coakley, *God, Sexuality*, 53.
50. Foucault, *History of Sexuality*, 24, 33; cf. Sigurdson, *Heavenly Bodies*, 436.

such a formulation might prove decisive for what is deemed rape in a legal context.

It was not so long ago, however, that there was a general refusal to think about, and, above all, talk about, occurrences such as rape or sexual coercion, particularly within the framework of marriage. Instead, precedence was given to the integrity of private life, which in practice often meant patriarchal notions of men's legitimate demands.

In our era, sexuality has increasingly become part of the public sphere. There are numerous examples of an ostensibly quite loveless sexuality in which continual new conquests seem to be the most important thing. "Let's talk about it," a Twitter conversation about good and bad sexual experiences, about grey zones between sex and assault, has shown how many women and not a few men still accept sex that does not feel good. Despite years of sexual liberation, it seems that people do not enjoy equal positions when it comes to framework and direction.

The origins of late-modern society's most influential disciplining project are anything but political, however. Rather, a mediatized and digitized culture is now establishing norms that encourage women to be subordinate and is urging young girls, but also boys, to objectify their bodies. It is sometimes claimed that the body cult, or perhaps body loathing, of the present moment is making people subject themselves to more serious damage and ascetic control than that which existed during certain periods of the monastic system which Luther criticized.[51]

Set against the centuries in which state and church jointly exercised control over people's sexuality, the sexual liberation of our era seems like a positive thing. At the same time, new disciplining institutions are emerging. As important as the question of which values governed the societal institutions of yesteryear—marriage and the family, for example—is the question of which values are today determining the framework and disciplining of people's gender and sexuality. Are they contributing to support, growth, and protection against assault, or are they abandoning the weaker parties to survive as best they can? According to the Lutheran view of humanity, a human being is a totality, which should be seen as both lost and saved. Likewise, there are no structures in the social body that Lutheran ethics regards as being beyond good and evil. Good and evil cut right across both individual and collectivity.

---

51. In "The Eschatological Body," Coakley, who adopts a very positive attitude to asceticism, wonders, "From what other site of control am 'I' pummeling [the body] into submission, beauty, or longevity?" (155).

While the Lutheran tradition often asserts the body as a working body, Luther's writings also contain a more complex view that includes desire, joy, and vulnerability. All is permeated by divine presence.[52] Luther expresses himself in terms surprisingly similar to contemporary discussion of sexuality as connected to health and a natural life.[53] On this point, both he and our own era are being challenged by a long tradition that has also discussed desire and *eros* in terms of longing, curiosity, and affection, and, not least, by a practice that has connected lust, eroticism, and the body to more than just procreation.

Ambivalence Then and Now

Reformation historian Kirsi Stjerna describes the Reformation as ambivalent with regard to the status of women. In the first place, women were active in the realization of the Reformation, often independently of men. They were visible in both words and actions. Despite this, the Reformation excluded women from clerical and official leadership positions. This was to some extent balanced by the new vocational ethic in which all tasks were viewed as vocations, and by the emphasis placed on individual freedom and the universal priesthood of all believers. Although the closure of the monasteries entailed a definite loss for many women, the emphasis on the universal priesthood of all believers and the Bible as the sole authority opened the door wide for women to see that they had a spiritual vocation. All vocations were viewed as having equal value, at least in theory. The consecrating of marriage and childbearing was extremely important for women, who, quite regardless, were expected to devote their lives to being wives and bearing children.

As Stjerna summarizes it, the Reformation thus entailed both wins and losses. It cannot be described as either a loss or a victory for women. The truth is more complex.[54] While there was a reduction in the number

---

52. WA 18, 275, "Christliche Schrift an W. Reitzenbusch, sich in den ehelichen Stand zu begeben" (1525) can be interpreted as saying that it is God's presence which, through His Word, creates new life. In the Cornelius chapter of *De servo arbitrio* (1525), Luther defends the unbaptized through reference to John the Baptist and his parents as well as to Mary, mother of Jesus, and Simeon, who, despite not having heard that Christ was risen, shared in the Holy Spirit. WA 18, 551–787; cf. LW 33.

53. This is almost blatantly obvious from his *Letter to Several Nuns*, WA Br 3, 327–28 (no. 766), "Luther an drei Klosterjungfrauen" (1524).

54. Stjerna, *Women and the Reformation*, 214.

of legitimate roles in society as a result of life becoming more difficult for unmarried women, among others, Luther's emphasis upon the universal priesthood of believers, for example, and his demand that everyone, both boys and girls, should receive education, would later be used by women in the nineteenth and twentieth centuries in their struggle for emancipation. This also meant that women's status as the lowest of the low was raised. In particular, everyday occupations such as cooking food and looking after children increased in value.[55]

This led in turn to a change in how the body was viewed. It was considered primarily as a gift to one's fellow humans. In one's everyday occupations, one gave one's body and labor to one's fellows, so that they could have freshly baked bread and newly brewed beer, clean new clothes, etc. In sexual desire and sexuality, people gave their bodies to each other. There is an obvious presence in the bodily, something almost God-given. Bodies form part of God's creating and preserving of the world. Here, too, there is a presence, one in which the divine can be sensed as if behind a mask.

Despite Luther's ambivalence towards powerful sexual desire, it, too, belonged to created, natural life.[56] The blessing of sexual intercourse lived on after the Fall. Danish theologian Niels Henrik Gregersen contends that it would therefore be more sensible to speak of original godliness than original sin.[57] Luther breaks with the tradition of disciplining and suppressing sexuality. Instead, he affirms it as a part of life. But he stands close to Augustine and saves sexuality by connecting it to marriage and procreation. Meanwhile, the body does not become a path to the divine, to union with God, either through libertinism or by controlling it in order to approach closer to God. The body is regarded as something good, but it is there for humanity and its well being. As a means of transformation—for saving the body and the soul from death—it is of no interest. As an earthly, living body, here and now, by contrast, it is anything but unimportant. For Luther, the spectacles of faith become a way to interpret the gifts of creation as signs of God's love and presence. The confidence of faith reveals to us God's presence in the midst of the temporal.

---

55. Gerle, "Luther, erotik och tvetydighet," 33–34.
56. WA 18, "Christliche Schrift."
57. Gregersen, "Skabelse og forsyn," 78.

As we saw in chapter 6, union with God is something given immediately, as a gift without conditions. It is not the result of purification and illumination but constitutes an instantaneous transformation for whoever receives God as a gift.[58]

From a Lutheran perspective, contemplative and charismatic prayers, pilgrimages, and retreats are neither merits nor ways to draw closer to God. They can rather be described with the term *adiaphora*, something one can both have and lack, since it makes no difference to salvation. On the other hand, all this can, of course, help to create the space and time needed for a hard-pressed modern person to experience a meeting with God. For those who have neither the means nor the time, however, it can be a comfort to know that the divine presence is also to be found in daily toil, in the sighs of prayer when things feel oppressive, and in the joy at the good things that life brings. For a Lutheran ethics, the song of praise comes from gratitude at life, the material good, the beautiful, and the delightful, and from the struggle against evil, rather than by seeking emptiness and purification. For Luther, self-reflection and meditation were a path that risked leading to self-absorption. He therefore recommended fellowship, music, and song, in order to drive away evil.

The classic Reformation image of redemption is being wrapped up, as if in a new and different garment. An equally apt image would be to speak of this as a loving embrace. It is also a way to avoid the legal imagery that for so long has characterized Lutheran theology.

Traditional Lutheran theology has foregrounded the body's work and its heavy toil for itself and others. This has often been described as being a Christ to one's fellow human beings and bearing one's cross for the sake of love. But we also catch glimpses of joy and sexual desire in Luther's writings. Joy at forgiveness, childlikeness, and perhaps union with God—at least nearness to God—all lend work a new tone

Tomas Appelqvist claims that "*theosis* recurs as a 'motif' throughout Luther's theological output, even if the clearest and the most examples occur in his early writings."[59] Luther started from a classical definition of love that involved seeing love as the force that unites the lover and the loved with each other.[60] Love changes people and creates an abundance.

---

58. Kleinhans, "Christ as Bride/Groom"; see also chapter 6.
59. Appelqvist, *Bönen*, 39.
60. Ibid., 37; cf. Peura, "Christ as Favor and Gift," 42–69.

When contemporary theologians emphasize the body as a gift and as grace, they are offering points of overlap with Luther's thought. When the relationship between language and body is described as a mystery, it is being connected to God and life as mysteries.[61] This represents a challenge to the reductionist view of knowledge and means that theology is once again opened up "to horizons beyond metaphysics and modernism."[62]

The search for a theology beyond patriarchy, violence, and metaphysics unites scholars from different traditions. Today concepts such as presence are being counterposed to the suspicion that what we imagine as reality is impossible to describe.

Poetry and Music as Theology

Music was important to Luther. He played the lute and composed verse. Poetry, song lyrics, and music represented different ways to express faith and live in faith, but were also signs of God's presence in the midst of the sensual. For Luther, joy was a means of scaring away the devil, that is, doubt and temptations.[63] "Luther claims that after theology, he honors and values music the highest.[64] Poetry, music, and dogmatics belonged together in Luther's view. The sensual had a close relation to the aesthetic. That Martin Luther wrote hymns and psalms—and not merely pamphlets, polemics, sermons, and dogmatic commentaries—is well known. There are artistic representations of an apparently jovial Luther playing the lute. This image is usually associated with his table talk, which records what seem to have been lively and cheerful entertainments. The large household managed by Katharina von Bora could grow to as many as around twenty-five people.[65]

Hymns were a part of pedagogy. The gospel was to be sung and presented so simply that even small children could understand. The psalm song has long been seen as central in evangelical churches. It was a matter of singing the gospel into the hearts of people as well as a way of creating

---

61. Beattie, *New Catholic Feminism*, 48.
62. Ibid.
63. Bainton, *Luther*, 323; cf. Stolt, "*Laßt uns fröhlich springen!*"
64. WA 30 II, 696; cf. Bainton, *Luther*, 323.
65. Bainton, *Luther*, 259.

a community of individuals by song, but also of singing as a way to dispel doubt and mistrust.

A dissertation from Helsinki emphasizes that Luther loved music as an "innocent pleasure." All musical expressions are seen as God's gift, the music of the spheres, birdsong, the human voice, and, not least, artistic music.[66] What is really interesting, however, is not how innocent music is but that something happens immediately, at the very instant the ear or the brain, the whole body in fact, is touched by music. For Luther, this paralleled the way in which the liberating words of forgiveness create anew, in that very moment. Miikka E. Anttila argues that Luther proceeds from a notion of the triune God as the giving God. When human beings receive God's gifts, a song of praise, a musical phenomenon, is awoken. In Luther's thought, what makes music special is precisely that it awakens people's feelings. This emphasis is bound up with Luther's view of theology as affective, indeed, sensual. The power of music is related to the way in which the word can be heard. Faith comes from hearing the word, something that is at once a musical and an emotional experience.

Faith is thus expressed not only intellectually but also as the emotional trust of the heart. In the same way as music can touch the human heart and persuade by means of its sweetness, so, too, can the good news of the gospel. Anttila is arguing, then, that one can see Luther's theology as a theology of joy and desire. Joy is a gift of the Holy Spirit that fills the heart and finds expression in voice and gestures. In Anttila's reading, desire is a central aspect of Luther's theology. One of the problems that Luther highlights in the enslaved will is our inability to feel desire in God's will. Christians thus ought not to avoid delighting in a visible and tangible creation. On the contrary, not to delight in the goodness God has created is, for Luther, a sign of lack of faith and ingratitude. The material is not a threat to the spiritual, but a sign of God's goodness. To be able to interpret life in this way is a part of faith, one that brightens the world and dispels darkness and doubt. Faith is described as the light of God's face since it involves a divine illumination of the senses and a semblance of the divine that fills the heart of the believer, a recognition of and a trust in a present God.[67]

---

66. Anttila, "The Innocent Pleasure."
67. WA 5, 118:1–16 (AWA 2, 200:3–201:15), "Operationes in Psalmos" (1519–21).

The Sensual and Affective Luther

Luther was not afraid of physicality and expressive imagery. His recorded table talk reveals an appreciation of food and drink, song, conversation, and poetry that seems far removed from modernity's counterposing of spiritual and material, reason and feeling, but also of God's agency in everyday life or the material and in the spiritual or sacral.

Martin Luther was an expressionistic, emotional person and preacher, who aimed at people's hearts. Despite this, theologians have often interpreted Luther more systematically than he comes across in his writings. The powerful rationalism that has characterized Lutheran theology and ethics for several centuries can therefore be questioned. As we have seen, a number of German scholars have argued that moral duty and great distance from everything pleasurable was, rather, an innovation of Kant's. It seems alien to the passionate, affective, and often-contradictory style in which Luther advanced his ideas. The conflicts in which he found himself during his lifetime were continually creating new fronts. He polemicized fiercely against his opponents. To read his texts without regard to his context, or to identify what or whom he was raging against, is to do a kind of violence to his thinking. Above all, it runs the risk of missing several important themes that we now have considerable sympathy for.

Martin Luther was not afraid to talk about his own experiences. He is famous for expressing faith and what it means specifically for me, as a human being here and now, that God has created me and that Christ has reconciled me to God, an experience that the Holy Spirit helps me to live in.[68]

Unlike Romanticism and the later focus on one's own feelings as decisive in deciding whether something is true or false, Luther nonetheless uses declarations of faith to reject feelings of doubt and depression, what he called trials of the devil. He referred to what he wrote as objective truth. At the same time, he himself played a decisive role in ensuring that certain interpretations were fixed as truths, while others were declared to be misleading and false. This process involved feelings and intuitive experiences just as much as historical events. There is a greater interaction between the subjective and the intersubjectively testable than the rationalist tradition allows.

Luther's images and verses suggest that his faith has more in common with poetry than with an investigative text. Fellowship with Christ

---

68. See, for example, Luther's explanations of the Articles of the Creed.

as a loving embrace and marriage bed have been recurrent examples in this study.[69] Luther's hymns are often formulated out of despair and anguish, to encourage faith and confidence, but also as a pedagogical tool for telling the gospel narratives in a simple way.

Faith as Trust and Re-creation

Just as the heart is touched by music, so too does something happen in the heart and body when the ear hears the words of God's grace. The words create anew. Instantaneously. The Lutheran tradition has for this reason spoken of a Living Word. Within a particular pietistic tradition, the division between faith and action has been presented as if knowledge leads to action. Yet this is a post-hoc reconstruction. For Luther, faith involves trust that in an instant can disrupt people's self-absorption and make them open to their fellow humans, the other. But this trust is continually threatened. It must therefore be restored and recreated time and again. The word, the address, is thus of vital importance. "Given for you." The words, in tandem with the taste of bread and wine on the tongue, create new hope, courage, and trust. The loving embrace meets people in simple bread and wine, as well as when words and water are joined in the baptismal address: Be not afraid! You are mine, I have called you by name.

The Lutheran tradition speaks of two sacraments: baptism and the mass. Sometimes the Word is referred to as the third. This emphasis upon the Word with a capital *w* has meant that the Lutheran tradition has sometimes appeared incorporeal and more connected to the brain than to the rest of the body. But even the brain and the heart are part of the body. Luther emphasized hearing and the importance of the ear. The mouth that speaks the words of forgiveness, the ear that hears, and the heart that is touched so that something new occurs—all are important. But also the tongue that tastes and licks, the hand that strokes and bakes bread, changes nappies, washes, and cooks food.

Luther is considerably more sensual than what the rationalistic reading of his works typically claims. He invoked the traditional marital metaphorics of sensual love between God and the soul, but also used similar imagery for the relations between people. It is not just words that move, then. The community of bodies, music, and other people's

---

69. WA 7, 12–38, cf. LW 31 "Von der Freiheit" (1520).

encouragement and comfort are also signs of caring and grace. For Luther, all this becomes an address, a love letter from God, something that touches the body and all its senses: hearing, sight, smell, taste, and feeling. Does this mean that one can speak of a sensual ethics? Yes, I would argue that this is quite clearly a highly bodily theology with physical consequences, not least in everyday life.

This is an important contribution to an ethics that not merely emphasizes the demands of our fellow human beings but seeks inspiration and a desire to do good in a curiosity about the other and a trust in life. There can be no doubt here that Luther's feeling for and experience of the loving embrace, which we encountered in chapter 6, provide a reason for loving actions in everyday life. And such actions are highly physical. Physical community creates trust between spouses and makes each of them trust all they have to the other.[70]

God's love is bound up with love for our fellow human beings. This also becomes clear in Luther's commentaries on the ten commandments, each of which begins with the words "We should fear and love God . . ." Caring for one's nearest is described in commentaries four to ten as a direct consequence of this.

---

70. WA 34, 52:5–21, "Eine Hochzeitpredigt über den Spruch Hebr 13, 4" (1531). "[5] Wol haben die alten Doctores geprediget, das der ehestand der frucht, [6] trew und lieb halben zuloben sey, Jst aber nicht auch die leibliche nuetzung [7] ein koestlich ding, das die erste tugent des ehestands geruemet ist, das sich ein [8] man auff sein weib verlassen darff, sein leib und gut auff dieser erden dem [9] weib troestlich befehlen, das es bey jhr als wol bewaret sey als bey jhm, Diese [10] frucht were auch wol eine, Aber wir wollen die selbigen nicht erzelen, befehlen [11] solchs den Rhetoren. Christlich und gottlich davon zu reden, ist das das [12] hochste, das Gottes wort an deinem weibe und an deinem man geschrieben ist, [13] wenn du dein weib also ansihest, als were nur eins und keins mehr auff [14] dieser welt, und wenn du deinen man also ansihest, als were nur einer und [15] sonst keiner mehr jnn der welt, das kein koenig, ja auch die Sonne nicht [16] schoener scheinen und jnn deinen augen leuchten sol als eben dein fraw odder [17] dein man, Denn alhie hastu Gottes wort, welchs dir die fraw odder den man [18] zuspricht, schenckt dir die fraw oder den man, Spricht: der man sol dein [19] sein, die fraw sol dein, das gefelt mir so wol, alle Engel und Creaturn haben [20] lust und freud darob, Denn es ist jhe kein schmuck uber Gottes wort, damit du [21] dein weib ansihest als ein Gottes geschenck, Also kanstu kein bloeds gewissen haben."

Sacred and Profane

As Wendte points out, modernity and technology often encompass a number of dualisms. One such dualism is the division between private and public. In this division the private has been seen as a woman's sphere and nowadays often as a sphere, the only one, where religion can be permitted. At the same time the ordinary meal and the home have been desacralized within theology but not within popular culture. There a well-cooked meal and a beautiful home are becoming signs of the good life, almost something sacred. Theologically, however, the ordinary meal has been made subordinate to the stylized meal, as the Latin American theologian Primavesi, among others, has argued. She claims that the male representatives of institutionalized religion have been given the power to spiritualize the latter by making it into a part of Christ's body.[71]

The notions of presence that I have summarized using the work of Martin Wendte can here become an important challenge for bringing the Eucharist and the ordinary meal in the home closer to each other. The meal of the divine service is a concentrated form of God's gift, which is always given in material form. It includes atonement and presence as physically tangible. Luther's delight in Katharina's supper table and in community is evident in his table talk. There, as we saw in chapter 5, he also gives the advice to seek the company of good friends, to eat, drink, and perhaps think about girls, in order to drive away depression and doubt.[72] All this was viewed as essential to the good life. In the material we meet God as creating, sustaining, and healing.

In an era glutted with television cooking programs and ever more sophisticated cook books, there are many points of overlap. Here, too, can be seen a cultural critique that goes along with a view of life as a gift. We are then challenged to widen the circle also to include those who lack the means to satisfy their hunger, not just spiritually or mentally, but physically, tangibly. For Niels Henrik Gregersen, the insight that our environment can be both taken for granted and under threat is a "creation-theological realism" and an expression for creation's continued need for God as creator.[73]

For a short period in historical terms, women have also been able to celebrate mass. Yet the liturgy has not been substantially influenced

---

71. Primavesi, *From Apocalypse to Genesis.*
72. WA TR 1, 49–50 (no. 122), "Tischreden" (1531).
73. Gregersen, "Skabelse og forsyn," 62.

by this development, even though inroads have been made from various quarters in an attempt to connect the mass to the everyday meal and ordinary life.[74] People's bodies and the things that characterize an ordinary meal, namely, smell and being full, continue to end up on the margins in a way that denies the concept of incarnation.[75] Despite decades of liturgical development, much remains to be done by way of connecting the mass more closely to the sanctity of everyday life.

Luther's unhesitating appreciation for everyday life can here serve as an inspiration for making porous the boundary between sacred and profane. For Luther is continually tracing God's care in the everyday. Several barriers between sacred and profane were therefore called into question by his theology. All of life was seen as sacred, a sacrament.

Which Institutions Are Influencing Current Attitudes?

The Lutheran tradition's view of marriage and married life has fluctuated between a more Reformatory view and one influenced by Roman Catholicism. A Catholic sacramental understanding of marriage presents it as a *natural* order and thus indissoluble even when unhappy.[76] Gustafsson describes this as a conflict "between a view of the subject shaped by modernity in which the subject is to a large degree allowed to act independently, and one influenced by tradition in which the subject is seen as needing tradition in order to act in a morally correct way."[77] Johanna Gustafsson has shown that, while the Reformist view, as well as a secularized understanding of marriage, are seen as resting upon the consent of each party, representatives of the church have long argued that Christian marriage is characterized by fidelity and is decided by the will of God with regard to marriage.[78]

Today, marriage in the West is characterized by the view that a relationship should proceed from mutual consent, something that seems reasonable and necessary in our part of the world.[79] In the debate, a soci-

74. Edgardh, *Gudstjänsten i tiden*, 116.
75. Grenholm, "Makt under inkarnationens villkor."
76. Gustafsson, *Kyrka och kön*, 145 (my italics).
77. Ibid.
78. Ibid.
79. Child marriage and arranged marriages are practiced in many parts of the world, but also rejected on good ground from a perspective of human rights and the rights of the child.

ologist such as Zygmunt Bauman describes and criticizes what he calls a de-ethicized intimacy.[80] Ethicists and many legal scholars in this debate are advancing claims for protection and legislation for the most intimate of relations, calling among other things for clear consent to sexual relations. For decades, theological feminism has demanded reciprocity in sexual relations, not merely consent but mutual pleasure as well as the rights and integrity of the body in sexual relations. This is even more radical. Invoking an international debate, theologian Sólveig Anna Bóasdóttir argues that the failure to include one's partner in sexual pleasure is a violation of the Christian injunction to love thy neighbor.[81]

The ambivalence of desire and intimacy is bound up with contemporary discourse to a very great degree. An idealized, or de-ethicized, love risks finding itself in a state of permanent dissatisfaction that drives human beings on. The gap between ideal and reality, as well as between different visions of the good life, is enormous.

The institutions that, then and now, have had as their aim the regulation of sexuality and its consequences have always proceeded from the view that material circumstances and different views of the body and sexuality operate in tandem. During certain periods, the rights of the weaker party have been emphasized. Even the severe legislation enacted during the period of Lutheran orthodoxy sought to treat women and men alike, that is, in a gender neutral fashion.[82] Marriage has often been described as a way to protect women and children. At the same time as this institution has aimed to protect women and children, it has in practice often been the most dangerous place for them. This has not disappeared, but perhaps become even more so, now that marriage and the family have come to be regarded as a part of the private sphere, in a way that was unknown in Luther's day.

Contemporary Challenges and the Political Consequences of Rereading

Late modern society is often described as eclectic. Both individuals and institutions can choose among a great many alternatives when shaping their identity or brand. This goes for moral attitudes, too. What this

---

80. Bauman, *Postmodern Ethics*, 106.
81. Bóasdóttir, "Bodyrights and Christian Sexual Ethics," 24.
82. Cronberg, *Synd och skam*, 133.

means is individuals are forced to construct not merely an identity but an entire life project.[83] A number of sociologists point out that the individualization processes of the twentieth century also entailed a profound detraditionalization. The individual has been successively detached from all collective ties. This freedom of choice and "disengagement from traditions and ideologies" can nevertheless give rise to a "desire for belonging, for understanding oneself as a part of something more collective."[84] The present moment thus exhibits a tension between the individual's freedom and a desire for belonging, or between security and freedom.[85]

Although scholars refer to our period as either late- or post-modern, the concept "modern" still has a positive connotation. To be modern signifies foresight and a willingness to be part of the present as well as a dose of optimism about the future. It also encompasses the notion that individuals to a large degree create their own future. Modernity has long been criticized for its pervasive individualism. It risks, in other words, becoming atomistic and ignoring the fact that we become human through interaction with our significant others. Despite this, the word modern is still a highly valued term in public discourse. This, too, is an area where a rereading of Luther serves to highlight contradictions.

Luther and other reformers are sometimes described as having inaugurated the early modern era. But perhaps Luther was not in fact so narrowly individualistic. Even as he emphasized a personal relationship to God, he saw people as part of a wider fabric of relations. Human beings were part of a larger narrative than their own. When Luther in *On the Freedom of a Christian* described a Christian as both the most liberated of all people and at the same time the slave or servant of all, he was underscoring precisely this fact that people live in relation to other people.[86] In relation to God, *coram Deo*, human beings are free. At the same time, they are tied by relations to other people, *coram hominibus*. He himself continually invoked tradition, but chose which narratives and themes to foreground. Following Kristeva, we can today speak of intertextuality and heteroglossia when we see how his texts are connected to a complex fabric of contemporary and earlier discourses within his own

---

83. Gustafsson Lundberg, *Medlem 2010*, 7.
84. Ibid.
85. Bauman, *Community*, 20.
86. WA 7, 12–38, "Von der Freiheit" (1520); cf. LW 31.

culture.[87] Luther works intertextually, then. When he uses already established motifs, such as those of the erotic bridal mystery, in new and more earthly, everyday contexts, something new happens. In his commentaries on Genesis, he aligns himself with a more traditional view of masculine and feminine, yet in other contexts he breaks new ground with regard to views on men and women. He sees them, for example, as radically equal before God. As we saw in chapter 6, he follows earlier mystics in using a language that disrupts traditional gender patterns and that ought more precisely to be described as queer.

A number of contemporary critical perspectives have been important touchstones for my ambition to move beyond dichotomies and a rationalist reading of Luther that differentiates between hearing and giving, between understanding cognitively and motivating to do, and between the individual as a person and the individual as part of a larger community. This does not mean that I am allowing the present context to be the final arbiter of what is right and wrong. As the phenomenological tradition since Hans-Georg Gadamer has made us aware, we can never fully locate ourselves outside of the tradition to which we belong.[88] But from a late-modern perspective, it is important to try to become conscious of the way that we are continually asking ourselves what we choose to retain from the tradition of the modern and what we wish to reject—what is important to emphasize and what should be, if not ignored, then at least nuanced.

Approaches to Knowledge

At the risk of simplification, we can say that people are today widely regarded as mechanical, biological, or economic. The mechanistic approach, which can be traced back to Descartes, sees human beings as machines, while the biological approach sees them as a result of evolution. To consider human beings as in the final instance engaged in maximizing profit and utility involves reducing them to an economic being,

---

87. See Kristeva, *Desire in Language*, 69, on notions such as intertextuality and heterologssia coined by M. Bakhtin. These terms substitute for the dialogical, in contrast to the monological in texts, by emphasizing that texts are part of a web where they relate to, are critical of, or develop other texts, including the texts of others. Cf. Bakhtin, *The Dialogic Imagination*, contrasting "the 'dialogic' and the 'monologic' work of literature."

88. Gadamer, *Truth and Method*.

homo oeconomicus. All these approaches to human beings, which can operate together in different ways, are considered scientific. By contrast, the tradition going back to Plato for which a human being is also a spirit, one capable of wisdom, is seen as anything but scientific. It is simply not measurable in the same way. In our own era, reductionist approaches to human beings rest upon an approach to knowledge as something that can be separated from the body and measured. For this approach to knowledge, the Platonic tradition's idea of wisdom poses a challenge, a challenge reinforced by the last few decades of research into the body and consciousness.

The theory of knowledge that has long dominated in the West and its universities has emphasized the distance between researchers and their object of research. An external perspective has been seen as furthering objectivity. This is now strongly contested, in particular by phenomenologists who emphasize that no-one can fully stand outside of their body and environment, and that all knowledge is reflexive.[89] Chinese-American theologian Kwok Pui-lan claims that theological research at universities has adapted itself to modernity's conceptions of scientific objectivity and its ideals of objective truth. She is critical of this development, which, she argues, has taken place because theology has chosen to retain its place as an academic discipline within a secular university. This attitude, which is influenced by the Enlightenment's faith in science, reason, and positivism, is not new. Nor is the critique of it. Kwok Pui Lan nonetheless questions the putatively objective and value-neutral modern paradigm that today appears in de-Christianized and universalized form with all the trappings of secularism.[90] Time and again, it has shown itself to be anything but objective; rather, it should be seen as a modern construction by which the secular is presented as objective while the religious is described as subjective and biased.

The critique of modernity's simplistic universalism and secular hegemony may offer some new approaches for a study of Luther and Lutheran theology and ethics.[91] The Lutheran tradition has suppressed

---

89. See more on this in chapter 3. That knowledge is reflexive does not mean that it is relative but, rather, that it can never be separated from personal perspective. It is always experienced by the mind as situated. The universal always proceeds from the particular. The interesting question is therefore how the particular and the universal relate to each other.

90. Kwok, *Postcolonial Imagination*, 187–89.

91. I have earlier, following Jürgen Habermas, drawn a distinction between

ritual in favor of the oral and the auditory: the word as written and read aloud. The language of rationality has been prioritized over the language of poetry.[92] The striving for objectivity and intersubjectivity has barred the way to an acknowledgment of the subject's derived knowledge of reality. The personal and affective language that characterizes so much of Luther's writings could here serve as an inspiration for emphasizing physical presence and the concrete, rather than a language that opens onto representation and rationalism.

Contemporary researchers have begun reading this tradition in ways that range beyond modernity. Such readings include a renewed interest in ritual, embodied knowledge, and what is seen as the most important knowledge. Research on ritual is foregrounding action, particularly those things we do together. Ritual as a practical expression is valued today as a source of theological reflection.[93] Research on rituals and the ritualizing of life-cycles and seasons shows that these can acquire the character of a manifestation of the ecosystem's unity and of God's immanence.

Theologian Maria Jansdotter argues with regard to research on ritual, and from an ecofeminist perspective, that theological knowledge, like philosophical and scientific knowledge, rests on an abstract mode of reasoning that in principle was long available only to privileged men. For women and men outside this privileged group, there remained a daily and experience-based form of knowledge that as a rule was not considered knowledge.[94] Following the Brazilian theologian Ivone Gebara, Jansdotter claims that both the Western theory of knowledge and Christian theology have foregrounded the autonomy of the individual. From this perspective, the ability to think and plan represents an argument for human beings' special status within nature as well as for an anthropocentric worldview.[95] This narrow view to the world is being challenged in a time when ecological consciousness is becoming increasingly necessary. The questioning of our approach to knowledge, which defines contemporary research and ethical debate, must be allowed to have a corresponding

---

secular and secularist in which a secularist perspective becomes totalitarian. A secular society is, for instance, not free from faith and religion, whereas this is an ideal for secularism. See Gerle, *Farlig förenkling*.

92. Jansdotter refers to Jone Salomensen and her research into rites. Jansdotter, "Makten och måltiden," 183.

93. Ibid., 184.

94. Ibid., 185.

95. Ibid.; Gebara, *Longing for Running Water*, 71, 84.

impact on our readings of Luther. It includes the question of how we gain knowledge, what knowledge is valued, and, not least, what significance the body has for how knowledge arises.

Practical knowledge is currently attracting attention from many quarters. Philosopher of religion Grace Jantzen, for example, argues that this represents a theory-of-knowledge challenge to a worldview that has given priority to purely intellectual knowledge. She has criticized this hierarchy of values in which philosophers of religion have primarily concerned themselves with the question of God's existence and the knowledge content of philosophy of religion, something that has led to a focus on coherence and rationality. Jantzen has instead advocated an approach that concerns itself with doing—how the subject works together with its surroundings. A knowledge of God is replaced by a practice of God. A more holistic epistemology means not merely knowing *that* but knowing *how*. A crucial question is thus which people's experiences we should proceed from.[96] As we have seen, Luther often takes examples from what in his time was women's world when describing God. Even the much-criticized rote learning form of the catechism takes on another significance if it is seen not as knowledge for the purposes of insight, or as a demonstration to others, but as knowledge for the heart, for creating freedom within.[97]

Theologically, Martin Luther was obsessed by the idea of God being with us—Jesus Christ here and now in joy—but perhaps even more by what is difficult, by suffering. This presence is often described as a comfort or as a defiant encouragement amidst our everyday work. Desire and joy, but also God's presence in suffering, are paradoxically both important aspects. Both exist at once.

In her study guide to Luther's Small Catechism, Margareta Brandby-Cöster observes that Luther was a professional theologian. At the same time, it was a matter of "himself before the word of God." He was an existential theologian. For Luther, it was "not problematic to seek to understand theology and the words of the Bible and to understand oneself in relation to God. This, too, is *simul*, i.e., at the same time. As a theologian, Luther worked as a professional in his time but he did not situate himself outside of the theologian's task."[98]

96. Jansdotter, "Makten och måltiden," 184–86; Jantzen, *Becoming Divine*, 20–26, 89.
97. See Cöster, "Tvånget i frihetens katekes."
98. Brandby-Cöster, "Sökvägar och ledtrådar," 58.

Connecting to the body, vulnerability, and humility is important for all theology that emphasizes incarnation. A God who becomes flesh and thus relinquishes power is a key element of Luther's theology of the cross.

Body, Femininity, and Incarnation

In Western symbolism, the body has been associated with femininity and with affect. The self has thereby been associated with reason and masculinity. In a hierarchical order, then, the body, feeling, and femininity are associated with each other. It is seen as something inferior to the soul, reason, and masculinity. But although this schema exists within the Christian church, the doctrine of incarnation means that this hierarchy is sometimes disrupted.[99]

I have repeatedly argued that Luther emphasizes belief in God as creator. At the same time, he belongs to a tradition that strongly emphasizes incarnation. I wish also to argue, then, that Luther has a number of points of overlap with the mystical tradition.[100] This will become clearer by dissociating his texts from their reception history and reading them instead from the perspective of the texts and traditions that preceded him as well as in relation to issues of our time.

Luther breaks with the tradition that had viewed the body and sexuality as an obstacle to one's relation to God. Hence, the Reformation was a historical threshold. All at once it was no longer a Christian ideal to refrain from sexuality and procreation. On the contrary, this became central, so important that it affected those who did not fit into the new era's normality, in which man and wife were considered partners. Although we today interpret physicality in medieval mysticism, and spirituality, in new ways, Nietzsche's challenge remains. Is the case, as he says, that "Christianity gave Eros poison to drink; he did not die of it, certainly, but degenerated to Vice"?[101] How should we view *eros* and sexuality? What role does the body play for theology? As we saw in the last chapter, *eros* theology affirms sexual desire as something positive. *Eros* is emphasized as the fundamental creative force of life, a source of creativity, curiosity, and openness to the future. Instead of the old opposition between *eros* and *agape*, what is now being proposed is a collaboration between different forms of love.

99. See, for example, Sigurdsson, *Det postsekulära*, 333.
100. See, e.g., Wiberg Pedersen, *Bernhard af Clairvaux*.
101. Nietzsche, *Beyond Good and Evil*, §168 (71).

Our own era is posing new questions. One relates to how the physicality seemingly advocated by Luther looks different to the transformation of the body that was a part of medieval mysticism. I think this is right. For Luther, it is in everyday life that the body is transformed and sanctified and acquires a deeper knowledge of God. The everyday becomes the site of quite ordinary human sensuality, which is at the same time interpreted as divine presence. Life and the body are seen, as we noted in an earlier chapter, as a gift in themselves, the fruit of God's ongoing creation. Moreover, Resurrection is regarded as a gift from God, not dependent upon human effort but given freely, through grace. For Luther, the bread in the mass is not connected to any transformation of the bread or of the human body, which might thereby attain eternal life, but is closely bound up with the ordinary meal. Just as the body gains nourishment and pleasure from eating and drinking together with others, so, too, are people restored to pleasure and freedom when the words "given to you" are spoken as the bread is given out and shared. It is a gift, granted here and now, to human beings just as they are.[102]

Another question is, what significance does it have for theology today that human beings are bodily creatures who have a personal relation to the divine? Is this Lutheran emphasis of any importance for current thought? I contend that Luther ends up in neither making a cult of the body nor despising it. He affirms what he sees as the natural body. At the same time, he delights in the church, which mediates the words of liberation. Yet the church as a body never becomes identical with the church as organization, but remains available to human bodies that need to encounter the liberating word, given shape by actions. Here, then, is a bodily theology in which both vulnerability and desire have a place. It is particularly expressed in the everyday, where it affects our spirituality. It is a place in which to atone and care for our fellow human beings. It may not always look spiritual but is sustained and nurtured by a view of life that creates the courage and assurance with which to resist evil.

The ideals of our own era foreground reciprocity and equality. The latter was foreign to Luther's world, where he in particular emphasized that all people had their assigned places within a structure of relationships defined by superiority and subordination. This also affected his image of God. His struggle often appears to have hinged on the question of being able to believe and trust in a forgiving father. The paradoxical aspect of his theology may perhaps stem from the fact that he, like Anselm,

---

102. See also chapter 6.

throughout his life saw God as a severe arbiter, with Christ as the mediator. It can sometimes seem as though Luther is using the bridal metaphor as an incantation for belief in a forgiving and merciful God. The image of lovemaking is the most intimate and loving he can find. It also belongs to the tradition of mysticism. In the Christ relation there is a closeness that excludes all threats. It dissolves all boundaries. However, particularly after the Peasant Revolt, when Luther did not know how to handle the violent protests by those who wanted to inaugurate the kingdom of heaven by force of arms, it seems to have become important to him to establish, in a way that now seems strange, a boundary between the Christ mystery and politics. Today, by contrast, we hold up the vision of the kingdom of heaven as something to strive towards. For Luther, the intimacy of the bridal mystery became something to invoke for the earthly love between people. To be sure, it could be only a pale reflection of the divine, but nonetheless something to strive towards and allow oneself to be inspired by. Today, the Christ mystery should constitute a challenge in relation to unjust social structures.[103]

Contemporary theology emphasizes relationality and wrestles with questions of how autonomy and heteronomy, that is, lack of control, relate to each other. The existential questions of the present moment also awaken a longing for intimacy, closeness, and physical union as well as for a Christ mystery in which Jesus becomes both mother and lover.[104]

Alongside the Christ mystery, Luther emphasized paternal care in a continual process of creation. He argued that God shows his care for human beings in the material. The hidden God was also at work in the incomprehensible and the intractable.[105] We find here a strong awareness of the ambiguousness of life. Human beings are urged to flee from the hidden God to the revealed God whom they encounter in Christ's love. Yet practical care is encountered through other human beings. As a Bible exegete, Luther foregrounds the way in which God reveals himself to our eyes and ears through visible signs that are nonetheless not direct. This

---

103. This will also be dealt with in the next chapter.

104. Heyward, *Saving Jesus from Those Who Are Right*.

105. The term *larva Dei* is important for Luther as a notion connoting external forces in the universe: other human beings, Satan, but also Christ, through whom God is covertly caring for humanity and the church. See, e.g., WA 14, 1–91, "Die ander Epistel S. Petri und eine S. Judas gepredigt und auslegt"; cf. LW 30 (1523–24); WA 14, 92–488, "Predigen über das erste Buch Mose" (1523–24); WA 14, 578, "Deuteronimion Mosi cum annotationibus"; cf. LW 9 (1525).

line of thinking in Luther derives from the words in Exod 33:20 about no one being able to see God and live. God, in his holiness, must therefore approach human beings indirectly, behind a mask or a veil. Luther illustrates this with the cloud that shows the children of Israel the way through the desert and the Red Sea, and with the manna in the desert, and the copper snake.[106] For Luther, human beings cannot recognize God or understand his nature on their own or by means of their own wisdom.

When Luther describes God as creator, he emphasizes how God gives us food, clothing, and a roof over our heads. Luther's explanations emphasize the now, the present moment. "I believe that God has made me and all creatures . . . that He richly and daily provides me with food and clothing, home and family, property and goods, and all that I need to support this body and life," as the text of Luther's Small Catechism has it.

Does this imply that we meet the divine in eroticism, in sexuality, as some *eros* theologians have argued.[107] Perhaps Luther had similar experiences. Could this help to eroticize our spirituality and spiritualize our eroticism? Maybe. The old opposition between eroticism, sexuality, and spirituality that runs like a thread through Western history is being challenged every bit as much as its polar opposite, the notion that the divine should be sought through bodily pleasure alone.

Luther often highlights physical vulnerability, whether of the infant in its cradle or of the Nazarene who bore his cross. Christ's presence in vulnerability is thus an important element of Lutheran ethics, an inspiration to be a Christ to one's fellow human. A new approach to the body affects politics: the body is not only young, healthy, and fit but vulnerable; it is through the body and its senses that we are part of the world, a world that reveals and opens itself to us precisely through our bodies. The rigid division between spiritual and material thus becomes doubtful, like the self-evident but often arbitrary divisions between private and political. Once again, we see a challenge to an approach to knowledge that emphasizes distance and the capacity of reason to stand above and beyond the object of study. The emphasis is instead placed upon presence in the midst of the temporary, the historical, and the material.

---

106. WA 42, 1–263, "Genesisvorlesung"; cf. LW 1:248 (1535–45); cf. WA 18 *De servo arbitrio*; cf. LW 33 (1526).

107. Heyward, *Saving Jesus*, 64.

10

Passion That Transforms: Patriarchy and Paradise, Personal and Private

Talk of bodies, desire, and sexuality can have a hidden subtext. It can be a way to avoid talking about, or to hide, something else. So there are often good reasons for asking what is not being said when religions and states around the world, rather than inquiring about reciprocity and sensitivity between partners, talk about who is sleeping with whom, what gender they are, and whether or not it is happening within certain approved institutions. What can we find in the subtext concealed by this discussion of bodies? Why are we talking about this right now? If morality solely concerns the framework of sexuality, then who is discussing limits and frameworks that are bound up with economics and technology?

When politicians and religious leaders feel constrained, language often becomes a way for them to retain power. At that point there is a danger that a socially critical theology gives way to what might be called "church theology." In chapter 1 I coined the term "churchification" as a designation for an exaggerated interest in the church—precisely at the cost of human beings. Where prophetic, socially critical theology poses critical questions about power, responsibility, and asymmetry that affect all of society, church theology runs the risk of showing the greatest interest in its own affairs. One of the most important questions in this study is how love, *eros*, and *agape* can interact so that ethics becomes, not slavishly adhering to the law, but driven by curiosity and desire in a way that safeguards all life. The previous chapter highlighted the meaning of presence in Lutheran theology. When we encounter the divine in the material and the physical, it naturally follows that we should take an interest in bodies.

In Common and Individually

My focus here is on bodies in relation to theology because taking the concrete body as a starting point affects theology. Bodies can look different. Skin color, gender, sexual orientation, age, and strength all vary. Not infrequently, one or many of these factors serve to separate people and to divide them into groups. But Christian faith is about all human beings having something in common as humans. By virtue of being created they share something decisive. The Church Father Augustine held that every person partly has something in common with all other people and partly is a unique being. For Augustine, the uniqueness of a human being is bound up with the fact that (s)he is created and therefore unique. What they share with other human beings is connected to their other "parent" Adam, or, to use a more inclusive idiom, with Adam and Eve.[1] Since I am a woman and ethicist, I often pose the question of what consequences a statement has for Eve. I am well aware of Eve's changing appearance and status, not only in different parts of the world but from city block to city block. Skin color, ethnic and religious affiliation, and social standing provide different identities and possibilities for changing one's situation. Nor does everyone have a unitary gender identity or sexual orientation.

Despite this intersectional perspective, I believe that women share certain fundamental conditions across the world. Just like Adam and Eve, they are unique at the same time as they share something with others. In part, this comes from being human, but it is also bound up with the feminine as a gender. If one too readily discusses people's rights regardless of gender, as often happens when human rights are being invoked, or when Christians refer to all people as created in God's image, there is a risk that what is particular disappears. But as people we are all both alike and different. What we share by virtue of being human bodies can be a way of seeing—both what unites us and what separates us.

---

1. Kampowski, *Arendt, Augustine, and the New Beginning*.

Body Theology and Church

Body theology is a trend. Much body theology, however, comes down to notions of church—a desire to exchange the idea of church as an organization with a view of church as the body of Christ. This view of church wants to make visible the church's social body. Community and contrast are central notions. When power is secularized, religion in many European countries has in fact come to be seen as something private, feminine, and purely subjective.[2] On the other hand, countries in South America, Africa, and Asia are seeing the entry into politics of Christian conservatives with deeply patriarchal qualities, not infrequently influenced by the United States and prosperity theology. One can also find Muslim, Jewish, Hindu, and even Buddhist versions of this phenomenon. The role of religion globally is complex and ambivalent.

To emphasize what Christians have in common with all people can, in my view, enable the church's own message—of incarnation, crucifixion, and resurrection—and inspire a social defense of people's bodies in everyday life. However, many discussions of the church and its mission specifically emphasize the church as body, as visible community, and, above all, as the body of Christ. People's bodies in everyday life are named and described, but easily become mere props. They are presented as parts of the body of Christ, which is said to accommodate hetero as well as homo and trans people. Yet the focus is on Christ's organic body, not on people's bodies in everyday life. Graham Ward argues that the loss of Jesus as a Jewish, gendered body involves the birth of the church as a body in which other bodies are situated and find their significance in light of Gal 3:28, where there is neither Jew nor Greek, neither slave nor free, nor is there male and female.[3] However, the equality of this baptismal formula, cited by St. Paul in his letter to the Galatians, risks becoming something spiritualized, something that holds in Christ but not in the world. Ward connects this line of reasoning to Gregory of Nyssa, who argues in his thirteenth sermon on the Song of Songs that whosoever beholds the church is looking directly at Christ.[4] I see here a danger of reductionism: the human, earthly body made abstract.

---

2. Sigurdson, *Det postsekulära tillståndet*.

3. "Within it all other bodies are situated and given their significance. We are all permeable, transcorporeal, transpositional." Ward, "Displaced Body," 176.

4. Ibid., 177.

This viewpoint possibly better suits other ecclesiastical traditions, such as the Radical Orthodoxy that is often to be found within so-called Anglo-Catholicism. Evangelical Lutheran churches, by contrast, have emphasized the church as an institution. It is constituted by its mission to spread the good news and to administer the sacraments.[5] Luther explicitly insisted that the bridegroom—that is, Christ—was unique, with regard to the institutional church's claim to be Christ's representative.[6] No one but Christ can be both husband and bridegroom, he says in a 1527 lecture on the Epistle to Titus.[7] He sharply criticizes both the popes' claims to be the bridegroom of the Christian church and the bishops' self-characterization as the bridegrooms of their dioceses. Luther calls them procurers, pimps.[8] He additionally describes the community of the holy as invisible.

However, an evangelical church is to be found everywhere the good news is offered to people, through word and deeds, spiritual and physical. It is therefore not institutionally or confessionally bound. And yet, amidst the ecumenical openness, certain Lutheran characteristics appear. These include a preoccupation with the everyday and with presence here and now. The empowerment of every person, like the personal address, is important.

Martin Luther emphasized oneness not only with the heavenly Christ but also with Jesus the human being who once walked about in Palestine.[9] Luther holds together the gospel as both story and gospel, a message in a unity of history and message.[10] The personal relationship to the stories is decisive. When Luther comments on the birth stories, it is important that Christ was born for each of us. A savior is born *to you*.[11] I argue that this is significant for how human beings are viewed in every-

---

5. Bruno Latour's theory of networks as connecting individuals and groups offers a possible way forward her. See Latour, *Reassembling the Social*.

6. WA 2, 143-52; cf. LW 31, *Sermo de duplici iustitia* (1519); Kleinhans, "Christ as Bride/Groom," 130.

7. WA 25, 60-69; cf. LW 29:18, "Vorlesung über die Briefe an Titus und Philemon" (1527); cf. Kleinhans, "Christ as Bride/Groom," 130.

8. Quoted in chapter 7, WA 47, 156:16; cf. LW 22:440; cf. Kleinhans, "Christ as Bride/Groom," 130.

9. Hägglund, *Arvet från reformationen*, 130; cf. WA 10 I 1, 73:14-19; cf. LW 52, 7-31 "Evangelium in der Christmetz" (1522).

10. Ibid.

11. WA 10 I 1, 79:14-16; cf. LW 52, 7-31 "Evangelium in der Christmetz" (1522).

day life. The whole human being is affected—as spirit, soul, and body. A relationship to the human and the communal is an indispensable part of the Christian view of life, not least from a Lutheran perspective. The protagonists of the Bible are often described in highly physical, human, and bodily ways.

The movements sometimes described as the New Materialism take seriously the body, the material, and poverty.[12] In this chapter I offer some reflections upon so-called embodied theology. The latter poses critical questions about what happens to working, worn-out, ageing, and malnourished bodies. Physicality, gender, and sexuality affect all of this. Appearance, age, and sexual orientation influence attitudes in one's milieu, something that has significance for not only one's mental but also one's physical health. Newborn girls often get less food and attention than boys. As a result, they sometimes do not even survive. In several countries female fetuses are aborted. One's opportunities, health, survival, and access to a decent life are thus often connected to gender, skin color, and bodily appearance. Human bodies have significance.

Paradise, Passion, Procreation, Patriarchy, Property, and More

In the presentation above, I have considered aspects and phenomena that I now want to survey with the help of some concepts that researchers Elizabeth Stuart and Adrian Thatcher have used in their examination of what churches teach about sex. The primary reason why I find it useful to deploy their schema is that it makes it possible to summarize and argue about crucial differences between the various views of sensuality, gender, sexuality, and the body that have emerged in the history of the church. Stuart and Thatcher argue that the concepts of *patriarchy, property, purity, parousia* and *procreation* are connected. It is essential, they argue, to reflect on the problems that these lead to, both singly and collectively, in order to reignite *passionate love*.[13] They also remark that all these phenomena were challenged by Jesus, who eats with those who were called unclean and challenges prevailing ideals of the family.[14] In the present

---

12. Coole and Frost, *New Materialisms*.
13. Stuart and Thatcher, *People of Passion*, 5.
14. Ibid., 9–20.

era, many of these challenges have become part of a secular culture that does not tolerate holding up a narrow ideal of the family as the norm.[15]

As we have seen in previous chapters, different conceptions of paradise affect people's value and goals in life. I should therefore like to add a seventh key term beginning with *p*, namely paradise, to my analysis of the current predicament of human beings, an analysis inserted into a story about the past and the future. This also concerns concepts such as privacy and poverty. These terms disassemble and reassemble familiar themes and texts in a new way. Throughout history, ethics and politics have been affected by how these concepts were understood. This remains the case. While some repetition of what has been said in other chapters will be unavoidable, the context is different.

Paradise and Purity

People in all cultures have understood their origins and their situation by retelling and referring to myths of origin. The biblical term *paradise* comes from the Persian Empire, in which it denoted the king's gardens.[16] In Song 4:12, the bride is described as a "garden" and in verse 13 as an "orchard of pomegranates, with choice fruits." Luther's 1531 translation speaks of "Ein Lustgarten von Granatäpfeln." Revelation 2:7 talks about the tree of life in the midst of the Paradise. In Luther's comments on Genesis the tree of Life represents church, before the fall, a place to praise God.

Since the myth of paradise virtually always deals with a vanished originary state of grace, it is not strange that our thoughts are always going back to "Paradise Lost."[17] Many religions include the notion of a lost golden age. In Islam, it is usually the time of the Prophet; in Judaism, the time before the destruction of the Temple. As Eva-Lotta Grantén notes, the current state of evolutionary theory makes it impossible for theology to sustain the notion that once upon a time everything on earth was

---

15. Within the UN, there have been many conflicts over how to define a family. See, for example, Gerle, "Various Interpretations." Today the notion of the *star family* is being promoted, as referring variously to the one-parent family, extra or "bonus" parents, adoptive parents, or donating families many of whom have no biological connections.

16. Ekerwald, *En fritänkare läser Bibeln*, 47.

17. Milton, *Paradise Lost*.

benign and peaceful.[18] Yet this longing, like the feeling that such a state once existed, is connected to the dissonances in life and a desire for a life without suffering and evil.

The notions that one forms about an originary good life nonetheless have considerable importance for ethics. If one sees salvation as a restoration of and/or return to a paradise of good, then the way that good is represented has an impact on people's efforts in the here and now. As we saw in chapter 4, different interpretations of the first human beings and their creation, within the Judaeo-Christian tradition, have been highly significant. Christians share with the Hebrew worldview a belief that God made the world good. During certain periods of the history of Christianity, it is also possible to discern the influence of the Platonic creation story. This is especially visible during the first centuries of the Common Era, but it can also be found in the present moment.

Plato, who lived between 427 and 347 BC, associated femininity with sexuality and masculinity with virginity. Distance from the originary good determined whether one was born a man or a woman. As we saw in chapter 4, Plato in the *Timaeus* describes the creation of human beings thus: the longer the Creator stirs the kettle, the greater the distance between the created human being and the divine. In this narrative, the woman ends up further from the divine than the man.[19] For Plato, divine love only rarely has anything to do with the feminine. The feminine is primarily associated with material things, childbearing, and death. A similar vein of thinking can be discerned in the writings of philosophers inspired by Plato, in which humanity's original state is interpreted as virginal, that is, angelic and masculine. For example, the Hellenistic Jewish philosopher Philo, who lived ca. 20 BC–AD 50, considered Adam a perfectly asexual human who contained within himself both feminine and masculine and thus lacked any sexual inclinations of his own. This human being was considered perfect, angelic, androgynous, and virginal. At the same time, Philo held that this was a man. Sexuality, according to his interpretation, was introduced by woman and resulted in the Fall. Since Adam was androgynous, he maintained a balance between reason and emotion. The creation of Eve upset the balance. She thereby caused the Fall, argued Philo.[20]

18. Grantén, *Utanför Paradiset*, 95.
19. Plato, *Timaeus*.
20. Aspegren, *Male Woman*, 14, 90–93

This classical conception of an angelic, originary creation lived on in the writings of the Greek Church Fathers. Origen, for example, argued that in paradise there was neither sexual intercourse nor childbearing.[21] Accordingly, the ideal to strive towards was of an angelic body that might thereby overcome death. Asceticism was a means of reaching this goal. The original state of paradise describes a pure human being, one free from sin. Restoring this asexual, virginal state was thus a step towards unification with God.

Augustine partly deviates from this view. He sees both men and women as created in God's image. But this concerns their rational capacity. In line with the differentiation of the sexes in Gen 1:28, woman seems to lose her divinity, which she can nevertheless regain by renouncing her biology. Augustine also holds notions about reason being purer than the body and the material, of which sexuality forms a part. As we saw in chapter 4, Augustine emphasizes control. Spirit must govern the bodily and the material. Even if he regards Adam and Eve as created man and woman, and as having conjugal relations in paradise, this was a physical relationship that could be controlled and that existed solely for the purpose of procreation. For Augustine, sexual relations were thus pure so long as they were not governed by the body and by desire. Because sexual desire lay beyond a human being's capacity for control, he unfortunately saw it as connected to sin and its transmission

Our cultural heritage includes different interpretations of creation, which have often influenced each other. These play a major role in the way human beings are regarded. Are they considered as originally sexless, as androgynous, or as created in God's image, as precisely man and woman? When human beings were seen as originally sexless, the angelic ideal became something to strive for. This longing for virginity and eternal life nevertheless tended to deny women full validity as human beings. Women were associated more with physicality, desire, and sexuality. They were thereby regarded as ephemeral and thus the antithesis of the eternal life that was associated with the eternal. They were a reminder of transience, materiality, and death—the opposite of the eternal. For almost the entire history of the church, woman has therefore been represented as having brought sin into the world. This perspective often also includes

---

21. Brown, *Body and Society*, 175; cf. chapter 4.

an ideal of purity according to which people, in their longing for divine passion, have turned away from sexual love.[22]

Luther breaks with this ideal of purity. He does not see reason as purer from sin than the body. For Luther, it is always a question of the whole person—spirit, soul, and body. An angelic, asexual state is thus nothing to be sought after. On the contrary, it is important to affirm all of God's creation. This includes the material good, which in itself entails an encounter with the divine, and a reminder of God's care and love. It also entails living amidst the ambiguousness that defines all life since the Fall. Because good and evil permeate all things, there is no more chance of establishing a sphere that is "pure" as there is of establishing one that is free of sin.[23] The body and sexuality are to be seen, not as impure, but as a part of God's creation. The purity ideal is therefore changed. As Eva-Lotta Granténargues, conviction as to the ambiguousness of life—that people do not live in a paradisical world—leads to realism.[24] The title of her book summarizes the Lutheran attitude as living outside of Paradise.[25]

In contemporary political debate, three ethical approaches can be distinguished. As I see it, these correspond to different notions of the paradisical or, put differently, of perfection and the possibility of realizing it. One approach believes that it can establish the good society, a kind of paradise, through state or church. One version is Christian millenarianism, the belief in a peaceful realm lasting for a thousand years. Another example is the efforts of communist utopias to achieve a classless society. Transhumanism is an example of a contemporary movement that seems convinced of the possibility of attaining a perfect body and of eventually conquering death. Unfortunately, all utopias that make totalitarian claims have a tendency to ossify into control and surveillance, creating new hierarchies and divisions among people.

The second approach is generally skeptical about the possibility of establishing some paradisical state. Conservative interpretations reject any attempt at social improvement from a stance of fundamental pessimism. At several moments in history Lutheran theologians, by invoking divinely ordained hierarchies, have effectively defended unjust

22. Stuart and Thatcher, *People of Passion*, 16.

23. I refer here to spiritual purity but am well aware that physical cleanliness deteriorated after the Reformation. I am not speculating about a possible connection here.

24. Granténn, *Utanför Paradiset*.

25. Ibid.

structures.²⁶ Even some contemporary trends, which are critical of a modernity that they associate with nihilism and individualism, have a tendency of deprecating everything that is regarded as part of the modern, such as gender equality, human rights, and the belief in progress. At the same time, they ignore the oppressive and authoritarian elements in the Bible and in the writings of the Church Fathers. According to Rosemary Radford Ruether, the ideal for Radical Orthodoxy theologians such as Stephen Long is an Augustine or a Thomas Aquinas.²⁷

Finally, a third approach affirms the ambiguousness of life, thereby preserving a certain skepticism towards the great utopias, particularly if they make totalizing claims. However, this approach also claims that people should do everything in their power to improve their own and other people's conditions of life. This can also include working for peace and justice as well as taking part in the struggle against the threats entailed by climate change. The view held by the early Church Father Irenaeus—that restoration, growth, and fulfilment are a part of salvation—*recapitulatio* here becomes a theological ally. The progressive pedagogy of N. F. S. Grundtvig was inspired by Irenaeus, among others, but also by a trust in one's own experience. Gustaf Wingren argues that in the early 1800s Grundtvig was that rare thing, a democrat by theological conviction.²⁸ Wingren additionally claims that an orthodox faith that is forcibly imposed has the effect that the church tends to become locked within itself, as a kind of defense against an unbelieving world. The idea of restoration flourished in the early church, by contrast, "in its radical openness towards those who lay without: it was for *them* that the church lived."²⁹ The function of Christ, in other words, was to make believers human.³⁰ In the second century and during the Reformation in the sixteenth, he argues, believing and being liberated were the same thing. Such was the case at a purely emotional level, but it was also something that had consequences for civic freedom.³¹ He defines salvation as "liberation where unfreedom prevails, forgiveness where guilt prevails, and life where death prevails." As a rule, what is human or inhuman can "be answered in the same way

26. I have earlier referred to Thielecke and Brunner.
27. Ruether, "Interpreting the Postmodern as Premodern," 77f.
28. Wingren, *Växling och kontinuitet*, 148.
29. Ibid.
30. Cf. Kristensson Uggla, *Becoming Human*.
31. Ibid., 148. However, Wingren claimed that *after* the Reformation it was usually the religious minorities of the left that wanted freedom in issues of faith.

by atheists as by Christians," even if they differ in their efforts to establish a human world. By contrast, there has never been and will never be a wholly unproblematic society—"evil merely moves to another place."[32]

Ruether highlights the future dimension of Christology. In modern thinking this has been grounded in various forms of Christian messianism, within both liberalism and liberation theology, which view God as someone who continues to come to us from the future. This future will culminate in the kingdom of God, when God's *logos*, through which God created the world and which is present in every created being and every culture, will be revealed. Although incarnation is the normative expression of classical Christian theology, theological reflection ever since the time of the New Testament has looked forward to God's kingdom as a coming fulfilment. The reign of God had not come fully through Christ's incarnation. The crucifixion demonstrated that the "powers of evil still reign." Resurrection "triumphs over this reign of evil that killed Christ, but in a way that looks forward to a future completion." This future can be seen both "as the return of Christ in clouds of glory definitively ending the reign of evil. It can also be seen as an "ongoing process (progress) within history by which we grow into better lives that more fully realize God's redeeming and transforming presence in creation."[33]

Luther's realism, and even his pessimism, may constitute a vaccine against the belief that everything is possible. At the same time, there is a risk that his heavy emphasis upon freedom of conscience, rather than healing of the body, risks standing in the way of what is possible. The interpretation of Church Father Irenaeus, that salvation is the restoration of a lost paradise, but also a development towards the realization of the kingdom of God, shows a third approach that avoids totalitarian, utopian claims, and conservative resignation. The notion of *recapitulatio* provides the inspiration to reach for the good, which, according to Christian belief, belongs to the future even as it is everywhere present in the here and now. The emphasis thus rests on the Johannine motif of life as defeating death.[34] As I see it, it is important to follow a vision that regards the material as something good and that does not conceive of the paradisical as "pure." The good then appears, not as unsullied by body, beyond gender or skin color, or as unitary and delimited, but rather with an understand-

32. Ibid., 153f.
33. Ruether, "Interpreting the Postmodern as Premodern," 84.
34. See chapter 7 and references to Sallie McFague.

ing of creation and redemption as affirming the joyful multiplicity and hybridity of superabundance.

The Divinely Ordained Becomes the Norm

Reformation brings with it a renegotiation and a reinterpretation. The body is affirmed as a part of creation and the "natural." Political, theological, and personal motifs form part of what is understood as natural and divinely ordained. Philosopher Martha Nussbaum distinguishes between four different meanings of nature: (1) something innate—its opposite then becomes that which is acquired or assimilated; (2) something so ordinary that everything else becomes strange and unusual; (3) something one cannot conceive of as being different—its opposite then becomes amazing and repulsive; (4) something suitable, whose opposite becomes what is unsuitable.[35] Each of these usages can be found in Luther's writing.

He understands the human body partly on the basis of highly concrete notions of creation, partly on the basis of the harm incurred by the Fall, which makes all human life seem ambiguous. As a monk, he had seen and experienced sexual impoverishment. He had also seen how it could lead to a double morality. Even outside the monastery he observes what he sees around him and what he himself experiences. Concrete experiences from everyday life in sixteenth-century Germany contribute to his worldview. When Luther criticizes the monastery for its pretensions to be a more spiritual, Christian way of life, he instead emphasizes what he saw as "natural" and universal. Childbearing and procreation were a part of that. Yet that which is described as normal becomes a norm that was not positive for everyone.[36]

Stuart and Thatcher argue that the postponement of Christ's return brought a return to a Hebraic outlook. Procreation once again takes center stage. At the same time, the church increasingly adapts itself to the Levitical rules on sexual purity. Masturbation, homosexuality, and other sexual activities that cannot be directly connected to procreation thereby became suspect and were for a long time met with severe punishments.[37] Luther, who spent much time translating the Bible, would naturally have

---

35. Nussbaum, *Sex and and Social Justice*, 255; see also Grenholm, *Motherhood and Love*.

36. See the final chapter.

37. Stuart and Thatcher, *People of Passion*, 17.

been strongly influenced by a Hebraic outlook that emphasizes God's continued creation through procreation.

Procreation—Propagating

In the biblical origin stories, argues Danish theologian Niels Henrik Gregersen, two attributes connect human beings to other living creatures, namely, sexuality and death.[38] Sexuality is connected to the godliness of human beings in Gen 1:27, in which they are said to be created in God's image, as man and woman. This is repeated in Adam's family tree in Gen 5:1–3. In Gregerson's reading, the blessing of sexual relations endures beyond the abyss of the Fall. Exegetically speaking, then, one should talk about original divinity rather than original sin.[39] Through sexuality, and with their bodies, human beings take part in a creation that is ongoing. A sign of this blessing of sexual relations can be glimpsed in the covenant given to Abraham (Gen 12:1–3) and when it is related that God allows Sara to feel desire again and makes her womb fertile (Gen 18:9–18).[40] Since human beings are regarded as a unity of body and soul, it is also meaningful to talk of a human body created in the image of God. There is much to suggest that Luther drew deeply on this view of life, something that is unremarkable insofar as he had translated the scriptures from Hebrew into German.[41]

During Luther's time, however, a great deal had happened. The New Testament itself took a very different line on the issue of procreation.[42] Because the end of the world was imminent, sexuality was less important. Those awaiting the kingdom of heaven did not have time for procreation, according to Luke 20:27–35. According to Paul, in 1 Cor 7:1–7, it was better not to marry. Marriage was nonetheless seen as a way to avoid illicit sexual relations. Genitalia were still regarded as a part of God's creation, but ideals other than Hebraic notions of creation prevailed in

---

38. Gregersen, "Skabelse og forsyn," 78.
39. Ibid.
40. Ibid.
41. In the medieval period the Latin Vulgate version was used. Luther's German Bible, which he translated from Hebrew and Greek, had an enormous influence on the development of national languages.
42. Gregersen, "Skabelse og forsyn," 78.

Greek society.⁴³ In the latter, there were powerful movements towards asceticism and abstinence.

As we saw in chapter 4, Augustine defended sexual relations and marriage as part of a good life. Sexual relations were nonetheless to be exclusively directed towards childbearing. An ascetic life of chastity was preferable. Marriage came next. Martin Luther, who was an Augustinian monk, shares many of these notions, but distanced himself from the ascetic ideal, above all that of chastity. Nor does he imagine human beings prior to the Fall as androgynous virgins. Instead, he follows Augustine, emphasizing that God created humans as man and woman, as material, gendered, sexual beings. The material does not make them sinful but should be seen as something good.

But after the Fall, everything becomes defined by ambiguity and the struggle between good and evil. This holds for reason just as much as the body and sexuality. Living in chastity as the monastery prescribed, however, ran counter to nature, that is, God's creation, Luther claimed.⁴⁴

Unlike Augustine, Luther did not believe that people could suppress their sexuality and desires. Marriage therefore became a means of salvation, a *remedium ad peccatum*.⁴⁵ In principle, all sexuality outside the framework of marriage was forbidden.⁴⁶ But having children was even more important. Luther's focus on childbearing means that he can advise a women who is unable to conceive a child with her husband to make discreet arrangements to do so by another man.⁴⁷ This seems not to clash with his purity ideal. By contrast, Luther's tract on marriage shows contempt for all those who do not want or are unable to have children.

Luther places a heavy emphasis on sexuality as something intrinsic to human beings. It is created and given by God and thus natural, so self-evident and irresistible that everything else becomes strange.⁴⁸ But he offers more reasons for marriage than Augustine does. Procreation is not the only one. Luther also talks lyrically about companionship and the sharing of responsibility.

---

43. Ibid., 79.
44. WA Br 3, s 327–28 (no. 766), "Luther an drei" (1524). Cf. earlier chapters.
45. WA 42, 88, "Genesisvorlesung" (1535–45).
46. WA 10 II, 275–304, "Vom ehelichen" (1522).
47. Ibid.
48. WA Br 3, s 327–28 (no. 766), "Luther an drei" (1524).

Sexual desire, however, is interpreted ambivalently. On the one hand, it is equated with Christ and God's creating Word. On the other, Luther regards it has having been brutalized after the Fall. But, according to Luther, since sexual desire is necessary for the continuance of the family, God hides its failings under the mantle of his grace.[49] One discernable threat is the lack of control. Human beings have no capacity to think about God during intercourse, argued Luther. He compares it to an epileptic fit or a stroke.[50] This can also be regarded as an interpretation that proceeds from the male experience. Many women and men today would not describe intercourse or orgasm in this way, but perhaps rather as a star fall, as becoming one with the cosmos.

The lack of control is nonetheless an idea that recurs in the writings of Kierkegaard, albeit formulated in terms of the inability of human beings to think during the exercise of their sexuality. The intensity of sexuality is thus seen as something threatening for Kierkegaard, Luther, and Augustine, while for Carter Heyward it becomes something that creates the possibility for an encounter and relationship with God.

Luther highlights both what is given by creation and community as good things. Sexuality and sexual desire exist for the purposes of community and are a part of God's ongoing creation. When rejecting the enforced celibate, he refers to the fact that it is not good for human beings to be alone. They are created for company. Having children is thus not the sole reason for marriage. Luther speaks warmly about a companionship that includes physical intimacy between spouses. He longs to sleep with Katharina,[51] something that indicates that this had a value of its own. There would therefore seem to be an ambivalence in Luther's thinking about this subject. Sometimes he follows Augustine closely, trying to "save sexuality," as it were, by connecting it to procreation. However, after his marriage to Katharina, he also emphasizes companionship and intimacy, for instance in his letters.

Luther's celebration of closeness between the sexes is also reflected in his view of animals and of all creation. In one of his table conversations, he talks lyrically about how animals, trees, and plants are created for each other and lovingly lean towards each other and open themselves to each other. His language is sensual. Just as God created man and woman, so is

49. WA 49, 19, "Predigten des Jahres 1540."

50. WA 42, 53, "Genesisvorlesung" (1535–45).

51. "... liege oft meiner Käthen an der Seiten, et est tamen mulier digna amari ..." WA TR 1, 210, "Tischreden" (no. 476) (1533).

all creation gendered. If it is the case that animals, and perhaps also plants and trees, are gendered, then they are happier and grow better if male and female species are mixed. The masculine stretches its branches towards those of the feminine in order to embrace them, and the female raises its branches towards the male. Luther finds the same pattern in stones and mammals, in minerals and corals. Marriage is inscribed into everything, even the hardest stones, he contends.[52] He sees it as a splendid magnification of marriage. Although his description of the sexual relations in all creation is joyful and sensual, masculine and feminine are interpreted in accordance with tradition. The man is viewed as stronger, like the sun or the sky, with a duty to impregnate the woman. At the same time, his figurative language gives expression to both sensuality and mutuality.

Luther's celebration of marriage is bound up with his stubborn dismissal of the celibate as something superior. The so-called third sex— namely, men who have taken a vow to live like angels, in celibacy—is a continual target of his scorn.[53] Both men and women are filled with sexual desire, he argues, and men possibly more than women. Susan C. Karant-Nunn claims that it can be argued on this basis that men represent a greater threat to the social order than women.[54] Since the sexual urge

---

52. Luther, WA TR 1, 561 (no. 1133), "Tischreden." "Bild des Ehestandes in allen Creaturen" (A. 431; St. 429 b; [2] [1. Mose 1, 27] S. 392). "Jm ersten Buch Mosi stehet geschrieben vom Ehestande: Gott schuf ein Männlein [3] und Fräulein, und segenet sie. Wiewol nu dieser Spruch fürnehmlich von dem Menschen ist [4] geredet worden, jedoch soll man ihn auch ziehen auf alle Creaturen in der Welt, als auf die [5] Vogel unter dem Himmel, auf die Fische im Wasser und alle Thier, so auf Erden sind. Da [6] findet man einen Mann und Weib, eine Henne und Sie, die sich zusammen halten und vergatten, [7] sich züchten und mehren. Daß also Gott uns den Ehestand in allen Creaturen fur die [8] Augen gestellet hat und wir desselbigen Bild und Contrafactur an den Bäumen, am Himmel [9] an den Vogeln, auf Erden an den Thieren und im Meer an den Fischen, ja auch an den [10] Steinen haben sollen. Denn Jedermann bewußt, daß auch unter den Bäumen Mann und Weib [11] gefunden werden, als Aepfel und Birn, da der Aepfelbaum der Mann ist und der Birnbaum [12] das Weib, und dergleichen Art mehr an den Bäumen gefunden werden; und wenn man sie bey [13] einander pflanzet, da wachsen sie und kommen besser mit einander fort denn sonst. Der Mann [14] streckt seine Zweige alle nach dem Weibe aus, als wollt er sie in Arm nehmen; wiederum, so [15] richtet das Weib ihre Zweige auch auf zu dem Manne. Also ist der Himmel auch der Mann [16] und die Erde das Weib; denn die Erde wird vom Himmel fruchtbar gemacht durch der Sonnen [17] Hitze, Regen und Wind & c., daß aus ihr allerley Kräuter und Früchte wachsen. Darnach so [18] findet man auch den Ehestand abgemalet in den harten Steinen, sonderlich an den Edelgesteinen, [19] als an den Corallen, Smaragden und andern" (1530–35).

53. Karant-Nunn, "Masculinity of Martin Luther," 172.

54. Ibid.

that God has implanted in everyone is impossible to resist, this means, according to Luther, that prelates, monks, and bishops will be unable to find satisfaction. When the pope enjoins celibacy for priests, this means in practice that he prefers various kinds of immorality.[55] Since they are unmarried, they will create disorder in all directions, Luther argues. He is therefore convinced that God requires marriage of every human being, except for the rare exceptions who have received God's gift of living in abstinence.[56] Nonetheless, he shows no concern for or empathy with those who cannot or will not marry.[57]

As Gregersen observes, Luther lived at a time before Romanticism transformed intimacy into something that intensified eroticism while simultaneously detaching it and making it free-floating. In this way, the loving aspect of sexual intercourse and companionship were pushed to the background. "For Luther, man and woman do not face each other, in the style of modern wedding photographs, but stand together facing the world.[58] Sexual relations are thus put in a wider context in which the fruits of sexuality and love lead to a concrete responsibility for children. Just as sexuality connects human beings to animals, argues Gregersen, so, too, does it connect their bodies to a larger community:

> If sexuality can only be legitimated through childbearing (as in premodern times), it becomes instrumental. Nor can sexuality be limited to the paired closeness of monadic life without it having difficulties in breathing (as in modern times). Like everything else in God's creation, sexuality is also an ambivalent force, which can both open and close, soften and ossify.[59]

Present-day scholars have also shown that what we understand as natural only rarely corresponds to what is actually found in nature. Nature contains considerably greater variety. Gender is revealed as relatively fluid. If virginity seems to have been an inspiration from the early Greek Church Fathers, Sarah Coakley, for example, argues that you can also find a desire to transform gender. She argues that from an eschatological perspective gender is not fixed, regardless of place or reason for oppression,

---

55. WA TR 3, 129 (no. 2978b), "Tischreden" (1533).
56. Karant-Nunn, "Masculinity of Martin Luther," 172.
57. WA 10 II, 267–304, "Vom ehelichen" (1522).
58. Gregersen, "Skabelse og forsyn," 79.
59. Ibid., 79–80.

but presents a potential tool for embodied salvation.[60] The significance of gender remains but becomes less static, more fluid.

Today, we talk not only about gender fluidity but about multiple sexual orientations. In 2013, legislation was passed in Germany to allow the possibility of choosing a third gender and of waiting to determine a child's gender, on the grounds that a number of children are born with ambiguous genitalia.[61] For example, a woman who has been forced to surgically remove her testicles becomes, not a woman, but a eunuch.[62] A desire to have children exists in many people, but not all. Ethical debates in our time often proceed from a conception of justice that is centered on autonomy. It thereby becomes a right to "have children" just as much as it is to choose not to. Affirming one's sexuality is also viewed as a right. Procreation is not the only option. Sexuality is tied to identity and the possibility of prospering as a person.

Parousia: The Coming of Christ Is at Hand

People in the medieval society in which Luther was born were convinced that Christ would soon return. They believed themselves to be living in the end time. But God was someone to be feared. Late in his life, in around 1545, Luther wrote of his terrible dread of the last days.[63] How would he find a merciful God? For Luther, the wretched conditions in the world, the church, and society were signs of Christ's imminent return. The most prominent sign was the Antichrist, which, according to Luther, was not some emperor or false prophet but the head of the Christian church, the pope.[64] Christ's return would put an end to all corruption, all conflicts, and all death. Luther felt this longing profoundly.

This longing is bound up, then, with an absence in which the fullness of life, victory, is concealed. It was therefore important for Luther to speak of hope and restitution as a promise to grasp here and now.

---

60. Coakley, *God, Sexuality*, 54.

61. This third gender has nothing to do with Luther's critique of enforced chastity.

62. T. Lundin, "Tyskland ger plats." Disorder of sex development (DSD) is used to describe people with ambiguous genitalia.

63. WA 54, 179, "Vorrede zum ersten Bande" (1545).

64. Ibid., 250–51.

Patriarchy and Property

Androcentric thinking proceeds from the man's perspective. Thinking of people primarily as men is a deeply rooted habit, not only in churches but generally in the world. Today we more often speak of patriarchy than of androcentricity or man-centeredness. The word patriarchy comes from *pater*, father, and *arche*, to rule or govern. A patriarchal society is thus one in which the father is the head of the family. In such a society women are expected to listen and obey. Men should be able to assert control. If this control is threatened, it can lead to violence.

As we saw, Augustine argued that a gender hierarchy formed part of the original creation. Man should rule over woman and the rest of creation. Even in Luther's writings, the gender order remains. But the angelic ideal is rejected and with it virginity and the ideal of monastic celibacy. From a perspective of what is natural, Luther instead focuses on the earthly, bodily life in which physical relations between man and women form a part.

In some respects Luther retains a conventionally male-centered point of view. In his radicalizing of the presence of sin, however, he does not mark a boundary between good and evil along the lines of gender, or between body and soul. Neither man nor reason is above such considerations, nor do they lie beyond the struggle between good and evil, life and death.

The Bible's creation stories describe what Luther sees as natural. Genesis teaches that the "natural" body is created by God and thus good. The body expresses itself as man and woman, but after the Fall the woman appears as a weaker version of the man. Luther also envisions different tasks for women and men. He follows a traditional line on the issue of man's superiority when in his commentaries on Genesis he describes the latter as sun and the woman as moon. Despite Luther's theological conviction as to the equality of all people before God, including their having been created in God's image and being at once sinners and redeemed, this is not something that makes him challenge either the gender order or other hierarchical institutions in society. During our earthly lives, we live under conditions of sin. The Pauline conviction expressed in Gal 3:28 that all—Jews, Greeks, slaves, women, and men—are one in Christ thus entails no challenge to societal injustices.

The Fall becomes a screen that in our eyes seems to legitimate inequality. Inequality between the sexes and between different groups of people was not, however, regarded as a threat to a good life, but as maintaining a good order, at least for those with the power to interpret and decide. Like patriarchy, domination and subordination in various contexts were long considered as divinely ordained.[65] They could be interpreted as givens within creation, but always as bulwarks against evil, never as a vision of God's kingdom and the revolutionary divine proximity that the stories about Jesus convey. A firm emphasis on the divinely ordained therefore risks becoming conservative if it is not linked to a dynamic view of creation and to the trinitarian perspective.

The ethical and political conversation today is characterized by notions of equality and mutuality, respect and trust, both in close intimate relations and in professional life and politics. In dialogue with Luther, the question arises as to the place of love and mutuality then—and now. Currently we conceive of intimacy as an oasis of love in a civilization that rests on the suppression of human beings' natural instincts.[66] Such oases may also be glimpsed in the conjugal relations enjoyed by Martin and Katharina, in the midst of a life defined by struggle, conflict, and many hardships. But Luther generally describes relations as asymmetrical, in terms of domination and subordination. This holds for sovereign and subject, parents and children, but also for husband and wife.

Obedience and respect need not necessarily exclude love and reciprocity. Luther's powerful and tender feelings for his family are evident in both his sermons and letters. A mother's love is a recurrent image of God's love for humanity. God loves human beings even though they sometimes smell bad, just as the mother loves the child whose diaper she is changing. Here, too, Luther often chooses to put the emphasis on a giving love, agape. Desire, longing, and reciprocity are implied by Luther, but more in his actions and life than in dogmatic, systematic writings. Desire and longing can be discerned in his letters, sermons, and table talk, not least in Martin's affectionate letters to Katharina during his many and long journeys. But the structures remain patriarchal.

After the Reformation, marriage becomes one of society's key institutions. As I noted earlier, the Lutheran body seems heteropatriarchal. However, this was not limited to the Lutheran societal body. This was typical for the time. It need hardly be pointed out that political and

---

65. See, for example, Emil Brunner and Helmut Thilelicke, who can be considered examples of the second ethical approach described above.

66. Both Theodor Adorno in *Minima Moralia* and Herbert Marcuse in *Eros and Civilization* argue that a repressive culture constitutes a threat to intimacy.

religious power relations have colluded with the claims to power made by the masculine exegetical tradition. For Luther, the freedom of a Christian is to a large extent an inner, not an outer, freedom. Emphasis on freedom of conscience often overshadows any healing of the body or changes to structures. But after the Reformation, a freedom emerges from canon law. Even in matters of liturgical practice, considerable freedom is allowed. Important institutions are changed on the basis of fundamental theological notions about the equality of all people before God.[67]

Poor relief and schooling emerge as the administrative concerns of non-ecclesiastical authorities.[68] The political and religious revolt against papal power thus has sweeping social and political consequences. Women play a prominent role in the early stages of the Reformation.[69] However, patriarchy survives within all spheres and estates. Apocalyptic ideas and a conviction about living in the end times put the focus on people's relation to God. The visions of a heavenly realm conjured up by the evangelists lead to a longing for God's kingdom, yet this does not always mean that these take the form of social and political challenges to the prevailing system. For a Lutheran ethics today, it is therefore important to allow visions of God's kingdom, and a belief in a God who makes everything new, to once again result in challenges and changes to unjust structures and areas of life. This should include an emphasis upon healing and redeeming the whole of a person, including the body.[70]

Ideas about ownership are closely associated with patriarchy. This is a question not merely of property but of being a person who has the right to rule over other people, especially women and children. In the Ten Commandments, the Decalogue, a wife is considered as part of the household goods. In Deut 22:23–27, a man who commits rape is to be stoned for having injured his neighbor by raping his wife, not for having injured her. She should be stoned for not having cried for help. While very few churches take their precepts for life from Deuteronomy, it is nonetheless remarkable that these Bible texts do not see the crime as an offense against the woman.[71]

---

67. Witte, *Law and Protestantism*.
68. Ibid.
69. Stjerna, *Women and the Reformation*.
70. See what I have previously designated a third ethical attitude.
71. Anderson, *Women, Ideology and Violence*, 87.

This perspective is not confined solely to history. In many countries in Africa, these kinds of texts, which Phyllis Trible argues can be described as terror texts, still have great influence.[72] Even though current legislation proceeds from the individual and asserts the equal value of all, it is not a given that women have full autonomy and the right to make decisions about themselves and their bodies. Nor is it self-evident that women enjoy a religious freedom that allows them to be involved in the interpretation of their tradition and its sacred texts. Often, they are instead expected to adapt themselves to others' interpretations and perspectives or to some "customary," traditional practice. Here and elsewhere can be detected the view that "his woman" is considered a piece of property which he has the right to control. Her role is to wait on him and "his" children. For him, a woman's body entails a risk of losing control over his sexual desire and his sexuality. Such a view is already discernable in the Testament of Reuben, and when Paul discusses the need for women to wear a veil as protection for the sake of the angels.[73]

Sociologist Meredith McGuire claims that both religion and human sexuality are important sources of power. Whoever holds religious power in a group thereby also seeks to gain control over sexual power, since the latter is seen as its competitor. Women's sexuality becomes especially threatening.[74] Woman thus becomes a threat to his control. In so doing, she risks being accused for how she behaves and dresses. If he violates her, she is said to be at fault. Such a perspective has not only been prevalent for large parts of the history I am concerned with. It is also apparent in courtrooms around the world.

Privacy

The boundary between private and public has never been neutral or innocent. In Luther's time it hardly existed, or at least looked very different. During modernity this boundary came to be drawn in a way that meant that the man belonged to the public and the woman to the private.[75] Even

---

72. Trible, *Texts of Terror*; Nadar, "Towards a Feminist Missiological Agenda," 96; Nadar, "'Texts of Terror.'"

73. In her doctoral dissertation, Johanna Gustafsson Lundberg shows how sexual ethics have often been a way of exercising power over women. Gustafsson, *Kyrka och kön*, 46–58.

74. McGuire, *Religion*, 119.

75. See, for example, Elshtain, *Public Man, Private Woman*.

the religious was increasingly seen as something that only belonged to the private. This was wholly alien to Luther. The gender order also looked different from that which followed upon modernity's dualism of private and public. In the Lutheran large household, it was Katharina von Bora who was the family's provider. Her lodging business and brewery made it possible for Luther to work as an author, poet, and theologian. Within the large household they seem also to have had access to an oasis of intimacy, something that can be glimpsed in their letters. The supper table was, however, a place for discussions of theology and politics in which students, guests, and, of course, Katharina von Bora, took part—something Martin Luther, but not everyone else, appears to have regarded as natural and welcome. Food, wine, music, and good friends offered a space of sensuality and presence. This is not exactly the image of Luther one encounters in contemporary media, and it is therefore perhaps important to highlight. Not only the intimacy of a couple, but also a larger company, represents an oasis. The close, intimate relationship is turned towards a larger community. The private is not counterposed to the public. The modern dualism quite simply did not exist.

People today freely put large parts of their private life onto social media sites. The internet has had the result of eliding the boundary between private and public in new ways. Zygmunt Bauman interprets this as part of a consumer society's demand that we make ourselves ever more adaptable. Making a show of having satisfied a real and urgent need is alternated with public confessions. Bauman claims that "portable electronic confessionals," particularly for teenagers, involve a mode of training oneself in "the art of living in a confessional society" that eradicates the boundary between private and public, with it instead becoming a "public virtue and obligation to publicly expose the private."[76] He defines consumerism as a type of social arrangement in which human needs and desires become "the most important driving force in society." In his Marxism-inflected idiom, he argues that, unlike consumption performed by individual people, consumerism is becoming an attribute of all of society. The individual's capacity to need, desire, and long for is differentiated from the individuals. Instead it is materialized as an external force that sets "the consumer society" in motion.[77]

---

76. Bauman, *Consuming Life*, 2.
77. Ibid.

This desire to be seen and affirmed in new ways is reforming the private. The ethical questions about how people relate to each other have not disappeared however—quite the contrary. The question of what responsibility we have as people simply takes new forms.

Everyone Is a Person—with Responsibilities and Autonomy

Martin Luther emphasized the responsibility and authority of the individual person. In this book I have drawn particular attention to his letter *To Several Nuns*. In it, he refers to their consciences and freedom, what we today call autonomy. The woman is addressed as an individual with her own responsibility, not as the property of her parents or husband or church/convent. She cannot hide behind decisions that others have taken for her.

Luther refashions the Ten Commandments so that the prohibition of graven images disappears. Yet women remain as possessions, something men should not covet or desire in their neighbor, according to the tenth commandment. The husband is the one who has the right and who can be injured. The androcentric, masculine perspective is taken as a given, including by Luther. The woman is still seen as a part of the household goods. Within marriage the woman is viewed as a partner. It was the man, however, who was expected to rule in the home and in society. But, as we saw in chapter 6, Luther argues that the union of the bride and groom requires the consent of each. Prior to his own marriage, it appears to have been Katharina who proposed and he who accepted. People are thus seen as individuals with a will of their own, in their loving relationships with both God and their fellow human, their partner.

Luther's table talk additionally reveals him as daring to be contradicted by a strong wife. He seeks her advice and views her as his equal before God. He does not treat his wife as a possession, charged with bearing his children. Having children is their joint project. Luther's view is therefore contradictory. Sometimes an androcentric and patriarchal attitude remains; sometimes his conviction of the equality of all before God leads to a greater degree of equality and reciprocity making its way into everyday relations.

Luther understands the whole world as belonging to God. God is the Creator and the one who gives counsel. At the same time, human beings can turn their back on God. While sin has traditionally been defined as disobedience, Niels Henrik Gregersen refers to it as "lack of sensitivity."[78] The notion of obedience presupposes a hierarchically defined structure that no longer exists, he argues. A lack of sensitivity, by contrast, is indicative of a tendency to avoid demanding situations and an inability to read situations in which one's fellow human being, though expected to be equal and strong, is in practice rarely that, but instead needs compassion and sympathy.[79]

In Luther's reading of the Fall, this tendency, of turning away from God with all one's body, soul, and spirit, is to be found in all people, regardless of gender. It makes them locked within themselves, *incurvatus in se ipse*. They become trapped within themselves. Then their mistrust of both God and their fellow humans grows. For this reason, regulations are needed in order to prevent the evil that follows upon self-absorption. Laws, regulations, and the sword of the sovereign are portrayed as bulwarks against evil. A patriarchal worldview such as that within which Luther is working looks at the world hierarchically, with God on top, then man, woman, child, and the rest of creation. The importance of ruling is emphasized, as is control. But still greater emphasis is placed upon the mode of address, a "language encouraging life" to stand against despair, darkness, and death. There are grounds for confidence and light. This is fundamental and what must come first. The last will be first. These surprising, absurd, irrational elements are continually interrupting, creating disorder and a tension around "the rationality of knowledge, manipulation, and overview."[80] This "life courage" creates sensitivity and new structures.

Responsibility and Relationship

Certain elements within the Christian tradition have powerfully confirmed the difference between Creator and created. This has often gone hand in hand with an emphasis upon the special status of human beings, particularly men. Theologically, this special status has served to justify the right to rule over and even to exploit the rest of creation. In recent years theology has questioned this one-sided interpretation of *dominio*, in the sense of "rule over." The concept of stewardship has been foregrounded in

78. Gregersen, "Skabelse og forsyn," 96.
79. Ibid.
80. Cöster, *Livsmodets språk*, 9.

its stead.[81] To be the image of God, in the sense of representative, does not then mean to dominate and exploit without responsibility for creation. And yet a paternalistic aspect remained.

Elizabeth A. Johnson remarks that the Protestant emphasis upon the four *solae* or foundational principles—through Christ alone, by faith alone, by grace alone, and by Scripture alone—reinforced an anthropological perspective. The question of a merciful God came to dominate. The Augustinian notion that God teaches in two ways or by means of two books, partly through holy Scripture, partly through nature, was also suppressed because of its emphasis upon humanity's fallen nature.[82] Today we need to appreciate the entire universe as a sacrament, she argues, where human beings are seen as a part of that universe, not as "lords of the manor" but as a family member in a community of life in which we are "sisters and brothers, friends and lovers, priests and prophets, co-creators and children of the earth, all God's good creation."[83] Luther's joyful description of all creation as having a soul and as filled with attraction may be one way to connect with this perspective, along with his emphasis upon the sacredness of the everyday.

As we have seen throughout this study, there have been different voices in history. Views on the body and sexual desire have shifted. Erotic writings authored by medieval female mystics indicate a direct relation to the divine, in which both body and sexual desire are essential. What is more, these mystics are fairly independent in relation to the hierarchies to which they were subordinated at the time.

Medieval piety viewed the body as integrated within a transformation of matter intended to conquer death. As Caroline W. Bynum and others have shown, the body thereby became important as an instrument of salvation. Sacred anorexia and mortification became ways of getting closer to Christ. Female mystics in particular sometimes portray unification with Christ as an erotic, physical union in the here and now.[84] For Mechtild von Magdeburg, however, the distance and polarity between God and human beings is an important component that makes impossible a total union.[85] *Eros* is bitter-sweet. As we saw in chapter 6, Luther

81. See, for example, Maguire and Rasmussen, *Ethics for a Small Planet*.
82. Johnson, "Losing and Finding Creation," 6–9.
83. Ibid., 18
84. See chapter 4.
85. Bornemark, *Kunskapens gräns, gränsens vetande*, 352–59, 367–70.

emphasizes presence as an embrace in the present moment. Within contemporary *eros* theology, however, there has been a questioning of the idea that desire can only be associated with lack and longing. As we saw in chapter 8, theologians have instead sought to foreground its potential in relation to surplus, being, the gift, creativity, and joy.[86]

Property, Autonomy, Heteronomy

The concept of property raises new questions today when we ask how the body, sexual desire, and the place of sensuality is viewed. While patriarchal interpretations have imagined God as a man, and the man as the ruler of a hierarchical system, other notions are being emphasized today. The dominant approach today centers on autonomy. Its opposite is described as heteronomy.[87] To be heteronomous means to lack independence, to be governed from without. A certain degree of heteronomy forms the basis of all human life since everyone lives in relationships.

In her book *Motherhood and Love*, Cristina Grenholm uses the concept of heteronomy in an analysis of what motherhood means. A pregnant woman does not have control over what is happening in her body. Motherhood cannot be reconciled with outright autonomy, only with relative autonomy.[88] Accordingly, there need not be a complete antagonism between autonomy and heteronomy. Autonomy, the possibility of taking one's own decisions and having control over one's life, is always relative and limited since people live in relationship. Between autonomy and heteronomy lies relationship, human coexistence in various forms, something that involves, as during pregnancy, physically making room for another person.[89] Heteronomy, which is often associated with women and their lack of control, is a condition of life, something unavoidable. That it has been associated with femininity, according to Grenholm, derives from gender models. Nonetheless, she cautions that vulnerability can be changed into exposure if it is elevated as an ideal.[90]

In her reading, heteronomy is part of life. It represents a vulnerability that humans encounter in a range of different relationships, such

---

86. See, for example, Shults, "Introduction: Saving Desire?," viii.
87. See, for example, Hampson, "On Autonomy," 1–16.
88. Grenholm, *Motherhood and Love*, 163.
89. Ibid., 164f.
90. Ibid., 166–68.

as that of parent and child, couple relationships, and in one's relationship to God. When both members of a couple are aware of their vulnerability, it can become a source of power.[91] Carter Heyward, whom I mentioned in chapter 8 in connection with *eros* theology, argues that the connection between vulnerability and power is not limited to erotic relationships. Courage, for example, can come out of fear, even if one is surrounded by friends helping one to "swim through one's fear."[92] Instead of the great gulf between God and human beings that we have encountered throughout history, Heyward speaks of a space that exists in every kind of relationship, even one's relationship with God. What is required of us is respect for that space. An unavoidable intervening space is necessary in order to understand love, both divine and human.[93] According to Heyward, this is connected to a loneliness that can never be fully bridged: "I am referring to a loneliness that reflects an emptiness at the heart of God, a void that, try as we may, we cannot fill . . . It is a place of an insatiable desire that cannot be met except in "intimations and glimpses" on the read we experience together as life.[94]" She here articulates the challenge we have encountered in *eros* theology. The bitter-sweet *eros* that emphasizes the unattainable recurs in talk of what can only be experienced in fleeting glimpses. Cristina Grenholm emphasizes that Heyward is defining God as longing and a desire for justice, compassion, solidarity, and friendship.[95] This space creates a mystery that human beings neither can nor need to control: all of the unknown. Reaching towards the good lies close to the third model I sketched above. It includes the insight that people can never fully attain perfection, but that their longing for justice and love leads to changes in the present. Longing gives the strength to work for change. As Grenholm additionally argues,

> we need to train our eye on heteronomy. Among other things, this means that we must endure unanswered questions about God, others, and ourselves. We have not even chosen our children, even if we have chosen to have them. We do not know them. Their mother is in some sense always inescapably alone, even in relation to their father. So, too, are partners with their loved ones. No relationship can be described fully. We must

---

91. Ibid., 183f.
92. Heyward, *Saving Jesus*, 98.
93. Ibid., 21.
94. Ibid.
95. Grenholm, *Motherhood and Love*, 184f; cf. Heyward, *Saving Jesus*, 22.

always allow what we do not know about each other to take up a space in every setting.⁹⁶

This space and this vulnerability should not be concealed, argues Grenholm. On the contrary, it should be "respected and also protected in public." She claims that even public debates need concepts such as love, vulnerability, and space.⁹⁷

This emphasis on vulnerability and the space that exists in between is an important contribution to contemporary theological debate, particularly within what I have presented as *eros* theology. It is a rupture within the hierarchical system. Even God encounters us in this in-between space, in the mystery.

I have previously shown that there is a break with *eros* spirituality when Luther, in *On the Freedom of a Christian*, emphasizes the mutual embrace in the place of *eros*'s continual longing and seeking for the divine. In it, the experience of faith becomes something that transforms in that moment. Luther aligns himself, then, with parts of the mystical tradition. What he attacks are all notions of one's own merits and of the power of reason to elevate itself above the temporary and the ambiguous aspects that characterize all life. Human vulnerability remains, as does physicality. For Luther, the human Jesus is God incarnate, a presence here and now. A comfort, aid and joy that finds expression in everyday love for one's fellow human being. The present is transformed by love.

At the same time, Luther puzzles over the hidden god, when life affects us in ways we cannot understand. He continually urges the believer to turn from the hidden god to the revealed one, that is, to the God whom human beings encounter in Jesus Christ. This indicates that he is aware that people can only imagine the divine in glimpses. His strong emphasis upon community also shows that he sees God in relationships. In the good that other people give, he sees the actions of God, as if behind a mask. God is revealed most clearly in Jesus Christ.

Luther's ideas have some points in common with the emphasis placed by several *eros* theologians upon human vulnerability, which in the midst of its lack of control can generate a power and an energy in which Christ's love flows. As I showed in my discussion in chapter 6 of Luther's use of erotic imagery, his figurative language is not tied to traditional hierarchical thinking. He reverses gender stereotypes in a way that

96. Grenholm, *Motherhood and Love*, 185.
97. Ibid.

recalls earlier mystics. His emphasis is upon the intimate relationship. But where late-medieval mystics emphasized physical union with Christ in his suffering, Luther instead describes the union of the married couple as something happy and joyful. It is a union with Christ in his victory.[98] To give oneself, to sacrifice oneself, or to approach the divine through asceticism—these are not things that Luther advocates. The embrace of bride and groom, the union with God, is not the result of effort. It is a gift to be received in faith. Human beings do not need to first distance themselves from their sinful nature, something often interpreted as their physical aspect. They will be united with God as they are, as whole people, possessed of spirit, soul, and body. There is thus room here for a healthy autonomy that does not require victims to be a part of love. That a loving relationship can include suffering, because one party suffers with the other, is something different from the relationship itself creating or glorifying suffering.

When it comes to property, one might say that it is primarily God, the Creator, who decides. Traditionally, a human being has been regarded as a man. In Luther's writings, however, women and children are at all times visible, as persons in their own right. The special attributes that he ascribes to them do not detract from their humanity or equality before God, either in creation or salvation.

Both men and woman are described as bodies. Their hardships and joys take different forms, however. Luther has a clearly medieval perspective. Today we might perhaps describe it as an essentialist view of gender. However, for Luther, women are always involved in theological reflection as their own subjects. They are not absent, rendered invisible, or presented merely as a temptation or something threatening to one's relation with God. Women's hardship and joy are highlighted as distinctive. In addition, all people are viewed primarily in relation to each other. No one is merely themselves.

In contemporary debate, various feminists claim that we still need to safeguard autonomy. Theologian Pamela Sue Anderson argues from a neo-Kantian perspective for what she calls "principled autonomy." She argues on the basis of this principle for an ethics that is not based upon self-sacrifice: "As 'non-sacrificial,' this love would not require self-sacrifice as a necessary condition for ethical and ritual practices

---

98. Kleinhans, "Christ as Bride/Groom," 129.

in (Christian) societies today."[99] As feminist theologians have shown, a strong emphasis upon *agape* and a giving love has often meant that women in particular have been expected to live in accordance with this ideal. Luther's theology of the Cross has also been criticized on this point for not considering the differing possibilities that women and men have to exercise control over their lives.[100] Throughout history, an emphasis upon the complementariness of men and women has often been used to legitimate gender hierarchy and injustice.[101] For this reason women have fought for the right to view themselves as independent human beings, in which they are not only considered on the basis of how they relate to men and children, as spouses, sisters, sisters-in-law, maidservants, or mothers. Lesbian theologians in particular have led the way in, as Monica Wittings puts it, undermining "the straight mind."[102] Elise Boulding, who herself lived in a fairly traditional marriage with her husband Kenneth, argued that same-sex couples had the potential to pave the way for new, more reciprocal forms of social life.[103] Feminist and *eros* theologians have also foregrounded the body as a meeting-point for sexual desire and the divine.[104] Today this in-between space is emphasized as the place where God, relationship, exists.

Authonomy Challenged—and Defended

That people live in relationships does not mean that everything is as clearly demarcated as we sometimes would like. Relationships change. Those between children and parents are different from those between adults. As Cristina Grenholm has shown, a certain measure of heteronomy exist in all relationships, not least those between parents and children. This can lead to vulnerability and exposure. Everyone knows that children are particularly exposed. Parents, too, can be exposed and can experience feelings of powerlessness and an inability to protect their children. Indifference and disinterest can creep into any relationship. What we know is that no human being can live entirely independently of others. People's

---

99. See Anderson, "Sacrifice as Self-Destructive Love," 29.
100. Guðmundsdóttir, *Meeting God on the Cross*.
101. Stuart and Thatcher, *People of Passion*.
102. Ibid., 161.
103. Boulding, *One Small Plot of Heaven*.
104. On *eros* theology, see chapter 8.

lives are affected not merely by family and friends but by politicians, bureaucrats, lawyers, employers, employees, bus drivers, cashiers, daycare staff, and social workers.

Luther can be criticized for not challenging the patriarchal worldview and the concepts of property that it entails. At the same time, it is anachronistic to judge him by latter-day values. He was far from alone in holding these views during his lifetime, but he also departed from them on key points. As we have seen, he affirmed the freedom and the right of individuals to follow their own conscience. This held for women, too. Luther's perspective was androcentric in a way that was common for the Middle Ages. Despite this, he made some important advances with regard to the view of woman as created in God's image and as having autonomy and a conscience of her own and a place in the communal priesthood.

A number of contemporary theological movements seek to revive the perspective of earlier traditions. There is, I believe, a risk here of idealizing a distant past as a vanished golden era. Sara Coakley often invokes the Greek Church Fathers and their asceticism, while trying to interpret them in the light of contemporary demands for greater gender mobility. For example, Coakley argues that gender is not inconsequential for Gregory of Nyssa but that he seeks for a gender fluidity:

> Even if our genitalia are finally irrelevant to our "bodily" condition before God, that does not mean that we are released from what Butler would (rather differently) term the "performances" of gender. On the contrary, the whole point of a life of virginity (as Gregory argues in his early work *De Virginitate*, bemusingly enough written at a time when he was probably married), is to become spiritually "fecund." And the continual purgative transformations of the ascetical life involve forms of gender fluidity and reversal (as we shall show) that undercut and subvert what could be expected of someone living according to the late-antique norms of married gender roles.[105]

In her 2012 Gifford Lectures, Coakley seeks to re-establish sacrifice as an ascetic form for Christian altruism.[106] In her fourth lecture she goes back to medieval practices of ascetic sacrifice and gender mobility, something she identifies in the Cappadocian Fathers.[107] She claims to be able to differentiate what in the sacrifice is divinely transformed from what is

---

105. Coakley, "Eschatological Body," 163–64.
106. Coakley, "Sacrifice Regained."
107. Ibid., 17.

demonically perverse.[108] Not everyone is convinced that this is possible, however. Philosopher of religion Pamela Sue Anderson claims, in a sharp rebuke to Coakley, that it is still important to safeguard autonomy and women's right to be independent subjects. She warns against an uncritical restoration of medieval practices and a presumption of medieval gender mobility:

> However, I would insist that it is necessary to be cautious here before making a leap and simply assuming this medieval fluidity. The gendering of ritual acts of submission and sacrificial love in which feminine and masculine subjects have been given religiously specific and often unequal roles creates the very serious danger of merely re-enforcing historical forms of gender oppression.[109]

Instead of the gender fluidity that Coakley argues for, Anderson maintains that there is an imminent danger that this practice instead serves to support subordination and perhaps unconsciously impresses coercive heterosexual norms, including the subjugation and self-sacrifice of women. She continues:

> It is just not clear that treating gender as fluid can overcome specific forms of injustice which are already embedded in the social and material conditions of both the recent and the past history of Christianity. That ritual and social practices of submission in self-sacrificial love have been ethically self-destructive becomes most apparent in the psycho-sexual and anthropological roles played by women in religions traditionally dominated by men. As already argued, patriarchal conceptions of sacrificial love in Christianity have been premised upon heteronomy and gender inequality.[110]

Anderson connects heteronomy to inequality. As we saw earlier, Cristina Grenholm also warns against elevating heteronomy and the vulnerability that forms part of every human life into an ideal. This is particularly risky when it is connected to the feminine gender.[111]

---

108. Ibid., 1, 9, 18–19.

109. Anderson, "Sacrifice as Self-Destructive Love," 35. See also the discussion on "gendering" in Anderson, "The Lived Body," 163–80; also Anderson, *Re-visioning Gender*, 49–52, 59–62, 89–92.

110. Anderson, "Sacrifice as Self-Destructive Love," 35.

111. Grenholm, *Motherhood and Love*, 169.

As we have seen, Luther strongly emphasizes that people live in relationships. And yet, even in the meeting between human beings and God, he emphasizes that the bridegroom must await the bride's response before any union can occur. At the same time as closeness and union are emphasized, in both the meeting between God and that between spouses, there emerges a reciprocity between two distinct partners in which not even the consummation of the wedding entails the absorption or incorporation of one partner by the other. It is, rather, a matter of wanting to be *with* the other, not of *being* the other. It is therefore not identical with merger, nor with subordination.

At the same time, every relation involves my changing as an individual. Kathryn A. Kleinhans expresses this as "I am who I am in a relationship with others."[112] Christ too is changed. The Word that became flesh is different following incarnation. If the First Council of Nicaea pronounced Jesus to be one in being with God, *homoousious*, then the Council of Chalcedon emphasized the relationships between God and Jesus as well as between the divine and the human. Christ is described as wholly divine, with the Father, and as wholly human, with us.[113]

Today there is a dawning realization among philosophers that there are no homogenous beings. This creates a space for new ideas. Catherine Keller argues that the "togetherness of life, the bios of co-existence" is a form of symbiosis. This connects to the theory of *symbiogenesis*, which proceeds from the idea that new organisms arise when two different ones are joined. If this is seen as fundamental for evolution, then collaboration becomes less a competition than a prerequisite for natural selection. Keller invokes Deleuze and Guattari, who argued that all diversity is symbiotic and that there are connective links between animals, plants, and micro-organisms—an entire galaxy.[114] A polydox theology in which many different concepts are contrasted with each other, Keller argues, entails taking pluralism seriously. It proceeds from a diversity in all creatures, which becomes in the present a "creaturely multiplicity of us all, now, becoming." She proposes that we call this the cohabitation of creation, a social life of creation.[115] A communal life of this kind, she

---

112. Kleinhans, "Christ as Bride/Groom," 129.

113. Ibid., 130.

114. Keller, "Be a Multiplicity," 83; cf. Nancy, *Being Singular Plural*, 12; Deleuze and Guattari, *Thousand Plateaus*, 250.

115. Keller, "Be a Multiplicity," 83.

argues, should be lived in an "atmosphere of gracious commensality, of unsentimental care and celebration."[116]

Despite being separated by five hundred years, an entirely different language, and an entirely different worldview to Luther's, this focus upon a shared life and on an unsentimental care, combined with songs of praise and festivity, fairly well summarizes some of Luther's ideas. This is especially the case when he draws upon the erotic language of the marital mystery. He would agree that all people and all creation belong to the same fabric of life, and that our response to God's gifts should be festivity and caring. I am arguing, then, that Luther's sensuality and life-affirmation contains points in common with contemporary *eros* theology that can be further developed in a critical dialogue.

Niels Henrik Gregersen, who works within a Danish Lutheran tradition, argues that we must take the risk of deforming the Christianity we know in order to develop new interpretations.[117] He is critical of the bloodless Late Protestantism that, particularly during the nineteenth century, imagined that reformation could be formulated by means of abstract principles. Like Elizabeth Johnson, he criticizes the four *soli*—through Scripture, the Word, Christ, and faith—and argues that they must be given force by means of lived Christianity. He polemicizes against nineteenth-century thinkers such as Hegel and Schleiermacher as well as modern attempts to differentiate between spirituality and institutionalized religion. Both approaches, he argues, are disembodied and individual. Instead, he claims that people, particularly in the Nordic countries, who live in cultures that are profoundly shaped by a Lutheran understanding of Christianity, are continually alternating between personal and organizational aspects of religion. Some are more church-oriented, others more critical of institutionalized forms, but they are both united in a view of the Lutheran churches as places with sufficient space for different forms of Christianity, in the border zone between church and culture. In them, therefore, there arise creative spaces for interpretation in which the personal and the organizational are intertwined.

Gregersen's perspective is characterized by a view of human beings that he defines as "a four 'e' anthropology." First, he argues that faith traditions are "emerging out of evolution" and are developing within

---

116. Ibid.

117. Gregersen, "Incarnate vs. Disincarnate Protestantism." Below I introduce some of the themes of this article. Cf. Gregersen, "Protestantisme med kød og blod," 253–70.

long-lived but gradually changing traditions. Second, they are "embodied in rituals," which means that they find expression in rituals that contain shared bodily movements and attention. Third, they are "embedded in linguistic traditions" with a wide repertoire of publicly available semantic meanings and practical ways of orienting themselves. Last but not least, they are "environmentally sensitive" towards what is happening in nature and in society at large.[118]

Summary

In this chapter I have proposed that a strong focus on sexuality and how it is practiced can be a way to conceal other important questions. I have therefore argued for an approach in which people are allowed to be different and yet seen as equal, and are given the opportunity to affirm their passion both for each other and for the divine. As we have seen in this chapter, there is a continual renegotiation of concepts such as passion, paradise, patriarchy, and procreation, particularly during a time when the boundaries between private and public are shifting. Today we think it self-evident that women should be treated as individuals responsible for themselves. This view experienced an important breakthrough during the Reformation, which emphasized the equality of all before God. However, it was not immediately applied to the family, society, or the church. Only gradually did this theological insight affect the regulation of society.

While personal autonomy is often foregrounded in contemporary debate, contemporary theological trends include a certain idealization of medieval practices around differentiating sharply between masculine and feminine, sacred and profane. I have here discussed the risks entailed by the return of this angelic ideal. Can asceticism's ideal of purity lead to a re-marginalizing of women as sexual, gendered bodies? In the midst of all the talk of gender mobility there are reasons to defend women as whole human beings, with both bodies and intellects, and with an autonomy that is easily pushed aside when emphasis is placed on sacrifice and subordination. Luther's underscoring of real, physical people, joy and trust instead of asceticism, was one way to re-establish the everyday body. My point here is that we should move forward so that people of different genders and sexual orientations can affirm one another as different but equal without being locked into either traditional Lutheran notions

---

118. Ibid.

of what is "normal" or medieval practices that emphasize subordination, something that perhaps unconsciously encourages the subjugation and self-sacrifice of women.

Gregersen's approach to his own Lutheran tradition is one example of how traditions are continually subjected to critical scrutiny and reinterpretation. Feminist thinkers have emphasized the body's importance precisely as a body, and how it affects theology. Grace Jantzen, whom we met in chapter 4, highlights birth and prosperity. She argues that these are life-affirming concepts and interpretations. They are important to emphasize in relation to a tradition that has often viewed the world with a man's gaze and focused upon the rational and even rationalistic.

In the next chapter, I wish to introduce some of these constructive contributions, by which the insight into the body's vulnerability does not lead to a focus upon suffering and death, but rather becomes the starting point for a cultural critique that defends vulnerable people by affirming birth and prosperity, life in abundance.

11

Birth and Blossoming: Passionate Vision for the Future and Contrast to Greed

A constant theme in this book has been that the body, sexuality, and experience affect theology, that is to say, how one talks about and imagines the divine. How one talks about God affects, in turn, one's view of people, animal, and the cosmos. Passion, whether desire, intense craving, or suffering, is something that transforms people and all of society. In the previous chapter I showed that many concepts that seek to describe the conditions for human life in the here and now, between past and future, are in a state of continual renegotiation. For instance, how should we understand the idea of paradise? Is it something we have left behind, or something we are heading towards? How do these notions affect our desires and our passion? Hierarchical relations between people have been called into question by demands for greater reciprocity. Society today emphasizes desire over duty and responsibility. But precisely this emphasis on reciprocity, between human beings and between human beings and God, is also emerging as a political challenge to inhuman structures. Responsibility is returning. The body's vulnerability is concrete.

Many of the contemporary theologians from whom I have taken inspiration highlight words such as relation, birth, life, and prosperity. The word abundance gestures beyond competition and limited resource. A life of abundance implies that there will be bread and wine left over when it is shared. Even the emphasis upon prosperity and abundance thereby becomes a critique of the culture of greed.

Luce Irigaray argues that the history of the West can be read as a phallic culture in which masculinity, virginity, and rationality are placed in opposition to femininity, physicality, and irrationality.[1] In place of the fixation with death that she detects in Heidegger, Levinas, and Derrida, she and several other scholars foreground birth. Grace Jantzen invokes Hannah Arendt's ideas about natality: "men, though they must die, are not born in order to die but in order to begin."[2] As far back as her doctoral dissertation on Augustine, Arendt saw natality as a meaningful philosophical category. In her writings, she makes repeated use of a passage from the *City of God* (12.20): "That a beginning might be made, man was created, before whom nobody was."[3] In *The Life of the Mind*, Arendt comments upon this passage as follows: "This very capacity for beginning is rooted in *natality*, and by no means in creativity, not in a gift but in the fact that human beings, new men, again and again appear in the world by virtue of birth."[4] As we saw earlier, Luther considered every new child as a gift, not on the basis of the child's creativity, but by virtue of having been born and created in order to live in relationships. It is not a person's special gifts—their appearance, intelligence, or creativity—that matters most, but new life. Giving birth and making a new start are part of the ongoing process of divine creation.

However, according to Luther, the ambiguity of life includes a fixation with one's own concerns, something that threatens relationships and hence life itself. The loving embrace liberates human beings to live openly. The anxious preoccupation with oneself is interrupted. For Luther, this is a kind of rescue, a salvation. Instead of the word "salvation," Grace Jantzen wishes us to speak of a blossoming. She argues that this relates to the early Christian values that Arendt actualizes via her notion of natality. Jantzen writes, "Natals . . . are free to contest and reshape the cultural symbolic even while also being constituted as subjects by their entry to it."[5] Jantzen emphasizes a presence in the here and now, in this world, that may be said to have certain points in common with Luther's ideas. As we saw in chapter 4, she is skeptical of those ascetic traditions, which have emphasized sacrifice and subordination of the physical senses. Jant-

---

1. Irigaray, *Ethics of Sexual Difference*; Irigaray, *This Sex which Is Not One*.
2. Jantzen, *Becoming Divine*, 231ff.
3. Arendt, *Love and Saint Augustine*, 147.
4. Arendt, *Life of the Mind*, 2:84.
5. Jantzen, *Becoming Divine*, 203.

zen argues that we instead need to develop that which leads to life and growth. As I see it, this also entails a defense of the most vulnerable.

The word *salvation* means rescue. For many, this is a question of a daily struggle for life, for survival. Marcella Althaus-Reid claims that theology today must take the very poorest as its point of departure.[6] She talks about those she calls "the scavengers." They make use of what they find on the street and turn it into art. She also draws attention to those who are transported in trains labelled as "not for passengers." But there are passengers. They are transported in overladen so-called *Tren Blanco*, white trains without seats and with broken windows, brought into cities as cleaners. At the same time other trains are leaving from the same platforms, full of people who are considered passengers. So it is with theologies, too, she writes. Some theologies are not for people. For this reason she highlights the plight of the most vulnerable, pointing to the homeless who rifle garbage cans for bread to share as their eucharists. They are the martyrs of our time, she argues.[7]

The poor are not confined to Latin America. In Stellenbosch, a city regarded as one of South Africa's more affluent, impoverished Africans are drawn to the garbage cans as soon as they are put outside the locked gates. When not excluded by legislation, migrants in many countries in Europe do the same. And so, too, do the homeless in the United States. Everywhere there are people looking for scraps near food stores and transport hubs. The poor exist in the midst of affluence.

Vulnerability is not an ideal in itself, however, especially not for women or other groups who are presented as particularly vulnerable on the grounds of skin color or ethnicity. All human life is vulnerable. A parent's instinct is to protect the weak child. How a society takes care of its weak is a sign of its maturity. Indeed, vulnerability is part of the human condition. It is part of birth and death. Finitude, transitoriness, and precariousness are other terms that gesture towards this vulnerability that is a part of life but that are also unequally distributed as a result of political decisions and on the basis of where and by whom a person happens to be born.

When we return to our archive of traditions, we can use the ancient texts and documents in order to challenge anew our notions of law and

---

6. Althaus-Reid, "'Saint and a Church,'" 108–18.

7. Ibid., 116.

justice. They can help to disrupt the boundaries once again.[8] This chapter will be about passion as suffering, but, above all, as desire, childbearing, and prosperity. Vulnerability presents a challenge to structures and politics. So, too, does the vision of prosperity and abundance. Prosperity and multiplicity are like the creation. They disrupt boundaries.

The erotic meeting is a matter of tenderness, of enticing the other to a meeting that can lead to a union in which the divide within myself and the other is abolished. But it is also a deeply ambivalent meeting. It can be abused if one party seeks to destroy the other's subjectivity and transform it into an object. Rape is the most brutal expression of this, when someone takes possession of the other and seizes something that can only be given. The desire and vulnerability of eroticism defines all of creation, as does ambivalence. Vulnerability can be abused.

The Abundance of Creation and the Christ Mystery

We live in a world in which the line between destitution and abundance runs between different neighborhoods. People in all times have sought to rationalize the differences between rich and poor, while in the Bible the creation story describes a God who allows his sun to rise on good and evil, rich and poor. The question then arises as to how our world distributes the surplus of life and its good gifts, and what responsibility we assume.

Martin Luther emphasized a creation in continual progress. Unlike a shoemaker, who could withdraw once his shoe was finished, Luther claimed that God could not abandon his creation but continuously created new life. Every day, every breath, thus involves receiving life anew. Every casual glance, every caress, is a greeting from the Creator, when human beings are viewed as co-creators. To plant an apple tree, even if the world is to end tomorrow, to have and look after children, to take care of one's fellows, all can be interpreted as a means of taking part in an ongoing act of creation.

Love, according to Luther, is inscribed into everything created, from trees and forests to the mollusks, minerals, and corals in the sea. Everything breathes love and sexual desire. Because of their self-absorption, however, human beings are often blind to this. The temptation to

---

8. Ibid., 113.

appropriate and to seize violently is not a new phenomenon, either as regards gender or particular groups of people.

Luther saw all creation in terms of traditional oppositions between masculine and feminine, which, in longing and sexual desire, sought each other out. He therefore described the creation as a marriage upon a grand scale.[9] Desire, prosperity, and giving birth lay at the heart of his worldview. Biologists today talk of the multiplicity and complexity of what theologians call creation, of "emergence" and "intertwinement" as the expressions of endlessly new and increasingly complex life forms. This shatters the traditional polar opposites that, in an exclusive fashion, have traditionally asserted the gender polarity between Adam and Eve. It is not only man and woman who have been created to complement each other and to live in a relationship. This is something that defines all life. It is a matter of multiplicity rather than polarity.

From Gender Polarity to Multiplicity

In the first chapter of the Bible, Genesis 1, we are told that God created "male and female" in his image. In chapter 2, another narrative begins. In other words, the Bible opens with two substantially different creation stories. However, both assign a special place to human beings. In the second narrative, human beings are created first—not last, as in chapter 1. Then all animals are created. But no animal is an adequate companion for the first human. The first human, according to chapter 2, feels alone until God takes one of his ribs to create another human, who is simultaneously alike and different. The very first human, who is sometimes imagined as being androgynous, is called Adam. This means, quite simply, human or earthly being. Only later did it become the given name for a man. The second human is given the name Eve and is described as a "helpmeet" or "help" for Adam. This word is reminiscent of "home help," but the Hebrew term, *ezer*, is the word usually used when God intervenes to rescue, redeem, or help.[10]

From a rabbinical perspective, more than one interpretation is possible. Hebrew has two words for help: *ezer* and *neged*.[11] The word most often translated as "help" has been the object of much debate and can

---

9. WA TR 1, 561, "Tischreden" (1530–35).
10. Trible, *Texts of Terror*.
11. Eskenazi, "Att läsa Bibeln," 220.

variously denote "a challenging obstacle," "a confrontation," or "finding oneself before someone." There are, then, different interpretations of these words within Judaism. Eve can be viewed, as not merely a strong counterpart, someone whom the Hebrew term *neged* counterposes to Adam, but someone who can be the opponent or ally of another woman, of her friends or children, as a leader or workmate.

That humans are different is an asset. Polarity as well as multiplicity exist not merely between man and woman. All people live in relationships. Friends, life partners, children, parents, and family are often what people think of when the word "relationship" comes up. But relationships can be found everywhere, including in relation to those who are unknown and even those who one finds threatening.[12] Although people have special relationships to each other, for many the essential thing is their relationship to a loved animal. The approach taken by creation theology is that everyone has a relationship to creation, to God, and to Life.

Contemporary scholars have shown that a multiplicity of different relations forms part of lived, natural life for humans and animals alike. Since everyone is dependent upon the web of ecology, even our relationship to nature and the cosmos should be emphasized. Concepts such as giving birth are thus interpreted not only literally but also, by extension, as a beginning, a challenge, and a re-creation of old symbols. For Luther, love as an embrace and a continual rebirth presented an ethical challenge. Free though human beings were in their relation to God, they were obligated to their fellows.[13]

Luther was a child of his time. He read the Bible in a pre-critical way, interpreting the creation stories in terms of traditional and contemporary understandings. Like Augustine, he read the narratives of the Fall as descriptions of the human condition. After the Fall, human life became different. Woman could now give birth, painfully, to children, and man worked by the sweat of his brow and with a great burden to provide, things Luther at times sighs about. Following Augustine, he also interprets man's sovereignty as a part of the human condition since the Fall. The same went for human beings' self-absorption. This self-absorption made it necessary to stave off evil and elicit good, through laws and even by the sword. By contrast, Luther saw the physical body or sexuality not

12. For Levinas, the encounter with the Other is a challenge, a threat, and actualizes the injunction not to kill or to hurt. See Levinas, *Alterity and Transcendence*; Levinas, *Totality and Infinity*.

13. WA 7, 12–38, "Von der Freiheit" (1520).

as something evil but as God's instrument in an ongoing creation. The body and sexuality were a part of the original good creation. This blessing lived on even after the Fall. Instead of imagining an originary asexual and angelic ideal, he emphasized Adam and Eve as gendered, sexual beings—indeed, so strongly that almost everything else disappeared from view. As we saw in earlier chapters, this view of what was considered natural affected both those without children and women, whose range of choices narrowed.

Even so, Luther advocated an affirmative approach to life. His focus was life, continual rebirth, rather than death and suffering. Suffering was unavoidable since the Fall, but every day was a new gift. Union with Christ, in the figurative language of the marital mystery, was a union with Christ in joy.[14] Baptism was a continual rebirth, a purifying, and a new beginning.[15] Life conquers over death.

Blossoming Life Breaks Boundaries

Seeing this new beginning as "an abundance of life" is a motif that goes back to the Gospel of John (John 10:10). Luther's Pauline emphasis upon the gift as a liberation from the law and judgement has sometimes obscured his own emphasis upon life and abundance. Luther can be described as an existential theologian. For the most part he wrote while acutely aware of situation and context. He became caught up in various conflicts but also in the joy of the moment. No millenarian, he did not believe that one might reach the kingdom of God, with all its abundance, in the here and now. But he lived his life in expectation of this fulfillment. It was no coincidence that the Hebrew aphorism about the apple tree has been linked to him: "Even if the world ends tomorrow, I shall plant an apple tree today." To affirm the goodness of every day formed a part of faith and of trust. Giving life to new family members meant being God's co-creator. His theology interpreted everyday activities as divine service. They encompassed gratitude for God's gift and service to one's fellow human beings. Blossoming and abundance, all were signs of God's care. Fragmentation and fixation with oneself, by contrast, were interpreted as signs of a lack of trust. It meant missing one's goal, losing one's sensitivity.

---

14. See chapter 6.

15. WA 2, 724-37, "Ein Sermon von dem heiligen hochwürdigen Sakrament der Taufe" (1519).

Contemporary theologians who emphasize healing and human blossoming claim that the splitting of subject and object is often an effect of trauma, such a slavery or rape. A caress, by contrast, can elicit and create security. The erotic encounter that becomes a physical union can result in one's person becoming entirely incarnated, above and beyond any division of subject and object, in order to emerge as a complete presence in the world. A holistic approach joins hope and struggle, eschatology and history, argues South African theologian Denise Ackermann.[16] Healing is seen as a part of God's love in a world in which God is at home with us.[17] In the background of this talk of abundance lie trauma, fragmentation, and violence. What Luther called self-absorption and sin find concrete expression in today's world. A longing for healing becomes a cry: *Kyrie Eleison*, Lord have mercy.

Luther's Christ mystery emphasizes healing, abundance, and transformation. Union—the embrace in which Luther sees himself as bride and Christ as bridegroom, sometimes vice versa—affects his view of the relationship between spouses and the ideal marriage.[18] Forcing yourself upon the other becomes impossible. Both must agree, by mutual consent, in order for the meeting, the union, to take place. He reconciles the figurative language of the marital mystery with everyday physical relationships. This, in my opinion, is something that can inspire us even today. Before God all are equal. For more holistic contemporary perspectives, both gender equality and what we today call gender fluidity can become an eschatological challenge in the midst of history—when eschatology and history are brought together.

The Language of Love Challenges Violence against Bodies

When the vision of the impending kingdom of heaven becomes present in history, the language of love can be used to examine and renegotiate structures and institutions that control people's bodies. In many countries, people are threatened and persecuted because of their sexual orientation, even though science in our era has shown that both gender determination and sexual orientation are more complex and flexible than previously realized. This therefore makes it deeply problematic in the

---

16. Ackermann, "Engaging Freedom," 13–23.
17. Ackermann, "Found Wanting and Left Untried?," 267–83.
18. WA 34 I, 50–82 (1531); cf. Hägglund, *Arvet från reformationen*, 146.

present day to read the Bible's narratives, for example, about the creation, as if they offer scientifically accurate descriptions.

Interpretation and hermeneutics take new research findings seriously. This has considerable significance for our view of the body and gender.

Charismatic groupings and evangelically influenced preaching and liturgy often take as their starting point songs of praise and worship. An erotic, sensual, figurative language speaks of a nearness to God. In a Lutheran tradition, however, it is important to recall that this Christ love, even if expressed sensually, is not in competition with earthly love. Luther went against the thinking of his day in refusing to idealize celibacy. For him, the fact that people take part in God's creation through bearing and caring for children was an argument against celibacy and monastic life as a more spiritual life path. His critique grew out of his conviction that it was impossible to acquire merit in the eyes of God.

Today, expressions of love have expanded to include different forms of sexuality, both hetero and homo, not all of which lead to procreation. People live longer and sometimes begin new relationships after the time for having children has passed. If politics and theology are not to continue giving heterosexual men exclusive priority, this must be reflected in both institutions and preaching. It grates, therefore, to connect a love song to Jesus with contempt for women and condemnation of homosexuals. It is quite possible to view heterosexual marriage as a fine arrangement and a bulwark of a shared life at the same time as one seeks to protect other forms of partnership and to work towards equality and reciprocity.

The battlegrounds of our era are different than those of Luther's. For this reason we must reject a moralism that implies that certain people stand closer to God because they live in a more traditional way, that is, in accordance with heteropatriarchal norms. In a world in which those already born and now living need love and tenderness, mothering has come to involve far more than just biological parents.[19] Moreover, the churches' views on sexuality and eroticism have broadened such that the latter are now seen as a part of the abundance and variety of life, not as something solely intended for reproduction. When violence against people's bodies becomes visible, perspectives change, challenging structures that sustain such violence. The violence that is exercised within the family and in close relationships particularly affects women and children.

---

19. *Mothering* can be used of all caring for others, independent of biological relation.

For this reason, even the frameworks that exist for protecting people's shared life must be continually renegotiated and changed, so that they truly are a help and a support. For the freedom of the Gospel not to ossify, it must live in both change and continuity.[20] This holds for personal, intimate structures as much as for political.

Changing Political Frameworks

National states and regional entities create regulations that determine how people are treated when they seek work or are forced into exile and to seek asylum. Our fears build walls and reinforce borders. But *homo sacer*, the naked body who, lacking passport and valid papers, is exploited and violated, is made into a fellow human being, a Christ, by the power of love and of creation.[21] As Judith Butler reminds us, there is no biological naked life, only "highly juridified states of dispossession."[22] Seeing such people precisely as our fellow human beings involves a challenge to structures that have placed a geographical limit upon empathy, compassion, and rights, one in which the rights of the citizen are counterposed to universal human rights.

In such boundary drawing between people, Lutheran ideas have for long periods played an ambiguous role. The one-sided focus on heterosexual marriage is one example. The Lutheran connection to power—that is, sovereign and nation—has also been allowed to contribute to the creation of boundaries between different peoples and faiths. The Lutheran churches in the Nordic countries for a long time worked closely with the state. Everyone was expected to be evangelical-Lutheran, to know their catechism, and to take Communion at least three or four times a year.

What, following the French Revolution, we call citizenship was thereby connected to religious affiliation. Freedom of religion as abundance and multiplicity has never been a given. Freedom of religion is thus interpreted by many to be freedom from religion, and there is a tendency to treat the secular, preferably atheist, individual as the only truly reliable citizen.[23]

---

20. Wingren, *Växling och kontinuitet*.
21. The notion "homo sacer" is being used by Italian philosopher Georgio Agamben. See Agamben, *Homo sacer*.
22. Butler and Spivak, *Who Sings the Nation-State?*, 42.
23. See more in Gerle, *Farlig förenkling*.

New institutions, both within and outside of the state, also affect our view of citizenship and affiliation. Media reporting not infrequently forms attitudes that define who is worth caring about, looking after, grieving for.[24] Not only citizenship but freedom of choice, capacity for initiative, and a healthy body are decisive factors in determining who is permitted to belong. The intensive discussion of the limits of sexuality risks not only making life unbearable for those who do not fit into the heteropatriarchal norms about what should be viewed as natural, but also as leading the conversation away from other relevant political and economic questions.[25] Making a scapegoat out of homosexuals or feminists can be a way to conceal other societal problems that politicians cannot or will not address, such as questions about education and healthcare.

Drawing attention to the vulnerable body can, however, provide a cultural critique that points the way out of the prison of the present. Similarly, play and the reversal of roles, with Christ being alternately described as bride and bridegroom, offers a way out of the anxious defense of patriarchy's ideal masculinity, which connects homosexuality with femininity and weakness. As early as 1909, the Futurist Manifesto presented a glorification of technology and speed combined with contempt for weakness, women, and tradition.[26] Perhaps it is no coincidence, either, that *eros* as postponement, when sexual desire is denied release or closure, is specially cultivated in homosocial settings that, outwardly at least, stress celibacy and abstinence.[27]

As we saw in chapter 6, the concept of bride/groom can be interpreted as saying that it is precisely as gendered human beings that we live in relationships, both with each other and with the divine. The goal is not to attain an angelical, genderless status, without genitalia, as in the writings of Gregory of Nyssa.[28] Kleinhans emphasizes instead that we are

24. See Butler, *Frames of War*.

25. In many countries homosexuals are still threatened with capital punishment or so-called "correction" rapes.

26. Marinetti, "The Founding and Manifesto of Futurism."

27. An interesting parallel is the so-called "hostess clubs" in Japan. Many companies visit hostess clubs after work to boost the ego of their male employees, whom the clubs' women affirm through flirting but without having sex. In this way the men are strengthened in their male identity and in male bonding even as true closeness and intimacy with a woman, as friend and lover, remains impossible. See Allison, *Nightwork*.

28. Gregory of Nyssa held that humans were originally created without genitals and that we ought to expect to become desexualized and degendered at the end of time and thereby regain this angelic status. While Coakley in her introduction to

gendered beings before God, but with a flexibility of gender that means it does not become confining.[29] It seems likely that Kleinhans is closer to Augustine, who was convinced that we would recognize each other as men and women in heaven.[30]

Luther's Christ mystery contains important elements of earlier mystics from the history of the church. However, he expressly rejected virginity as an ideal. Instead, he emphasized what he regarded as natural bodies and their lives as gendered, sexual beings.[31] It is as whole human beings, *totus homo*, that we stand before God, the world, and ourselves, *coram Deo, coram hominibus/mundo/meipso*.

The body, Gregersen argues, is an "expressive organ." It faces others and expects a response. According to biblical faith, the soul is more than the body, but the body is a complete form of revelation for the soul, something that, according to Gregersen, can be seen in the glint of an eye, the tone of a voice, and the intensive listening of the body.[32] One might thus say that the body is created for relationships. Eroticism is an expression of this. Moreover, incarnation means that the divine lives in the deepest possible relationship to the human. Daring to see God as vulnerable body is not merely a way to reconcile creation and salvation. It is a mode of cultural critique centring on tenderness and closeness instead of the strength that comes from distance and power.

Shared Life: A Vision

The world of economics and politics shapes the framework and circumstances to which we relate as citizens. For Theodor Adorno, the sphere of intimacy can serve as an oasis of love.[33] In intimate relationships, something resembling a model for true living can emerge. The unguarded trust that shared life can create may, however, become toxic when that relationship is broken.[34] At the same time, Adorno, like Marcuse, argues

---

Religion and the Body describes this as a gender fluidity by which gender becomes unimportant, I use the notion of gender fluidity to denote the way that gender remains important but less static.

29. Kleinhans, "Christ as Bride/Groom."
30. Ibid., 250.
31. Gerle, "Eros, Ethics, and Politics."
32. Gregersen, "Skabelse og forsyn," 94.
33. Adorno, *Minima moralia*.
34. Bauman, *Postmodern Ethics*.

that that no real liberation is possible without that of society.³⁵ Love, not merely justice, must therefore challenge and reshape every area of life. Luther warned against an unpolitical interpretation of the Song of Solomon that would focus upon the intimate relationship between God and the soul as something private. Instead of privatizing the text, he presented the Song of Solomon as a political text written by King Solomon about God's love of the state.³⁶

The Song of Solomon in this way became a defense of temporal authority, of the sovereign's mandate. The sovereign's love was idealized and in principle placed beyond criticism. Bo Kristian Holm notes that this utopia of a harmonious public sphere means that everything which threatens harmony must be silenced—that is, zealots, peasants, and nobles.³⁷ "The consequence of Luther's reading is that the political realm, with the help of the nuptial imagery, is interpreted under the headline of the utopia of the harmonized public domain, marked by tranquility, harmony and peace."³⁸ As we know, Luther vacillated in his attitude towards the Peasant Revolt. From having initially sought to mediate, he instead urged the princes to strike down the uprising.³⁹ Few today want to defend the brutal silencing of peasants who rise up against inhumane conditions. At the same time as we rightly lament Luther's attitude, we can observe in contemporary politics a similar effort to silence and obscure those who disrupt the order of things. Refugees and poor migrants are made invisible and treated as non-persons. There are, then, real risks in idealizing a harmonious, uniform political community.⁴⁰ Moreover, Christ's love must also present a challenge to the exercise of public office.⁴¹

Luther's reading of the Song of Solomon as defending political authority feels tendentious. Yet he read it simultaneous with the Magnificat, in which Mary gives praise to God who "put down the mighty from their seats, and exalted them of low degree."⁴² For Luther, the ideal king was humble and truly cared for his people. It is interesting, too, that

35. Marcuse, *Eros and Civilization*.
36. WA 31 II, 586-769, "Vorlesung über das Hohelied" (1530-31).
37. Gutman, *Über Liebe und Herrschaft*, 225; see also Holm, "Dynamic Tensions".
38. Holm, "Dynamic Tensions."
39. WA 8, 676-87; WA 18, 291-334; WA 18, 357-61; WA18, 384-401, also WA 11, 245-80.
40. See Gerle, "Eros, Ethics, and Politics."
41. Hägglund, *Arvet från reformationen*, 146.
42. Luke 1:52 KJV.

his reading of the Song of Songs blurs the boundary between economics and politics. Even within the political sphere, claims Bo Holm, Luther sees it as a matter of reciprocal care.[43] In Luther's day, this meant care within a limited political area. In the Nordic countries, this responsibility came to be associated primarily with the household and the parish, and to some extent the nation. Today this challenge must be understood in an increasingly globalized world.[44] Christian faith lives in a tension between change and continuity.[45]

God's spheres of promise to humanity, *oeconomia, politia, ecclesia,* can be read as leading to a static class society. It can also be (mis)construed as saying that the good news of every person's worth should only be granted validity within *ecclesia,* that is, within the church, education, and culture. For Luther, however, all areas were subordinate to God's justice and mercy, including the sphere of politics, which in his time belonged almost exclusively to the sovereign. Yet this was not to say that that all spheres fell under the church's jurisdiction.[46] Every sphere of promise had its integrity and all office-holders had a duty in their relationship to God and their fellow humans. Forgiveness, grace, and mercy therefore cannot be limited to certain areas. On the contrary, need and forgiveness everywhere alternate with each other. Within every sphere of human existence, according to Lutheran theology, God wishes to establish and promote good, healthy life. Demands and laws as well as forgiveness, gospel, and grace—all are needed.

Without law, we cannot recognize evil and instead allow ourselves to be terrorized by those who, sometimes in God's name, serve only themselves. But sometimes the law must be exploded in order to get beyond it, in order to establish justice. As Derrida reminds us, justice is an experience of the impossible: a will, a longing, a demand for justice.[47]

43. Holm, "Dynamic Tensions."

44. Gerle, "Eros, Ethics, and Politics."

45. For Gustaf Wingren this is one of the criteria for Christian faith. See *Växling och kontinuitet*.

46. Luther's position is here very different from, for example, that of American theologian Stephen Long, whom I earlier referred to in the context of radical orthodoxy. See Ruether, "Interpreting the Postmodern as Premodern," 76, 80. In Gerle, "Lutheran Theology as a Resource," I describe different interpretations of Luther's thinking on the Two Regimens. Each of them denounces theocracy or Church's authority over other areas.

47. Derrida, *Acts of Religion*, "Justice is an experience of the impossible: a will, a desire, a demand for justice..." (244).

Law, he argues, is not the same as justice. The law can be calculated, but not justice. The latter demands that we factor in that which cannot be calculated.[48]

Earlier I highlighted the idea that ethics and *eros* should alternate with each other. Without gospel, finding joy in work becomes a heavy burden. In a secularized society, it is important to foreground the Reformation's fundamental precept: as a person I am free. Therefore I am God's collaborator. When I realize that I need not justify my existence by being better than others, I become free to embrace my fellow human beings, free to be responsible. Then I become able to see the needs of my fellow human beings, since they can rest easy knowing that they are loved and cherished by God, by life, and can thus live openly and with sensitivity.

Many Christians today take it as a given that God created all people in his image. This involves a political challenge to various forms of injustice. The notion of a pact recurs in talk about "covenants" within the field of human rights. In South Africa, there has been an end to interpretations by which the story of the Tower of Babel and the confusion of languages served to legitimate a policy of racial apartheid. Nowadays, concepts such as ethnicity, culture, and religion are instead used to mark boundaries, especially in Europe and the West.[49] Christ's love, and his challenge to love even your enemy, is even more challenging when it comes to how strangers and opponents should be treated, even in politics. Contemporary theology's emphasizing of relationships, abundance, and blossoming here becomes essential.

The Latin American Roman-Catholic theologian Ivone Gebara writes that, in East and West, North and South, an urgent need is growing "to reinvent our dreams of love and justice and our capacity for communion, mercy, and solidarity. We have a growing sense of weariness in the face of the endless violence that assaults us and the absence of respectful ways of struggling for a world that embodies justice and solidarity." In such a situation, she continues, "the collective search for God becomes the task not just of so called theologians but of all those who share a passion for life."[50]

What Gebara means is that relatedness is fundamental for human beings. She sees relatedness as "the primary and the ultimate ground of all that exists," something that "goes beyond the human world and beyond

---

48. Ibid., 244.
49. See, for example, Gullestad, *Plausible Prejudice*.
50. Gebara, *Longing for Running Water*, 102f.

all we can articulate." It is on the basis of this experience, and beyond it, that we "can thus affirm that God is relatedness." It speaks of God as "possibility, as opening, as the unexpected, the unknown; as physical and metaphysical." This relatedness, she continues, has no exact definition: "It cannot be reduced to a given being, a given species, or a given system." She summarizes, "Relatedness is not an entity apart from beings; rather, it is a mystery that is associated with all that exists."[51]

To describe God and human beings using relatedness as a key term results in a cultural critique that calls into question arbitrary divisions and boundaries between people, regardless of whether they are based on merits or received assumptions.

Human Value: Only for Successful and Hard-Working People?

Our era is full of expressions that value people. "You are worth it," people say to each other, and even to themselves when they are indulging themselves. But what does it mean to say this? Sometimes it can sound as though only someone who has performed well is deserving of reward in the form of the good things in life. Presumably this is an influence from the United States, where a secularized version of an extreme Calvinist position sees a connection between success and God's blessing.

As Max Weber showed in his study of capitalism and the Protestant ethic, there is a connection between Puritanism and capitalism and the faith that God has predestined human beings to heaven or hell.[52] All reformers, especially Luther, foregrounded working for one's fellow human beings as a good. Calvinistic Puritanism, however, saw the emergence of attempts to decipher the signs of whether one was predestined to heaven or hell. Those who found success in this life were taken to have God's blessing. Success, in business and in love, was thus interpreted as having been made possible by God. Similar notions persist in secular form. The successful are worth it; they have made themselves deserving.

This line of thinking has also had considerable impact within prosperity theological circles. All around the world, growing mega-churches preach that whoever gives to the church will become correspondingly rich. The notion is a foreign one to Lutheran ethics. Such haggling runs

---

51. Ibid., 103.
52. Weber, *The Protestant Ethic*.

contrary to Lutheranism's emphasis upon grace and God's care. It revives memories of Luther's critique of indulgences, which in his time were described as a way to buy oneself free from sin, while prosperity theology today promises material wealth based upon one's performance. In fact, for Lutheran theology, the gift has nothing to do with performance. Seeing oneself as God's child, or as loved by God like a partner, is not the result of effort and labour. It is a gift that resembles a loving embrace. It is not conditional upon success or merit, but is given to those who long for it. Like Jean Calvin, Luther thought that human beings themselves could not affect the gift but merely receive it and be open to the moment when it was offered. But—and this is a crucial difference—the outward form of one's life gave no indication as to whether one had been chosen by God. The poorest and most miserable, no less than the sovereign in his palace, might be blessed by God. Appearances are not a guide.

Paradoxically, this emphasis upon what lies within, something I have often criticized in this book, resulted in it becoming impossible to connect divine selection to social and economic standing. Before God there can only be radical equality. In Luther's time, however, relations between people were defined less by equality than asymmetry. In everyday life, too, it was emphasized that there was a connection between working and doing one's part for one's fellow human beings. Criticism of the mendicant friars could be harsh. Those who did not work should not eat. According to Birgit Stolt, in peasant communities this work ethic became a joyless obligation to work.

"Idleness teaches many evils" (Sir 33:29) became proverbial as "the devil makes work for idle hands" (Prov 16:27). This work ethic, combined with a Bible verse such as "if any would not work, neither should he eat" (2 Thess 3:10), was ideally suited to Nordic peasant communities. However, what got entirely lost in the process was the unbounded joy, the heart that "dances and overflows with delight," that is, work attended by joyful song and joking.[53]

Stolt claims that Luther emphasized joy and sexual desire, but that his emphasis upon the everyday, particularly in connection with unequal structures, could be abused by sovereigns and masters, often with dire consequences for women, ordinary people, the poor, the sick, and those from elsewhere. In this book, therefore, I have chosen to challenge Lutheran ethics, to allow that which is deemed crucial in relation to God,

53. Stolt, *Luther själv*, 38.

such as joy and freedom, to be more strongly emphasized in the world. In consequence, it becomes imperative to enquire about the political, ethical consequences of the radicality of the gift.

If the gift is unrelated to how people are valued by others, what emerges is a radical cultural critique of the growing tendency to make belonging and acceptance conditional upon an individual's performance.[54] Those who are sick, who are getting old and running out of steam, or who are quite simply talented in ways that do not fit in, all run a grave risk of being punished by attitudes and societal legislation. For Luther, the boundary is not between intellect and body. Despite his appreciation for reason, he does not look down on the body and the material as something inferior or of lesser value. This ought to have consequences for how we today value the body and the body's work. Yet Luther no more idealizes the body than he disdains it. His position therefore poses a challenge both to disdain for the body and to the body cult.

When Luther encouraged eating and drinking, it had nothing to do with the words "because you are worth it." It was, rather, a matter of driving out the devil. By turning in faith to God, people might dispel doubt and despondency. Friends, wine, food, and music were one aid. All are equal before God. A spouse or partner, creates a special space in which trust and shared responsibility can be nourished. The bride's embrace, the mutual love between God and human beings are for Luther a gift that liberates human beings for their fellows. A relationship to God and a loving human relationship should not be seen as in competition. Ongoing creation, healing, and care go hand in hand. Sensuality moves and becomes present in the material, earthly life. The emphasis is on the present, here and now, as well as on a sensitive presence and reciprocity.

A Bodily Luther

In this book I have emphasized a more affective and bodily Luther than the one we encounter in the theology of rationalism. The rationalist Lutheran tradition has systematized Luther's thoughts about God and human beings into a comprehensive system, yet his extensive writings show a more contradictory and ambivalent Luther. *Eros* theologians such as Catherine Keller, Rita Nakashima Brock, and Carter Heyward call into question the clear distinctions between God and human beings, between

---

54. See also Gerle, "Eros, Ethics, and Politics."

different forms of love, and between different forms of divine intervention in the world. This involves a challenge to much of the traditional Lutheran view, which perhaps unconsciously has ended up in binary opposites, as it counterposes masculinity and rationality to femininity, body, and irrationality.

Where a rationalist interpretation has emphasized knowledge and insight, I want to underscore the importance of feelings for ethics and one's relationship to God, human beings, and animals. The cognitive reading of Luther, in my view, has obscured other important aspects. This does not mean that reason or intellect are unimportant for Lutheran ethics—quite the contrary. But physicality and vulnerability have great importance, as do sensuality and abundance. The bodily senses are not in competition with our relationship to God, but should be seen as an aid. For Luther, the intellect is not superior to feelings and the body. Body, soul, and spirit—to invoke a classical division—are involved in the struggle between good and evil, or, as Luther would put it, God and the devil. His view of human beings was influenced by Hebrew thought. It was a matter of the heart being good or evil, physically and psychologically.[55] Luther had a dualistic worldview, but the opposition lay not between body and soul or between body and spirit. All of a human being was created by God but also, as he saw it, damaged by the Fall. This means that even reason was clouded. Intellect and thought, which Luther prized highly, accordingly did not lie outside of, or above, the physical or material.

Justification means that all of a human being is drawn into God's force field and enveloped in love. In Luther's dualistic perspective, this is interpreted as a protection against the forces of darkness. Human beings were now ridden by God instead of the devil. But which of them was to be in the saddle was not decided once and for all. Conversion, or, rather, taking refuge in God's mercy and grace, must happen daily. Baptism is described as dying to the old human being every day and arising in Christ. At the same time, God's promise in baptism holds for all time. However, the words of forgiveness heard from outside, the stories of God's grace and care in the creation, and the experience of Christ's love are not primarily a matter of knowledge and understanding but create trust and joy, an abundance and an inspiration that are reminiscent of falling in love. They change the present. Faith and trust are inspired by

---

55. Bainton, *Luther*, 254.

the living word but also by music and poetry. The senses become an aid, not a threat.

Body and Senses: A Gift

The focus of this study has been sensuality and the body's significance for theology. Its working title for a long time was "Luther and Eroticism." Sexuality was revolutionized in Luther's time. As a consequence of his total focus upon the fact that human beings would be saved by grace alone, not deeds, the earthly, ordinary, and everyday life of eroticism, sexuality, and childbearing came to be regarded as something good and natural. Distancing oneself from this was no longer viewed as a path to the divine. Luther therefore rejected the ascetic piety that the monasteries had fostered since the very first centuries of Christianity. Since those who needed human deeds were one's fellow humans, not God, ordinary life came to be regarded as a vocation. This calling was for everyone. The mission undertaken at baptism, to be a Christian, was made real in everyday life. An emphasis on the universal priesthood meant that believers should be a Christ to their fellow human beings, partly by giving their time and labor, partly by comforting and guiding, like the Holy Spirit, Christ here and now. Luther and the early reformers claimed this, not only as a theory but as a practice, something that led to great changes in ways of living in early modern Europe.[56]

Ordinary life, with its sexuality, childrearing, and families, had always existed, of course. For monks and nuns and for the clergy, who had chosen a more spiritual mode of life, this nonetheless seemed like a threat to divine union. A rejection of family life was also a way for them to define their freedom from these commonalities. Striving for spirituality and to come closer to God, those in holy orders viewed it as important to control and minimize the physical body's need of food, sleep, and sexuality. Intellect was underscored. Physical love in this way became a rival to divine live. For many, the path to the spiritual seemed to be less body, or by disciplining the bodily senses. It was this thinking that Martin Luther fundamentally challenged. He claimed that we do not for a moment get closer to God by being less body. In denouncing the monastery's merit-based thinking, he also elevates the physical and material aspects

---

56. Witte, *Law and Protestantism*.

of everyday life. For this reason his theology had profound social and political consequences.[57]

Summary

Passionate Embrace: Luther on Love, Body, and Sensual Presence reveals a different Luther from the one we encounter in the media. Instead of a Luther responsible for our working too hard, this book shows a Martin Luther who accepted sensualism and sensuality. Food, wine, music, and good friends were a means of keeping depression and doubt at bay. The body was not a threat to the spiritual. Sexuality was seen as natural and created by God.

Luther broke with a monastic tradition that viewed the physical senses as competitors of the spiritual. Love for another human being did not thereby become a competitor of love for God. God's love was a gift that no one could earn by their own merits, but only receive. Luther compared it to the amorous embrace of two lovers. Both give and receive at the same time. The encounter is full of joy. Union involves wanting to be with, not to become, the loved one. A loving relation is defined by reciprocity and respect. The consent of the other is necessary.

This study shows how Luther used the figurative language of mysticism in the Song of Solomon in a new way. He emphasized union with Christ as something joyful. The relationship is characterized by joy and abundance, not suffering.

In order to offer a perspective on the body cult and body loathing of our own era, I have in this book discussed views of sensuality, the body, sexuality, and eroticism in a dialogue between "the sensory Luther" and contemporary scholars. Accounts of earlier mystics, from Origen to Bernard of Clairvaux, have provided depth and context. Bernard's formulations about the married couple who share everything—bed, table, home, and inheritance—makes a revolutionary appearance in Luther's sermon on marriage from 1531. But now these formulations gesture, not to God and the soul, but to the relationship between husband and wife. Luther extolled the physical advantages that enable spouses to rely upon each other and to entrust to each other all they own on this earth.

---

57. Ibid., 21–24. I have elsewhere (e.g., Gerle, "Var dags") argued against Ernst Troeltsch and his thesis that the Reformation did not have societal consequences.

Luther criticized a spirituality that became private and apolitical. He argued that God's love interrupted our self-absorption and paved the way for relationships and shared responsibility. In this, he idealized marriage in a way that negatively affected all those outside of it as an institution. What he saw as natural in the relationship between a woman and a man accords badly with what science has today established about different genders and sexuality. In similar fashion, he idealized the power of the sovereign and political authority.

This book does not seek to present a flattering portrait of Luther, but rather to highlight what is contradictory and ambiguous in his thought. At the same time, I have argued here that the passion to be found in Luther's love mystery ought to have a greater impact on politics, local as well as global. Luther used a gender-transgressing idiom in his nuptial mystery, offering new and political interpretations for our shared lives. Yet Luther's sexual revolution did not go far enough, becoming stuck in a mode of social repression in which only heterosexual marriage was permitted. His conviction that everyone is equal before God should have political consequences today and direct states towards greater justice, fair distribution, and generosity.

A Lutheran ethics should allow itself to be inspired by contemporary *eros* theology, which challenges traditional Lutheran approaches that counterpose different forms of love to each other. Instead, *eros* and *agape* should be seen as working together in a continually renewed dance and challenge. An emphasis on longing for the other and a community that radically transforms structures have an ally in Luther. A sensual presence that recognizes God in another human being has political consequences for how we come together in the mystery of life as both spiritual and physical beings.

Bibliography

Martin Luther

Luther, Martin. *D. Martin Luthers Werke*. Kritische Gesamtausgabe. 73 vols. Weimarausgabe (WA): Hermann Böhlaus Nachfolger, 1930–85.

———. *Works*. Edited by Jaroslav Pelikan and Helmut T. Lehmann. 55 vols. American ed. Philadelphia: Muchlenberg and Fortress; St. Louis: Concordia, 1955–86.

Luther, Martin. 1516, *Zu Taulers Predigten* (Notes to Taulers' Sermons) WA 9.

———. 1514–17, *Sermone aus den Jahren 1514–1517* (Sermons) WA 1 (LW 51).

———. 1519, *Sermo de duplici iustitia* (Two Kinds of Righteousness) WA 2 (LW 31).

———. 1519, *Ein Sermon von dem heiligen hochwirdigen Sacrament der Taufe* (The Holy and Blessed Sacrament of Baptism) WA 2 (LW 35).

———. 1519, *Resolutiones super propositionibus Lipsiae disputatis* (The Leipzig Debate) WA 2 (LW 31).

———. 1519, *In epistolam Pauli ad Galatas commentaries* (Galatians) WA 2 (LW 27).

———. 1519–21, *Predigten Luthers* (Luther's Sermons) WA 9.

———. 1519–21, *Operationes in Psalmos*, (Psalms) WA 3II (LW 14).

———. 1520, *Von der Freiheit eines Christenmenschen* (On the Freedom of a Christian) WA 7 (LW 31).

———. 1521, *Das Magnificat verdeutschet und ausgelegt* (Magnificat) WA 7 (LW 21).

———. 1522, *Evangelium in der Christmetz* (The Gospel for Christmas Eve) WA 10 I 58–95 (LW 52, 7–31).

———. 1522, *Wider den falsch genannten geistlichen Stand des Papsts und der Bischöfe* (Against the Spiritual Estate of the Pope and the Bishops Falsely so called) WA 10 II (LW 39).

———. 1522, *Vom ehelichen Leben* (The Estate of Marriage) WA 10 II (LW 45).

———. 1523–24, *Die ander Epistel S. Petri und eine S. Judas gepredigt und ausgelegt*, (2 Peter and Jude) WA 14 (LW 30).

———. 1523–24, *Vorlesung über das Deuteronomium* (Lectures on Deuteronomy) WA 14 (LW 9).

———. 1524, *Luther an drei Klosterjungfrauen* (Luther's Letter to Several Nuns, translated by Erika Bullmann Flores) WA Br 3.

———. 1523–24, *Predigten ber das erste Buch Mose* (Genesis) WA 42 (LW 1).

———. 1525, *De servo arbitrio* (The Bondage of the Will) WA 18 (LW 33).

———. 1525, *Deuteronimion Mosi cum annotationibus* (Deuteronomy 1–34) WA 14 (LW 9).

———. 1526, *Vorlesung über den Prediger Salomo* (Ecclesiastes) WA 20 (LW 15).
———. 1527, *Vorlesung über die Briefe an Titus und Philemon* (Titus and Philemon) WA 25 (LW 29).
———. 1527, *In Genesin Declamationes* (Sermons over Genesis) WA 24, 90–91.
———. 1527, *Ob man vor dem Sterben fliehen möge* (Whether One May Flee from a Deadly Plauge) WA 23 (LW 43).
———. 1527–30, *Vorlesung über Jesaias* (Lecture over Isaiah) WA 31 II (LW 17, 342).
———. 1528, *Vom Abendmahl Christi* (Confession Concerning Christ's Supper) WA 26 (LW 37).
———. 1528, *Christliche Schrift an W. Reißenbusch, sich in den ehelichen Stand zu begeben,* (Open Letter on Marriage) WA 18, 275.
———. 1529, *Deutsch Catechismus* (Catechism) WA 30 I (LW 51).
———. 1529, *Der kleine Catechismus für die gemeine Pfarrherr und Prediger* (Small Catechism) WA 30 I (LW 51).
———. 1530, *Letter to Ludwig Senfl*, WA, Br 1727.
———. 1530, *Predigten des Jahres 1530* (no. 33) (Sermons from 1530) WA 32, 274, 7f.
———. 1530–31, *Vorlesung über das Hohelied* (Song of Solomon) WA 31 II (LW 15).
———. 1530–32, *Wochenpredigten über Matth. 5–7* (The Sermon on the Mount) WA 32 (LW 21).
———. 1530–35, *Tischreden* (Table Talk) WA TR 1.
———. 1530–35, *Tischreden* (Table Talk) (no. 1133) WA TR 1, 561.
———. 1530–35, *Tischreden* (Table Talk) (no. 2978 b), WA TR 3.
———. 1531, *Einleitung zur Vorlesung über das Hohelied* (Introduction to Song of Solomon) WA 31 II (LW 15).
———. 1531, *Eine Hochzeitpredigt über den Spruch Hebr 13, 4* (Sermon on a Marriage) WA 34 I
———. 1532–33, *Praelectio in psalmum 45* (Psalm 45) WA 40 II, 581–584 (LW 12:279).
———. 1532–33, *Vorlesungen über die Stufenpsalmen,* (Psalm121:3) WA 40 III, 63:17f.
———. 1531–35, *In epistolam S. Paulus ad Galatas Commentarius* (Galatians) WA 40 I (LW 26–27).
———. 1533, *Tischreden* (Table Talk (no. 476), WA TR 1.
———. 1533, *Tischreden*) (Table Talk) (no. 437). WA TR 1.
———. 1535–45, *Genesisvorlesung* (Lectures on Genesis) WA 42 (LW 1–3).
———. 1536, *Die Disputation de homine,* (Disputation on the Divinity and Humanity of Christ) WA 39 I (LW 39).
———. 1537–38, *Auslegung des ersten und zweiten Kapitels Johannis in Predigten* (John 1–2) WA 46 (LW 22).
———. 1538–40, *Auslegung des dritten und vierten Kapitels Johannis in Predigten* (John 3–4) WA 47 (LW 22).
———. 1538–42, *Genesisvorlesung* (Genesis) WA 43 (LW 4, 5).
———. 1539, *Vorrede zum 1 Bande der Wittenberger Ausgabe der Deutschen Schriften,* (Preface to the Wittenberg Edition of Luther's German Writings) WA 50, 659:22–35, (LW 34).
———. 1540–45, *Predigten,* (Sermons) WA 49 (LW 51).
———. 1545, *Vorrede zum ersten Bande der Gesamtausgaben seiner lateinischen Schriften,* (Preface to the Complete Edition of Luther's Latin Writings) WA 54 (LW 34).

———. 2011, *Lilla katekesen*. Introduction, translation, and commentary by Carl Axel Aurelius and Margareta Brandby-Cöster. Uppsala: Trossamfundet Svenska kyrkan.

Other Works

Ackermann, Denise M. "Engaging Freedom: A Contextual Feminist Theology of Praxis." *Journal of Theology for South Africa* 94 (1996) 32–49.
———. "Found Wanting and Left Untried? Confession of a Ragbag Theologian." In *Ragbag Theologies: Essays in Honour of Denise M. Ackermann, a Feminist Theologian of Praxis*, edited by Miranda Pillay, Sarojini Nadar, and Clint Le Bruyns, 267–82. Stellenbosch: SUN, 2009.
Adorno, Theodor W. *Minima Moralia: Reflections on a Damaged Life*. Translated by E. F. N. Jephcott. London: Verso, 2005.
Agamben, Giorgio. *Homo Sacer: Sovereign Power and Bare Life*. Translated by Daniel Heller-Roazen. Meridian: Crossing Aesthetics. Stanford: Stanford University Press, 1998.
Allison, Anne. *Nightwork: Sexuality, Pleasure, and Corporate Masculinity in a Tokyo Hostess Club*. Chicago: University of Chicago Press, 1994.
Althaus-Reid, Marcella. "'A Saint and a Church for Twenty Dollars': Sending Radical Orthodoxy to Ayacucho." In *Interpreting the Postmodern: Responses to "Radical Orthodoxy"*, edited by Rosemary Radford Ruether and Marion Grau, 107–18. New York: T. & T. Clark, 2006.
———. "Queer I Stand: Lifting the Shirts of God." In *The Sexual Theologian: Essays on Sex, God and Politics*, edited by Marcella Althaus-Reid and Lisa Isherwood, 99–109. London: T. & T. Clark, 2004.
Althaus-Reid, Marcella, and Lisa Isherwood, eds. *The Sexual Theologian: Essays on Sex, God and Politics*. London: T. & T. Clark, 2004.
Anderson, Cheryl B. *Women, Ideology and Violence: Critical Theory and the Construction of Gender in the Book of the Covenant and Deuteronomic Law*. London: T. & T. Clark, 2005.
Anderson, Pamela Sue. "The Lived Body, Gender and Confidence." In *New Topics in Feminist Philosophy of Religion: Contestations and Transcendence Incarnate*, edited by Pamela Sue Anderson, 163–80. Dordrecht: Springer, 2010.
———. *Re-visioning Gender in Philosophy of Religion: Reason, Love and Epistemic Locatedness*. Farnham, UK: Ashgate, 2012.
———. "Sacrifice as Self-Destructive Love." In *Sacrifice and Modern Thought*, edited by Julia Meszaros and Johannes Zachhuber, 29–47. Oxford: Oxford University Press, 2013.
Anttila, Miikka E. "The Innocent Pleasure: A Study on Luther's Theology of Music." PhD diss., University of Helsinki, 2011.
Appelqvist, Tomas. *Bönen i den helige Andes tempel: Människosyn och kyrkosyn i Martin Luthers böneteologi*. Skellefteå: Artos, 2009.
Arendt, Hannah. *The Human Condition*. Chicago: University of Chicago Press, 1998.
———. *The Life of the Mind*. 2 vols. London: Secker & Warburg, 1978.

———. *Love and Saint Augustine*. Edited and with an interpretive essay by Joanna Vecchiarelli Scott and Judith Chelius Stark. Chicago: University of Chicago Press, 1996.
Aspegren, Kerstin. *The Male Woman: A Feminine Ideal in the Early Church*. Edited by René Kieffer. Uppsala: Almqvist & Wiksell, 1995.
Augustine. *The City of God against the Pagans* (*De civitate Dei contra Paganos*). Vol. 7, *Books XXI–XXII*. Translated by William M. Green. Cambridge, MA: Harvard University Press, 1972.
———. *The Good of Marriage* (*De bono conjugali*). Translated by David G. Hunter. In *Theology and Sexuality: Classic and Contemporary Readings*, edited by Eugune F. Rogers Jr., 71–86. Oxford: Blackwell, 2002.
———. *On the Holy Trinity*. Translated by Arthur West Haddan. In vol. 3 of *Nicene and Post-Nicene Fathers*, Series 1, edited by Philip Schaff, 1–228. New York: Cosimo Classics, 2007.
———. *Soliloquies: Augustine's Inner Dialogue*. Translated by Kim Paffenroth. Edited by John E. Rotelle. New York: New City, 2000.
Aulén, Gustaf. *Den kristna försoningstanken: Huvudtyper och brytningar*. Stockholm: Svenska kyrkans diakonistyrelse, 1930.
Aurelius, Carl Axel. *Luther i Sverige: Svenska Lutherbilder under tre sekler*. Skellefteå: Artos, 2015.
Bacon, Hannah. "Expanding Bodies, Expanding God: Feminist Theology in Search of a 'Fatter' Future." *Feminist Theology* 21 (2013) 309–26.
Bainton, Roland. *Luther, mannen som blev en epok*. Stockholm: Diakonistyrelsen, 1950.
———. *Women of the Reformation in Germany and Italy*. Minneapolis: Augsburg, 1971.
Bakhtin, Mikhail Mikhailovich. *The Dialogic Imagination: Four Essays*. Edited by Michael Holquist. Translated by Caryl Emerson and Michael Holquist. Austin: University of Texas Press, 1981.
Bauerschmidt, Frederick Christian. "Aesthetics: The Theological Sublime." In *Radical Orthodoxy: A New Theology*, edited by John Milbank, Catherine Pickstock, and Graham Ward, 201–19. New York: Routledge, 1999.
Bauman, Zygmunt. *Community: Seeking Safety in an Insecure World*. Cambridge: Polity, 2001.
———. *Consuming Life*. Cambridge: Polity, 2007.
———. *Postmodern Ethics*. Oxford: Blackwell, 1995.
Bayer, Oswald. *Martin Luther's Theology: A Contemporary Interpretation*. Translated by Thomas H. Trapp. Grand Rapids: Eerdmans, 2003.
Beattie, Tina. *New Catholic Feminism: Theology and Theory*. London: Routledge, 2006.
Bergmann, Sigurd. "Fetishism Revisited: In the Animistic Lens of Eco-Pneumatology." *Journal of Reformed Theology* 6 (2012) 195–215.
———. "'Millions of Machines Are Already Roaring': Fetishised Technology Encountered by the Life-Giving Spirit." In *Technofutures, Nature and the Sacred: Transdisciplinary Perspectives*, edited by Celia Deane-Drummond, Sigurd Bergmann, and Bronislaw Szerszynski, 115–38. Farnham, UK: Ashgate, 2015.
Bernard of Clairvaux. *On the Songs of Songs*. Translated by Kilian Walsh. 4 vols. Spencer, MA: Cistercian, 1971–80.
———. *Treatises*. Vol. 2, *The Steps of Humility and Pride; On Loving God*. Spencer, MA: Cistercian, 1974.

Blåder, Niclas. *Lutheran Tradition as Heritage and Tool: An Empirical Study of Reflections on Confessional Identity in Five Lutheran Churches in Different Contexts*. Eugene, OR: Pickwick, 2015.

Bóasdottir, Sólveig Anna. "Bodyrights and Christian Sexual Ethics." *NIKK Magasine* 1 (2007) 23–29.

———. *Violence, Power, and Justice: A Feminist Contribution to Christian Sexual Ethics*. Uppsala: Acta Universitatis Upsaliensis, 1998.

Bornemark, Jonna. *Kunskapens gräns, gränsens vetande: en fenomenologisk undersökning av transcendens och kroppslighet*. Huddinge: Södertörns högskola, Biblioteket distributör, 2009.

Børresen, Kari Elisabeth. *From Patristics to Matristics: Selected Articles on Christian Gender Models*. Edited by Øyvind Norderval and Katrine Lund Ore. Rome: Herder, 2002.

———, ed. *The Image of God: Gender Models in Judeo-Christian Tradition*. Minneapolis: Fortress, 1995.

Boulding, Elise. *One Small Plot of Heaven: Reflections on Family Life by a Quaker Sociologist*. Wallingford, PA: Pendle Hill, 1989.

Bråkenhielm, Carl Reinhold. "Ethics and Ecclesiology: Burning Issues for Church of Sweden—and Beyond." In *Exploring a Heritage: Evangelical Lutheran Churches in the North*, edited by Anne-Louise Eriksson, Göran Gunner, and Niclas Blåder, 79–96. Eugene, OR: Pickwick, 2013.

Brandby-Cöster, Margareta. "Sökvägar och ledtrådar: Reflektioner kring arbetet med att översätta Martin Luthers lilla katekes." In *Lilla Katekesen*, translated by Carl Axel Aurelius and Margareta Brandby-Cöster, 53–75. Uppsala: Trossamfundet Svenska Kyrkan, 2011.

Brock, Brian. "Why the Estates? Hans Ulrich's Recovery of an Unpopular Notion." *Studies in Christian Ethics* 20 (2007) 179–202.

Brock, Rita Nakashima. *Journeys by Heart: A Christology of Erotic Power*. New York: Crossroad, 1988.

Brown, Delwin. *Boundaries of Our Habitations: Tradition and Theological Construction*. Albany: State University of New York Press, 1994.

Brown, Peter. *The Body and Society: Men, Women, and Sexual Renunciation in Early Christianity*. London: Faber and Faber, 1988.

Burrus, Virginia. *Begotten Not Made: Conceiving Manhood in Late Antiquity*. Stanford: Stanford University Press, 2000.

———. "Introduction: Theology and Eros after Nygren." In *Toward a Theology of Eros: Transforming Passion at the Limits of Discipline*, edited by Virginia Burrus and Catherine Keller, xiii–xxi. New York: Fordham University Press, 2006.

———. "Queer Father: Gregory of Nyssa and the Subversion of Identity." In *Queer Theology: Rethinking the Western Body*, edited by Gerard Loughlin, 147–62. Oxford: Blackwell, 2007.

———. "Radical Orthodoxy and the Heresiological Habit: Engaging Graham Ward's Christology." In *Interpreting the Postmodern: Responses to "Radical Orthodoxy"*, edited by Rosemary Radford Ruether and Marion Grau, 36–53. London: T. & T. Clark, 2006.

———. *The Sex Lives of Saints: An Erotics of Ancient Hagiography*. Philadelphia: University of Pennsylvania Press, 2004.

Butler, Judith. *Frames of War: When Is Life Grievable?* London: Verso, 2009.

Butler, Judith, and Gayatri Chakravorty Spivak. *Who Sings the Nation-State? Language, Politics, Belonging.* London: Seagull, 2007.

Bynum, Caroline Walker. *Christian Materiality: An Essay on Religion in Late Medieval Europe.* New York: Zone Books, 2011.

———. *Fragmentation and Redemption: Essays on Gender and the Human Body in Medieval Religion.* New York: Zone Books, 1991.

———. "Jesus as Mother and Abbot as Mother: Some Themes in Twelfth-Century Cistercian Writing." In *Medieval Religion: New Approaches*, edited by Constance Hoffman Berman, 20–48. New York: Routledge, 2005.

———. *Jesus as Mother: Studies in the Spirituality of the High Middle Ages.* Berkeley: University of California Press, 1982.

———. *Resurrection of the Body in Western Christianity, 200–1336.* New York: Columbia University Press, 1995.

Camnerin, Sofia. *Försoningens mellanrum: En analys av Daphne Hampsons och Rita Nakashima Brocks teologiska tolkningar.* Uppsala: Acta Universitatis Upsaliensis, 2008.

Carlsson, Petra. *Theology beyond Representation: Foucault, Deleuze and the Phantasms of Theological Thinking.* Uppsala: Uppsala Universitet, 2012.

Carson, Anne. *Eros the Bittersweet: An Essay.* Princeton: Princeton University, 1998.

Casanova, José. *Public Religions in the Modern World.* Chicago: University of Chicago Press, 1994

———. "Religion, Politics and Gender Equality: Public Religions Revisited." Geneva: UNRISD, 2009. (Quoted with the approval of the author).

Clack, Beverley. *Sex and Death: A Reappraisal of Human Mortality.* Cambridge: Polity, 2002.

Clark, Elizabeth, ed. *St. Augustine on Marriage and Sexuality.* Washington, DC: Catholic University of America Press, 1996.

Coakley, Sarah. "The Eschatological Body: Gender, Transformation and God." In *Powers and Submissions: Spirituality, Philosophy and Gender*, 153–66. Oxford: Blackwell, 2002.

———. *God, Sexuality, and the Self: An Essay "On the Trinity".* Cambridge: Cambridge University Press, 2013.

———. "Introduction: Religion and the Body." In *Religion and the Body*, edited by Sarah Coakley, 1–12. Cambridge: Cambridge University Press, 1997.

———. "Sacrifice Regained: Evolution, Cooperation and God." Gifford Lectures. Aberdeen: University of Aberdeen, 2012. http://www.giffordlectures.org/lectures/sacrifice-regained-evolution-cooperation-and-god.

Cobb, John, Jr., and David Griffin. *Process Theology: An Introductory Exposition.* Louisville: Westminster John Knox, 1977.

Coole, Diana, and Samantha Frost, eds. *New Materialisms: Ontology, Agency, and Politics.* Durham: Duke University Press, 2010.

Cooper, Melinda. "Why I Am Not a Postsecularist." *Boundary 2: An International Journal of Literature and Culture* 40 (2013) 21–39.

Córdova Quero, Martín Hugo. "Friendship with Benefits: A Queer Reading of Aelred of Rievaulx and His Theology of Friendship." In *The Sexual Theologian: Essays on Sex, God and Politics*, edited by Marcella Althaus-Reid and Lisa Isherwood, 26–46. London: T. & T. Clark, 2004.

Cortright, Charles Lloyd. "'Poor Maggot-Sack that I am': The Human Body in the Theology of Martin Luther." PhD diss., Marquette University, 2011.
Costa, Mario. "For the Love of God: The Death of Desire and the Gift of Love." In *Toward a Theology of Eros: Transforming Passion at the Limits of Discipline*, edited by Virginia Burrus and Catherine Keller, 38–62. New York: Fordham University Press, 2006.
Cöster, Henry. *Kyrkans historia och historiens kyrka*. Stockholm: Symposion, 1989.
———. *Livsmodets språk: Förkunnelse och sakrament i en luthersk teologi*. Lund: Arcus, 2009.
———. "Tvånget i frihetens katekes." In *Luther som utmaning: Om frihet och ansvar*, edited by Elisabeth Gerle, 109–33. Stockholm: Verbum, 2008.
Crockett, Clayton, ed. *Secular Theology: American Radical Theological Thought*. London: Routledge, 2001.
Cronberg, Marie Lindstedt. *Synd och skam: Ogifta mödrar på svensk landsbygd 1680–1880*. Tygelsjö: Cronberg, 1997.
Daly, Mary. *Beyond God the Father: Toward a Philosophy of Women's Liberation*. Boston: Beacon, 1973.
D'Arcy, Martin Cyril. *The Mind and Heart of Love: Lion and Unicorn; A Study in Eros and Agape*. London: Faber & Faber, 1945.
Davies, Jon. "Sex These Days, Sex Those Days: Will It Ever End?" In *Sex These Days: Essays on Theology, Sexuality and Society*, edited by Jon Davies and Gerard Loughlin, 18–34. Sheffield: Sheffield Academic Press, 1997.
Deleuze, Gilles, and Félix Guattari. *A Thousand Plateaus: Capitalism and Schizophrenia*. Translated by Brian Massumi. Minneapolis: University of Minnesota, 1987.
Derrida, Jacques. *Acts of Religion*. Edited by Gil Anidjar. New York: Routledge, 2002.
Driel, Francien Th. M. van. *Poor and Powerful: Female-Headed Households and Unmarried Motherhood in Botswana*. Saarbrücken: Breitenbach, 1994.
Eckhart, Meister. *Meister Eckhart: A Modern Translation*. Edited and translated by Raymond Bernard Blakney. New York: Harper, 1941.
Edgardh, Ninna. *Gudstjänsten i tiden, Gudstjänstliv i Svenska kyrkan 1968–2008*. Lund: Arcus, 2010.
Ekerwald, Carl-Göran. *En fritänkare läser Bibeln*. Lund: Ellerströms förlag, 2014.
Elshtain, Jean Bethke. *Public Man, Private Woman: Woman in Social and Political Thought*. Princeton: Princeton University Press, 1981.
Erikson, Erik H. *Kulturkris och religion: Analys av den unge Luthers personlighetsutveckling*. Stockholm: Diakonistyrelsens förlag, 1966.
Eskenazi, Tamara Cohn. "Att läsa Bibeln i vår egen tid, ett judiskt perspektiv." In *Att tolka Bibeln och Koranen: Konflikt och förhandling*, edited by Hanna Stenström, 45–66. Lund: Studentlitteratur, 2009.
Farley, Edward. "Interpreting Situations: An Inquiry into the Nature of Practical Theology." In *Practicing Gospel: Unconventional Thoughts on the Church's Ministry*, edited by Edward Farley, 29–43. Louisville: Westminster John Knox, 2003.
Farley, Margaret A. "Sexual Ethics." In *Sexuality and the Sacred: Sources for Theological Reflection*, edited by James B. Nelson and Sandra P. Longfellow, 54–67. Louisville: Westminster John Knox, 1994.
Farley, Wendy. "Beguiled by Beauty: The Reformation of Desire for Faith and Theology." In *Saving Desire: The Seduction of Christian Theology*, edited by F. LeRon Shults and Jan-Olav Henriksen, 128–47. Grand Rapids: Eerdmans, 2011.

Foucault, Michel. *Discipline and Punish: The Birth of the Prison.* Translated by Alan Sheridan. 2nd ed. New York: Vintage, 1995.
———. *The History of Sexuality.* Vol. 1, *An Introduction.* Translated by Robert Hurley. New York: Pantheon, 1978.
———. *The Order of Things: An Archeology of Human Sciences.* New York: Pantheon, 1970.
Freud, Sigmund. *Civilization and Its Discontents.* Translated by Joan Riviere. London: Hogarth, 1949.
———. *The Ego and the Id.* Translated by Joan Riviere. London: Hogarth, 1949.
———. *An Outline of Psychoanalysis.* Translated by James Strachey. New York: Norton, 1949.
Fulkerson, Mary McClintock. "Interpreting a Situation: When Is 'Empirical' also 'Theological'?" In *Perspectives on Ecclesiology and Ethnography,* edited by Pete Ward, 124–44. Grand Rapids: Eerdmans, 2012.
Gadamer, Hans-Georg. *Truth and Method.* Translated by W. Glen-Doepel. Translation edited by Garrett Barden and John Cumming. New York: Seabury, 1975.
Gebara, Ivone. *Longing for Running Water: Ecofeminism and Liberation.* Translated by David Molineaux. Minneapolis: Fortress, 1999.
Gerle, Elisabeth. "Eros, Ethics, and Politics: Nuptial Imagery in Luther Read as a Challenge to Traditional Power Structures." In *Lutheran Identity and Political Theology,* edited by Carl-Henric Grenholm and Göran Gunner, 222–41. Eugene, OR: Pickwick, 2014.
———. *Farlig förenkling: Om religion och politik.* Nora: Nya Doxa, 2010.
———. "From Homogeneous Nations to Pluralism and Global Spheres of Solidarity." *Dialog: A Journal of Theology* 52 (2013) 283–85.
———. "Kön, genus och religion." In *Mänskliga rättigheter och religion,* edited by Dan-Erik Andersson and Johan Modée, 61–77. Malmö: Liber, 2011.
———. "Kristna fristående skolor—en front mot vad?" In *Religiösa friskolor i Sverige: Historiska och nutida perspektiv,* edited by Jenny Berglund and Göran Larsson, 47–80. Lund: Studentlitteratur, 2007.
———. "Luther and the Erotic." *Currents in Theology and Mission* 37 (2010) 198–208.
———. "Luther, erotik och tvetydighet." In *På spaning . . . Från Svenska kyrkans forskardagar 2009,* edited by Hanna Stenström, 353–367. Stockholm: Verbum, 2010.
———, ed. *Luther som utmaning: Om frihet och ansvar.* Stockholm: Verbum, 2008.
———. "Lutheran Theology as a Resource for Future Society." In *Transformations in Luther's Theology: Historical and Contemporary Reflections,* edited by Christine Helmer and Bo Kristian Holm, 210–28. Leipzig: Evangelische Verlagsanstalt, 2011.
———. *Mångkulturalism för vem?* Nora: Nya Doxa, 2005.
———. *Mänskliga rättigheter för Guds skull: Tolka text, tro och tradition.* Nora: Nya Doxa, 2006.
———. "Mot ömsesidighetens teologi." In *Etiska undersökningar: Om samhällsmoral, etisk teori och teologi,* edited by Elena Namli, Per Sundman, and Susanne Wigorts Yngvesson, 291–315. Uppsala: Uppsala Studies in Social Ethics 40, 2010.
———. "Nationalism, Reformation and the Other in Denmark and Sweden." In *Yearbook Societas Ethica.* Oxford, 2006.

———. "Var dags och varje människas upprättelse." In *Luther som utmaning: Om frihet och ansvar*, edited by Elisabeth Gerle, 15–54. Stockholm: Verbum, 2008.

———. "Various Interpretations of Human Rights for Women: Challenges at United Nations' Conferences." In *Human Rights Law: From Dissemination to Application*, edited by Jonas Grimheden and Rolf Ring, 343–74. Leiden: M. Nijhoff, 2006.

Giddens, Anthony. *The Transformation of Intimacy: Sexuality, Love and Eroticism in Modern Societies*. Cambridge: Polity, 1992.

Grant, Colin. "For the Love of God: Agape." *Journal of Religious Ethics* 24 (1996) 3–21.

Grantén, Eva-Lotta. *Utanför Paradiset: Arvsyndsläran i nutida luthersk teologi och etik*. Stockholm: Verbum, 2013.

Gregersen, Niels Henrik. "Dybdeinkarnationen: Kristologien og de universelle sammenhaenge." In *Gudstankens aktualitet*, edited by Else Marie Wiberg Pedersen, Bo Kristian Holm, and Anders Christian Jacobsen, 255–76. Copenhagen: Anis, 2010.

———. "Incarnate vs. Discarnate Protestantism: Martin Luther and the Disembodiment of Faith." In *Justification in a Post-Christian Society*, edited by Carl-Henric Grenholm and Göran Gunner, 173–91. Eugene, OR: Pickwick, 2014.

———. "Protestantisme med kød og blod." *Dansk Teologisk Tidsskrift* 73 (2010) 253–70.

———. "Skabelse og forsyn." In *Fragmenter af et speil: Bidrag till dogmatiken*, edited by Niels Henrik Gregersen, 59–130. Frederiksberg: Anis, 1997.

Gregory of Nyssa. *Commentary of the Song of Songs*. Translated by Casimir McCambley. Brookline, MA: Hellenic College Press, 1987.

———. *The Life of Moses*. Translated by Abraham J. Malherbe and Everett Ferguson. New York: Paulist, 1978.

Grenholm, Carl-Henric. *Tro, moral och uddlös politik*. Stockholm: Verbum, 2014.

Grenholm, Cristina. "Makt under inkarnationens villkor: Teologiska perspektiv på maktbegreppet." In *Makt i nordisk teologisk tolkning*, edited by Sigurd Bergmann and Cristina Grenholm, 209–24. Trondheim: Tapir, 2004.

———. *Motherhood and Love: Beyond the Gendered Stereotypes of Theology*. Translated by Marie Tåqvist. Grand Rapids: Eerdmans, 2011.

Grisar, Hartmann. *Martin Luther: His Life and Work*. Adapted from the 2nd German ed. by Frank J. Eble. Edited by Arthur Preuss. Westminster, MD: Newman, 1955.

Gullestad, Marianne. *Plausible Prejudice: Everyday Experiences and Social Images of Nation, Culture, and Race*. Oslo: Universitetsforlaget, 2006.

Guðmundsdóttir, Arnfríður. *Meeting God on the Cross: Christ, the Cross, and the Feminist Critique*. Oxford: Oxford University Press, 2010.

Gustafsson, Johanna. *Kyrka och kön: Om könskonstruktioner i Svenska kyrkan, 1945–1985*. Eslöv: Brutus Östlings förlag, 2001.

Gustafsson Lundberg, Johanna. "Feministiska perspektiv på teologi och etik: En introduktion." In *Kön, teologi och etik: En introduktion*, edited by Maria Jansdotter Samuelsson, Johanna Gustafsson Lundberg, and Annika Borg, 11–26. Lund: Studentlitteratur, 2011.

———. *Medlem 2010: En teologisk kommentar*. Uppsala: Svenska kyrkans forskningsenhet, 2012.

Gustavsson, Matilda. "Min bok är en rad förvrängda självporträtt." *Sydsvenska dagbladet*, September 16, 2012. http://www.sydsvenskan.se/2012-09-16/forvrangda-sjalvportratt.

Gutiérrez, Gustavo. *A Theology of Liberation: History, Politics and Salvation*. Translated and edited by Sister Caridad Inda and John Eagleson. Maryknoll, NY: Orbis, 1973.

Gutmann, Hans-Martin. *Über Liebe und Herrschaft: Luthers Verständnis von Intimität und Autorität im Kontext des Zivilisationsprozesses*. Göttingen: Vandenhoeck & Ruprecht, 1991.

Habermas, Jürgen. *Between Naturalism and Religion: Philosophical Essays*. Translated by Ciaran Cronin. Cambridge: Polity, 2008.

Hägglund, Bengt. *Arvet från reformationen: Teologihistoriska studier*. Gothenburg: Församlingsförlaget, 2002.

———. *De Homine: Människouppfattningen i äldre luthersk tradition*. Lund: C. W. K. Gleerup, 1959.

Hallonsten, Gösta. "Sexualiteten och traditionen." *Svensk Teologisk Kvartalsskrift* 80 (2004) 120–23.

Hammar, Inger. *Emancipation och religion: Den svenska kvinnorörelsens pionjärer i debatt om kvinnans kallelse ca 1860–1900*. Stockholm: Carlsson, 1999.

Hampson, Daphne. "On Autonomy and Heteronomy." In *Swallowing a Fishbone? Feminist Theologians Debate Christianity*, edited by Daphne Hampson, 1–16. Reading: SPCK, 1996.

Heidegger, Martin. *Being and Time*. Translated by Joan Stambaugh. Albany: State University of New York Press, 1996.

Henriksen, Jan-Olav. "Desire: Gift and Giving." In *Saving Desire: The Seduction of Christian Theology*, edited by F. LeRon Shults and Jan-Olav Henriksen, 1–30. Grand Rapids: Eerdmans, 2011.

Heyward, Carter. *Saving Jesus from Those Who Are Right: Rethinking What It Means to Be Christian*. Minneapolis: Fortress, 1999.

———. *Touching Our Strength: The Erotic as Power and the Love of God*. San Francisco: Harper & Row, 1989.

Hirdman, Yvonne. *Genus: Om det stabilas föränderliga former*. Malmö: Liber förlag, 2001.

Holm, Bo Kristian. "Dynamic Tensions in the Social Imaginaries of the Lutheran Reformation." In *Lutheran Theology and the Shaping of Society: The Danish Monarchy as Example*, edited by Bo Kristian Holm and Nina Javette Koefoed. Göttingen: Vandenhoeck & Ruprecht, forthcoming.

———. *Gabe und Geben bei Luther: Das Verhältnis zwischen Reziprozität und reformatorischer Rechtfertigungslehre*. Berlin: de Gruyter, 2006.

Holmberg, Carin. *Det kallas manshat: En bok om feminism*. Stockholm: Modernista, 2003.

hooks, bell. *All about Love: New Visions*. London: Women's Press, 2000.

Hornborg, Alf. "Technology as Fetish: Marx, Latour, and the Cultural Foundations of Capitalism." *Theory, Culture and Society* 31 (2014) 119–40.

Hunter, Richard L. *Plato's Symposium*. Oxford: Oxford University Press, 2004.

Inglehart, Ronald, Miguel Basáñez, and Alejandro Menéndez Moreno. *Human Values and Beliefs: A Cross-Cultural Sourcebook; Political, Religious, Sexual, and Economic Norms in 43 Societies*. Ann Arbor: University of Michigan Press, 1998.

Irenaeus. *Ad haereses*. Leipzig: Weigel, 1853.

———. *Against the Heresies*. Vol. 3. Translated by Dominic J. Unger. With further revisions by John J. Dillon. New York: Newman, 2012.

Irigaray, Luce. *An Ethics of Sexual Difference*. Translated by Carolyn Burke and Gillian C. Gill. London: Continuum, 2004.

———. *This Sex which Is Not One.* Translated by Catherine Porter with Carolyn Burke. Ithaca: Cornell University Press, 1985.
Irwin, Alexander C. *Eros Toward the World: Paul Tillich and the Theology of the Erotic.* Minneapolis: Fortress, 1991.
Jansdotter, Maria. "Makten och måltiden: Ett ekofeministiskt perspektiv på nattvarden." In *Makt i nordisk teologisk tolkning*, edited by Sigurd Bergmann and Cristina Grenholm, 181–92. Trondheim: Tapir, 2004.
Jantzen, Grace M. *Becoming Divine: Towards a Feminist Philosophy of Religion.* Bloomington: Indiana University Press, 1999.
———. *Power, Gender and Christian Mysticism.* Cambridge: Cambridge University Press, 1995.
Jeanrond, Werner G. "Augustinus teologi om kärlek." In *Eros och Agape: Barmhärtighet, kärlek och mystik i den tidiga kyrkan*, edited by Henrik Rydell Johnsén and Per Rönnegård, 221–43. Skellefteå: Artos, 2009.
———. "Kärlekens praxis, utmaningar i vår samtid." In *Kärlekens förändrade landskap*, edited by Mikael Lindfelt and Johanna Gustafsson Lundberg, 221–43. Stockholm: Verbum, 2009.
———. *A Theology of Love.* New York: T. & T. Clark. 2010.
Jocic, Andreas. "Tron är aldrig allena: En undersökning av Kristusföreningsmotivet i den finska Lutherforskningen." Master's thesis, Göteborgs universitet/Institutionen för litteratur, idéhistoria och religion, 2012.
Johannesson, Karin. *Helgelsens filosofi: Om andlig träning i luthersk tradition.* Stockholm: Verbum, 2014.
Johnson, Elizabeth A. "Losing and Finding Creation in the Christian Tradition." In *Christianity and Ecology*, edited by Dieter T. Hessel and Rosemary Radford Ruether, 3–21. Cambridge: Harvard University Press, 2000.
Kampowski, Stephan. *Arendt, Augustine, and the New Beginning: The Action Theory and Moral Thought of Hannah Arendt in the Light of Her Dissertation on St. Augustine.* Grand Rapids: Eerdmans, 2008.
Kant, Immanuel. *Critique of Judgment.* Translated by J. H. Bernard. New York: Hafner, 1974.
Karant-Nunn, Susan C. "The Masculinity of Martin Luther: Theory, Practicality, and Humor." In *Masculinity in the Reformation Era*, edited by Scott H. Hendrix and Susan C. Karant-Nunn, 167–89. Kirksville, MO: Truman State University Press, 2008.
Käßmann, Margot. *Schlag nach bei Luther: Texte für den Alltag.* Frankfurt am Main: HDV Verlagsleitung Edition Chrismon, 2012.
Keller, Catherine. "Afterword. A Theology of Eros, After Transfiguring Passion." In *Toward a Theology of Eros: Transforming Passion at the Limits of Discipline*, edited by Virginia Burrus and Catherine Keller, 366–74. New York: Fordham University Press, 2006.
———. "Be a Multiplicity: Ancestral Anticipations." In *Polydoxy: Theology of Multiplicity and Relation*, edited by Catherine Keller and Laurel C. Schneider, 81–102. New York: Routledge, 2011.
———. *Cloud of the Impossible: Negative Theology and Planetary Entanglement.* New York: Columbia University Press, 2015.
———. *Face of the Deep: A Theology of Becoming.* London: Routledge, 2003.
———. *From a Broken Web: Separation, Sexism, and Self.* Boston: Beacon, 1986.

———. "Is That All? Gift and Reciprocity in Milbank's *Being Reconciled*." In *Interpreting the Postmodern: Responses to "Radical Orthodoxy"*, edited by Rosemary Radford Ruether and Marion Grau, 18–35. New York: T. & T. Clark, 2006.

———. *On the Mystery: Discerning Divinity in Process*. Minneapolis: Fortress, 2008.

Kleinhans, Kathryn A. "Christ as Bride/Groom: A Lutheran Feminist Relational Christology." In *Transformative Lutheran Theologies: Feminist, Womanist, and Mujerista Perspectives*, edited by Mary J. Streufert, 123–34. Minneapolis: Fortress, 2010.

Kristensson Uggla, Bengt. *Becoming Human Again: The Theological Life of Gustaf Wingren*. Eugene, OR: Cascade, 2016.

Kristeva, Julia. *Desire in Language: A Semiotic Approach to Literature and Art*. New York: Columbia University Press, 1980.

Kwok, Pui-lan. *Postcolonial Imagination and Feminist Theology*. London: SCM, 2005.

Landry, Donna, and Gerald MacLean, eds. *The Spivak Reader*. New York: Routledge, 1996.

Laqueur, Thomas. *Making Sex: Body and Gender from the Greeks to Freud*. Cambridge: Harvard University Press, 1990.

Latour, Bruno. *Reassembling the Social: An Introduction to Actor-Network-Theory*. Oxford: Oxford Univeristy Press, 2005.

Levinas, Emmauel. *Alterity and Transcendence*. Translated by Michael B. Smith. New York: Colombia University Press, 1999.

———. *Totality and Infinity: An Essay on Exteriority*. Translated by Alphonso Lingis. Pittsburgh: Duquesne University, 1969.

Lind, Martin. "Kristen tro och det allmänmänskliga" In *Där främlingskapet bryts kan en ny värld börja*, edited by Kristina Hellqvist, 30–43. Lund: Arcus, 2010.

Lindberg, Carter. *The European Reformations*. Oxford: Blackwell, 1996.

Lindfelt, Mikael. "Olof Sundbys Luther i vår tid." In *Uppdrag samliv: Om äktenskap och samlevnad*, edited by Mikael Lindfelt and Johanna Gustafsson Lundberg, 255–93. Stockholm: Verbum, 2007.

Lindfelt, Mikael, and Johanna Gustafsson Lundberg, eds. *Uppdrag samliv: Om äktenskap och samlevnad*. Stockholm: Verbum, 2009.

Lindmark, Daniel, ed. *Alphabeta Varia: Orality, Reading and Writing in the History of Literacy; Festschrift in Honour of Egil Johansson on the Occasion of His 65th Birthday, March 24, 1998*. Umeå: Forskningsarkivet, Arbetsenheten för religionsvetenskap, 1998.

Lindström, Fredrik. "Guds långa näsa och blödande hjärta. Gränser för Guds makt i Gamla testamentet." *Svensk Teologisk Kvartalsskrift* 77 (2001) 1–12.

Lindström, Martin. *Bibeln och bekännelsen om kvinnliga präster*. Stockholm: Verbum, 1978.

Løgstrup, K. E. *Den etiske fordring*. Copenhagen: Gyldendal, 1969.

Loughlin, Gerard. "Sex after Natural Law." In *The Sexual Theologian: Essays on Sex, God and Politics*, edited by Marcella Althaus-Reid and Lisa Isherwood, 86–97. London: T. & T. Clark, 2004.

Louth, Andrew. *The Origins of the Christian Mystical Tradition, from Plato to Denys*. Oxford: Oxford University Press, 2009.

Lundin, Susanne. *Guldägget: Föräldraskap i biomedicinens tid*. Lund: Historiska media, 1997.

―――. *Organs for Sale: An Ethnographic Examination of the International Organ Trade*. Translated by Anne Cleaves. New York: Palgrave Macmillan, 2015.
Lundin, Tomas. "Tyskland ger plats för tredje kön." *Svenska dagbladet*, October 30, 2013. http://www.svd.se/tyskland-ger-plats-for-tredje-kon.
MacIntyre, Alasdair. *Whose Justice? Which Rationality?* Notre Dame: University of Notre Dame Press, 1988.
Maguire, Daniel C., and Larry L. Rasmussen. *Ethics for a Small Planet: New Horizons on Population, Consumption and Ecology*. Albany: State University of New York Press, 1998.
Mannermaa, Tuomo. *Christ Present in Faith: Luther's View of Justification*. Edited and introduced by Kirsi Stjerna. Minneapolis: Fortress, 2005.
Marcuse, Herbert. *Eros and Civilization: A Philosophical Inquiry into Freud*. London: Routledge and Kegan Paul, 1956.
Marinetti, Filippo Tommaso. "The Founding and Manifesto of Futurism." 1909. In *Futurist Manifestos*, edited by Umbro Apollonio, translated by R. W. Flint, 19–24. New York: Viking, 1973.
Marion, Jean-Luc. *God without Being: Hors-Texte*. Translated by Thomas A. Carlson. Chicago: Chicago University Press, 1991.
McFague, Sallie. *Models of God: Theology for an Ecological, Nuclear Age*. London: SCM, 1987.
McGinn, Bernard. *The Foundations of Mysticism: Origins to the Fifth Century*. New York: Crossroad, 2002.
McGuire, Meredith B. *Religion: The Social Context*. 4th ed. Belmont, CA: Wadsworth, 1997.
Merleau-Ponty, Maurice. *Phenomenologie de la perception*. London: Routledge, 2012.
Mikkola, Sini. "Gendered Sexuality in Martin Luther's Anthropology in the Treatise *Estate of Marriage* 1522." Paper presented at the 12th International Congress for Luther Research, Helsinki, Finland, August 7, 2012.
Milbank, John. *Theology and Social Theory: Beyond Secular Reason*. Oxford: Blackwell, 2006.
Milton, John. *Paradise Lost*. London: Macmillan, 1952.
Mogård, Anders. *Förtröstans hermeneutik: Nathan Söderbloms Lutheranvändning och traditionsbearbetningens problematik*. Skellefteå: Artos, 2012.
Mulinari, Diana. "Ett postkolonialt feministiskt samtal." In *Religionens offentlighet*, edited by Hanna Stenström, 205–16. Skellefteå: Artos, 2013.
Nadar, Sarojini. "Beyond the 'Ordinary Reader' and the 'Invisible Intellectual': Shifting Contextual Bible Study from Liberation Discourse to Liberation Pedagogy." *Old Testament Essays* 22 (2009) 384–403.
―――. "'Texts of Terror': The Conspiracy of Rape in the Bible, Church, and Society; The Case of Esther 2:1–18." In *African Women, Religion and Health: Essays in Honour of Mercy Amba Ewudziwa Oduyoye*, edited by Isabel Apawo Phiri and Sarojini Nadar, 77–95. Maryknoll, NY: Orbis, 2006.
―――. "Towards a Feminist Missiological Agenda: A Case Study of the Jacob Zuma Rape Trial." *Missionalia* 37 (2009) 85–102.
Nahnfeldt, Cecilia. *Luthersk kallelse: Handlingskraft och barmhärtighet*. Stockholm: Verbum, 2015.

Nancy, Jean-Luc. *Being Singular Plural.* Translated by Robert D. Richardson and Anne E. O'Byrne. Meridian: Crossing Aesthetics. Stanford: Stanford University Press, 2000.

Neuhaus, Sinikka. *Reformation och erkännande: Skilsmässoärenden under den tidiga reformationsprocessen i Malmö 1527-1542.* Lund: Centrum för teologi och religionsvetenskap, Lunds universitet, 2009.

Nietzsche, Friedrich. *Beyond Good and Evil: Prelude to a Philosophy of the Future.* Translated and edited by Marion Faber. Oxford: Oxford University Press, 1998.

Nordbäck, Carola. "Kyrkohistorisk historiebruksforskning." In *Minne och möjlighet: Kyrka och historiebruk från nationsbygge till pluralism*, edited by Urban Claesson and Sinikka Neuhaus, 14-43. Gothenburg: Makadam, 2014.

Nussbaum, Martha. *Sex and Social Justice.* New York: Oxford University Press, 1999.

Nygren, Anders. *Agape and Eros.* Translated by Philip S. Watson. New York: Harper & Row, 1969.

———. *Eros och Agape.* Stockholm: Verbum, 1930.

Ochoa Espejo, Paulina. "Does Political Theology Entail Decisionism?" *Philosophy and Social Criticism* 38 (2012) 725-43.

Origen. *Contra Celsum.* Translated by Henry Chadwick. Cambridge: Cambridge University Press, 1953.

———. *An Exhortation to Martyrdom; Prayer; and Selected Works.* Translated by Rowan A. Greer. Classics of Western Spirituality. New York: Paulist, 1979.

Österberg, Eva. *Folk förr: Historiska essäer.* Stockholm: Atlantis, 1995.

———. *Vänskap: En lång historia.* Stockholm: Atlantis, 2007.

Outka, Gene. *Agape: An Ethical Analysis.* New Haven: Yale University Press, 1972.

Pateman, Carole. *The Disorder of Women.* Cambridge: Polity, 1989.

Persson, Per Erik. *Att tolka Gud i dag: Debattlinjer i aktuell teologi.* Lund: Gleerups, 1970.

Peura, Simo. "Christ as Favor and Gift: The Challenge of Luther's Understanding of Justification." In *Union with Christ: The New Finnish Interpretation of Luther*, edited by Carl E. Braaten and Robert W. Jenson, 52-63. Grand Rapids: Eerdmans, 1998.

Plato. *Symposium.* Translated by Christopher Gill. New York: Penguin, 2003.

———. *Timaeus.* Translated by Henry Davis. In vol. 2 of *The Works of Plato.* Bohn's Classical Library. London: H. G. Bohn, 1850.

Plummer, Marjorie Elizabeth. *From Priest's Whore to Pastor's Wife: Clerical Marriage and the Process of Reform in the Early German Reformation.* Burlington, VT: Ashgate, 2012.

Poster, Mark. "Foucault, the Present and History." *Cultural Critique* 8 (1987-88) 105-21.

Primavesi, Anne. *From Apocalypse to Genesis: Ecology, Feminism, and Christianity.* Minneapolis: Fortress, 1991.

Reyes, Paulina de los, and Diana Mulinari. *Intersektionalitet: Kritiska reflektioner över (o)jämlikhetens landskap.* Malmö: Liber, 2005.

Roper, Lyndal. *The Holy Household: Women and Morals in Reformation Augsburg.* Oxford: Clarendon, 1989.

Rubenson, Samuel. "Äktenskapet i den tidiga kyrkan." In *Uppdrag samliv: Om äktenskap och samlevnad*, edited by Mikael Lindfelt and Johanna Gustafsson Lundberg, 179-224. Stockholm: Verbum, 2007.

———. "Eros och Agape: Om himmelsk åtrå i den tidiga kyrkan." *Vår Lösen* 8 (1998) 587–95.
———. "Himmelsk åtrå: Höga visan i tidigkristen tolkning." In *Eros och Agape: Barmhärtighet, kärlek och mystik i den tidiga kyrkan*, edited by Henrik Rydell Johnsén and Per Rönnegård, 105–27. Skellefteå: Artos, 2009.
Ruether, Rosemary Radford. "Asceticism and Feminism." In *Sex and God: Some Varieties of Women's Religious Experience*, edited by Linda Hurcombe, 229–50. New York: Routledge and Kegan Paul, 1987.
———. "Interpreting the Postmodern as Premodern: The Theology of D. Stephen Long." In *Interpreting the Postmodern: Responses to "Radical Orthodoxy"*, edited by Rosemary Radford Ruether and Marion Grau, 76–90. New York: T. & T. Clark, 2006.
———. *Sexism and God-Talk: Towards a Feminist Theology*. Boston: Beacon, 1983.
Scanlon, Michael J. "Arendt's Augustine." In *Augustine and Postmodernism: Confession & Circumfession*, edited by John D. Caputo and Michel J. Scanlon, 159–72. Bloomington: Indiana University Press, 2005.
Schmitt, Carl. *The Concept of the Political*. Translated by George Schwab. Expanded ed. Chicago: University of Chicago Press, 2007.
Schott, Robin May, ed. *Feminist Interpretations of Immanuel Kant*. Rereading the Canon 8. University Park: Pennsylvania State University Press, 1997.
Schweiker, William. "Against the Seductions of Transhumanism: Responsibility for the Human Future." Villanova University Theology Institute Conference, Villanova, PA, March 2011. www.youtube.com/watch?v=o5tutXOYnEI.
Shell, Susan Meld. *The Embodiment of Reason: Kant on Spirit, Generation, and Community*. Chicago: University of Chicago Press, 1996.
Shults, F. LeRon. "Introduction: Saving Desire?" In *Saving Desire: The Seduction of Christian Theology*, edited by F. LeRon Shults and Jan-Olav Henriksen, vii–ix. Grand Rapids: Eerdmans, 2011.
Sigurdson, Ola. *Det postsekulära tillståndet: Religion, modernitet, politik*. Munkedal: Glänta, 2009.
———. *Heavenly Bodies: Incarnation, the Gaze, and Embodiment in Christian Theology*. Translated by Carl Olsen. Grand Rapids: Eerdmans, 2016.
———. *Himmelska kroppar: Inkarnation, blick, kroppslighet*. Gothenburg: Glänta, 2006.
———. "Kristna kroppar som könade kroppar." In *Kärlekens förändrade landskap, Teologi om samlevnad*, edited by Mikael Lindfelt and Johanna Gustafsson Lundberg, 217–43. Stockholm: Verbum, 2009.
Smith, Bruce R. "Premodern Sexualities." *Publications of the Modern Language Association of America* 115 (2000) 318–29.
Söderblom, Nathan. *Luther och melankoli och andra Lutherstudier*. Stockholm: Proprius, 1983.
Sölle, Dorothee. *Christ the Representative: An Essay in Theology after the Death of God*. Translated by David Lewis. London: SCM, 1967.
Søltoft, Pia. "Kaerlighed og krop- den problematiske sexualitet." In *Kroppens teologi—teologiens kropp*, edited by Kirsten Busch Nielsen and Johanne Stubbe Teglbjærg, 119–42. Copenhagen: Anis, 2011.
Stadin, Kekke. *Stånd och genus i stormaktstidens Sverige*. Lund: Nordic Academic Press, 2009.

Stenqvist, Catharina. "Nygrens dilemma och isärhållandets logik." *Svensk teologisk kvartalsskrift* 82 (2006) 123–34.
Stenström, Hanna. "Den irriterande rösten." In *Tolkning för livet: Åtta teologer om bibelns auktoritet*, edited by Anne-Louise Eriksson, 66–90. Stockholm: Verbum, 2004.
Stjerna, Kirsi. *Women and the Reformation*. Oxford: Blackwell, 2009.
Stolt, Birgit. *"Laßt uns fröhlich springen!" Gefühlswelt und Gefühlsnavigierung in Luthers Reformationsarbeit: Eine Kognitive Emotionalitätsanalyse auf Philologischer Basis*. Berlin: Weidler, 2012.
———. *Luther själv: Hjärtats och glädjens teolog*. Skellefteå: Artos, 2004.
Stuart, Elizabeth, and Adrian Thatcher. *People of Passion: What the Churches Teach about Sex*. London: Mowbray, 1997.
Svalfors, Ulrika. *Andlighetens ordning: En diskursiv läsning av tidskriften Pilgrim*. Uppsala: Acta Universitatis Upsaliensis, 2008.
Tegborg, Lennart. "Från kyrkolag till enhetsskola: Undervisning och fostran genom tre århundraden." In *Normer och normlöshet: Essäer kring skolmoral och samhällsmoral*, 42–75. Stockholm: Liber, 1980.
Thielicke, Helmut. *Theologische Ethik*. Vol. 2, *Ethik des Politischen*. Tübingen: Mohr, 1987.
Tillich, Paul. *Dynamics of Faith*. New York: Harper & Row, 1958.
———. *Systematic Theology*. 3 vols. Chicago: University of Chicago Press, 1951–63.
Tracy, David. *The Analogical Imagination: Christian Theology and the Culture of Pluralism*. New York: Crossroad, 1981.
Trible, Phyllis. *God and the Rhetoric of Sexuality*. Philadelphia: Fortress, 1978.
———. *Texts of Terror: Literary-Feminist Reading of Biblical Narratives*. Philadelphia: Fortress, 1984.
Turner, Mark. *The Literary Mind: The Origins of Thought and Language*. New York: Oxford University Press, 1998.
Ulfers, Friedrich, and Mark Daniel Cohen. "Nietzsche's Amor Fati: The Embracing of an Undecided Fate." Published by the Nietzsche Circle, June 2007. http://www.nietzschecircle.com/Nietzsches_Amor_fati.pdf.
Ulrich, Hans G. "On the Grammar of Lutheran Ethics." In *Lutheran Ethics at the Intersections of God's One World*, edited by Karen L. Bloomquist, 27–48. Geneva: Lutheran World Federation, 2005.
Vikström, Björn. *Den skapande läsaren: Hermeneutik och tolkningskompetens*. Lund: Studentlitteratur, 2005.
Ward, Graham. "The Displaced Body of Jesus Christ." In *Radical Orthodoxy: A New Theology*, edited by John Milbank, Catherine Pickstock, and Graham Ward, 163–81. London: Routledge, 1999.
———. "On the Politics of Embodiment and the Mystery of All Flesh." In *The Sexual Theologian: Essays on Sex, God and Politics*, edited by Marcella Althaus-Reid and Lisa Isherwood, 71–85. London: T. & T. Clark, 2004.
Webb, Stephen H. *The Gifting of God: A Trinitarian Ethics of Excess*. New York: Oxford University Press, 1996.
Weber, Max. *The Protestant Ethic and the Spirit of Capitalism*. Translated by Talcott Parsons. London: Routledge, 2001.
Wendte, Martin. "'This is My Body, Which is for You': Exploring the Significance of Luther's Theology of the Eucharist in a Technological Age." In *The Body Unbound:*

Philosophical Perspectives on Politics, Embodiment and Religion, edited by Marius Timmann Mjaaland, Ola Sigurdson, and Sigridur Thorgeirsdottir, 89–106. Newcastle: Cambridge Scholars, 2010.

Westhelle, Vítor. *Eschatology and Space: The Lost Dimension in Theology Past and Present*. New York: Palgrave Macmillan, 2012.

Wiberg Pedersen, Else Marie. *Bernhard af Clairvaux: Teolog eller mystiker?* Copenhagen: Anis, 2008.

———. "A Man Caught between Bad Anthropology and Good Theology? Martin Luther's View of Women Generally and of Mary Specifically." *Dialog: A Journal of Theology* 49 (2010) 190–201.

———. "One Body in Christ? Ecclesiology and Ministry between Good Theology and Bad Anthropology." In *"Like Living Stones": Lutheran Reflections on the One, Holy, Catholic, and Apostolic Church*, edited by Hans-Peter Grosshans and Martin L. Sinaga, 59–82. Minneapolis: Lutheran University Press, 2011.

———. "This Is Not about Sex? A Discussion of the Understanding of Love and Grace in Bernard of Clairvaux's and Martin Luther's Theologies." *Dialog: A Journal of Theology* 50 (2011) 15–25.

Wingren, Gustaf. *Creation and Gospel: The New Situation in European Theology*. 1979. Reprint, Eugene, OR: Wipf & Stock, 2004.

———. *Creation and Law*. 1961. Reprint, Eugene, OR: Wipf & Stock, 2003.

———. "Livets mening." Review in *Sydsvenska Dagbladet*, April 27, 1976.

———. *Luther frigiven: Ett tema med sex variationer*. Lund: Gleerups, 1970.

———. *Luther on Vocation*. 1957. Reprint, Eugene, OR: Wipf & Stock, 2004.

———. *Luthers lära om kallelsen*. Lund: Gleerups, 1942.

———. *Man and the Incarnation: A Study in the Biblical Theology of Irenaeus*. 1959. Reprint, Eugene, OR: Wipf & Stock, 2004.

———. *Människa och kristen: En bok om Irenaeus*. Skellefteå: Artos, 1997/1983.

———. *Öppenhet och egenart: Evangeliet i världen*. Lund: Liber, 1979.

———. *Skapelsen och lagen: Evangeliet och kyrkan*. Skellefteå: Artos, 2013/1958.

———. *Teologiens metodfråga*. Lund: Gleerup, 1954.

———. *Theology in Conflict: Nygren, Barth, Bultmann*. Translated by Eric H. Wahlstrom. Philadelphia: Muhlenberg, 1958.

———. *Växling och kontinuitet: Teologiska kriterier*. Lund: Gleerups, 1972.

Witte, John, Jr. *Law and Protestantism: The Legal Teachings of the Lutheran Reformation*. Cambridge: Cambridge University Press, 2002.

Woodhead, Linda. "Sex in a Wider Context." In *Sex These Days: Essays on Theology, Sex and Society*, edited by Jon Davies and Gerard Loughlin, 96–121. Sheffield: Sheffield Academic Press, 1997.

Young, Iris Marion. *On Female Body Experience: "Throwing Like a Girl" and Other Essays*. New York: Oxford University Press, 2005.

www.ingramcontent.com/pod-product-compliance
Lightning Source LLC
Chambersburg PA
CBHW030433300426
44112CB00009B/982